The Making of Islamic Economic Thought

Interrogating the development and the conceptual framework of economic thought in the Islamic tradition as it pertains to ethical, philosophical, and theological ideas, this book provides a critique of modern Islamic economics as a hybrid economic system. From the outset, Sami Al-Daghistani is concerned with the polyvalent methodology of studying the phenomenon of Islamic economic thought as a human science in that it nurtures a complex plenitude of meanings and interpretations associated with the moral self. Studying legal scholars, theologians, and Sufis in the classical period, Al-Daghistani looks at economic thought in the context of *Sharīʿa*'s moral law. Alongside critiquing modern developments of Islamic economics, he puts forward the idea of a plural epistemology of Islam's moral economy, which advocates for a multifaceted hermeneutical reading of the subject in light of a moral law, embedded in a particular cosmology of human relationality, metaphysical intelligibility, and economic subjectivity.

SAMI AL-DAGHISTANI is a postdoctoral fellow at the MF Norwegian School of Theology, Religion and Society in Oslo, an associate faculty member at the Brooklyn Institute for Social Research in New York, and a research scholar at the Middle East Institute at Columbia University. He is the author of *Ethical Teachings of Abū Ḥāmid al-Ghazālī: Economics of Happiness* (2021) and translator to Slovenian of *Ibn Ṭufayl's Ḥay ibn Yaqẓān* (2016) and *Ibn Baṭṭūta's Riḥla* (2017).

The Making of Islamic Economic Thought

Islamization, Law, and Moral Discourses

SAMI AL-DAGHISTANI
MF Norwegian School of Theology, Religion and Society

CAMBRIDGE
UNIVERSITY PRESS

University Printing House, Cambridge CB2 8BS, United Kingdom

One Liberty Plaza, 20th Floor, New York, NY 10006, USA

477 Williamstown Road, Port Melbourne, VIC 3207, Australia

314–321, 3rd Floor, Plot 3, Splendor Forum, Jasola District Centre, New Delhi – 110025, India

103 Penang Road, #05–06/07, Visioncrest Commercial, Singapore 238467

Cambridge University Press is part of the University of Cambridge.

It furthers the University's mission by disseminating knowledge in the pursuit of education, learning, and research at the highest international levels of excellence.

www.cambridge.org
Information on this title: www.cambridge.org/9781108845755
DOI: 10.1017/9781108990813

First published 2021

A catalogue record for this publication is available from the British Library.

Library of Congress Cataloging-in-Publication Data
Names: Al-Daghistani, Sami, 1986– author.
Title: The making of Islamic economic thought : Islamization, law and moral discourses / Sami Al-Daghistani, MF Norwegian School of Theology, Religion and Society.
Description: New York : Cambridge University Press, 2021. | Includes bibliographical references and index.
Identifiers: LCCN 2021009527 (print) | LCCN 2021009528 (ebook) | ISBN 9781108845755 (hardback) | ISBN 9781108990813 (ebook)
Subjects: LCSH: Economics – Religious aspects – Islam. | Islam – Economic aspects. | Wealth – Religious aspects – Islam. | Islamic law – Economic aspects. | BISAC: BUSINESS & ECONOMICS / Economics / General | BUSINESS & ECONOMICS / Economics / General
Classification: LCC BP173.75 A4173 2021 (print) | LCC BP173.75 (ebook) | DDC 297.2/73–dc23
LC record available at https://lccn.loc.gov/2021009527
LC ebook record available at https://lccn.loc.gov/2021009528

ISBN 978-1-108-84575-5 Hardback

Contents

List of Figures — *page* vii
Acknowledgments — viii

Introduction — 1
The Premise — 1
Western Philosophical Tradition and the Birth of Economic Science — 6
The Genealogy of Modern Islamic Economics — 26
Classical Scholarship and the Moral Self — 31
Methodology and Theoretical Framework — 34
Scholarly Relevance of Premodern Economic Teachings — 42

1 The Force of Revivalism and Islamization: Their Impact on Knowledge, Politics, and Islamic Economics — 43
1.1 The Socioeconomic Paradigm against the Backdrop of a Colonial Past — 44
1.2 Contextualizing Muslim Reformists' Understanding of Socialism, Capitalism, and Spirituality — 48
1.3 Abū al-Aʿlā Mawdūdī and the Twentieth-Century Transition from Nation to Islamic State — 64
1.4 Islam and the Economic System between the 1930s and the 1970s — 73
1.5 Islamization of Knowledge Process and Contemporary Islamic Thought — 81
1.6 Islamization of the Islamic Economy (1979–Present) — 87
1.7 Concluding Remarks — 95

2 The Present: Muslim Economists and the Constellation of Islamic Economics — 97
2.1 Introductory Remarks — 97
2.2 Theories and Definitions: Recent Developments and Contentions — 102
2.3 Methodologies of Contemporary Islamic Economics — 109

2.4 Islamic Economics and Forms of Conventional Knowledge 120
2.5 Islamic Jurisprudential Economics and Islamic Law 128
2.6 Contemporary Muslim Economists' Views on Classical Muslim Scholars 139
2.7 Concluding Remarks 141

3 The Past Perfect: *Sharīʿa* and the Intellectual History of Islamic Economic Teachings 145
3.1 Widening the Scope of Classical Economic and Legal Thought in Islam 145
3.2 *Sharīʿa*'s Legal Supremacy versus Moral Cosmology 149
3.3 *Maqāsid*, *Istiḥsān*, *Maṣlaḥa*, and Economic Preservation in *Sharīʿa* 157
3.4 *Siyāsa Sharʿiyya*: Between the Moral and Legal Realm 168
3.5 Metaphysics and the History of Islam's Moral Economics 173
3.6 The Nature of Markets, Price Control, and the Notion of Fair Price 182
3.7 The Value of Wealth (*Māl*) and the Hereafter 187
3.8 Productivity, Value of Labor, and Cooperation 203
3.9 Islamic Authority (*Wilāya*) and the Principle of Moral Integrity 210
3.10 Concluding Remarks 219

4 The Appraisal: Contemporary Islamic Economics and the Entrenchment of Modernity 221
4.1 Introductory Remarks 221
4.2 Modern Divergence of *Sharīʿa*'s Moral Principles 224
4.3 Critiquing the Discipline of Islamic Economics 235
4.4 The Islamization of Economics 247
4.5 Concluding Remarks 252

5 Pluralistic Epistemology of Islam's Moral Economics 256
5.1 Introductory Remarks 256
5.2 Moral Cosmology and Pluralistic Epistemology in Islamic Tradition 259
5.3 Economic Development in Light of Spiritual Prosperity 269

Conclusion: Moral over Legal, Pluralistic over Monolithic 274

Appendix 277
Bibliography 279
Index 310

Figures

1 History and development of economic thought in Islamic tradition *page* 277
2 *Kasb–zuhd* amalgam under the banner of *Tawakkul* 278
3 Categorization of the contingent fields of economy, society, and ecology within the cosmological order 278
4 Economic behavior and pluralistic epistemology of *Sharī'a* 278

Acknowledgments

I have been fortunate to be surrounded by scholars in Islamic Studies from whose scholarship I have benefited, immensely. They have helped me form and nuance my arguments, enthusiastically reading chapters of my thesis and offering key insights. I would like to thank my advisor at Leiden University, Maurits Berger, who persistently and diligently supervised every step of my PhD studies, and whose bi-weekly meetings, in order to discuss the thesis and its progress, contributed to its end product. At Leiden University, I am also grateful to professors, colleagues, and staff members, including the Leiden Center for the Study of Religion, Leiden Institute for Area Studies, Leiden University Center for the Study of Islam and Society, and Netherlands Interuniversity School for Islamic Studies, as well as to Leiden University Funds.

I would like to credit my co-advisor at WWU Münster, Marco Schöller, for his supervision, advice, and encouragement and Dr. Monika Springberg-Hinsen for her prompt assistance and support at the Institut für Arabistik und Islamwissenschaft. Likewise, I would like to sincerely thank Taner Yüksel and Murat Şahinarslan from DITIB Türkisch-Islamische Union der Anstalt für Religion e.V. in Cologne for their generous academic and financial support.

My utmost gratitude and appreciation for his time, knowledge, and mentorship goes to my advisor at Columbia University, Wael Hallaq, who not only read, commented, and discussed in detail Chapters 3, 4, and 5 of this book but who also helped shape my understanding of the nuances within Islamic intellectual and legal history. Professor Hallaq's seminars and workshops on Islamic intellectual history, and numerous discussions with him in and outside of his office hours, remain some of my most cherished academic moments of my PhD research. At the Department of Middle Eastern, South Asian, and African Studies, (MESAAS) I am grateful to Timothy Mitchell for reading and providing comments for Chapter 1 and to Hossein Kamaly for his invaluable commentaries and suggestions. Likewise, I would like to express my sincere thanks to Katherine Pratt Ewing, the former director, and to Walid Hammam, the associate director of the Institute for Religion, Culture, and Public Life (IRCPL) at Columbia University, for providing me with an academic platform, workspace, and wonderful colleagues; to Gil Anidjar at the Religion Department for his backing; as well as to Marnia Lazreg at Hunter College in New York for her insightful analysis and discussion. The time spent first as a visiting scholar at MESAAS and at the IRCPL between 2015 and 2017, and then as a research scholar at IRCPL between 2017 and 2019, deepened my critical orientation and provided me with numerous academic incentives, projects, and collaborations that stretched well beyond my PhD studies.

At McGill University, where I spent the winter term of 2014, I would like to extend thanks to Ahmad Ibrahim, whose courses on Islamic law prompted me to carry on ongoing research and teaching activities in this domain, as well to Adina Sigartau for her invaluable help at the institute and the fellow students I met during my studies in Montreal.

At Amsterdam University, I am indebted to Michael Kemper for his time and the commentary he provided for one of the very first drafts of the thesis.

At Oxford University, I would like to extend my gratitude to Paul Flather for supporting my presentations at the Sorbonne, Oxford University, and in Madrid, within the framework of the Europaeum.

Moreover, I am deeply grateful to Seyyed Hossein Nasr, Alexander Knysh, and Aamir Mufti for meeting me in person and for enriching my critical thinking on the processes within Sufi epistemology, ethics, and economic thought.

Likewise, I extend my appreciation to my friends and colleagues at the MF Norwegian School of Theology, Religion and Society in Oslo, the Middle East Institute at Columbia University, and the Brooklyn Institute for Social Research in New York for their conversations and intellectual input. The three institutions have been my academic home for the past several years. MF has been particularly welcoming to my academic orientation and also granted me generous institutional support.

At Cambridge University Press, I would sincerely like to thank the former commissioning editor Daniel Brown for believing in my project and for meeting me in 2019 at MESA's annual meeting, the current acting commissioning editors Maria Marsh and Atifa Jiwa, the copy-editor Anny Mortada, the project manager Malini Soupramanian, the content Manager,Thomas Haynes, and their team for their support, and the two reviewers for their valuable suggestions and comments, as well as to Zachary Hendrickson for helping out with the index.

Personally, in New York, I am thankful to my dear friend and a rising musician in the jazz scene, Jan Kus. Hours spent together in Harlem, Queens, the Bronx, and Brooklyn, in any weather and under any conditions, provided me friendship and smiles. To colleagues and friends at Columbia University – Rajbir Singh Judge, Fatima-Ezzahrae Touilila, Zachary Hendrickson, Kevin Witkow, Marianna Pecoraro, Mohamad Mezian, Ibrahim Bechrouri, and Ayah Dosougi, I will always appreciate the amity of our time and engaged intellectual discussions in my favorite city; in the Netherlands, I am grateful to Mahmood Kooriadathodi and Eftychia Mylona for their friendship and immense help surrounding my PhD defense process, as well as to Chryssa Vergidou (Chrysulaki), Hayat Ahlili, Bart and Elenore Geuzebroek, Marcela Probert, Tijmen Baarda, Faryaneh Fadaei, Gulnaz Sibgatullina, Tamás Szenderák, Amin Ghodratzadeh, Samuela Etossi, Arshad Muradin, Arnold Yasin Mol, Brigitte Van de Pas, Alain Corbeau, Haris Mexas, Saeko Kitamae, as well as to the Leiden Hikma community, for their friendship and a wonderful time spent in Leiden and abroad; at the European University at St. Petersburg, to Alfrid Bustanov and Anna Matochkina, for their invitation and hospitality; in Slovenia, to Mirt Komel, a solid friend, philosopher, fellow co-editor, and intellectual companion, to Nastasja Škrelj-Grat and her family for her long-lasting and beautiful friendship, and to Matea Pregelj for her backing.

I am also thankful to my Slovenian, Iraqi, Iranian, American, Serbian, and Filipino family for their love, inspiration, and support. My love and gratitude go to my beloved parents, Marija and Nabil, whose affection and encouragement followed me to the four corners of the Earth. Despite the physical distance, their voice on the other side of the line always reassured me of their unconditional love. I would also like to thank my wonderful wife and intellectual partner, Kristin Soraya Batmanghelichi, who persevered with me throughout the last two years of my PhD studies in New York and whose love, care, and motivation supplied me with much needed affection, understanding, and guidance. To our daughter who brings unsurmountable amount of joy to my life – Lina Jocelyn – I love you, immensely.

Sections of this book have been presented at various fora at Columbia University, Leiden University, McGill University, European University at St. Petersburg, Rotterdam College, Nijmegen University, Exeter University, International University of Sarajevo, University of Ljubljana, Oxford University, George Mason University, University of Oslo, University of Bergen, University of Berkeley, as well as in Tunis, Amman, New Orleans, Cologne, Madrid, and elsewhere. Parts of Chapters 2 and 3 have appeared in my book *Ethical Teachings of Abū Ḥāmid al-Ghazālī: Economics of Happiness* (London: Anthem Press, 2021) and in two articles, "Al-Ghazali and the Intellectual History of Islamic Economics," *ZIT Jahrbuch für Islamische Theologie und Religionspädagogik: Islamische Gelehrten neu gelesen*, vol. 3 (2014): 97–134; and "Semiotics of Maṣlaḥa and Islamic Economic Theory," *International Journal for the Semiotics of Law*, vol. 29, no. 2 (2016): 389–404.

Introduction

The Premise

Economic thought in Islamic tradition is not about economics as we understand it in modern terms, with respect to material prosperity, economic development, and consumption and transfer of wealth. In fact, one could state that economic thought as analyzed by classical Muslim scholars is least concerned with such pursuits. Rather, it pertains to much broader human and Divine relations, as well as behavioral patterns of spiritual, metaphysical, and, above all, moral qualities, irreducible to merely the natural order.

This book does not analyze the field of economics and finances per se or the *fiqh* works that discuss economic provisions but the discourse and conceptual framework of economic thought in Islamic tradition pertaining to moral, philosophical, legal, and theological ideas of classical and contemporary Muslim scholars. Also, it does not aim to address and/or compare the relations between and among neoliberal capitalist,[1] Marxist, and Islamic economic thinking.[2] Instead, it interrogates how the subject matter and the discourse of Islamic economics emerged, what forces contributed to its development, and, even more so, how different the contemporary subject is from classical economic philosophy in the Islamic tradition. It is hence centered on the *making* of Islamic economics as an intellectual endeavour and as a discipline.

[1] By neoliberal economics, I mean neoliberal political philosophy, whose public policy and assumptions often refer to neoclassical economics and uphold free trade, low taxes, and low government regulations. The neoclassical economic movement, which started between 1960 and 1980, relates to the intellectual tradition of classical liberalism. See e.g. Richard D. Wolff and Stephen Resnick, *Contending Economic Theories: Neoclassical, Keynesian, and Marxian* (Cambridge, MA: MIT Press), 336–338.

[2] On the comparison between neoliberal, Marxist, and Islamic economic ideas, see for instance Maxime Rodinson, *Islam and Capitalism* (New York: Pantheon Books, 1974); Muḥammad Bāqir al-Ṣadr, *Iqtiṣādunā* (Tehran: World Organization for Islamic Services, 1982), vol. 1, parts 1 and 2.

Despite the fact that Chapters 2 and 4 analyze the methodological shortcomings of contemporary Islamic economics, this project neither attempts to engage with political criticism of the contemporary Islamic economic project nor does it seek to underpin its religious ideas. Rather, it attempts to analyze the classical economic tradition, as put forward by several Muslim scholars, and its distinguished and distinguishing features, which I argue have been lost in the modern era. It does so through tracing the sociology of knowledge that occurred in the shift within the structural processes from colonial to postcolonial Muslim states and by peering into Muslim scholars' writings that elaborate how local structures foresaw socioeconomic development through constructing possible "Islamic" solutions.

The importance of the moral understanding of economic life that was present in the classical Islamic intellectual tradition seems to be understood differently in the contemporary subject of Islamic economics and finance for various reasons. The birth of contemporary Islamic economics was colored by the evolution of the natural and social sciences and the European classification of modern social sciences,[3] including the economic discipline, which is concomitant with a particular worldview and vision of knowledge that espouses primarily a material understanding of economic relations. Contemporary Islamic economics also draws from socioeconomic and political developments that occurred in the Middle East and South Asia in the nineteenth century as many Muslim reformists[4] across the region envisioned an Islamic society with *Sharīʿa*[5] as a central paradigm. This

[3] See Thumas Khun, *The Structure of Scientific Revolutions* (Chicago, IL: University of Chicago Press, 1970).

[4] In this book, I use the terms reformists/revivalists, Islamists, and *nahḍa* scholars interchangeably, unless otherwise indicated. It is important to note though that the Arabic terms *tajdīd* (renewal) and *iḥyāʾ* (revival) are often used concurrently, even though renewal is more akin to the very notion of reform or *iṣlāḥ*. For more details about the reformist period, its main representatives, and their ideas, see Chapter 1.

[5] All Arabic (and Persian) characters, words, and phrases are transliterated according to the *Encyclopaedia Islamica* style. At times, the letter "h" is omitted at the end of certain Arabic words (e.g. *ḥisba*, *Sharīʿa*). "System of Transliteration of Arabic and Persian Characters," *Encyclopaedia Islamica*, last modified 2017, http://referenceworks.brillonline.com/entries/encyclopaedia-islamica/system-of-transliteration-of-arabic-and-persian-characters-transliteration. In the Bibliography and in the footnote citations, works by Sayyid Abū al-Aʿlā Mawdūdī, Maḥmūd Tāliqānī, Sayyid Quṭb, and Alī Sharīʿatī have

impacted the Muslim development of contemporary Islamic economics vis-à-vis the Islamists' call for an Islamic state. It also influenced the process of Islamizing sciences, which has been narrated as one component of Islamic identity. This is, however, only part of the story. Europe's incursions into the Middle East in the nineteenth century amounted to a paradigmatic geopolitical and economic shift in Muslim countries.[6] Economic ideas expounded by Muslim scholars in the first half of the twentieth century (as will be indicated in Chapters 1 and 2) emerged as a call for an Islamic vision of (state) economy, which went hand in hand with early twentieth-century Islamists' vision of an Islamic state. This was followed in the latter half of the same century by a flourishing of Islamic economic theories and the establishment of an Islamic banking system.

The problem of contemporary Islamic economics is, however, not so much about the question of identity but rather the position of science, the perception of knowledge, and the role of *Sharīʿa* in constructing such an identity in relation to the colonial restructuring of the social fabric. As will be evident in the following pages, Islamic economics has been trapped in this construction of scientific positivism, colonial sociopolitical determinations, and the call to Islamize knowledge. It eventually surfaced as a reconfigurative economic system, only to yet again be incorporated in the domain of mainstream or orthodox economic narratives.[7]

From the very outset, this book is concerned with the plural and polyvalent methodology of studying the phenomenon of Islamic economic thought as a human science in that it displays and nurtures a complex plenitude of meanings and interpretations that are often associated with the moral self.[8] As such, it studies economic thought in

been listed under the spellings here, even if the publication uses a different spelling.

6 Tomoko Masuzawa, *The Invention of World Religions* (Chicago, IL: University of Chicago Press, 2005), 180.

7 By orthodox or mainstream economics, I refer to economic theories often described and considered as part of the neoclassical economics tradition. Mainstream economics applies rational choice theory and emphasizes individual maximization of one's own utility. Moreover, such theories at times use statistics and mathematical models to demonstrate economic developments. For more see e.g. Wolff and Resnick, *Contending Economic Theories*.

8 For more on Islam as a religion and its plural forms, see Shahab Ahmed, *What Is Islam? The Importance of Being Islamic* (Princeton, NJ: Princeton University Press, 2016), 5.

the Islamic tradition and *Sharīʿa* through a multitude of approaches in what I call the plural epistemology of Islam's moral economy,[9] which advocates for a multifaceted hermeneutical reading of the subject in light of a moral ethos. This moral law is embedded in a particular cosmology of human relationality, metaphysical intelligibility, and economic subjectivity. Since epistemological reasoning is also concerned with the question of justification and the limits of this field, the epistemological inquiry poses questions about what sources are utilized by religious scholars and Muslim economists and how a plural epistemology can be presented as an alternative hermeneutical process in economic thought. I propose to approach the phenomena of (contemporary) Islamic economics through a genealogical, epistemological, and social analysis of the historical conditions that formed the very subject and to further introduce the mechanisms and methodology to study economic teachings in Islamic tradition as complex polyvalent phenomena based on *Sharīʿa*'s moral cosmology.

Hence, this project sets forth to demonstrate that the popular discipline of Islamic economics often obstructs the complexity of historical, sociopolitical, intellectual, and especially moral structures and boundaries between ethics, *Sharīʿa*, and economic conduct. If one were to claim that there is no functional Islamic economy, this would be done in light of renouncing the existing platform of contemporary Islamic economics with its financial and banking aspects that have been put into practice, which retrospectively justifies the validity of the discipline. An epistemological and hermeneutical reading of Islamic economic thought via classic Islamic scholarship, which nurtured a multiplicity of major paradigms (e.g. *Sharīʿa*, *taṣawwuf*,[10] *falsafa*, *kalām*), can provide both a metanarrative of viewing economic teachings in Islamic tradition as a method to bridge the gap between the heavenly and the mundane and a reconciliation of seemingly unlikely

9 See Chapter 5.

10 Throughout the book, I do not equate *taṣawwuf* with mysticism. While it is more appropriate to understand mysticism as belief that union with the absolute is inaccessible to the intellect, *taṣawwuf* (and Sufism) is essentially concerned with experiential knowledge and the validity and authority of that knowledge. Throughout the history of Islam, there have been diverse Sufi movements; Sufism was mystical in only some of them. For more on *taṣawwuf* see e.g. Muhammad Abul Haq Ansari, *Sufism and Sharīʿa* (Leicester: Islamic Foundation, 1986); Alexander Knysh, *Sufism* (Princeton, NJ: Princeton University Press, 2017).

concepts, such as responsibility with economic conduct, morality[11] with law, spirituality with *Sharīʿa*, and *ʿilm* with *ʿamal*. Thus, in order to explicate the *making* and *unmaking* of an Islamic economic discipline, it is of utmost importance first to discern the legal supremacy of economics from its moral normativity and second to provide a clear picture of systemic divergences and disparities between classical and contemporary ideas by analysing Muslim scholars and their texts. In order to first analyze and second de-essentialize and define the subject matter of Islamic economics with all its peculiarities and specifics, this book will examine the historical development of Islamic economic thought. It includes two different stocks of knowledge, that is, materials and sources from Islamic intellectual tradition and major works in Western philosophy and economics. Various religions and cultures have aimed to present the best economic model for humanity, advocating the aspect of justice and morality.[12] This is also the case for the Islamic tradition. What differs substantially, however, is the very concept of the *economic* as an extension of the *moral* in Islamic and Western traditions, especially after the Enlightenment period.

Deconstructing and de-essentializing contemporary Islamic economics involves deciphering the metanarrative from its subject matter and exploring its genealogy and interconnectedness with the positivist social sciences, Islamists' political orientation, and financial mechanisms of modern market-driven economics. This suggests that the history and genealogy of economic science in general, and economic thought in Islamic tradition in particular, cannot be conceived in a linear, monolithic manner as an incremental narration with nomothetic social sciences. Instead, it must be thought through as an epistemologically plural hermeneutical field within the classical tradition.

[11] As it will be shown in the following pages, primarily in Chapters 3 and 5, the moral self is the center of restructuring of social fabric in the selected texts I analyze within the Islamic tradition. Morality is not concerned only with rules and principles but with the cultivation of certain inner dispositions and traits of character that pertain to *Sharīʿa*'s moral cosmology. Hence, in view of *Sharīʿa*'s moral cosmology as it appears in many of the classical texts discussed in Chapter 3, morality is in line with virtuous standards based on pure will and intrinsic predisposition (*niyya*) and is not born out of a need to fulfill obligations. See e.g. Abū Ḥamid al-Ghazālī, *The Alchemy of Happiness*, trans. Claud Field (London: J. Murray, 1910); H. A. Prichard, "Does Moral Philosophy Rest on a Mistake," *Mind*, vol. 21, no. 81 (January 1, 1912): 21–37, https://doi.org/10.1093/mind/XXI.81.21.

[12] On the history of economics in Christianity, see Dotan Leshem, *The Origins of Neoliberalism* (New York: Columbia University Press, 2016).

In what follows, I briefly present the major aspects of the book, which concern some of the trends of Western economic history and philosophy, as well as the social and intellectual history of Islamic economic thought, and how the two systems vary in their historical development and epistemic (as related to position of knowledge and its justification) reasoning of what constitutes the realm of *economic*. In the second part of the Introduction, I present the main research question. Finally, I survey each chapter of the book and its major elements in more detail and discuss the need for and relevance of such scholarly research.

Western Philosophical Tradition and the Birth of Economic Science

References to the philosophy of positivism in this book do not serve only to underline its structural critique in comparison to classical economic thought in Islamic tradition but rather to display its far-reaching implications for contemporary Muslim economists who aimed to devise a new economic paradigm.

Economic science as a purely objective branch of knowledge neither existed in the classical Islamic tradition, nor in pre-Enlightenment Europe.[13] Nowadays, economics is often defined through the understanding that scientific method is the only way to accrue knowledge, which is often purported as scientism, an ideological construction of science that views only scientific claims as meaningful. On the relation between natural sciences and economics, one can observe that

> From the mid-nineteenth century onwards economics has fancied itself as methodologically akin to physics. Therefore, almost inevitably economists saw the physics-related revolution in the philosophy of science as relevant to economics as well. Meanwhile the identification of economics with physics in the economist's mind had become so strong that it almost completely obscured the most fundamental difference between the practice of physics (and indeed of all the natural sciences) and the practice of economics.

[13] See for instance scholasticism and the theory of natural law. Thomas Aquinas, *Summa Theologica*, trans. Fathers of the English Dominican Province (Perrysburg, OH: Benziger Bros., 1947); Joseph A. Schumpeter, *History of Economic Analysis* (Abingdon, UK: Taylor & Francis, 2006), chapter 1.

Whereas physics invents and chooses its methods on the basis of the nature of the phenomena that it studies, economics does not.[14]

The science–religion divide depicts religious knowledge as incompatible with scientific reasoning and suggests that it has to be put under the same scrutiny. This divide is the result of various factors, including a shift in attitudes from liberal to evangelical Christianity in Europe, the rise of creationism in America, and advances in physics and biology; it is most noticeable in Western traditions. Yet, this view is antithetical to Islamic tradition, in which the material constitutes a part of the cosmological. The quest for scientific (natural) economic laws and development of economics as an independent science (as organized knowledge) dates back to the very beginnings of philosophical thought and its relation to economic science. Despite its rich and diverse history, orthodox economic thought as it emerged in early modern Europe can be read as an effort to separate ideological taints from objective research in order to establish its scientific status. The divorce of economics and ethics, the two of which were formerly entangled with religion, took place first through the process of secularization during the Renaissance, given the rise of the market and the subduing of the moral to the necessities of the commodity exchange: "Secularization, thus understood, is properly described as a general orienting concept that causally links the decline of religion with the process of modernization."[15]

The first issue this book is concerned with is the so-called Cartesian bifurcation,[16] which dissociated philosophy from theology, a move that in turn secularized the sciences of nature. The Cartesian

14 Edward Fullbrook, "Introduction: Lawson's Reorientation," in *Ontology and Economics: Tony Lawson and His Critics*, ed. Edward Fullbrook (London: Routledge, 2009), 3.

15 "[S]ecularization theory has not been subjected to systematic scrutiny because it is a doctrine more than it is a theory. Its moorings are located in presuppositions that have gone unexamined because they represent a taken-for -granted ideology rather than a systematic set of interrelated propositions." Jeffrey K. Hadden, "Toward Desacralizing Secularization Theory," *Social Forces*, vol. 65, no. 3 (1987): 588, 598; see also Larry Witham, *Marketplace of the Gods: How Economics Explains Religion* (Oxford: Oxford University Press, 2010), chapter 8.

16 See Wolfgang Smith, *The Quantum Enigma: Finding the Hidden Key* (Hillsdale NY: Sophia Perennis, 2005), 7ff.; Wolfgang Smith, *Cosmos and Transcendence: Breaking through the Barrier of Scientistic Belief* (San Rafael, CA: Sophia Perennis, 2008), 21–38; Wolfgang Smith, *The Wisdom of Ancient Cosmology:*

bifurcation elevates quantitative measurement of science and theory while denigrating the direct experience of qualities. The distinction between false and true, uni- and multidimensional aspects of the universe is encapsulated in the scientific revolution[17] and its main representative is the philosophy of René Descartes, who believed that only that which is measurable is true.[18] This theory goes hand in hand with the assumption that the external world is a mechanical structure, which bisects quality from quantity, since the modus operandi of physics is based upon measurements. In relation to measurements, Wolfgang Smith states that

> The first thing to be noted is that one measures, not directly by sight, or by any other sense, but by means of an artefact, an appropriate instrument. What counts, in fact, is the interaction between object and instrument: it is this that determines the final state of the instrument, and hence the outcome of the measurement. And that outcome, moreover, will be a quantity .... The experimental physicist makes use of his senses at every step; and it is by way of sense perception, in particular, that he ascertains the final state of the instrument. But this does not mean that he perceives the quantity in question .... What one perceives are corporeal objects of various kinds – including scientific instruments .... But one does not perceive measurable quantities. And that is the reason why one needs an instrument. The instrument is required precisely because the quantity in question is *not* perceptible. It is thus the function of the instrument to convert the latter, so to speak, into the perceptible state of a corporeal object, so that, by means of sense perception, one may attain to the knowledge of something that is not in itself perceivable.[19]

Contemporary Science in Light of Tradition (Oakton, VA: Foundation for Traditional Studies, 2009).

17 For more on the scientific revolution and the interplay between mechanical philosophy and mathematical order, see Richard S. Westfall, *The Construction of Modern Science: Mechanisms and Mechanics* (Cambridge: Cambridge University Press, 1978). On the critique of the progress in "normal sciences," see Khun, *Structure of Scientific Revolutions*. On the history and influence of scientific development in Islamic tradition, see George Saliba, *Islamic Science and the Making of the European Renaissance* (Cambridge, MA: MIT Press, 2007).

18 "Somit darf ich als allgemeine Regel festsetze, daß alles das wahr ist, was ich ganz klar und deutlich auffasse." (videor pro regulâ generali posse statuere, illud omne esse verum, quod valde clare & distincte percipio). René Descartes, *Meditationes III*, trans. Gerhart Schmidt (Stuttgart, 1986) in Thomas Bauer, *Die Kultur der Ambiguität: Eine andere Geschichte des Islams* (Berlin: Verlag der Weltreligionen, 2011), 55–56.

19 Smith, *Quantum Enigma*, 29–30.

The scientific revolution was superseded by the Age of Enlightenment[20] as an intellectual and philosophical movement that favored reason and ideas such as liberty, rationalism, progress, and separation of church and state. The Enlightenment is often regarded as the foundation of modern Western political and intellectual culture, whose main figures include Voltaire, Denis Diderot, Jean-Jacques Rousseau, David Hume, Adam Smith, and Immanuel Kant. Various Enlightenment philosophers overthrew traditional (religious) authority and exuberantly supported empiricism and rational thought, which was concomitant with progress. One such proponent was David Hume.

Closely related to the Cartesian bifurcation is the second perspective pertaining to classical economics and the inner association between "positive" and "descriptive" statements. This division is a consequence of Hume's "is–ought" dichotomy, whereby the "is" describes the way something "is," while the "ought" denotes "what ought to be."[21] It was this distinction that helped create the paradigmatic shift in the modern sciences that dichotomized fact from value,[22] which culminated in the making of the modern bureaucratic state[23] – a fact that bears significance also for the Islamic economic project. Even though social sciences as a separate field emerged in the nineteenth century, since the Enlightenment the majority of economists have been seeking to mathematize the field of economics. The result was the process of deductivism in economics (morphing developments within the discipline of mathematics into mathematical deductivism),[24] while practitioners were oblivious to the given inconsistency between scientific and

[20] See e.g. Immanuel Kant, "Was ist Afklärung?," *UTOPIE kreativ*, vol. 159 (2004): 5–10; Michel Foucault, "What Is Enlightenment?," in *The Foucault Reader*, ed. P. Rabinow (New York: Pantheon Books, 1984), 32–50.

[21] David Hume, *A Treatise of Human Nature* (Auckland, New Zealand: The Floating Press, 2009).

[22] See e.g. Alasdair MacIntyre, *After Virtue* (Notre Dame, IN: Notre Dame Press, 2007).

[23] "This paradigm shift finds attestation in nearly all modern phenomena, beginning with the creation of a distinction between fact and value and Is and Ought and ending with the modern bureaucratic state, modern capitalism, and nationalism." Wael Hallaq, *The Impossible State* (New York: Columbia University Press, 2013), 10, 75.

[24] "Academic economics is currently dominated to a very significant degree by a mainstream tradition or orthodoxy, the essence of which is an insistence on methods of mathematical-deductivist modelling." Tony Lawson, *Reorienting Economics*, (London: Routledge, 2003), 3, 5.

mathematical modeling, as well as about the ontological presuppositions of the nature of social reality. The rise of mathematical deductivism has culminated in positivism as a philosophical system that recognizes only that which can be scientifically verified, while rejecting metaphysics.[25] Its well-known representative, Auguste Comte (d. 1857), developed a threefold theory of social evolution, which concludes in positivism.[26] Namely, methods found to be successful in natural sciences were applied in social sciences. Tony Lawson holds that the world that mainstream economists analyze is the empirical world. Instead, economics ought to embrace a "social ontology" to include the underlying causes of economic phenomena: "The futile search for constants in human behavior condemns econometrics to sterility; it disregards the basic truth that human beings act."[27] This dichotomy was, however, unknown to the classical Islamic intellectual tradition in which the economic, legal, and political were placed under the banner of the moral. In view of the positivist foundations of modern (Islamic) economics and its financial aspect, this tradition is rendered undesirable since mathematical axioms often do not correspond to the reality on the ground and have little to do with the epistemological axioms of premodern economic thought.

On the level of economic policies and international trade, between the sixteenth and eighteenth centuries mercantilism as a type of national economic policy dominated parts of Europe. It was designed to maximize the export and trade of a nation by accumulating gold and silver while minimizing costs.[28] Mercantilism developed during a time of major economic transition in Europe, when feudal estates were transforming into nation-states and the accumulation of monetary

[25] See e.g. Bruce Caldwell, *Beyond Positivism: Economic Methodology in the Twentieth Century* (London: Routledge, 1994); Milton Friedman, "The Methodology of Positive Economics," in *Essays in Positive Economics* (Chicago, IL: University of Chicago Press, 1953), 3–43.

[26] Auguste Comte, *A General View of Positivism* (Cambridge: Cambridge University Press, 2009).

[27] Further, he argues "for a theory of social ontology that includes forms of social structure, including social relationships, rules, positions, processes and totalities, etc., that collectively constitute a relatively autonomous realm, being dependent upon and resulting from human interaction, but with properties that are irreducible to human interaction, though acting back upon it." (Lawson, *Reorienting Economics*, 68).

[28] For an overview of mercantilist literature, see Schumpeter, *History of Economic Analysis*, chapter 7.

reserves from foreign nations prompted colonial expansions. One of the responses to mercantilism was the physiocrats – a group of Enlightenment economists, such as François Quesnay (d. 1774) and Anne-Robert-Jacques Turgot (d. 1781) – whose advocating for productive work in a national economy preceded the classical economic school. The term mercantilism or rather mercantilist system was, however, first used by one of its critics, Adam Smith (d. 1790), who vindicated the idea that not only consumption but also production ought to be considered in a national economy. The secularization of production processes as part of a modern discipline of economics with the idea of a rational individual who acts in their own self-interest, as well as the labor theory of value, took place in the eighteenth century with Adam Smith. Smith's *The Theory of Moral Sentiments* (1759) tackles the questions of moral sense, self-interest, and utility. On the other hand, *The Wealth of Nations* (1776) as an analytical book addressed political economy in the context of the Industrial Revolution, division of labor, free markets, and international cooperation.[29] Smith regarded natural or private liberty as a means to achieve the betterment of man, by deploying and allocating his own resources.[30] Government has a rather limited task to protect the nation from external enemies and upholds public works and advances education,[31] yet Smith's notion of justice in economic activities is considered as one of the key features of human society.[32] Justice, which Smith argued can be taught and is to be followed, is necessary in a commercial society, for "beneficence is less essential to the existence of society than justice. Society may subsist, though not in the most comfortable state, without beneficence; but the

[29] See Adam Smith, *The Wealth of Nations* (MetaLibri, 2007), electronic version.
[30] Smith, *Wealth of Nations*, 106, 252–253, 533.
[31] "According to the system of natural liberty, the sovereign has only three duties to attend to; three duties of great importance, indeed, but plain and intelligible to common understandings: first, the duty of protecting the society from violence and invasion of other independent societies; secondly, the duty of protecting, as far as possible, every member of the society from the injustice or oppression of every other member of it, or the duty of establishing an exact administration of justice; and, thirdly, the duty of erecting and maintaining certain public works and certain public institutions which it can never be for the interest of any individual, or small number of individuals, to erect and maintain; because the profit could never repay the expense to any individual or small number of individuals, though it may frequently do much more than repay it to a great society." (Smith, *Wealth of Nations*, 533–534).
[32] Smith, *Wealth of Nations*, 550.

prevalence of injustice must utterly destroy it."[33] On justice, Smith states that

Commerce and manufactures can seldom flourish long in any state which does not enjoy a regular administration of justice, in which the people do not feel themselves secure in the possession of their property, in which the faith of contracts is not supported by law, and in which the authority of the state is not supposed to be regularly employed in enforcing the payment of debts from all those who are able to pay. Commerce and manufactures, in short, can seldom flourish in any state in which there is not a certain degree of confidence in the justice of government.[34]

This also presupposes cooperation between merchants and various elements of society, as well as creation of social bonds.

Some economists believe that Smith was not only the founding father of modern economic thought but also a forerunner of neoliberal economic policies, yet his critique of government's involvement in economic affairs can be interpreted as his mistrust in state apparatus due to officials' corrupt and exploitative approach to socioeconomic challenges.[35] Although Smith was an antimercantilist and a moral economist who also discussed poverty, the beginnings of classical economic thought[36] in the West also marks Smith's pursuit of laws of economic motion as found in physics by Isaac Newton, and David Ricardo's proposition of the moral laws of distribution.[37] Even though Smith argued for a limited governmental interference in economic matters and *laissez faire*, he should not be read from a modern neoliberal standpoint but rather as someone who was skeptical of state's involvement in economic affairs. In this sense, *Wealth of Nations* ought to be read in tandem with the *Moral Sentiments*. Despite Smith's trust in the Enlightenment project, he anchored his economic theory also in a moral philosophy. Some of the subsequent economic theories comprise also of William Stanley Jevons's mechanic utility theory, as they

33 Adam Smith, *The Theory of Moral Sentiments* (MetaLibri, 2005), electronic version, 77–78.

34 Smith, *Wealth of Nations*, 710.

35 Smith, *Wealth of Nations*, 146.

36 Although Smith's economic theory was appropriated by neoclassical economists, there is a discrepancy in reading Smith's theory of the invisible hand and the notion of self-interest between classical and neoclassical economists. See Smith, *Theory of Moral Sentiments*; Smith, *Wealth of Nations*.

37 David Ricardo, *On the Principles of Political Economy and Taxation* (Kitchener, Ontario: Batoche Books, 2001), chapter 4.

were – in spite of their multitude – delineated according to the natural sciences and laws, especially mathematics and physics.[38] The utilitarian philosophical tradition inspired by psychological hedonism influenced economic theories by justifying that there is no distinction between needs and wants.[39] Psychological hedonism indicates that the benefit of an item is qualitatively different but quantitatively similar, which further implies rationalizing future needs for wants. Such a philosophical tradition extends to economics, finances, property rights, the notion of distribution, and other domains of economic activities. Yet, the separation of economics and ethics, as it is known nowadays, occurred in the late eighteenth and early nineteenth centuries, when economics became its own distinct science, as conceived also by John Stuart Mill, who advocated for the application of scientific method in social sciences,[40] whereby laws were discovered through observation and induction, which required empirical verification. Despite his stance on limited interventionism in economic affairs by governments and his support for economic democracy, Mill believed in a utilitarian society,[41] whereby economic development is measured through a combination of function of land, labor, and capital.[42] Mill referred to utilitarianism as

[38] See Jeremy Bentham, *An Introduction to the Principles of Moral Legislation* (Kitchener, Ontario: Batoche Books, 2001); John Stuart Mill, *The Collected Works of John Stuart Mill*, volume IV: *Essays on Economics and Society*, part I, ed. John M. Robson (Toronto: University of Toronto Press, 1967); John Stuart Mill, "On the Definition and Method of Political Economy," in *The Philosophy of Economics: An Anthology*, ed. Daniel Hausman (Cambridge: Cambridge University Press, 2007), 41–58; Ricardo, *On the Principles of Political Economy and Taxation*; Waleed Addas, *Methodology of Economics: Secular vs. Islamic* (Kuala Lumpur: International Islamic University Malaysia, 2008), 53.

[39] This stems from Bentham's theory that the ultimate object of desire is pleasure. "Nature has placed mankind under the governance of two sovereign masters, pain and pleasure." (Bentham, *Introduction to the Principles of Moral Legislation*, 14). See also John S. Mill, *Utilitarianism* (London: Parker, Son and Bourn, 1863).

[40] John Stuart Mill, *A System of Logic* (Harper & Brothers, 1882), electronic edition by eBooks@Adelaide; "John Stuart Mill not only turned economics primary concerns away from production and distribution to those of value, he also made the case that economics, and the social sciences in general, should ape the methodology of astronomy and physics." (Fullbrook, "Introduction: Lawson's Reorientation," 3).

[41] See Mill, *Utilitarianism*.

[42] See Mill, *Collected Works*.

> The creed which accepts as the foundation of morals, Utility, or the Greatest Happiness Principle, holds that actions are right in proportion as they tend to promote happiness, wrong as they tend to produce the reverse of happiness. By happiness is intended pleasure, and the absence of pain; by unhappiness, pain, and the privation of pleasure. ... If I am asked, what I mean by difference of quality in pleasures, or what makes one pleasure more valuable than another, merely as a pleasure, except its being greater in amount, there is but one possible answer. Of two pleasures, if there be one to which all or almost all who have experience of both give a decided preference, irrespective of any feeling of moral obligation to prefer it, that is the more desirable pleasure.[43]

The first phase was to set apart politics from morals and to establish economics as a respectable discipline, as an emancipated field that subjected various domains and disciplines to its logic. This later became known as the "imperialism of economics."[44] Classical economics included value theory and distribution theory.[45] Logic and mathematic science are often regarded as objective and infallible conceptual and analytic tools in natural sciences. This mathematical empiricism, which pertains to the domain of ontology, is a key methodical question for a scientist or a philosopher. What Comte, for example, aimed at with positivism is an arrangement of scientific knowledge in order to establish a hierarchy of sciences,[46] including sociology, out of which economics would eventually spring. Since he was concerned with social evolution, Comte styled a theory of natural progress.[47] For him, the epistemological perspective of positivism in physical sciences had to be implemented in the science of human society – sociology. Hence his view of positivism defines the methodology and empirical goals of sociological method by perceiving the theological stage subordinated to the metaphysical, which was further subordinated to the positive: "Methodologically, Comte's plan was to observe historical and ethnological facts and to build his science of society from such

43 Mill, *Utilitarianism*, 9–12.

44 Jesus M. Zaratiegui, "The Imperialism of Economics over Ethics," *Journal of Markets and Morality*, vol. 2, no. 2 (1999): 208.

45 See e.g. Michel Foucault, *The Order of Things* (New York: Vintage Books, 1994), 251–263.

46 See Comte, *General View of Positivism*.

47 Comte, *General View of Positivism*, 22, 48; Harriet Martineau, trans., *The Positive Philosophy of Auguste Comte* (Kitchener, Ontario: Batoche Books, 2000), 27; Anthony Giddens, *Positivism and Sociology*, 2nd ed. (Aldershot, UK: Ashgate Publishing, 1974), 1.

generalizations as these facts would suggest. This is, of course, a very familiar program that was, then and later, espoused by numerous writers, especially by historical economists."[48] However, it is, rather, an ontology (including a worldview) that decides the method and not the other way around.[49] Since classical economic science was conceived in relation to the physical realm of inquiry, it adopted and maintained the hermeneutical field of empirical knowledge, including mathematical statements.[50] Yet, purely scientific, objectifiable, and rational economic science was never established, for economic vision, epistemology, and methodology rest upon a particular worldview that is expounded by certain values.[51] Social sciences, including economics, sociology, political studies, anthropology, and human geography, and so forth deal not only with a different spatial reality but also with different structures and processes than natural sciences. In this sense, no field of knowledge, including economics, is value-free in its entirety.

The change in economic theory from classical to neoclassical economics – a term coined by Thorstein Veblen (d. 1929)[52] – is attributed to, among others, William Stanley Jevons (d. 1882),[53]

48 Schumpeter, *History of Economic Analysis*, 493.

49 By ontology, I refer to Lawson's study (or theory) of being or existence that is concerned with the nature and structure of an object in reality. See Lawson, *Reorienting Economics*, 12.

50 "The recent flurry of empiricist and quasi-empiricist views of mathematics is based on the assumption that mathematical statements are factual and empirical. The statement is perhaps stretchy. It could be correct only if the condition that mathematics is presented in theoretical terms capable of explaining some phenomenon or aspects of the physical reality. It has been convincingly shown that induction and analogy, albeit powerful tools of discovery, could not yet produce conclusive proofs or evidence for some well-known mathematical theorems. The use and failure of computers to verify the steps of mathematical logic in some cases – e.g. the four color theorem – implies that the conception of a proof can involve fallible arguments. Therefore, the falsifiability of a theory is taken as the main necessary condition for appraising theories against empirical evidence. In other words, falsifiability constitutes the true criterion of demarcation of 'scientific' propositions." (Addas, *Methodology of Economics*, 93).

51 For more see Tony Lawson, *Economics and Reality* (London: Routledge, 1997).

52 Thorstein Veblen, "The Preconceptions of Economic Science – III," *Quarterly Journal of Economics*, vol. 14, no. 2 (1900): 261; Thorstein Veblen, *The Theory of the Leisure Class* (New York: Macmillan Company, 1912).

53 See W. Stanley Jevons, *The Theory of Political Economy* (New York: Augustus M. Kelley, 1960).

Léon Walras (d. 1910),[54] and Alfred Marshall (d. 1924) and has been called the "marginal revolution."[55] However, in spite of orientational changes that neoclassical economic theory underwent and was associated with, such as the economic equilibrium, the epistemological and structural similarities with classical economics – pertaining to maximization of utility and the primacy of rational behavior – remained unvarying. Jevons for instance states that his

> theory of Economics, however, is purely mathematical in character. Nay, believing that the quantities with which we deal must be subject to continuous variation, I do not hesitate to use the appropriate branch of mathematical science, involving though it does the fearless consideration of infinitely small quantities. The theory consists in applying the differential calculus to the familiar notions of wealth, utility, value, demand, supply, capital, interest, labour, and all the other quantitative notions belonging to the daily operations of industry. As the complete theory of almost every other science involves the use of that calculus, so we cannot have a true theory of Economics without its aid.[56]

Walras, as the father of general equilibrium theory, also provided a definition of economic utility based on economic value as opposed to a theory of methodological subjectivism, which broke with the labor theory of value.[57] Furthermore, Veblen was critical of his contemporaries and their views on economy as an autonomous and static field. Although he disagreed with the neoclassical economics of the time and described economic behavior as socially determined, he developed a twentieth-century evolutionary economics based upon Darwinian principles and ideas emerging from other fields of social sciences, such as sociology, psychology, and anthropology. In spite of the fact that ethics does play a certain role in the economic and financial world, neoclassical economists believed that societal moral norms and codes can be assessed and analyzed from an economic point of view.[58] For

54 See Léon Walras, *Éléments d'économie politique pure, ou théorie de la richesse sociale* (Paris, 1926).

55 Jevons saw his economic theory as an application of Jeremy Bentham's utilitarianism. See Harro Maas, *William Stanley Jevons and the Making of Modern Economics* (Cambridge: Cambridge University Press, 2005); Alfred Marshall, *Principles of Economics*, 8th ed. (London: Macmillan and Co., 1920).

56 Jevons, *Theory of Political Economy*, 3.

57 J. R. Hicks, "Léon Walras," *Econometrica*, vol. 2, no. 4 (1934): 347–348.

58 Zaratiegui, "Imperialism of Economics over Ethics," 216.

instance, cost–benefit analysis in Western economic tradition is based on utility function,[59] in comparison to the classical Islamic concept of *maṣlaḥa* as an ethical mechanism that employs social good. The theory of (mono) utility revolves around needs and wants, which seems to be opposite to the Islamic approach to welfare, which includes moral needs.[60] The second phase of neoclassical theory upholds the claim that such economic theory was (meant to be) neutral.[61] Neoclassical economic theory coincides with the rational behavior approach, which asserts that people act rationally when engaging in economic decision-making. It stipulates that a particular commodity or service possesses value that goes beyond its initial input costs. That means that in addition to the value of a good that derived from the cost of material and labor, as identified by classical economists, there is also a perceived value of that very good by the consumer, which impacts its price and demand. The perceived value of a good by consumers further questions the very existence of and need for an upper limit of a commodity as well as a cap on financial gains or income. This ultimate rationalization and secularization of economic theory comes from the reduction of quality to quantity, which encompasses the whole of modern economic science. For Alfred Marshall, "Political Economy or Economics is a study of mankind in the ordinary business of life; it examines that part of individual and social action which is most closely connected with the

59 "Eighteenth-century economics stood in relation to mathesis as to a general science of all possible order; nineteenth-century economics will be referred to an anthropology as to a discourse on man's natural finitude. By this very fact, need and desire withdraw towards the subjective sphere – that sphere which, in the same period, is becoming an object of psychology. It is precisely here that in the second half of the nineteenth century the marginalists will seek the notion of utility." (Foucault, *Order of Things*, 257).

60 "Despite the problems with the notion of a single use value, the conventional economic literature never (to our knowledge) discusses the analytical tool necessary for cases involving multiple use values on one hand and a single end on the other, which Islamic and other religious values require." Waleed El-Ansary, "The Quantum Enigma and Islamic Sciences of Nature: Implications for Islamic Economic Theory," in *Proceedings of the 6th International Conference on Islamic Economics and Finance* (Jeddah: Islamic Development Bank, 2005), 154, see also 149.

61 "But since mono-utility functions cannot support the distinction between values and tastes or intrinsic 'good' and 'evil,' the neoclassical theory of choice favours libertarian policies while claiming to be neutral, thereby smuggling psychological hedonism into economic policy while suppressing the need for substantive philosophical debate over these policies." (El-Ansary, "Quantum Enigma and Islamic Sciences of Nature," 168).

attainment and with the use of the material requisites of wellbeing."[62] Yet, as explained below, economics became a technical science and a social mathematics, presupposing establishment of economic laws, and as such a narrower term than what political economy initially encompassed.

Moreover, Karl Marx (d. 1883) provided a critique of neoclassical economic theory[63] and refashioned the notion of commodity not only according to its use but as a socially specific kind of usefulness. He also reexamined the ideas of economic, utility, and efficiency as pseudo-concepts. The first is an illusion because there is no real-time economy. Utility ought not to be conflated with the notion of usefulness, since utility refers to the commensurability of things, whereas efficiency presupposes a false neutrality and one-size-fits-all neoclassical concept.[64] Yet, Marxism as a method of socioeconomic analysis is also entangled in this intricate web of science–value relations.[65] Despite its approach to renouncing normative philosophical ethics as well as the validity of the state as a structure of the bourgeois economic interest,[66] Marxist analysis of politics affirms the legacy of positive science by treating morality as a class ideology.[67] Marxism, despite its social mechanisms that promote well-being of society at large, as well as theoretical underpinnings

62 Marshall, *Principles of Economics*, 6.

63 See Karl Marx, *Das Kapital* (Hamburg: Verlag von Otto Meissner, 1883); Bob Rowthorn, "Neoclassical Economics and Its Critics: A Marxist View," *Social Scientist*, vol. 2, no. 3 (1973): 3–29.

64 See Dennis Badeen and Patrick Murray, "A Marxian Critique of Neoclassical Economics' Reliance on Shadows of Capital's Constitutive Social Forms," *Crisis & Critique*, vol. 3, no. 3 (2016): 24–27.

65 Even though Marx was not a moral philosopher and was opposed to the morality and ethics of his time, for it helped sustained the existing social order, he did have a moral theory of society. See Rodney G. Peffer, *Marxism, Morality, and Social Justice* (Princeton, NJ: Princeton University Press, 1990); Eugene Kamenka, *The Ethical Foundations of Marxism* (London: Routledge & Kegan Paul, 1962), electronic edition.

66 For Marx, economic classes are contingent upon a nation-state because a state is by definition an instrument of social control used by the members of one class to suppress or subordinate the members of another. Karl Marx and Friedrich Engels, *Die deutsche Ideologie* (Berlin: Akademie Verlag, 2003). Hallaq notes that classical Muslim scholars would – although for different reasons – affirm the idea of disappearance of the bureaucratic state as envisioned by Marx in the postcapitalist (communist) society. See Hallaq, *Impossible State*, 31.

67 Donald Clark Hodges, "Historical Materialism," *Ethics, Philosophy and Phenomenological Research*, vol. 23 (1962): 6. Marx was against the traditional notion of morality as an ethics of duty that is separated from the underlying

explaining the science of economic life and the means of production, entails dogmatic stipulations as would any other economic approach.

The formation of a modern nation-state – which established the norm of the legal as we understand it in Foucauldian terms as a top-down hegemonic approach and the subordination of citizens as legal subjects[68] – also impacted the development of national economies.[69] The legal is inextricably interrelated to the concept of the political, which also repercussions for the emergence of political Islam.[70] Wael Hallaq points out that the legal in any other era and society differs from the legal and the moral as they materialized in a modern state, for the very concept of the legal was, in premodern Islam, derived from the moral.[71] On the other hand, political theology (found within the Schmittian doctrine)[72] is only possible with the condition of the modern state. In Carl Schmitt's theory, law becomes a mechanism of politics, whereby the political is constituted by the state. The emergence of the nation-state is also intertwined with the idea of secularism and liberalism. Secularism is closely related to the project of the modern nation-state as a political doctrine in which economic behavior is enmeshed with the concept of the legal and the political and, according to Charles Taylor, defined as an independent and nonreligious political ethic. Considering such historical developments of secularism in

concerns of daily life. In this sense, Marx sought an approach that would unify daily concerns with moral concerns.

68 See e.g. Michel Foucault, *Discipline and Punishment* (New York: Vintage Books, 1979).

69 For Ludwig Mises (d. 1973), a leading spokesman of the Austrian School of Economics, the solution for a nation to avoid militaristic excursions was a return to rationalistic liberalism. See Ludwig Mises, *Nation, Staat, Wirtschaft: Beiträge zur Politik und Geschichte der Zeit* (Vienna: Manzsche Verlags und Universitäts-Buchhandlung, 1919).

70 Salvatore holds that the hermeneutical field of political Islam grounded revivalist Islam; Armando Salvatore, *Islam and the Political Discourse of Modernity* (Reading: Ithaca Press, 1997), 165–166. Bauer states that West-oriented Islamic revivalism through traditionalism provided for the birth of fundamentalist Islam (Bauer, *Die Kultur der Ambiguität*, 59–60).

71 Wael Hallaq, "Groundwork of the Moral Law: A New Look at the Qur'an and the Genesis of Shari'a," *Islamic Law and Society*, vol. 16 (2009): 248, 257.

72 Carl Schmitt, *Der Begriff des Politischen* (Berlin: Dunckner & Humbolt, 1979); for the English translation see Carl Schmitt, *The Concept of the Political*, trans. George Schwab (Chicago, IL: Chicago University Press, 1996); Giorgio Agamben, *The Signature of All Things* (New York: Zone Books, 2009).

Europe, the notion of sovereignty of a nation-state appears to have been defined in counter-theological terms.[73]

Ever since the dichotomization of the "is–ought" problematic, moral economics has been treated as a reductionist phenomenon. Many contemporary economists claim that economics can be treated either as a natural science, with its important yet problematic element of mathematical deductivism, under the pretext that it can be validated, objectified, and monitored; or it is handled as a social science, in that it is a spontaneous order that pertains to social institutions.[74] By doing the latter, one falls into the trap of ideological rationale, since the neoliberal economic paradigm has been driven by ideological force par excellence, treating economics according to market forces.

Economic ideas emerge out of social systems and as such within particular historical moments. In the modern era, concepts pertaining to economic theories and financial markets manifest epistemological and political realities in which economic provisions are made to be objectives themselves. This has been facilitated by modern nation-state apparatus, while universities and academic departments have furthered the study of conventional economics as science. For any economic system to be valid and to flourish, state laws and a particular political economy have to be enforced. The contribution of modern economic science, despite its variations and at times opposing theories, inevitably led to the emergence of a global economic outlook that obliterates cosmological and moral foundations of economic conduct, in that the ultimate value of economy became not welfare-oriented predispositions but the maximization of individual provision. Karl Polanyi (d. 1964), an economic historian who opposed the traditional outlook on economics, argued that market-based society was not an outcome of the natural order but was devised as such due to historical, political, social, and economic variables. He observed that

[73] Talal Asad, *Formations of the Secular* (Stanford, CA: Stanford University Press, 2003); Isaiah Berlin, *Liberty* (Oxford: Oxford University Press, 2002), 2.

[74] For the proponents of the neoliberal approach see e.g. Friedman, "Methodology of Positive Economics," 3–43; Hayek argues in favor of a society organized around a market order; see Friedrich Hayek, *Individualism and Economic Order* (Chicago, IL: University of Chicago Press, 1948); Friedrich Hayek, *The Road to Serfdom* (Chicago, IL: University of Chicago Press, 2007); Friedrich Hayek, *The Counter Revolution of Science* (London: The Free Press of Glencoe Collier-Macmillan, 1955).

A market economy can exist only in a market society.... A market economy must comprise all elements of industry, including labor, land, and money. (In a market economy money also is an essential element of industrial life and its inclusion in the market mechanism has, as we will see, far reaching institutional consequences.) But labor and land are no other than the human beings themselves of which every society consists and the natural surroundings in which it exists. To include them in the market mechanism means to subordinate the substance of society itself to the laws of the market.[75]

Polanyi stated that an economic system is embedded in and emerges from a particular sociocultural context. In this regard, a modern nation-state and a market society ought to be analyzed in conjugation. The market, whose final determinant is the state, is not a natural entity. The neoliberal conviction that views the market economy as the absence of the state is a relatively recent phenomenon,[76] whereby the state is becoming similar to a business enterprise. The nation-state treats citizens as its entrepreneurs, and it has proven that it is incapable of ensuring a healthy functioning of markets. Markets are not self-regulating, but they can ensure optimal conditions according to market regulations. In this sense, Adam Smith's invisible hand – which has been the driving force of classical economic conception – is practically nonexistent. Smith was doctrinarily not an advocate of laissez-faire but defended various approaches of government's activities. For later economist Milton Friedman (presented below), Smith's self-interest and the invisible hand represented the core axioms of scientific economics, which had political implications of advocating for a utility-based self-interest and the endless expanse of the market. Such interpretations of Smith's economic theory completely overshadowed his moral philosophy. Portrayals of Smith's theory of economics as an objective scientific field are encroached in the very history and politics of economic discipline. Economic solutions that are being presented thus ought not to be solely concerned with the material world but with interrogating the basic fundaments of human behavior. Hence, it would be naive to expect from economists systemic propositions and theoretical solutions on how to reorganize social life. For these reasons,

[75] Karl Polanyi, *The Great Transformation* (Boston: Beacon Press, 2001), 74–75.
[76] Thomas Piketty, *Capital in the Twenty-First Century* (Cambridge, MA: Belknap Press of Harvard University Press, 2014), 473–474.

it has been argued that today's economic activities are separated from ethical considerations and the natural world.[77]

John Maynard Keynes's (d. 1946) mixed economy was a response to some of the charges levied by Marx – that the capitalist system is not self-sustaining and self-correcting – as well as to the Great Depression. Keynes, however, saw this as an opportunity for state or government to justify its interference and existence.[78] As a pro-interventionist, Keynes believed that monetary policy does not play a decisive role in stimulating economy but advocated spending by government. The most influential economist in the twentieth century, with Keynes, is often regarded as Milton Friedman (d. 2006); he was a leading thinker of the Chicago school, whose free-market idea opposes traditional Keynesian economics. Friedman suggested that measured governmental monetary policy can provide solutions to economic recessions.[79] His quantity theory of money is based on a mechanical relationship between changes in the money supply and the price level, indicating that governmental money supply ought to be steady, which became known as monetarism, affected the development of twentieth-century economic theories. Moreover, Friedman's aim was to introduce economics to the masses and show that governmental failures and decisions have unintended consequences, while his economic postulates include the idea that economic results are more important than intentions. This is indicative of Friedman's aim to treat economics as a free-market-oriented "brute" scientific field that focuses purely on economic results. However, even though the free market is often associated with Friedman's economics, not all proponents of the free-market idea follow Friedman's economic model.

Friedrich Hayek (d. 1992) and the Austrian School of Economics also advocated for free-market capitalism and methodological individualism. Hayek, who was an adamant opponent of monetary policy, in line with the Austrian School of Economics, rejected mathematical modeling but sought to analyze and understand human actions. Hayek was skeptical of "hard science" and advocated a human understanding

[77] Ernst F. Schumacher, *Small Is Beautiful* (London: Perennial Library, 1973), 92.

[78] See John Maynard Keynes, *The Collected Writings of John Maynard Keynes*, vol. 7: *The General Theory of Employment, Interest and Money* (Cambridge: Cambridge University Press, 2013).

[79] See Milton Friedman, *Capitalism and Freedom* (Chicago, IL: Chicago University Press, 1962).

within social sciences and economics by stating that they should not impose a positivist methodology. Hayek states that

Against all this the persistent effort of modern Science has been to get down to "objective facts," to cease studying what men thought about nature or regarding the given concepts as true images of the real world, and, above all, to discard all theories which pretended to explain phenomena by imputing to them a directing mind like our own. Instead, its main task became to revise and reconstruct the concepts formed from ordinary experience on the basis of a systematic testing of the phenomena, so as to be better able to recognize the particular as an instance of a general rule. In the course of this process not only the provisional classification which the commonly used concepts provided, but also the first distinctions between the different perceptions which our senses convey to us, had to give way to a completely new and different way in which we learned to order or classify the events of the external world. The tendency to abandon all anthropomorphic elements in the discussion of the external world has in its most extreme development even led to the belief that the demand for "explanation" itself is based on an anthropomorphic interpretation of events and that all Science ought to aim at is a complete description of nature.[80]

Further, he believed that "all the 'physical laws of production' which we meet, e.g., in economics, are not physical laws in the sense of the physical sciences but people's beliefs about what they can do."[81] On the nature of social sciences, including economics, he states that

They deal, not with the relations between things, but with the relations between men and things or the relations between man and man. They are concerned with man's actions, and their aim is to explain the unintended or undersigned results of the actions of many men.... The social sciences in the narrower sense, i.e., those which used to be described as the moral sciences, are concerned with man's conscious or reflected action, actions where a person can be said to choose between various courses open to him, and here the situation is essentially different. The external stimulus which may be said to cause or occasion such actions can of course also be defined in purely physical terms. But if we tried to do so for the purposes of explaining human action, we would confine ourselves to less than we know about the situation.[82]

80 Hayek, *Counter-Revolution of Science*, 18.
81 Hayek, *Counter-Revolution of Science*, 31.
82 Hayek, *Counter-Revolution of Science*, 25, 26.

While Hayek affirmed the different nature and methodology of social sciences, he nonetheless advocated for maximizing consumption and methodological individualism in economic science – the idea that social phenomena result from the motivations of individuals.[83]

Economists routinely distinguish between "self-interest" (being interested in a material pursuit that might extend to others) and "selfishness" (being exclusively concerned with oneself) and complain that religious scholars and theologians do not recognize the difference between classical and neoclassical economic philosophy; on the other hand, in more technical-economic terms, selfishness entails a "continuity" axiom that implies psychological hedonism.[84] Various economists claim the so-called spiritual neutrality of the analytical tools of neoclassical theory,[85] which, as we shall see in Chapter 5, is erroneous since it smuggles psychological hedonism into economic theory and policy while suppressing the need for discussion over those philosophical theories and policies. Even though there is no single definition of neoclassical economics since it became increasingly diverse, according to Christian Arnsperger and Yanis Varoufakis[86] the three axioms that can be found in all neoclassical economic theories are methodological individualism, methodological instrumentalism, and methodological equilibration. Methodological individualism implies that economic processes at the macro level can only be attributed to the deeds and actions of individuals at the micro level. All economic processes and phenomena can be explained only by and through individual actions, which further implies that the individual is the sole source of moral values. In this context, values from any external source or institution (such as religion) are rejected. The emphasis on instrumental rationality and methodological

83 See Carl Menger, *Principles of Economics* (Auburn, AL: Ludwig von Mises Institute, 2007).

84 See for instance Hayek's distinction: "If we put it concisely by saying that people are and ought to be guided in their actions by their interests and desires, this will at once be misunderstood or distorted into the false contention that they are or ought to be exclusively guided by their personal needs or selfish interest, while what we mean is that they ought to be allowed to strive for whatever they think desirable." (Hayek, *Individualism and Economic Order*, 15).

85 For instance, Friedman claims that neoclassical economics is value-free (Friedman, "Methodology of Positive Economics," 3–43).

86 Christian Arnsperger and Yanis Varoufakis, "What Is Neoclassical Economics? The Three Axioms Responsible for Its Theoretical Oeuvre, Practical Irrelevance and, thus, Discursive Power," *Panoeconomicus*, vol. 53, no. 1 (2006): 5–18.

individualism generates an image of human as being autonomous of external sources but nonetheless seeking the maximization of utility. The very (economic) behavior of actors, related to the second axiom of methodological instrumentalism, presupposes fixed preferences that generate utility, whereby individuals continuously strive for the maximization of this utility, hence the close connection between the "continuity" axiom and hedonistic tendencies. The market is considered to be the most appropriate instrument to satisfy such tendencies. Neoclassicists believe their scientific analysis to be a natural method, which made neoclassical economic theories appear to be the most adequate method for studying economic variables and individual behavior. This anchorage in scientific economics and the radical absence of any possible critique of such neoclassical theories is essential to maintaining their discursive power.

Ernest Schumacher has correctly observed that "The trouble about valuing means above ends – which, as confirmed by Keynes, is the attitude of modern economics – is that it destroys man's freedom and power to choose the ends he really favours; the development of means, as it were, dictates the choice of ends."[87] Since modernity encompasses also processes of rationalization of the economic field, economy becomes an objectified reality where social order is based on an engineering design and causality.[88] Economy becomes a dominant field in human life, since the more one (or a state) engages into economic life, the more prosperous – and as an extension of that "civilized" – one becomes. In this regard, modern economically centered natural order undermines the doctrine of cosmological harmony and collective exchange. As a consequence, individual prosperity and fulfillment is given importance, whereby

> There is no collective agent here, indeed, the account amounts to a denial of such. There are agents, individuals acting on their own behalf, but the global upshot happens behind their backs. It has a certain predictable form, because there are certain laws governing the way in which their myriad individual actions concatenate. This is an objectifying account, one which treats social events like other processes in nature, following laws of a similar sort. But this objectifying take on social life is just as much part of the modern

[87] Schumacher, *Small Is Beautiful*, 51.

[88] Charles Taylor, *A Secular Age* (Cambridge, MA: Belknap Press of Harvard University Press, 2007), 176–177.

understanding, derived from the modern moral order, as the new modes of imagining social agency.[89]

As asserted by contemporary economists like Thomas Piketty and Tony Lawson, the term "economic science" must be thus tendered with caution. Even though for Piketty economics is part of the social sciences – which is, as will be discussed in Chapters 4 and 5, a problematic categorization due to the mechanisms borrowed from natural sciences[90] – he is very skeptical of the term "economic science." Piketty therefore advocates for using the term "political economy," for, despite its old-fashioned usage, it fits the narrative of economy much better and sets it apart from other social sciences, namely its political, normative-based, and moral intentionality.[91] Defined as political economy, economics is much more than just quantifications and formulas. It addresses the very core of social circumstances and analyzes various impacts on society, which is in Islamic tradition – unlike neoclassical economics – not devoid of a moral fiber. From this perspective, economics cannot be perceived as a science on its own like physics per se, for science depends on predictability and certitude. Economics, conversely, has too often been proven to be wrong, yet correct only when analyzing events in retrospect.

The Genealogy of Modern Islamic Economics

The modern perceptions of Islam and, later on, Islamic economics as politically motivated entity was also informed by the political developments in the backdrop of nineteenth century Europe.[92] Muslim

89 Taylor, *Secular Age*, 181.

90 On the development of social sciences, see Immanuel Wallerstein et al., *Open the Social Sciences* (Stanford, CA: Stanford University Press, 1996,) 9–14; "Sociology was born in the midst of profound tension between religion and liberal culture in Europe, and only in this context can we understand the discipline of sociology's understanding of religion." (Hadden, "Toward Desacralizing Secularization Theory," 589). See also Masuzawa, *Invention of World Religions*, 15.

91 Piketty explains, "I dislike the expression 'political science,' which strikes me as terribly arrogant because it suggests that economics has attained a higher scientific status than the other social sciences. I much prefer the expression 'political economy,' which may seem rather old-fashioned but to my mind conveys the only thing that sets economics apart from the other social sciences: its political, normative, and moral purpose." (Piketty, *Capital in the Twenty-First*, 573–574).

92 On the notion of the political, see Schmitt, *Der Begriff des Politischen.*

reformists in the nineteenth and twentieth centuries addressed political and social issues that eventually bolstered an economic Islam. In various classical treaties analyzed in Chapter 3, however, the individual did not exist for the sake of the state (government) but as part of the collective unit, at least in theory, governed by moral laws. The governmental authority promoted welfare to the individual,[93] which was part of the *umma* not as an abstract (worldly) entity but also as a concrete (local) one. Hence, it is incumbent upon Muslim scholars to think of Islamic economics outside the box of the nation-state.

This conspicuous aspect of the debate on Islamic economics pertains to the colonial period and the conception of the state, which was in many ways seen as a reaction to and a continuation of the writings by Muslim reformists during the period known as *al-nahḍa*.[94] While some Muslim reformists advocated those theoretical excursions as a means of consolidating the moral, educational, and political transformation of Muslim societies,[95] others later in the twentieth century attempted to restore the lost *adab* (moral and spiritual characteristics) of the Islamic civilization.[96] The reformists' ideas[97] were largely expressions of the sociopolitical and economic conditions of the time. They called for the reapplication of *Sharīʿa* as state law and defended the Muslim subject, while aiming to implement methods, theories, and concepts that were unique and profound to the Western intellectual makeup. According to Bjørn Olav Utvik, the driving force of Islamism as a political ideology is social as well as religious: "rather than being a hostile or negative reaction to change, Islamism could be seen as on the whole an effort

[93] See Sherman Jackson, *Islamic Law and the State: The Constitutional Jurisprudence of Shihāb al-Dīn al-Qarāfi* (Leiden: Brill, 1996), 224.

[94] For more on the intellectual history of *al-nahḍa*, see Jens Hanssen and Max Weiss, *Arabic Thought beyond the Liberal Age* (Cambridge: Cambridge University Press 2016).

[95] See e.g. Sayyid Abul Aʿlā Mawdūdī, *Islamic Economic System: Principles and Objectives* (Delhi: Markazi Maktabah Islami, 1980); "The decision to go for Islam as a political formula to the detriment of Islam as a culture assumes the shape of a contemporary call for tatbiq (implementation) of the shariʿa – it blatantly overlooks the history of the shariʿa and the related predicament." Bassam Tibi, *Islam between Culture and Politics* (New York: Palgrave Macmillan, 2005), 155.

[96] See Muhammad Naquib al-Attas, *Islam, Secularism and the Philosophy of Future* (London: Mansell, 1985); Muhammad Naquib al-Attas, *Islam and Secularism* (Kuala Lumpur: ISTAC, 1993).

[97] For the authors, see Methodology and Theoretical Framework below.

to promote modernisation while Islamising, domesticating and indigenising it."[98]

The social and cultural knowledge of Muslim societies changed during the colonial period. The consecutive decades saw the emergence of nationalistic sentiments in South Asia, the echoes of political Islam, and the resurgence of scholars who wrote on Islamic economics; scholars such as Muhammad Hamidullah, Abū al-Aʿlā Mawdūdī, and others[99] explored the concept of the Muslim state. Those religious scholars invoked the state – which was a uniquely European phenomenon – as a way to expand "authentic" Islamic ideas based on the Divine law. Consequently, the concept and institution of *Sharīʿa* as a moral law as it was practiced by their Muslim predecessors in the classical period was gradually being altered into a primarily legal understanding, which would correspond more to the modern classification of law.[100]

What followed in proceeding decades was the merging of an Islamization of knowledge process and Islamic economic theories as a methodological hybridity of Islamic terminology and neoclassical economics. Since Muslim scholars have taken the existence of the nation-state for granted, including many Islamist thinkers, I argue that contemporary Islamic economics is ideologically constructed through the mechanisms of secular economics, resting upon the neoclassical economic epistemology and the conditions of a modern nation-state that was made "Islamic" through the Islamization process. The Islamization of knowledge process, which aimed to Islamize domains of human action, has been coined and developed in the second half of the twentieth century primarily by Ismaʿil al-Faruqi[101] and Muhammad Naquib al-Attas.[102] Pertinent to the Muslim conception of knowledge is the notion of *ʿilm* and *maʿrifa*, translated as science and knowledge, not only as utilized and understood by the classical Muslim scholars themselves but also within the modern context. Following the philosophy of al-Faruqi and al-Attas, the Islamization process has at least two

[98] Bjørn Olav Utvik, *Islamist Economics in Egypt* (Boulder, CO: Lynne Rienner, 2006), 22.

[99] On the economic ideas in Islam between 1930 and 1970, see Chapter 1.

[100] See e.g. Tibi, *Islam between Culture and Politics*, 63–66, 148–166; for explanation of how *fiqh* changed from more ethical to legal understanding, see Abū Ḥamid al-Ghazālī, *Al-Mustaṣfāʾ* (Medina: Sharika al-Madīna al-Munawwara li al-Ṭabāʿat, 2008).

[101] Ismaʿil Raji al-Faruqi, *Islamization of Knowledge* (Herndon, VA: IIIT, 1989).

[102] E.g. al-Attas, *Islam, Secularism and the Philosophy of Future.*

strands that aim to accommodate various teachings stemming from Islamic sources and basic principles in order to attain a new understanding of knowledge that would be suitable and applicable in Muslim countries, while often resorting to the methods, concepts, and theories of their Western counterparts. The Islamization process as conceived by al-Faruqi was most successfully applied to economic models. Islamic economics and banking have, despite their theoretical critique of the neoliberal economic paradigm, endorsed the mainstream political-economic ideology instead of pursuing the postulates that are supposedly intrinsic to Islamic economic thought, such as the idea of socioeconomic justice and higher moral ends. Given the impact of the Islamization of knowledge process on Islamic economics, several reservations for that model exist, since Islamizing economics appears to be only a temporary solution. Consequently, this process constructs a self-perpetuated narrative of its own economic worldview that does not primarily aim to provide for the social benefit of society as a whole but rather sets to distinguish itself from other mainstream economic systems, or even operates within them. As explored in Chapter 1, from the 1970s onwards, Islamic institutions, universities, and educational centers advocated for an economic curriculum that accommodated Islamization of knowledge efforts, while involving mainstream economic structures and concepts.[103] This exposes the methodological confusion, which was seen only as a plan of action by modern Muslim economists. Muslim economists perceived such a methodology as dependent on the subject it studied.[104] Due to the deductive method in contemporary Islamic economics, "research remained focused on the 'ideal' situations and normative behavior given by Islamic rules and values."[105] As such, it prompted the study of economics as a subcategory of mainstream economic doctrine and did not correspond to social reality on the ground.

[103] Addas, *Methodology of Economics*, 5.

[104] Zubair Hasan, "Islamization of Knowledge in Economics: Issues and Agenda," *IIUM Journal*, Special Issue, vol. 6, no.2, (1998): 3.

[105] Abdulrahman Yousri Ahmed, "The Scientific Approach to Islamic Economics: Philosophy, Theoretical Construction and Applicability," in *Theoretical Foundations of Islamic Economics*, ed. Habib Ahmed (Jeddah: Islamic Development Bank, Islamic Research and Training Institute, 2002), 50.

As we shall see in Chapter 2, according to the majority of Muslim economists the subject of Islamic economics is approached from a legal-financial perspective, loosely embedded in *Sharīʿa* as a methodological tool. By establishing itself within the "scientific" parameters of knowledge, as it was known in nineteenth-century Europe, Islamic economics presented itself as an alternative economic system to capitalism[106] and socialism, while turning toward the scientific theories of neoclassical economic positivism and its episteme.[107] Such theories disregarded not only the scholarship but also the epistemic value of premodern Muslim scholars and their ideas on moral economic behavior. This eventually led to the coupling of Islamic economics and finances with a mainstream economic framework, which, to an extent, paid only lip-service to *Sharīʿa*'s legal impediments. In constructing an economic system, contemporary Muslim economists relied on neoclassical conceptions and religious scriptures. The inner structure of Islamic economics, despite its distinctly religious characteristics, rests upon the neoclassical economic paradigm and its tainted views on the universe through preconceived economic terms, concepts, and methodology. And since economic methodology differs from legal philosophy, Muslim economists faced a second methodological stalemate. Given the neoclassical economic system on one hand and the *fiqh* methodology with which modern Muslim economists

106 Capitalism is based on the neoliberal ideology of production and distribution of goods of the free-market economy, in which production activities are privatively owned. The exchange of commodities and services are floating free i.e. without any major systematic injunction of the state. Privatization of personal and public domains often results in secluding private ownership, exploitation of human psyche and labor, as well as privileging profit over people's needs. Historically, capitalism evolved in England in the nineteenth century, although formal modes of capitalism were known also in other regions before that time. It soon spread through Europe and beyond via mercantilism and colonial projects, which exploited natural resources and human force. Under capitalism, the means of production are privatized, including services, properties, and industries. This assumingly free utilization and appropriation of property by owners plays into the discussion of production activities by acquiring profit and expanding monopoly over the working force. By capitalism, I generally refer to "a system of economic life made distinctive by its combination of three spheres – the imaginative, the productive and the institutional." Charles Tripp, *Islam and Moral Economy* (Cambridge: Cambridge University Press, 2006), 3.

107 See Keynes, *General Theory of Employment, Interest and Money*. See also Friedman's notion of usefulness and the ideology of the so-called Chicago positivism (Friedman, "Methodology of Positive Economics," 3–43).

operated on the other, the Islamic financial sector was devised through Western conceptualizations of economic science, despite its reliance on Islamic terms.[108] Further, since there is no real-time existing Islamic economy, the data Muslim economists established indicates a methodological synthesis and hence epistemological discordances. These inherently asymmetrical and ambiguous classifications of Islamic economics in particular reflect the narrative of an Islamic economic science that was born out of the abovementioned twofold contestation. By doing so, Muslim economists, willingly or unwillingly, justified religious teaching with a mainstream economic narrative. Despite its distinct characteristics, contemporary Islamic economics is embedded into the global politico-economic amalgam and hence functions within this paradigm, unlike classical Islamic scholarship, which views *Sharīʿa* primarily as a moral category that intends to reform not just economic processes but also the moral self.

Classical Scholarship and the Moral Self

Even though ethics appears to be central to economic teachings in contemporary Islamic economics, the concept as such in contemporary writings and deliberations[109] is rarely used as a categorical imperative in line with premodern conceptions of their worldview. Making Islamic economic science compatible with mainstream economics is a feasible attempt, yet a futile venture for two reasons. First, modern economic science operates within a different epistemic field in comparison to classical economic thought in Islamic tradition. Merging two epistemic systems would hence presuppose that the Islamic notions of *ʿilm*, *akhlāq*, *māl*, and other core concepts have to be divested of their epistemic values. Second, in light of scientific empiricism, the value of the moral cosmology of *Sharīʿa* – as a totality of ethical standards, norms, and teachings in the context of economic-spiritual development in Islamic tradition[110] – has been cast as unscientific. The moral cosmology of *Sharīʿa*, as expounded by some of the major Muslim scholars, entails economic teachings as part of wider metaphysical considerations, whose ethical foundation ultimately

108 Addas, *Methodology of Economics*, 97.

109 See e.g. the writings of Choudhury, Naqvi, Siddiqi, Chapra in Chapter 2.

110 See e.g. Abū Ḥamid al-Ghazālī, *Iḥyāʾ ʿUlūm al-Dīn*, 4 vols. (Beirut: Dār al-Nadwah, n.d.).

functions as a technology of self-examination as it pertains to the most profound human behavioral patterns. It affects not simply exchange but also production processes and their spiritual significance. While the concept itself did not exist in classical Islamic milieu as such, this project aims to show that the classical scholars were cognizant of *Sharīʿa*'s ethical patterns in and of economic behavior, in that those patterns form part of one's daily-life obligations and religious duties. In that context, the economic teachings and ethical behavioral stipulations by, for instance, al-Shaybānī, Ibn Abī al-Dunyā, al-Iṣfahānī, al-Ghazālī, al-Muḥāsibī, Ibn Taymiyya, and Ibn Qayyim al-Jawziyya are all-encompassing and thus cosmological.

Every economic doctrine rests upon a certain philosophical system, and the same is true for Islamic economics. Economic imperatives in Muslim societies have never constrained people from engaging in economic activities;[111] on the contrary, they have encouraged purchase of what are regarded as "licit" commodities. Various classical Muslim scholars presuppose that economic thought was never parted from overall moral predicaments and that it shapes the very nature of human conduct through a particular worldview.[112] The argument I am putting forward is hence concerned with the idea that viewing economic teachings as an all-embracing moral cosmology of *Sharīʿa* is not only more justified from a historical perspective but also that it will do more justice to the central themes of economic thought in Islamic intellectual tradition as presented by the aforementioned modern thinkers. *Sharīʿa* as one of the central paradigms within Islamic thought was, according to Hallaq, never parted from moral fiber in premodern times.[113] Since moral philosophy predated political economy, which was also largely influenced by classical Muslim scholars, and since contemporary Muslim scholars rarely refer to their premodern counterparts, studying the historical scholarship on economic thought is in this context inevitable. Classical economic philosophy in Islamic tradition displays a vast array of seemingly legal content with an

[111] "Al-Ghazalijevi pogledi na ekonomske probleme i neka etičko-pravna pitanja značajna za ekonomsko ponašanje," in Sadeq Abdul-Hasan and Aidit Ghazali, eds., *Pregled islamske ekonomske misli* (Sarajevo: El-Kalem, 1996), 148.

[112] Sadeq, *Pregled islamske ekonomske misli*, 12.

[113] See Wael Hallaq, *The Origins and Evolution of Islamic Law* (Cambridge: Cambridge University Press, 2005).

overarching moral character, wherein excursions to theological, philosophical, Sufi, and metaphysical realms were intimately related. Many classical Muslim scholars operated not only within the legal realm but also within the broader theological and Sufi contexts, introducing concepts such as *ʿadl*, *maṣlaḥa*, *iḥsān*, *faqr*, *zuhd*, *tazkiyya* and so forth, which are vital in reconstructing the epistemology of the subject, for their deliberations did not depart from the moral understanding of the cosmos. In doing so, one has to go beyond the legal spectrum of *Sharīʿa*, since classical scholars expounded their theories not only as jurists but also through theological and Sufi discourses.[114] Although there is no economics in Islam per se, the term that was used historically referred to household management (*ʿilm tadbīr al-manzil*),[115] and ethical teachings – which Muslim scholars deduced from their religious scripture – have played an important role not only in economic thought but in establishing ethical categories. Obtaining material gains can, in such a tradition, be regarded as tantamount to defending the faith.[116] As will be indicated in the following chapters, one of the differences between modern and classical Islamic scholarship is that the latter viewed material gains within the scope of the Hereafter and thus as part of the moral worldview; contrastingly, modern scholarship approaches economic ideas primarily from a technical and legal-financial viewpoint.

Economic issues in Islamic tradition cannot be resolved only in mathematical terms, for they are sociological, philosophical, and above all ethical in nature. What are presented as economic solutions to modern problems are, in actuality, technical solutions to drawbacks that are profoundly more complex and as such inextricably related to the very composition of knowledge, which brings us back to the debate on morality and science. As will be discussed in Chapters 3, 4, and 5, classical Islamic scholarship and the sciences of

114 See Chapter 3, and the works of e.g. al-Shaybānī, al-Ghazāli, al-Dullāji, Abī al-Dunjā, Ibn Qayyim, etc.

115 Abdul Azim Islahi, *Contribution of Muslim Scholars to Economic Thought and Analysis, 11–905 AH/632–1500 AD* (Jeddah: Islamic Economics Research Centre, King Abdulaziz University, 2004), 15.

116 Taha J. al-Alwani and Waleed El-Ansary, "Linking Ethics and Economics," in *Islamic Finance: Islamic Finance into the 21st Century: Proceedings of the Second Harvard University Forum on Islamic Finance* (Cambridge, MA: Harvard University, 1999), 112.

nature[117] provide a total refutation of the quality to quantity reduction. Based on the abovementioned extrapolations of premodern economic teachings, it is necessary to approach the subject of economic thought in Islamic tradition by linking various fields of knowledge such as theology, philosophy, *taṣawwuf*, and jurisprudence with moral conduct.

Methodology and Theoretical Framework

Based on the abovementioned observations, the main question that this book intends to answer is what constitutes classical economic thought in Islamic tradition and how does it differ from contemporary considerations. This question is admittedly a broad one and will therefore be answered by proposing a set of sub-questions that extend to premodern and modern periods in Islamic tradition.[118] There are corresponding questions that are integral to the argument: How did the positivist logic of natural and social sciences impact the development of contemporary Islamic economic theories? How does the revivalist period and the emergence of the modern nation-state play into the making of the modern Islamic economic project? What are the structural implications of the Islamization of knowledge process for Islamic economics? How did the contemporary Islamic economic project form, and what is its epistemology? Is there a legally stipulated study of economic teachings in Islam and how is it related to the notion of morality and justice? What is the role of *Sharīʿa* (and its relation to *maṣlaḥa*) in establishing theories of Islamic economics and how are they perceived by contemporary Muslim scholars in comparison to their medieval counterparts? In relation to that, what are the specifics of economic reasoning in Islamic tradition, and how intertwined is economic reasoning with

117 "[W]ithout Islamic metaphysics and sciences of nature, there is no such thing as Islamic economics." Waleed El-Ansary, "The Quantum Enigma and Islamic Sciences of Nature: Implications for Islamic Economic Theory," in *Proceedings of the 6th International Conference on Islamic Economics and Finance* (Jeddah: Islamic Development Bank, 2005), 145.

118 Throughout this book, I refer to the premodern period in Islam as between the seventh and seventeenth centuries and the modern period as after the eighteenth century. For more detail, see Wael Hallaq, *Sharīʿa: Theory, Practice, Transformations* (Cambridge: Cambridge University Press, 2009), parts 1 and 3. Moreover, I use "classical," "premodern," and/or "traditional scholars" interchangeably.

Islamic jurisprudence or *uṣūl al-fiqh*, the objectives of Islamic law or *maqāṣid al-Sharī'a*, and other fields of knowledge, such as *kalām* and *taṣawwuf*? And finally, what is the role of ethical theories and a moral understanding of the universe in shaping the economic tradition in Islam?

This book hence explores several conspicuous aspects of the discourse and intellectual history of Islamic economic thought, including its ontology and genealogy. The overall approach of this book is historical-critical in analyzing several key texts on economic thought within Islamic intellectual history. It is analytical in the sense that it inquires into what contemporary authors have stated about Islamic economics, how the subject emerged, and what social, economic, and intellectual factors contributed to its fruition. Secondly, it is critical in that it seeks to understand the alteration of the knowledge processes of the economic paradigm in Islamic tradition before and after the colonial period. This approach will portray the genealogy, the sociology of knowledge, and the nature of the discipline. Moreover, it will delineate ideological contestations and theoretical shortcomings of the field due to the paradigm shift that occurred in the nineteenth century with colonialism and that flourished in the twentieth century with revivalism, political Islam, and Islamization of knowledge. To explore the epistemological and hermeneutical approaches to economic teachings in Islamic tradition, I propose a methodology that sets forth to analyze and/or deconstruct already existing theories on Islamic economics. This subsequently entails the deconstructing the perception of the established superiority of *fiqh*-based economic literature.

Each chapter has its own theoretical consideration as is indicated below. In this Introduction, I have briefly presented early modern Europe's economic philosophy through, chiefly, the Descartian reducibility of quality to quantity and Hume's "is–ought" distinction.

Chapter 1 is concerned with the sociopolitical and epistemological developments in Muslim countries at the turn of the nineteenth century and the formation of the modern nation-state as a distinctly European project. It focuses on Muslim reformists' vision of an Islamic state and society within the parameters of a modern state, as well as Muslim scholars' reappropriation of mainstream economic theories through the Islamization of knowledge process. I provide a broad overview of the colonial period and analyze Muslim reformists and their perspectives in order to place their view within a colonial historiography in

Muslim countries. In spite of different trends of reformists – whose seminal contributions to the political, legal, and theological reverberations of faith provided material for the next generation of scholars, who coined the subject of Islamic economics – and their ideas pertaining to socioeconomic configuration of the Middle East and South Asia, addressing the role of socialism, capitalism, and the state, the reformist scholars did not discuss Islamic economics as such. The reformists of the late nineteenth and early twentieth centuries were religious scholars who, according to Ahmed Khan, are divided into two groups: "the modernists," such as Jamāl al-Dīn al-Afghānī, Muḥammad ʿAbduh, Rashīd Riḍā, Muhammad Iqbal, Muhammad Asad, and Fazlur Rahman; and the "neo-revivalists" or "literalists," such as Ḥasan al-Bannā, Syed Quṭb, Abū al-Aʿlā Mawdūdī, Muḥammad Bāqir al-Ṣadr, Nejatullah Siddiq, Khurshid Ahmad, Umer Chapra, Muḥammad Anas Zarqa, Monzer Kahf, and others. Writing on Islamic economics was, however, pioneered by Muhammad Hamidullah and other South Asian scholars,[119] and advanced by Abū al-Aʿlā Mawdūdī and Ahmad Khurshid. In this chapter, I refer to primary literature of Muslim reformists in Arabic, original sources of early Muslim religious scholars and economists, and secondary sources addressing the historical, political, and cultural background of the colonial period in the Middle East and South (East) Asia.

In the second part, I present the Islamization of knowledge process and its key thinkers as it developed in relation to the discipline of Islamic economics. Early twentieth-century literature on economics in Islam contributed to the establishment of Islamic economics as a gradually self-sufficient discipline, which was attributed to Mawdūdī's text *The Economic Problem of Man and Its Islamic Solution.* This is not a coincidence and goes hand in hand with sociopolitical, national, and religious development in the twentieth century in South Asia. The Islamization of knowledge process, which emerged in the 1970s, encompasses all areas and fields of human activities under the Islamic banner and was presented as an alternative to Western theories of knowledge, including the study of economics. The proponents[120] of the Islamization

[119] Muhammad Hamidullah, "Islam's Solution to the Basic Economic Problems: The Position of Labour," *Islamic Culture*, vol. 10, no. 2 (1936): 213–233; Muhammad Hamidullah, "Haidarabad's Contribution to Islamic Economic Thought and Practice," *Die Welt des Islams*, vol. 4, no. 2/3 (1955): 73–78.

[120] See for instance Ismaʿil al-Faruqi, Muhammad Naquib al-Attas, Umer Chapra, Muhammad Choudhury, and Nejatullah Siddiqi; see also Chapter 1.

process argue that a multifaceted approach to the field of Islamic studies in general, and Islamic economics in particular, entails Western theoretical considerations as well as relying on the scriptural sources of Islamic tradition. They define the Islamization of knowledge as a process of coupling concepts rooted in modernization processes and aligning them with Islamic legal and theologically based arguments. On the other hand, the opponents[121] to this approach provide an insightful critique to the subject matter of Islamic economics through a severalfold perspective: the Islamization of Islamic economics serves its own narrative by "Islamizing" a human field of study; it develops a stock of knowledge to oppose an already-established economic system; and it does not serve the social needs of society by promoting economic justice, which appears vital in addressing the gist of economic thought in Islamic tradition. The self-fulfilling narrative of Islamic economics presents a temporary solution as well as a stalemate. The aim of this chapter is hence to present a twofold analysis of Islamic economic thinking through this process. First, Islamic economics emerged as a distinct field of study as a result of broader historical, socioeconomic, and political developments, as well as the Islamists' reappropriations of those paradigms. Second, since its development it has rested upon a dual conception – its own theological sources and Western mainstream politico-economic norms.

Chapter 2 reexamines the field of contemporary Islamic economics on the basis of selecting from the corpus of contemporary scholars and Muslim economists' writings by applying the following structure. The original writings of Muslim economists appear primarily in English – which is the unofficial language of Islamic economics – in addition to sources in Arabic, Urdu, and other languages. A selection of highly acclaimed contemporary Muslim economists, such as Haider Naqvi, Muhammad Akram Khan, Muhammad F. Khan, Alam Choudhury, Umer Chapra, and Nejatullah Sidiqqi, and their writings on economics will be analyzed on the basis of the key terms, methodology, and epistemology they used that espouses a continuation of both Western neoclassical economics and Islamic theological tenets. This selection is based on some of their authoritative writings, the frequency of

121 See for instance the writings of Thomas Philipp, Timur Kuran, and Vali Nasr. For details on the critique of the Islamization process and economics, see Chapter 4.

references made by other scholars have to their texts, and the penetrating theories and ideas they have provided for the overall study of economics in Islam, in spite of their differences. In addition, in this chapter I address the existence of multiple and at times opposing theories on and of Islamic economics as a structural problem that points to the uneven development of the discipline, also by consulting secondary literature on contemporary Islamic economics and ethics.[122] Contemporary Muslim economists often refer to the concepts of economic justice, law, and ethics, albeit in diverse ways and from different standpoints. The panoply of ideas to which these economists refer expresses an array of economic, ethical, and/or legal objectives, and the manner and construction of these concepts are of primary concern and ultimately lead to my critique of them in Chapter 4.

Chapter 3 which encapsulates the gist of the book, is about the intellectual history of classical Muslim scholars, and it analyzes primary textual sources on moral, metaphysical, and legal aspects of economic teachings in Islamic tradition and their relation to *Sharīʿa* as a moral cosmological system. The first part introduces the study of *Sharīʿa* as a moral category and not only as a legal device as it is understood by various contemporary Muslim economists. Since legal precepts and commercial laws are only one part of overall moral-economic conduct, the first part of this chapter will demonstrate that, although there is a strong correlation between Islamic law and economics, this correlation is based on the legal reading of economic conduct and is thus predominately associated with legal stipulations, inheritance law, contract-based rules, and so forth. Such a reading presupposes legal-technical reality of economic postulates and does not address the moral philosophy of economics and epistemological axioms that would explain the overall subject of economic behavior in Islamic tradition. Despite the importance of legal and *fiqh*-based material, economic thought in Islamic tradition stretches beyond the juristic framework, hence questioning the legal establishment is essential for an overall study of the subject at hand. Reading classical Muslim scholars who tackled economic issues reveals that, despite the strong connection to *Sharīʿa*, economic conduct was often

122 E.g. S. Mohammad. Ghazanfar, *Medieval Islamic Thought: Filling the "Great Gap" in European Economics* (London: Routledge, 2003); Islahi, *Contribution of Muslim Scholars.*

perceived as a natural extension of moral, theological, and what we would nowadays refer to as Sufi teachings, while also encapsulated in the Qur'anic ethos. Many questions on the historical relation between modern Islamic legal scholarship and economic theories (including those pertaining to *maqāṣid al-Sharī'a*, *maṣlaḥa*, *istiṣlāḥ*, and *istiḥsān*), in addition to questions about existing commercial activities in Muslim societies, have until today remained unanswered. Since economic activities stretch beyond *fiqh* rules, I propose to reexamine the correlation between the field of law and the subject of economics in classical texts by referring to the concept of *Sharī'a* as moral cosmology.

Central to this chapter is, however, the terminological and theoretical interpretation of the writings of selected classical Muslim scholars (some of them also legal specialists), which focuses on textual analysis of the key concepts (e.g. *kasb*, or acquisition of wealth; *zuhd*, or renunciation of the world; *māl*, or wealth/money; *'adl*, or justice; *maṣlaḥa*, or common good; *farḍ kifāya*, or connective obligations; *ḥisba*, or Islamic institution performing business accountability, and so forth) by inquiring into the context in which those terms were invoked in close connection to moral economic behavior. This will lead me to delve into the writings of Muslim scholars from the eighth to fifteenth centuries, since many ideas on economic activities and moral conduct stem from this period. Since the premodern Muslim scholars expounded their economic, philosophical, and Sufi ideas in proximity to the conception of *Sharī'a* as an overall ethical term, sometimes expressed via different theoretical concepts, the moral self and the metaphysical qualities of economic behavior appear to be of high relevance in the writings of classical authors. Among others, I analyze the readings by Abū Yūsuf, al-Shaybānī, Ibn Abī al-Dunyā, al-Rāghib al-Iṣfahānī, al-Ghazālī, al-Muḥāsibī, al-Dimashqī, Ibn Taymiyya, Ibn Khaldūn, Ibn Qayyim al-Jawziyya, al-Maqrīzī, and others. These authors made seminal contributions to the subject of ethical-economic thought. As will be indicated below, despite the fact that some authors can be regarded primarily as jurists and others as Sufis, they elucidated an infused moral-cosmological preeminence of economic ideas, encapsulated in terms such as *kasb*, *zuhd*, *adab*, and *maṣlaḥa*. This multifaceted discourse encapsulated man's behavior and his moral and spiritual predispositions rather than only juristic stipulations.

Chapter 4 provides a conceptual critique of the contemporary Islamic economic project as a hybrid discipline and Islamization of knowledge as a self-perpetuating narrative by referring to the works of Timur Kuran, Muhammad Akram Khan, Seyyed Vali Reza Nasr, Syed Farid Alatas, and other scholars. It views such economic theories either as subordinated to the positivist social sciences or neoliberal economic paradigm, as a subsystem of Islamic law, or in light of the Islamization process and its methodological reverberations. Drawing upon the findings in Chapter 3, which expounds that economic matters were in the premodern period not discussed only in legal or *fiqh* terms – which would historically fall under the category of *mu'āmalāt* – but as moral-cosmological categories, this chapter will interrogate the epistemological and methodological shortcomings of contemporary Islamic economics.

The methodological deadlock of modern Islamic economics is the result of the over-compartmentalization and scientific differentiations of concepts, categories, and disciplines of knowledge that occurred in Western sciences and that have had ramifications for the twentieth-century Muslim intellectual makeup. Accordingly, separate branches of knowledge such as Islamic politics, Islamic sociology, Islamic economics, and so on were formed.[123] Theoretical arguments asserted by some contemporary Muslim scholars are, despite their Islamic references, almost exclusively interwoven into the social, political, and epistemological imaginary of nineteenth-century Europe and its division of sciences. They are thus embedded in the fabric of neoclassical economic philosophy.[124] This chapter will look at contemporary Western and Muslim scholars who discuss the concepts of knowledge, Islamic reason, secularization, and economics. Though contemporary Muslim scholars rely on fundamental sources of Islam, classical thinkers merged legal rulings with the metaphysics of *Sharī'a*'s moral order and, unlike their contemporary counterparts, did not separate

[123] See some of the literature from the International Institute of Islamic Thought (IIIT), e.g. Isma'il Raji al-Faruqi, *The Essence of Islamic Civilization* (Herndon, VA: IIIT, 2013); Taha Jabir al-Alwani, *Issues in Contemporary Islamic Thought* (Herndon, VA : IIIT, 2005); al-Faruqi, *Islamization of Knowledge*. On the critique of positivist methodology from an Islamization of knowledge point of view, see Taha Jabir al-Alwani, *Islamic Thought: An Approach to Reform* (Herndon, VA: IIIT, 2006).

[124] Chapter 2 addresses the plurality of voices among Muslim economists. Despite this plurality, many Muslim economists conceive the discipline of Islamic economics as a science that combines orthodox economic and Islamic ethical postulates.

disciplines in a way that denuded them of moral cosmology, indicating very different (and distinct) epistemological foundations of economics.

Chapter 5 introduces the theory of pluralistic epistemology of economic teachings in Islamic tradition and attempts to answer the question, based on the analysis of previous chapters, "should a reconstruction of economic teachings in Islamic tradition be possible, and what kind of epistemology and reading does it presuppose?" By investigating the discourse of polyvalent economic theories in Islamic tradition which aims to establish a more equitable and just society, this chapter will determine the discourse and particularities of an economic model that is based on a moral cosmology. I analyze scholars who pinpointed that Islamic culture can be realized through a multitude of paradigms and multifaceted approaches in studying the historical discourse of economic Islam.[125] The moral dimensions of *Sharīʿa* introduce a human understanding that permeates legal, social, and economic processes. The study of economic ideas in Islamic tradition is possible only through a particular conceptualization, whereby *ʿilm* as knowledge and *ʿamal* as informed action or deed form the core of such an epistemology. Modern (Islamic) economics not only lacks an understanding of economic justice, which is according to classical scholars achieved through social insurance and social balance, but it also rests upon Western political dogmas and economic processes, embedded in the modern state apparatus, which presupposes a particular social history. While acknowledging the shortcomings of the contemporary field of Islamic economics, it is crucial to examine the genealogy of the subject by deconstructing its presumed narrative and to mediate mechanisms and terms that would accommodate postulates from the classical tradition. Bridging the historical gap between classical and modern economic thought furthermore gives incentives on how to build a more equitable and socially progressive society that rests on economic justice and the philosophy of common good. Therefore, I propose a new reading of and approach to economic thought in Islamic tradition, which does not eviscerate the intrinsic value of the moral predicaments that were swept away with the onslaught of modernity.[126]

125 See e.g. the writings of Bassam Tibi, Armando Salvatore, Thomas Bauer, and Shahab Ahmed.

126 By *modernity*, I refer to "the concrete facts of modern life" including industrial development and technological revolution, as well as the changes that occurred in material, cultural, communicational, and social life. On the

Scholarly Relevance of Premodern Economic Teachings

The necessity for such research stems from the dearth of contemporary scholarly investigation in the field of ethical economics as a metaphysical axiom, the historical underrepresentation of Muslim economic thought, and the claim that Islamic economics has to be scientific and objective as defined in early modern Europe in order to be considered mature and hence in concordance with the modern scientific apparatus. With this book, first, I expect to provide a clearer and synthetic picture of the moral cosmology of economic thinking in classical scholarship. Second, I aim to highlight the alteration in methodology and epistemology of Islamic economics as conceived by Muslim reformists, Islamists, and contemporary Muslim economists in how they conceptualized an Islamic state, society, and knowledge, in comparison to their classical predecessors. Examining the modern perceptions of Islamic economics, first, and the classical terminologies and definitions of economic postulates that are closely related to spiritual and moral worldview, second, will allow me to affirm the methodological, epistemological, and axiological cleavages between classical Muslim scholars and contemporary Muslim economists. This will further lead me to inquire into the specifics of what constitutes economic postulates and values, through which I will present a new hermeneutical approach. Nonetheless, since the questions that will be raised during this book are far more valuable than the answers themselves, I do not claim that I will provide the only solution to the problematic at stake. Hence, one of the aims of the book is to bring the economic tradition of aforementioned scholars to the table and back into modern discourse on economics, politics, the role of the state, and ethics.

Economic philosophy in Islamic tradition does not benefit Muslims alone, and it ought not to be exclusively run by and theorized upon by only Muslims. If the true value of future economic thought in Islam lies at the heart of wisdom, the sciences of nature, and the moral self, it can have the potential to address many of the world's economic (and other) dilemmas by extrapolating the ideas of classical Islamic scholarship on economic behavior.

other hand, *modernism* (or modernist discourse) denotes the perception and nature of conduct that arose in early modern Europe as a result of modernity and its predicaments. See e.g. Bjørn Olav Utvik, *Islamist Economics in Egypt*, 11.

1 The Force of Revivalism and Islamization

Their Impact on Knowledge, Politics, and Islamic Economics

After this basic constitutional problem of sovereignty, the only problem that remains to be answered is as to who enjoys the political sovereignty in this set up? Unhesitatingly the reply would be that political sovereignty too, as a matter of fact, belongs to God and God alone. Whatever human agency is constituted to enforce the political system of Islam in a state, will not possess real sovereignty in the legal and political sense of the term, because not only does it not possess de jure sovereignty, but also that its powers are limited and circumscribed by the supreme law, which it can neither alter nor interfere with. The true position of this agency [human agency to enforce that political system of the Islamic state] has been described by the Qurʾan itself. The term used by the Qurʾan for this agency is "khalifa," which means that such agency is not sovereign in itself but is the vicegerent of the de jure and de facto sovereign, viz, God Almighty.

Abū al-Aʿlā Mawdūdī, *First Principles of the Islamic State*, 24

There are limits to the meaning of things in the way they are meant to be known, and their proper places are profoundly bound up with the limits of their significance. True knowledge is then knowledge that recognizes the limit of truth in its every object.

Syed Muhammad Naquib al-Attas, *Prolegomena to the Metaphysics of Islam*, 15

Daß es sich beim Islamismus unserer Tage um keine restaurative, geschweige denn traditionalistische Bewegung handelt, ist in der Fachwissenschaft unumstritten. Vielmehr ist der Islamismus ein Phänomen der Modernisierung des Islams, der sich selbst in seinen epistemologischen Grundlagen nicht auf den klassichen Islam (der nach Ansicht der Islamisten ein verfälschter, dekadenter Islam war) berufen kann und will, sondern auf epistemologischen Grundlagen der Aufklärung und der Moderne.

Thomas Bauer, *Die Kultur der Ambiguität: Eine andere Geschichte des Islams,* 387

1.1 The Socioeconomic Paradigm against the Backdrop of a Colonial Past

This chapter is organized around two conspicuous phenomena that impacted the unfolding of modern Islamic economics: the Muslim revivalism in the late nineteenth and early twentieth centuries, with a focus on Mawdūdī as the ideologue (and not a progenitor) of an Islamic state and an Islamic vision of society, and the Islamization of knowledge process that rendered the discipline of contemporary Islamic economics and finance compatible within the science of economics. This chapter provides a historical survey of selected reformist writers, who at the turn of the twentieth century grappled not just with the weakening of their societies in the face of colonial strategies but also with formulating certain principles around achieving a moral Islam. More specifically, I analyze Muslim reformists and their ideas and reactions to the political, social, and legal changes sweeping through the region, focusing mainly on their notions of social justice, state, and economy. Their ideas, embedded primarily in theological, political, social, and legal discourses, were also applicable for the advancement of economic-related topics that were picked up by Islamists and Muslim economists in the twentieth century. Given the underlying correlations between the late nineteenth and early twentieth centuries' political and socioeconomic developments in the shadow of colonial domination of Muslim countries (in the Middle East and South Asia), the first part of this chapter discusses the sociology of knowledge that led to the development of Islamic economic theories. I explore Islamic economics – as an indigenous intellectual field – and its adaptation to global economic parameters in relation to the identity politics of Muslim societies by analyzing Muslim scholars' responses to colonialism, state formation, and the justification for the emergence of the Islamic economic paradigm.

The second part of this chapter offers an epistemological and historical analysis of the Islamization process and the ideological effects it generated for Islamic sciences, in general, and for Islamic economics, in particular. The authors who are analyzed in the first part of this chapter often wrote uncritically about the moral predicaments of economics in Islam and were impervious to the economic liberal paradigm, while accepting the agency of an Islamic state. The Islamization process in the second half of the twentieth century was neither conceived nor developed in a vacuum; it was indeed affected by sociopolitical conditions in the postcolonial states, especially in Pakistan and Malaysia, and their state-run political agendas of Islamizing their economies, which in turn shaped the very vision of Islamic economics via several distinct yet interconnected spheres. The emergence of nation-states is interlinked to the responses from the Muslim reformist movement to socioeconomic conditions in the Middle East and South Asia. Furthermore, efforts to construct a modern Islamic identity and society based on theological principles of *tawḥīd* and *umma* provided a theological frame for implementing the discipline of Islamic economics within those states.

The emergence of Islamic economics is hence entangled in the complex reaction to political repercussions of colonialism, the intricate correlation of authentic Islamic identity, and the conception of the modern state apparatus. Yet it is beyond the scope of this chapter to discuss in great detail the historical development of the colonial period in the Middle East and South Asia, in relation to the regional rulers and their interaction with Western colonial powers. However, the ramifications of this colonial period set the groundwork for much of the sociopolitical turmoil experienced in Muslim countries, thus it is crucial to consider their impact when configuring Muslim reformists' outlook on socioeconomic and political factors of the time and when understanding modern Muslim economists' major ideas on the subject.

The concept of Islamism as a political force is entangled with the ideas of later Muslim religious scholars and economists who, in the name of the Islamization of knowledge, formed the very discourse (and the discipline) of Islamic economics.[1] The weakening of the Ottoman Empire (1299–1923), given French and British economic and political incursions into its territories, was compounded by individual resistance and nationalist movements emerging in North Africa, and the Middle East. The Ottoman dynasty's dismantling of its Islamic legal and political systems in the Middle East and North Africa laid fertile ground for the expansion of Islamism in the early

[1] I refer to "Islamism" as a political ideology, which is distinguishable from Islam as a normative system. See Bassam Tibi, "The Renewed Role of Islam in the Political and Social Development of the Middle East," *Middle East Journal*, vol. 37 (1983): 3–13; Bassam Tibi, *Der Islam und das Problem der kulturellen Bewältigung des sozialen Wandels* (Frankfurt: Suhrkamp, 1985).

twentieth century.[2] Despite its politicized ideas, Islamism was, in essence, also a project about social justice and moral Islam. In the same vein, it was also regarded as a sociopolitical reaction to the interference and usurpation of chiefly British colonial rule and a product of it. State ideologues, such as Mawdūdī in Pakistan, who was one among many, reinforced this political approach.

Starting with Pakistan in 1947, several countries in the modern world have identified themselves as "Islamic states" and affirmed that Islam is their official religion.[3] The attempts in Pakistan, Malaysia, Iran, and other Muslim countries to Islamize societies and state apparatus, to implement *Sharīʿa* legislation, and to establish Islamic economic structures, despite their different implementation, are at most pursuits to reiterate a lost (Islamic) tradition or to challenge Western socioeconomic norms. However, those changes did not alter the prevalent modus operandi of the global politico-economic ideology. As will be evident in the course of this chapter, Islamists' reinforcement of legal monism and economic ideology within nation-states has exposed epistemological and historical inconsistencies of the two epistemic systems – the secular nation-state and the vision of an Islamic religious state.[4]

Between the Tanzimat reform period (1839–1876)[5] and 1923, the year marking the official dissolution of the Ottoman Empire, Western-inspired legal codes and penal laws were already being integrated into Ottoman state law or *qanūn*, in an attempt to modernize and force fundamental changes of the empire as it was being restructured into a modern nation-state.[6] This undoubtedly led to irreversible repercussions for the

2 For Bassam Tibi, formulation of re-Islamization or repoliticization of Islam arrived due to structural crisis and the appeal of Islam (and the Islamic state) as a solution for sociopolitical problems in Muslim societies. According to Thomas Bauer, re-Islamization of Islam emerged as a reaction to modernity. See Bassam Tibi, *Die Krise des modernen Islams: Eine vorindustrielle Kultur im wissenschaftlich-technichen Zeitalter* (Frankfurt: Suhrkamp, 1991 [first edition 1981]), 62; Bauer, *Die Kultur der Ambiguität*; Salvatore, *Islam and the Political Discourse of Modernity*, 173.

3 The Constitution of the Islamic Republic of Pakistan, 1973, Senate of Pakistan, accessed September 17, 2017, www.senate.gov.pk/uploads/documents/3.%20Special%20Publication%20to%20mark%20Constitution%20Day.pdf.

4 Hallaq, *Sharīʿa*, 360.

5 See Roderic H. Davison, *Reform in the Ottoman Empire, 1856–1876* (Princeton: Princeton University Press, 1963).

6 For example, see the Ottoman penal code from 1858, which, in the name of Islam, nonetheless adopted most of the French legal codes. *The Imperial Ottoman Penal Code*, trans. John A. Strachey Bucknill (Oxford: Oxford University Press, 1913).

sociopolitical and economic conditions in Ottoman territory[7] and in the greater Middle East. Not only did the transformation face a backlash on the Islamic legal scholars' input in providing legislation and authoritative teaching, but it also penetrated into the educational institutions that in the past played a vital role in social life.[8] As a response to that abrupt alteration of the local social systems and the negation of the cultural ambiguity of Islamic traditional culture,[9] many religious Muslim scholars pledged to re-establish Islam's "authentic" vision of the law and social life as the only solution to modernity, since they contested the positivist economic methodologies.[10] Consequently, and as an extension of the reappropriation of that "authentic" Islam from the colonial period, a discourse nowadays known as "Islamization" emerged, which in part owes its existence to the preceding revivalists and the intellectual makeup they generated.[11] The following context of the state–religion relation is vital to the subject of Islamic economics and economics as a discipline.

At least three movements emerged during the nineteenth century in the Middle East and South Asia that aimed to preserve traditional Islamic knowledge, to secularize Muslim societies and apparatus, or to reconcile these two trends. While the traditional movement called for a return to the scriptural teachings of Islam, the second movement sought to adapt to the secularization process. A third movement advocated the conjuncture of Islamic sources and non-Islamic philosophy.[12] For this analogous discussion of Islamization of knowledge and Islamic economics, the tertiary movement appears most relevant.

Efforts to develop an authentic Islamic vision of socioeconomic life stem from the reformist movements at the beginning of the twentieth century, yet Islamic economic literature, which would form the discipline, emerged in the following decades[13] with the writings of Hifzur

7 See e.g. Hallaq, *Sharīʿa*, 2, 3, 4, 6, 7, 10ff.; Iza Hussin, *The Politics of Islamic Law* (Chicago, IL: Chicago University Press, 2016), 12, 20; Salvatore, *Islam and the Political Discourse of Modernity*, 54.

8 See e.g. Hallaq, *Sharīʿa*, 357–370.

9 Bauer, *Die Kultur der Ambiguität*, 14, 16, 18.

10 See e.g. Maḥmūd Muḥammad Nūr, *Al-Iqtiṣād al-Islāmi* (Cairo: Maktabāt al-Tijārah wa Taʿāwun, 1978).

11 Bauer, *Die Kultur der Ambiguität*, 222–223.

12 Ahmed El-Ashker and Rodney Wilson, *Islamic Economics: A Short History* (Leiden: Brill, 2006), 315.

13 See the works of the South Asian Muslim scholars presented later in this chapter. See also Muhammad A. Khan, *What Is Wrong with Islamic Economics?* (Cheltenham, UK: Edward Elgar Publishing, 2013), xi.

Rahman Seoharwi, Manazir Ahsan Gilani, Shaikh Mahmud Ahmad, Muhammad Hamidullah, Khurshid Ahmad, and especially Mawdūdī's book *The Economic Problem of Man and Its Islamic Solution*,[14] of which at least some were influenced by the *nahḍa* scholars.[15] Still, it is only the systemic political and economic changes to gradually Islamize national economies and the Islamization of knowledge process, which commenced in the late 1970s with Isma'il al-Faruqi's and Muhammad Naquib al-Attas's philosophy of knowledge, that prompted the expansion and fruition of contemporary Islamic economics as a structural field and educational discipline. Despite being perceived as a spiritual quest, the Islamization of knowledge was utilized as a possibility to decolonize and dewesternize epistemic perspectives, while suggesting authentic contributions to the field of knowledge as a response to the politico-economic issues in the Muslim-majority countries of the Middle East and South and Southeast Asia. It succeeded, however, only in part.

1.2 Contextualizing Muslim Reformists' Understanding of Socialism, Capitalism, and Spirituality

The nineteenth-century Muslim revivalists, who are briefly analyzed below, barely opened the debate about the sources of Islamic knowledge. Muhammad Akram Khan distinguishes two revivalist movements that supported the development of modern Islamic

14 For Rodney Wilson and Timur Kuran, Mawdūdī is perceived as the pioneer of Islamic economics. See e.g. Timur Kuran, "Islamic Economics and the Islamic Subeconomy," *Journal of Economic Perspectives*, vol. 9, no. 4 (1995): 156.

15 Mawdūdī also inspired Sayyid Quṭb and his writings on Islam, state, and modernity. As will be evident later in this chapter, in the twentieth century the process of Islamic reformism (often described as the "re-Islamization": the creation of a new ideology that combined Islamic core beliefs with Western political and organizational structures), is presented as the only viable alternative to Western political ideologies. According to Bauer's theory of cultural ambiguity in Islam, all ideologies are intolerant toward ambiguity and multiplicity, including Islamism: "Im Laufe des 20. Jahrhunderts findet ein Prozeß statt, der oft fälschlich als 'Re-Islamisierung' bezeichnet worden ist, in Wahrheit aber die Neuschaffung des Islams als seiner Ideologie ist, die die Strukturen westlicher Ideologien aufnimmt und nach dem Scheitern der westlichen Ideologien in der islamischen Welt als die einzige 'eigene' Alternative versanden wird." (Bauer, *Die Kultur der Ambiguität*, 52).

economics;[16] The "modernist movement" resorted to *ijtihād* in reinterpreting the textual sources in the context of the socioeconomic conditions of the time.[17] Jamāl al-Dīn al-Afghānī,[18] Muḥammad ʿAbduh,[19] Rashīd Riḍā,[20] Muhammad Iqbal,[21] Fazlur Rahman,[22] and others form the modernist camp. The second group is comprised of scholars such as Ḥasan al-Bannā, Sayyid Quṭb,[23] Abū al-Aʿlā Mawdūdī,[24] Muḥammad Bāqir al-Ṣadr,[25] and Ismaʿil al-Faruqi,[26] who upheld a more literal reading of the sources of Islam and implemented their ideas with limited application of *ijtihād* into the socioeconomic sphere (one could also include in this group Muhammad Abdul Mannan[27] and Khurshid Ahmad,[28] among others). Yet, this division can be also reshuffled according to the contents of scholars' work. For instance, Ḥasan al-Bannā, Sayyid Quṭb, Jamāl al-Dīn al-Afghānī, Muḥammad ʿAbduh, Rashīd Riḍā, ʿAlī Sharīʿatī, and Muhammad Iqbal can be considered as reformists who did not directly address the

16 Khan, *What Is Wrong with Islamic Economics?*, xi–xii.
17 Khan, *What Is Wrong with Islamic Economics?*; Sami Al-Daghistani, "Semiotics of Islamic Law, *Maṣlaḥa*, and Islamic Economic Thought," *International Journal of the Semiotics of Law*, vol. 29 (2016): 395.
18 Jamāl al-Dīn al-Afghānī, *Al-ʿAmal al-Kāmilah*, ed. Muḥammad ʿImārah (Cairo: Dār al-Kitāb al-ʿArabī li al-Tabʿah wa al-Nahar, 1968).
19 Muhammad ʿAbduh, *Risālat al-tawḥīd* (*The Theology of Unity*), trans. I. Musaʾad and K. Cragg (London: George Allen & Unwin, 1966).
20 Rashīd Riḍā, *Al-Ribā wa al-Muʿāmalāt fī al-Islām*, ed. Muhammad Bahjat al-Bitar (Beirut: Dār Ibn Zaydūn, 1986).
21 Muhammad Iqbal, *The Reconstruction of Religious Thought in Islam*, electronic version, accessed March 12, 2017, https://ia902701.us.archive.org/31/items/cover_201501/the_reconstruction_of_religious_thought_in_islam.pdf.
22 Fazlur Rahman, *Islam and Modernity* (Chicago, IL: Chicago University Press, 1982).
23 Sayyid Quṭb, *Social Justice in Islam*, trans. John B. Hardie (New York: Islamic Publication International, 1953).
24 Sayyid Abū al-Aʿlā Mawdūdī, *First Principles of Islamic Economics* (Markfield, Leicestershire: Islamic Foundation, 2011); Sayyid Abū al-Aʿlā Mawdūdī, *Economic Problem of Man and Its Islamic Solution* (Lahore: Markazi Maktaba Jamaʾat-e-islami Pakistan, 1955).
25 Al-Ṣadr, *Iqtiṣādunā* (1982).
26 See al-Faruqi, *Islamization of Knowledge*; Ismaʿil Raji al-Faruqi, *Tawhid: Its Implications for Thought and Life* (Herndon, VA: IIIT, 1982).
27 Muhammad Abdul Mannan, *Islamic Economics: Theory and Practice* (Sevenoaks, Kent: Hodder & Stoughton, 1986).
28 Khurshid Ahmad, *Studies in Islamic Economics* (Leicester: Islamic Foundation, 1981).

subject of Islamic economics but together with their interlocutors tackled the socioeconomic problems that were looming in the backdrop of the colonial struggle. Conversely, Abū al-Aʿlā Mawdūdī, Khurshid Ahmad, Muhammad Abdul Mannan, Maḥmūd Tāliqānī, and Muḥammad Bāqir al-Ṣadr commenced and/or advanced the Islamization of economics.

Many Muslim reformists applied distinct theories to and held very different views on the socioeconomic restructuring of Muslim societies, yet the majority of them in their deliberations referred to the notion of an Islamic vision for transforming nineteenth-century Muslim societies, tackling concepts such as social justice, education, socialism, and colonial rule. The loss of autonomy and the immediate political and economic dissection of societal structures in the Middle East, North Africa, and South (East) Asia by the European colonial powers not only meant a transfer of administrative control over those societies but also an emersion of those very cultures into the commercial, industrial, and economic structures of an emerging nation-state.[29] The economic, administrative, financial, and social transformation took an immense toll on indigenous populations of the Middle East, which led to an array of reactions – one of them being the rising prominence and advancement of the idea of an Islamic state.

1.2.1 The Spiritual and Social Reconstruction of Colonial Life

There were various degrees of resentment toward adapting to Western political and legal structures that can be seen within the Muslim reformist camp.

Jamāl al-Dīn al-Afghānī (d. 1897) was an Islamic ideologue who wrote about the political and economic losses of the Muslim world and whose main theme was unity against European (especially British) imperialism.[30] Al-Afghānī's political views indicate an interest in adopting a constitutional government with active citizenship using a pan-Islamic model.[31] His ideology welded together traditional

[29] See Charles Tripp, *Islam and Moral Economy* (Cambridge: Cambridge University Press, 2006), 32; Hallaq, *Impossible State*, 141, 143, 144.

[30] See Nikki R. Keddie, *Sayyid Jamal ad-Din "al-Afghāni": A Political Biography* (Berkeley: UCLA, 1972).

[31] Keddie, *Sayyid Jamal ad-Din "al-Afghāni"*; Roy Jackson, *Mawlana Mawdudi and Political Islam* (London: Routledge, 2010), 103.

religious views of Islam, a critique of Western imperialism, and an appeal for Islamic unity with a call for adoption of Western sciences and institutions. Al-Afghāni advocated the moral crux of Islam by expounding the notion of social solidarity (*al-taḍāmun al-ijtimā'ī*) and social responsibility (*al-takāful al-ijtimā'ī*),[32] while addressing the concepts of socialism (*al-ishtirāqiyya*) and capitalism (*ra'smāliyya*), as well as their critiques. He perceived their materialism as a destructive force that would culminate in the breakdown of society. Al-Afghānī's critique[33] of socialism and materialism is expressed as a concern for the emerging potential for social disorder and the tearing apart of the social fabric.[34] He also preached about an "ideal" or "golden" Islam – one that he himself had neither known nor experienced but that had existed prior to his time.

Even though al-Afghānī and 'Abduh (d. 1905) agreed on reviving Islam through the application of *Sharī'a* as an anticolonial struggle,[35]

32 See Jamāl al-Din al-Afghānī, *Al-'Amal al-Kāmilah*, ed. Muhammad 'Imārah (Cairo: Dār al-Kitāb al-'Arabī li al-Tab'ah wa al-Nahar, 1968), 413ff; Muḥammad Abū Zahra, *Al-Takaful al-Ijtimā'i fī al-Islām* (Cairo: Dār al-Fikr al-'Arabī, 1964).

33 "The 'Refutation' has not seemed to Western readers to be a particularly convincing argument, yet it has had and continues to have considerable reputation among Muslims. With it Afghani seems to have accomplished several goals simultaneously: (1) He suggested to intellectuals the dangers of going too far in their open criticisms of Islam, since religion had the practical virtues of tying together the community and keeping men from vice. (2) To the same group he suggested a way of reform through stressing certain passages of the Koran and certain parts of the Islamic tradition. (3) He combated the pro-British influence of Sayyid Ahmad Khan and his followers by identifying them with the harmful materialists. (4) He suggested certain limits to politico-economic as well as religious reform. (5) He reinforced pride in Islam as the best religion, providing Muslims with a useful counterweight to the British claims of cultural superiority. It would seem that Western disappointment in the book stems from an expectation of finding in it what we would call a 'religious' document. It appears rather to be primarily an expedient, political tract; not necessarily even expressing the real opinions of the author, but written in order to accomplish certain goals .... The 'Refutation' is certainly not an attempt to 'rethink'; Islam, and any consistent public rethinking might in itself become sectarian, which was just what Afghani wanted to avoid." (Keddie, *Sayyid Jamal ad-Din "al-Afghāni,"* 180).

34 Al-Afghānī, *Al-'Amal al-Kāmilah*, 413–422; Keddie, *Sayyid Jamal ad-Din "al-Afghāni,"* 171ff; see also Nikki R. Keddie, *An Islamic Response to Imperialism: Political and Religious Writings of Sayyid Jamal ad-Din "al-Afghani"* (Berkeley: University of California Press, 1983).

35 Hussin, *Politics of Islamic Law*, 177.

they parted paths in how to incorporate Western sciences, knowledge, and political systems into an Islamic vision of society.[36] ʿAbduh and his early nationalist stance, which can be seen as a reaction to the British occupation of Egypt (1882–1956), influenced the flourishing of nationalist sentiment in Egypt and across the Middle East. For ʿAbduh, colonial rule was the embodiment of the decline of Egypt and the Middle East region as a whole. To extirpate this domination, he proposed to revise the social order in Muslim societies through Islam's political and moral reconstitution.[37] As a trained theologian and mufti, ʿAbduh was versed in Islamic studies and legal tradition, which he combined with his reformist views and incorporated into his writings.[38] While al-Afghānī believed that the source for revivalism ought to be found in Islam itself, ʿAbduh contended that pan-Islamism (and not Arab nationalism) was the answer to addressing the sociopolitical crisis. For him, there was no conflict between Islamic sciences and Western knowledge since the aim of his reform was to raise Muslim consciousness. Even though he called for the cessation of the four legal schools or *madhāhib* and held that, along with the Qurʾan, the main source should be deeds and views of the Prophet Muḥammad and the Rāshidūn caliphate, he believed in the immutability of doctrinal Islam but not of legislative Islamic practices.[39] Similarly to Mawdūdī, he emphasized the education of Muslims, which would integrate both an Islamic and Western pedagogy.

Rashīd Riḍā (d. 1935) also promoted the establishment of an Islamic state that would be fully in accordance with modernization, based on *Sharīʿa* as a legal-moral system,[40] whereas Ḥasan al-Bannā (d. 1949) of the Muslim Brotherhood, who lamented the loss of Islamic spirit due to the material gains that had enchanted Muslims of the time, called for the restoration of mutual responsibility and

[36] El-Ashker, Wilson, *Islamic Economics: A Short History*, 321.

[37] ʿAbduh, *Risālat al-tawḥīd*.

[38] See e.g. *Al-Manār* (*The Beacon*), which he published with Rashīd Riḍā (1865–1935).

[39] "Abduh believed that Islamic doctrine does not prescribe any specific form of government, provided it follows the general principles of consultation (shura) as well as supporting the Maliki principle of maslaha (public interest) as the basis for legal decisions." (Jackson, *Mawlana Mawdudi and Political Islam*, 104).

[40] Wilson, *Short History of Islamic Economics*, 323. On *fiqh al-muʿāmalāt* and *ribā*, see Rashīd Riḍā, *Al-Ribā wa al-Muʿāmalāt fī al-Islām*, ed. Muhammad Bahjat al-Bitar (Beirut: Dār Ibn Zaydūn, 1986).

social cohesion.[41] Unlike ʿAbduh, al-Bannā believed that elements of Western knowledge and modernization were alien to Islam. The revival or awakening of religious sentiments could be achieved through Islamic beliefs and its moral values, which would reinvigorate society, for capitalism would diminish its spiritual qualities. Armed with a social agenda, the Muslim Brotherhood entered the realm of politics as the largest mass movement in Egypt at the time; they addressed questions of poverty, property, state, and power. They used the political arena as a vehicle to restore an Islamic order and to recuperate the spiritual revival.[42]

Sayyid Quṭb (d. 1966), a leading member of the Muslim Brotherhood, criticized the impact of Western cultural and political values in Egyptian society and argued that social justice ought to be preserved in Islamic tradition.[43] Even though he flirted with socialist ideas,[44] Quṭb believed that Islam put forward basic principles of social justice and provided mechanisms to preserve the egalitarian structure between the poor and the wealthy.[45] However, he aimed to return to

41 Tripp, *Islam and Moral Economy*, 51.

42 On the notion of property, Tripp states that it hence became more than simply a discussion within the domain of *fiqh* (Tripp, *Islam and Moral Economy*, 49).

43 After his visit to the United States, he observed, "America is the inexhaustible material resources, strength and manpower. It is the huge factories, unequaled in all of civilization. It is the awesome, incalculable yields, the ubiquitous institutes, laboratories, and museums. American genius ... America's bounty and prosperity evokes the dreams of the Promised Land ... this country of mass production, immense wealth and easy pleasures. I have seen them [Americans] a helpless prey in the clutches of nervous diseases in spite of all their grand appearances .... They are like machines swirling round madly, aimlessly into the unknown .... That they produce a lot there is no doubt. But to what aim is this mad rush? For the mere aim of gaining and production. The human element has no place if their life is neglected .... Their life is an everlasting windmill which grinds all in its way: men, things, places and time .... What is the medicine to all this imbroglio? A peaceful heart, a serene soul, the pleasure which follows strenuous work, the relation of affection between men, the cooperation of friends." Sayyid Quṭb, "The America I Have Seen: In the Scale of Human Values," in *America in an Arab Mirror: Images of America in Arabic Travel Literature: An Anthology*, ed. Kamal Abdel-Malek (New York: St. Martin's Press, 2000), 10; Sayyid Quṭb, "Humanity Needs Us," trans. M. Hafez, *Al-Muslimūn*, vol. 3 no. 2 (1953): 3–4 in Tripp, *Islam and the Moral Economy*, 230.

44 "Similarly we have no good grounds for any hostility between Islam and the thought of social justice, such as the hostility that persists between Christianity and Communism." (Quṭb, *Social Justice in Islam*, 7–9).

45 "Islam prescribes the basic principles of social justice, and establishes the claim of the poor to the wealth of the rich; it lays down just principles for power and

the "lost" Islamic knowledge that would liberate Muslims: "Rather our summons is to return to our own stored-up resources, to become familiar with their ideas, and to proclaim their value and permanent worth, before we have the resources to an untimely servility which will deprive us of the historical background of our life."[46]

In South Asia, Muhammad Iqbal (d. 1938) also addressed the ideas of socialism (or proletariat, *nadar*) and capitalism (*sarmayahdar*). Iqbal was interested in socialist communal views (and not its materialist philosophy), while being skeptical of capitalism because of its economic inequality.[47] Even though he did not develop a reformed system of Islam, he nonetheless argued that the faculties of social norms, solidarity, and cooperation could contribute to the common well-being of society in the direction of a spiritual renewal.[48] Two interrelated key concepts in Iqbal's vocabulary for the resurgence of Islam were *khudi* and *tawḥīd*. Iqbal states that "Humanity needs three things today – a spiritual interpretation of the universe, spiritual emancipation of the individual, and basic principles of a universal import directing the evolution of human society on a spiritual basis."[49] *Khudi* is

for money and therefore has no need to drug the minds of men and summon them to neglect their earthly rights in favor of their expectations in heaven." (Quṭb, *Social Justice in Islam*, 41).

46 Quṭb also noted that "While we are examining this universal theory which takes its rise from the nature of Islamic thought about the world and life and humanity, we may study also the fundamental outlines of social justice in Islam." (Quṭb, *Social Justice in Islam*, 52).

47 The first book authored on economics in Urdu is believed to be Iqbal's *Ilmul Iqtisad*. Muhammad Iqbal, *Ilmul Iqtisad (The Science of Economics)* (Lahore: Khadimul-Taleem Steam Press of Paisa Akhba, 1904; 2nd edition, Karachi: Iqbal Academy, 1961).

48 Iqbal, *Reconstruction of Religious Thought in Islam*, 56.

49 "Modern Europe has, no doubt, built idealistic systems on these lines, but experience shows that truth revealed through pure reason is incapable of bringing that fire of living conviction which personal revelation alone can bring. This is the reason why pure thought has so little influenced men, while religion has always elevated individuals, and transformed whole societies. The idealism of Europe never became a living factor in her life, and the result is a perverted ego seeking itself through mutually intolerant democracies whose sole function is to exploit the poor in the interest of the rich. Believe me, Europe today is the greatest hindrance in the way of man's ethical advancement. The Muslim, on the other hand, is in possession of these ultimate ideas of the basis of a revelation, which, speaking from the inmost depths of life, internalizes its own apparent externality. With him the spiritual basis of life is a matter of conviction for which even the least enlightened man among us can easily lay down his life; and in view of the basic idea of Islam that there can be no further revelation binding on man,

a moral and existential term expressing the consciousness of *umma* as well as individual agency, since the individual is expressed through the communal.

Mawdūdī (d. 1979) had more frequent interaction with Iqbal than with other reformists. Like Mawdūdī, Iqbal seemed eager to pursue the idea of a Muslim-governed province in India,[50] while calling for an Islam that would adapt to modern conditions. Iqbal advocated a Muslim homeland in the 1930s but without offering a political organization to achieve that objective.[51] Yet, while Iqbal was openly using Western sources and literature, Mawdūdī, despite relying on Western thought, did not do so openly. This was in order to facilitate an image of Islam as a dynamic and revolutionary ideology that was primarily based on its own worldview. Mawdūdī asserted that Iqbal's influence on him was limited by saying that "the commonality of views between ʿAllamah Iqbal and me are limited to our belief that Islamic law should underlie the revival of our religion; my thoughts and intellectual probing are my own."[52] For Mawdūdī, the very concept of Islamism asserts a degree of intellectual independence; this stems from his interpretation of Iqbal's notion of *khudi* (selfhood), which

we ought to be spiritually one of the most emancipated peoples on earth. Early Muslims emerging out of the spiritual slavery of pre-Islamic Asia were not in a position to realize the true significance of this basic idea." (Iqbal, *Reconstruction of Religious Thought in Islam*, 106–107).

50 Iqbal, *Reconstruction of Religious Thought in Islam*, 8. See also Afzal Iqbal, *Islamisation of Pakistan* (Lahore: Vanguard, 1986).

51 "Iqbal's aim was evident in his letter to the rector of al-Azhar in Cairo, Shaikh Mustafa al-Maraghi, requesting a director for the intended daruʾl-ʾulum; Iqbal asked the Egyptian ʿalim for a man who was not only well versed in the religious sciences, but also in English, the natural sciences, economics, and politics. Iqbal arranged for him to come to Lahore and serve as the imam of the Badshahi (royal) mosque at a salary of 100 rupees per month and to partake in Iqbal's plans for the revival of Islam, ʿumraniat-i Islami ki tashkil-ijadid (reconstruction of the social aspects of Islam). Mawdudi turned down Iqbal's offer on the grounds that he did not want a paying job that would restrict his freedom. Mawdudi accepted Iqbal's scheme and agreed to use the waqf to train a number of capable Muslim students and young leaders in Islamic law as well as modern subjects. Although the project was essentially educational, the imprint of Mawdudi's politics was evident in its name, Daruʾl-Islam (Land of Islam)." Seyyed Vali Reza Nasr, *Mawdudi and the Making of Islamic Revivalism* (New York: Oxford University Press, 1996), 34.

52 Sayyid Abū al-Aʿlā Mawdūdī, *Fundamentals of Islam* (Delhi: Markazi Maktabah-i Islami, 1978), 21, in Nasr, *Mawdudi and the Making of Islamic Revivalism*, 37.

Mawdūdī read as Islamic self-confirmation against foreign political and ideological isms.[53] As such, Mawdūdī took historical Islam out of its context by making it politically viable for modern needs – especially his theory of an Islamic state. Iqbal's understanding of *tawḥīd* implied rejection of the dualistic projection of the world,[54] indicating a unity of spirit and matter and embodied in the term *khudi*.[55] The ultimate level of *khudi*, which is God, is both immanent and transcendent and points to the spiritual foundations of reality. Similar to Iqbal's, Mawdūdī's goal was the reintegration of *tawḥīd* in society, yet the former's concept appears more mystical, whereas the latter's appears more policy-oriented.

Further west, in Iran, ʿAlī Sharīʿatī (d. 1977) was developing a fully novel approach to Shiʿism and to interpretation of religion, while critiquing Marxism and liberal democracy.[56] His theory of Islam did not rest solely on an Islamic state but rather on the conception of God that is to be found in personal and practical aspects of human

53 "In perhaps his greatest work, Secrets of the Self (ʿAsrar-i-Khudīʾ), Iqbal writes of the need for Muslims to re-awaken their soul and act. Just as Mawdudi saw the Prophet Muhammad as a paradigm of the ideal Muslim and leader, Iqbal too saw the Prophet as the perfect Prophet-Statesman who founded a society based on freedom, equality and brotherhood reflected in the central tenet of 'unity' (tawhid). In the practical sense, Iqbal believed that a requisite of being a good Muslim was to live under Islamic law which acts as the blueprint for the perfect Islamic society, as envisioned by the Prophet Muhammad.... Iqbal – unlike Mawdudi – thought that the perfect Islamic state has never existed in past history and so to create such a state requires looking to the future, not the past." (Jackson, *Mawlana Mawdudi and Political Islam*, 52, 89).

54 For more on the Cartesian dualistic conception of the world and its critique, see Bauer, *Die Kultur der Ambiguität*, 2011.

55 See Muhammad Iqbal, *Asrar-i Khudī*, trans. by R. A. Nicholson as *The Secrets of the Self* (London, 1920).

56 "At any rate, Western bourgeois liberalism and Marxism both boast of their humanism. The former claims, by leaving individuals free to think and to pursue scientific research, intellectual encounter, and economic production, to lead to a blossoming of human talents. The latter claims to reach the same goal through the denial of those freedoms, through their confinement under a dictatorial leadership that manages society as a single organization, on the basis of a single ideology that imparts to people a monotonous uniformity."; "Democracy and Western liberalism – whatever sanctity may attach to them in the abstract – are in practice nothing but the free opportunity to display all the more strongly this spirit and to create all the more speedily and roughly arena for the profit-hungry forces that have been assigned to transform man into economic, consuming animal." Ali Sharīʿatī, *Marxism and Other Western Fallacies*, trans. R. Campbell (Berkeley, CA: Mizan Press, 1980), 21, 33.

endeavor.[57] He believed that Marxism could not provide the ideological means for its own liberation,[58] thus he focused on Islam as a revolutionary ideology and thought of Shi'ism as a complete party.[59] According to Sharīʿatī, even though historically the foundation of the human problematic is the emergence of private ownership, in modern times the development of machines would be a necessary transition for the human condition. Islam and Marxism are two ideologies that embrace all aspects of human life, yet in a very different form of ontology and cosmology. Marxism is based on materialism, while Islam is founded

> upon faith in the unseen – the unseen [*ghayb*] being definable as the unknown actuality that exists beyond the material and natural phenomena that are accessible to the senses and to our intellectual, scientific, and empirical perception, and which constitutes a higher order of reality and the central focus of all the movements, laws, and phenomena of this world.[60]

Sharīʿatī, who wrote on religious knowledge, stressed that Islam also addresses economic provision and social justice as principles of its social and cosmological order that pertain to moral growth.[61] His religious reform of Islam centered both on the Qurʾan, which is perceived to contain a revolutionary theory, and on *tawḥīd*[62] as an absolute unity of God and all things connected to God.[63]

57 Even though he contested against tyranny, he lived in the time where Islam was not only religiously but also politically and linguistically the most viable discourse. Barbara Celarent, review of *On the Sociology of Islam*; Marxism and Other Western Fallacies, by Ali Shariʿati, *American Journal of Sociology*, vol. 117, no. 4, January 2012, 1290.

58 "Since history, according to Marx, is 'the continuation of the movement of material culture', man, in the context of history, is ultimately returned to the mechanical nature of the naturalists, to be conceived of as a material entity. Thus, all the values that Marx bestows upon him in the context of society he takes back from him with the hand of dialectical materialism. (Here Chadel's very telling remark comes to mind: 'Marx the philosopher crushes all the substantive values of man under the wheels of the blind juggernaut of dialectical materialism; but Marx the politician and leader, with the most fervid and electrifying praise of these values, mobilizes people for power and victory.')" Sharīʿatī, *Marxism and Other Western Fallacies*, 29.

59 Hamid Dabashi, *Theology of Discontent* (New York: New York University Press, 1993), 116–117.

60 Sharīʿatī, *Marxism and Other Western Fallacies*, 65–66.

61 Sharīʿatī, *Marxism and Other Western Fallacies*, 73.

62 Dabashi, *Theology of Discontent*, 129–134.

63 See Ali Sharīʿatī, *On the Sociology of Islam*, trans. Hamid Algar (Berkeley, CA: Mizan Press, 1979).

Moreover, in Pakistan Fazlur Rahman (d. 1988), one of the key proponents of the modernization process of Islam,[64] who was also critical of Mawdūdī,[65] held that

> The most important and urgent thing to do from this point of view is to "disengage" mentally from the West and to cultivate an independent but understanding attitude toward it, as toward any other civilization, though more particularly to the West because it is the source of much of the social change occurring throughout the world. So long as Muslims remain mentally locked with the West in one way or the other, they will not be able to act independently and autonomously.[66]

While he favored the spiritual and metaphysical components of Muslim society,[67] he was nonetheless critical of Islamization of knowledge:

64 "The 'Wahhabi' movement and other kindred or parallel reform phenomena wanted to reconstruct Islamic spirituality and morality on the basis of a return to the pristine 'purity' of Islam. The current postmodernist fundamentalism, in an important way, is novel because its basic élan is anti-Western (and, by implication of course, anti-Westernism). Hence its condemnation of classical modernism as a purely Westernizing force. Classical modernists were, of course, not all of a piece, and it is true that some of these modernists went to extremes in their espousal of Western thought, morality, society, and so on. Such phenomena are neither unexpected nor unnatural when rapid change occurs, particularly when it derives from a living source like the West. But just as the classical modernist had picked upon certain specific issues to be considered and modernist positions to be adopted thereupon – democracy, science, status of women, and such – so now the neo-fundamentalist, after – as I said before – borrowing certain things from classical modernism, largely rejected its content and, in turn, picked upon certain specific issues as 'Islamic' par excellence and accused the classical modernist of having succumbed to the West and having sold Islam cheaply there. The pet issues with the neo-fundamentalist are the ban on bank interest, the ban on family planning, the status of women (contra the modernist), collection of zakat, and so forth-things that will most *distinguish* Muslims from the West. Thus, while the modernist was engaged by the West through attraction, the neo-revivalist is equally haunted by the West through repulsion." (Rahman, *Islam and Modernity*, 136–137).

65 Rahman, *Islam and Modernity*, 116ff.

66 Rahman, *Islam and Modernity*, 136–137.

67 "If metaphysics enjoys the least freedom from assumed premises, man enjoys the least freedom from metaphysics in that metaphysical beliefs are the most ultimate and pervasively relevant to human attitudes; it is consciously or unconsciously the source of all values and of the meaning we attach to life itself. It is therefore all-important that this very ground of formation of our attitudes be as much informed as possible .... Metaphysics, in my understanding, is the unity of knowledge and the meaning and orientation this unity gives to life. If

> The essence of the matter is that the neorevivalist has produced *no* Islamic educational system worthy of the name, and this is primarily because, having become rightly dissatisfied with much of the traditional learning of the *ulema*, he himself has been unable to devise any methodology, any structural strategy, for understanding Islam or for interpreting the Quran.[68]

Yet Rahman agreed with Mawdūdī that education is vital for the recuperation of the Muslims and that the Qur'an should be analyzed within the context of historical, social, political, and economic developments, in order to understand the pressing conditions of the time.

1.2.2 The Social Logic of the State and the Material Imprint of Capitalism and Socialism

The above-mentioned reformists deliberated over not only the sociopolitical conditions of the time but also the idea of morality and moral restructuring of man that could be attained through social mobility. This would be levied against the dangers of capitalism and communism. Islamic socialism merged the question of social norms and power with moral and spiritual components, reflecting on the premodern ideas of social cohesion, religious morality, and spiritual well-being. The underlying notions of mutual responsibility and cohesion led reformists to believe that the Islamic vision (of the state and society) would contest the ideas of individualism and property ownership, linking the economic and the ethical realms.[69]

this unity is the unity of knowledge, how can it be all that subjective? It is a faith grounded in knowledge." (Rahman, *Islam and Modernity*, 132).

68 Rahman, *Islam and Modernity*, 137.

69 Muṣṭafā Sibā'ī, *Ishtirākiyya al-Islām* (Damascus: Mu'assasat al-Matba'at al-'Arabiyyah, 1960); Seyyed Maḥmūd Tāliqānī, *Islām va Mālkīyāt*, trans. Ahmad Jabbari and Farhang Rajaee as *Islam and Ownership* (Lexington, KY: Mazda, 1983), 88–101. In relation to the notion of ownership, Tripp states that "Linking ownership to a goal greater than the mere satisfaction of individual wants would bring out the 'social function' (*al-wazifat al-ijtima'iyah*) of property – that is, the obligations of the proprietor to other members of society. This function corresponded partly to the conditionality of all property in a universe in which God had entrusted humans with its use, encapsulated in rules such as payment of zakat, which were associated with this conditional ownership. To participate in a system of zakat was not only obligatory in the terms laid down for the faith (as one of the five pillars of Islam), but was also a means whereby any individual could fulfil their ethically complete potential." (Tripp, *Islam and Moral Economy*, 56).

The notion of social balance that was discussed by the reformists in part invokes an understanding of moral economy, reflected in God's balanced and proportioned ordering of the universe. According to Tripp, some of the modernists have taken up the subject of wealth and property in light of the prophetic *ḥadīth* that insinuates the moral fortitude of the acquisition of wealth,[70] yet many of them have delved into the subject matter by resorting to the Western intellectual corpus. The question of wealth acquisition – one of the focal points of premodern Muslim scholars – has emerged as a major concern also among modern Muslim economists, especially in relation to twentieth-century capitalism.

The Islamic critique of the materialism and socialism of the 1940s and 1950s[71] influenced how Islamic economics would be conceptualized and treated during the 1970s. The early social critique centered on the notion of the state (*dīn wa dawla*), "which would both defend society against the depredations of capitalism and lay the foundations for its Islamic reassertion."[72] *Dīn wa dawla*, however, was not a traditional phrase invoked in premodern Islam but only appeared during the anticolonial movements toward the late nineteenth century.[73] This had irrevocable ramifications toward the development

70 "Every community has a test and the test of my community is money/wealth" (*Inna li-kul ummah fitnah wa-fitnah ummati al-māl*). Kitāb al-zuhd, no. 26 (*ḥadīth* no. 2336). Abū ʿIsa Muḥammad bin ʿIsā bin Surah al-Tirmidhī, *Al-Jāmiʿ al-ṣaḥīḥ*, ed. Ibrāhīm ʿAwaḍ (Beirut: Dār Iḥyāʾ al-Turāth al-ʿArabī, 1963), part 4, 569 in Tripp, *Islam and Moral Economy*, 65.

71 Sayyid Quṭb, *Al-ʿAdālat al-Ijtimāʿīyya fī al-Islām* (Beirut: Dār al-Shurūq, 1990), 10–11; Sharīʿatī, *Marxism and Other Western Fallacies.*

72 Tripp, *Islam and Moral Economy*, 77.

73 "Der Slogan, der Islam sei *dīn wa dawla*, 'Religion und Staat', ist kein klassicher islamischer Grundsatz und kein wesenhafter Bestandteil des Islams. Tatsächlich findet er sich erstmals in der islamischen antikolonialistischen Bewegung Ende des 19. Jahrhunderts. Bei den Vordenkern des 'politischen Islams' wie Abū l-'Alā' al-Mawdūdī und Sayid Quṭb nimmt er eine yentrale Stellung ein und wir schließlich yur Leitmaxime des modernen politischen Islams. Erstmals wird damit der Anspruch erhoben, alle Aspekte des öffentlichen Lebens, von der Kultur, über die Politik bis hin zur Wirtschaft, aus einer einheltichen islamischen Perspektive zu regeln. Es versteht sich von selbst, daß die alte Ambiguitätstoleranz hier keinen Platz findet." (Bauer, *Die Kultur der Ambiguität*, 342). "Its first documented presence in the Arab Middle East goes back to the end of the formative phase of a space of public communication during the end of last century. Even before, the similar expression *din-ü-develet* (where *islam* was implicitly present as the object to predicate) has been used in the Ottoman literature of 'political advice' at least since the end of the

of the political and economic systems of modern Islam – in particular, in South Asia, where the first scholars of Islamic economics emerged.

The institutionalization process of such endeavours across the Middle East and South Asia normalized the transition of religious ideologies into political systems, carried out by reformists. The difference between European concepts of the state and citizen and Islamists' designs of the state is apparent on an epistemological level, wherein the emancipation of the citizen in Europe occurred through their emancipation from religious authority; conversely, the revivalists supported the emancipation of their citizens from colonial powers (chiefly Britain and France) through Islamic moral teachings. This was paradoxically carried out through the homogenous structure of state formation, which was historically a uniquely European experience.[74] The popular movements for decolonization, national independence, and state activism that developed in the early twentieth century sought to justify an Islamic narrative, pitching social reforms and political developments in a framework of a new, ideal Islamic state, which would fulfill the sociopolitical and economic void created by the colonial powers. Such a narrative of social criticism, willingly or unwillingly, presupposed an authentic Islamic socio-politico-economic vision, which was, however, rooted in a liberalist logic.[75] The state authorities in the Middle East managed to hold onto state power and to idealize historic narratives of Islamic rule, giving leeway to facilitate and reconstruct the necessary mechanisms for the establishment of an Islamic state with popular support.[76] The secular logic of the state in the Middle East and

seventeenth century .... It is clear only that the slogan acquired a particular prominence after the demise of the Caliphate in Istanbul between 1922 and 1924, and in particular from the 1930s, especially through the sociopolitical activism of new, organized Islamist groups like the Egyptian Muslim Brotherhood." (Salvatore, *Islam and the Political Discourse of Modernity*, 58).

74 Hallaq, *Impossible State*, 38.

75 "Nowhere was this more in evidence than in Egypt, one of the principal sites for the development of a distinctive Islamic social critique of capitalism in the 1930s and 1940s. In the 1950s and 1960s, under the republican regime of Gamal 'Abd al-Nasir (Nasser), it became the terrain for competing visions of development – centralised socialist state planning versus free enterprise liberal capitalism – expressed both in a secular and a distinctively Islamic idiom." (Tripp, *Islam and Moral Economy*, 77).

76 In Egypt, for instance, Islamic socialism was closer to the ideas of secular and socialist developments than to the revivalist ideas of Jamāl al-Dīn al-Afghānī, Muḥammad Abduh, and Rashīd Riḍā. See Sami A. Hanna and George H. Gardner, eds., *Arab Socialism: A Documentary Survey* (Leiden: Brill, 1969).

South Asia, which also meant an opening for a later capitalist development, remained the dominant political and systemic force.

The Muslim religious scholars who wrote on Islamic economics (analyzed below) envisioned an Islamic state, which was, however, never fully parted from the capitalist, secular, and liberal functions, despite its Islamic character. It is exactly in this sense that the once-colonized and now formally "decolonized" subjects took upon themselves the same systemic structures of governance, for the (Islamic) state became the dominant guide in expounding the laws and norms of *Sharīʿa*, which would liberate the underprivileged from the colonial rule.[77] The secular-liberal logic of statehood has been the main agency of power since the 1950s in the emerging Islamic states of Iran, Pakistan, Malaysia, and others.[78] State formation meant also facing the handicaps of the socioeconomic, political, and historical circumstances of independence in those countries. Some leaders, such as Muhammad Zia ul-Haq from Pakistan and Ayatollah Ruhollah Khomeini from Iran, sought to increase state authority and to expand control over the economy by Islamizing economic and financial sectors.

The colonized countries of the Middle East (and South Asia), such as Egypt, Pakistan, and Malaysia, experienced capitalism in the twentieth century through the political power of colonialism and the subsequent expansion and exploitation of local structures embedded in the creation of the modern nation-state.[79] It was exactly the nation-state that encapsulated and generated the legal framework, institutional nature, and economic policies for the expansion of a market economy under the auspice of allegedly Islamic governments.[80] The gradual

[77] See e.g. Hussin, *Politics of Islamic Law*, 93–94.

[78] For instance, the Constitution of 1957 in Malaysia was predominantly secular in nature and followed the British order. See Constitution of Malaysia of 1957, accessed September 16, 2017, www.commonlii.org/my/legis/const/1957. See also Seyyed Vali Reza Nasr, *The Vanguard of the Islamic Revolution: The Jamaʾat-I Islami of Pakistan* (Berkeley: University of California Press, 1994), 28ff.

[79] J. M. Blaut, "Colonialism and the Rise of Capitalism," *Science & Society*, vol. 53, no. 3 (1989): 260–296.

[80] Market economy is inextricably related to the formation of a nation-state. Polanyi writes, "Market economy implies a self-regulating system of markets; in slightly more technical terms, it is an economy directed by market prices and nothing but market prices .... In the advent of the labor market common law played mainly a positive part – the commodity theory of labor was first stated emphatically not by economists but by lawyers. On the issue of labor

withdrawal of colonial rule and the achievement of formal independence in the region generated the sentiment among the local population that the moment to establish a society (and a state) driven by authentically Islamic norms had arrived. Such a society would be possible only within the context of the modern state, which would reinforce the narratives of prosperity, social cohesion, independence, and Islamic legal rule. Yet many questions remained unsettled that were germane to the legitimacy of such a state, its far-reaching consequences, the issue of territorial limits, and the concern of national sovereignty and religiously driven governance. The changing political and socioeconomic conditions from the 1970s onwards in Pakistan and Malaysia – the countries in which Islamization of knowledge and Islamic economics were most pronounced – did not replace the colonial state but rather took over its operations.[81] The change in the political arena in Pakistan, Malaysia, and Iran and the vast oil-price rises of the 1970s had altered the balance of economic power between many oil-producing countries across the Middle East and the industrialized states.

In what follows, I discuss how a key Muslim revivalist of Islamic economics, Mawdūdī, voiced the promulgation of healthy accumulation and launched a critical stance against capitalism, based on his theory of moral economy as something that should emerge from within a modern Muslim society. Since capitalist monetary economy uses money[82] both as a commodity and as a tour de force of development, the aforementioned Muslim reformists contested such an economic mode due to its power in colonizing all domains of life. The credit for envisioning and, more so, realizing an Islamic state and society, based

combinations and the law of conspiracy, too, the common law favored a free labor market." (Polanyi, *Great Transformation*, 45, 90).

81 Charles H. Kennedy, *Bureaucracy in Pakistan* (Karachi: Oxford University Press, 1987); Seyyed Vali Reza Nasr, *Islamic Leviathan* (Oxford: Oxford University Press, 2001), 48.

82 For more detailed discussion on money (*māl*) and its alienating faculties if used illicitly as stated by the classical Muslim scholars, see Chapter 4. Tripp notes that Marx also distinguished at least two aspects of money: "Marx appreciated the 'wealth-in-circulation' aspect of money, but also, as a critic of what this means for human relations, was aware of its alienating capacities. In this, he was following a long tradition of uneasy moralists who inveighed against the dangers inherent in the nature of money. Thus money is not simply 'protocapitalist' in a material sense, but also in an ethical or normative sense." (Tripp, *Islam and Moral Economy*, 64).

on the fundamental premise of the Qurʾan and equipped with an Islamic political economy, goes to Sayyid Abū al-Aʿlā Mawdūdī and his theory of theo-democracy.

1.3 Abū al-Aʿlā Mawdūdī and the Twentieth-Century Transition from Nation to Islamic State

One of the most influential and prolific contemporary Muslim thinkers, Sayyid Abū al-Aʿlā Mawdūdī (d. 1979), was an Islamic ideologue and proponent of the re-Islamization of Muslim society and state in India.[83] His interpretation and implementation of Islamic principles and of the notion of *Sharīʿa*, state, and economics is also visible in the writings of other revivalists. Mawdūdī was brought up in the historical context of India at a time of decline of British colonial power, witnessing a downswing of Muslim Mughal dominance and a subsequent rise of Hindu nationalism and secularism.[84] Between 1937 and 1939, after returning to Delhi, Mawdūdī expanded his vision of *daʿwa* as a call for an Islamic worldview. The founder of *Jamaʿat-i Islami* in 1941, he acted as its leader from its inception until 1972.[85] Between 1921 and 1924, he was involved in the *Khilafat* movement, and later in the *Jamiʿat-i Ulama-i Hind*.[86]

1.3.1 Mawdūdī's Key Islamic Concepts

The reintegration of the notions of *tawḥīd*, *Sharīʿa*, and *dīn* in the political discourse of the modern state are crucial for understanding Mawdūdī's vision of an Islamic state and society, which promulgated development of Islamic economics as a discipline through his disciples, such as Khurshid Ahmad and other Muslim economists. As the mastermind of political Islam,[87] Mawdūdī's key concepts expound his vision of the religion of Islam and its sociopolitical predicaments, which give

83 On nationalism and the historic development of colonialism, see Partha Chatterjee, *Nationalist Thought and the Colonial World: A Derivative Discourse* (London: Zed Books, 1993), 1–36.

84 Jackson, *Mawlana Mawdudi and Political Islam*, 83.

85 Nasr, *Vanguard of the Islamic Revolution*, 3.

86 Nasr, *Mawdudi and the Making of Islamic Revivalism*, 19–21.

87 For Mawdūdī, Islam is an all-embracing ideological system equal to Western political ideologies. Abū al-Aʿlā Mawdūdī, *Mabādiʾī al-Islām* (Dimashq: Dhakhāʾir al-Fikr al-Islāmī, 1961), 3–4, 62–63. See also Bauer, *Die Kultur der*

incentives also for the study of the revivalist vision of Islam's political economy. Mawdūdī holds that *Sharī'a* is "the detailed code of conduct or the canons comprising ways and modes of worship, standards of morals and life and laws that allow and proscribe, that judge between right and wrong."[88] As for *fiqh*, he maintains that it is a "detailed law derived from the Qur'an and the hadis covering the myriads of problems that arise in the course of man's life have been compiled by some of the leading legislators of the past."[89] In a similar vein, Mawdūdī's notion of *dīn* contains multiple meanings. The first pertains to the higher reality, reign, and heavenly kingdom, whereas the second is rather the opposite, denoting subordination and communality.[90] He understood that the underlying difference between *Sharī'a* and *dīn* was that religion, translated as *dīn*,[91] always remained the same, whereas *Sharī'a* contained multiple forms that have undergone alterations in order to adapt to new realities and times.[92] In light of his idea of an *umma*-based Islamic state, Mawdūdī opposed Hindu nationalism, while promoting the idea of Islam as a religion of unity. He observes

> The law of God (the Shari'a) has always aimed at bringing together mankind into one moral and spiritual frame-work and make them mutually assistant to one another on a universal scale. But nationalism at once demolishes this frame-work with the noxious instruments of racial and national distinction .... The Shari'a of God provide the highest opportunities of free contact between man and man because on this very contact depends the progress of human civilization and culture.[93]

In his writings, however, Mawdūdī often resorted to Western philosophical and political thought and invoked the postulates of an Islamic

Ambiguität, 100. Kuran has a similar opinion: Timur Kuran, *Islam and Mammon* (Princeton, NJ: Princeton University Press, 2004), 5.

88 Sayyid Abū al-A'lā Mawdūdī, *Towards Understanding Islam (Risalah Diniyat)* (Lahore: UKIM Dawah Center, 1960), 82.

89 Mawdūdī, *Towards Understanding Islam*, 82.

90 Sayyid Abū al-A'lā Mawdūdī, *Als Muslim leben* (Karlsruhe: Cordoba Verlag, 2001), 57.

91 "Mawdudi defined *din* primarily as absolute obedience to God. The *shari'ah* as the content of the *din* in turn provided linkages between the individual and the society and, hence, the manner in which *din* was to fulfill its objective." (Nasr, *Mawdudi and the Making of Islamic Revivalism*, 63).

92 Mawdūdī, *Als Muslim leben*, 59.

93 Sayyid Abū al-A'lā Mawdūdī, *Nationalism and India* (Lahore: Maktaba-e-Jama'at-e-Islami, 1947), 10–12, in Donohue and Esposito, eds., *Islam in Transition*, 95.

vision of society based on the notion of *tawḥīd*, as the absolute oneness of God. This allowed him to combine philosophical, sociopolitical, and economic theories with dogmatic religious interpretations, deploying an idiosyncratic methodology of *ijtihād* and literalist exegesis of Islamic sources.[94] Mawdūdī described *tawḥīd* as

> the most fundamental and the most important teaching of Prophet Muhammad (blessings of Allah and peace be upon him) is faith in the unity of God. This is expressed in the primary Kalimah of Islam as "There is no deity but Allah" (La-ilaha illallah). This beautiful phrase is the bedrock of Islam, its foundation and its essence. It is the expression of this belief which differentiates a true Muslim from a kafir (unbeliever), mushrik (one who associates others with God in His Divinity) or dahriyah (an atheist).[95]

His concept of *tawḥīd* – a central term that is also used by proponents of Islamization and Islamic economics – presents a building block for the advancement of his sociopolitical theory of the state. What I refer to as Mawdūdī's "modern Islamic nation-state" rests upon the conceptualization of religious terminology, yet reintegrated in the framework of a political economy of a state. He views *tawḥīd* through the sovereignty of God, which encompasses socioeconomic and moral systems.[96] As a result of this, he adopted a more literalist approach to the Qur᾽an but did not contest scientific knowledge, which he perceived as objective. A major point of contestation for him was how science is used and for what purposes. As long as it is rooted in the Islamic belief with accompanying ethical norms, it can be regarded as Islamic, a view that will also have repercussions for the field of Islamic economics. In this regard, he differentiated between modernization, which he accepted, and westernization – a feature that set him apart from other Islamists. Instead of criticizing the processes and modes of modernization for the decline of the Muslim *umma* – like some of the early revivalists did – he also directed his focus on the Muslims' inability and failures to emerge and succeed in establishing their own sociopolitical system.[97] His view

94 Jackson, *Mawlana Mawdudi and Political Islam*, 106.

95 Mawdūdī, *Towards Understanding Islam*, 50.

96 Sayyid Abū al-A῾lā Mawdūdī, *Islam: Its Meaning and Message*, ed. Khurshid Ahmad (London: Council of Europe, 1976), 147–148.

97 Mawdūdī states that "On the one hand we have to imbibe exactly the Qur᾽anic spirit and identify our outlook with the Islamic tenets while, on the other, we have to assess thoroughly the developments in the field of knowledge and changes in conditions of life than have been brought during the last eighteen

on the *umma* also correlates to his comprehension of *tajdīd* as renewal process, perceived as an inevitable outcome of applying Islamic worldview to the system of thought that commences within an individual and has far reaching paradigmatic consequences upon society as a whole.[98] His reading of the Qur'an does not suggest reinforcement of the seventh-century religious paradigm but rather an attempt to reformulate Islam's sociopolitical domain through the inception of *tajdīd* as part of the Qur'anic revelation.[99]

1.3.2 Colonial Legacy and Mawdūdī's Vision of an Islamic Society and State

Mawdūdī's views on Islamic state and society are, as will be analyzed in the following pages, crucial to the development of an Islamic economic system, due to the intersection of his theory on religious morality and the unfolding of the political economy embedded in the formation of a modern state of Pakistan. Since the reconstitution of political power of Muslims in India in the first half of the twentieth century was closely associated with the idea of modernity, the fusion of Islamic and Western concepts and ideas in Mawdūdī's writings was inevitable in order to achieve the political and economic autonomy of a postcolonial state.

Mawdūdī's actual turn to a more Islamic ideological formation took place in the 1930s when he accepted an offer from Nawab Salar Jang, a politician from Hyderabad, to propose and then promulgate an Islamic vision of society.[100] The geopolitical context and timeline of

hundred years." Muhammad Yusuf, *Maududi: A Formative Phase* (Karachi: Islamic Research Academy, 1979), 35.

98 For more on *tajdīd*, see Sayyid Abū al-A'lā Mawdūdī, *A Short History of the Revivalist Movement in Islam*, trans. al-Ash'ari (Lahore: Islamic Publication, 1963), 34–44.

99 On this point, it is crucial to reiterate that since the nineteenth century, *Sharī'a* law was deconstructed in commercial, general, and criminal law and, as a result, replaced with legal codes and laws of French and British origin. See e.g. Hallaq, *Sharī'a*, 371ff.

100 "'This city [Hyderabad] has for some 200 years been the seat of Islamic culture and civilization. Great ulama, men of virtue, generals and courtiers are buried here .... What a pity that their legacy is alive in stone [monuments of the city] and dead in the people .... In this old Islamic settlement my eyes have searched and found neither a great man of God nor a skilled traditional craftsman .... Every search of mine attests to the

this occurrence is important, since the Hindus and Muslims of India were facing the British Raj as the system of governance that was instituted in 1858. This had an impact on the political and socioeconomic landscape in the region.[101] Mawdūdī's understanding of Islam meant adhering to what later became his vision of political Islam, which would encompass his religious doctrine and his political engagement. It was in 1932 that Mawdūdī's politics reiterated his anticolonial stance and envisioned organization of society driven by Islamic norms, which for him was a natural consequence of the religious-spiritual and economic decline of Muslims under British rule. Yet his political stance was expressed more substantially in 1937 when he arrived in Delhi,[102] where he began commenting on nationalism, Islamic values, and India's politics after its independence. Notably, his political outlook on the state was entrenched in Western tradition and scholarship. This was evident in his usage of particular terms when articulating his political vision, integrating his Islamic revivalist agenda through concepts such as "religious ideology," "party," "state," "code," and so forth.[103] His articulation of his political views within the concept of a nation-state does not stem from a historical understanding that Islamic theology necessitates formation of a modern nation-state but rather from his conviction that a nation-state was best suited for his political agenda for the Muslim community, given the centrality of the

death of that nation.' He was so disturbed by what he saw in Hyderabad that he could envision no future that did not include an Islamic revival. Mawdudi gives 1933 as the year when his attitudes changed." (Cited in Khurshid Ahmad, "Jama'at-i Islami kiya hey, uski zarurat kiya thi," *Haftrozah Zindagi*, November 10–16, 1989, 13, in Nasr, *Mawdudi and the Making of Islamic Revivalism*, 27, 30.)

[101] For more, see e.g. John F. Riddick, *The History of British India: A Chronology* (Westport, CT: Praeger, 2006); Srinath Raghavan, *India's War: World War II and the Making of Modern South Asia* (New York: Basic Books, 2016); Lawrence James, *Raj: The Making and Remaking of British India* (New York: St. Martin's Griffin, 1997).

[102] Jamaat-e-islami Pakistan, accessed May 17, 2017, https://web.archive.org/web/20140418092730/http://jamaat.org/beta/site/page/3; Nasr, *Mawdudi and the Making of Islamic Revivalism*, 31.

[103] See Mawdūdī, *Nationalism and India*. See also Maryam Jameelah, "An Appraisal of Some Aspects of Maulana Sayyid Ala Maudoodi's Life and Thought," *Islamic Quarterly*, vol. 31, no. 2 (1987): 127. Nasr states that "Many of Mawdudi's views were formed in debate, rather than in conformity, with Western sources. His discourse produced an ideological orientation that was indigenous on the surface but was based on the very culture he sought to reject." (Nasr, *Mawdudi and the Making of Islamic Revivalism*, 33).

state and its social, judicial, and political imprint in colonial India.[104] Given that Muslim-dominated Punjab was the political heartland of British India, Mawdūdī's anticolonial voice and his *daʿwa* program had repercussions for the political makeup of the region. For Mawdūdī, the project of *Daru-l-Islam*, an educational organization over which he presided, became the objective of Muslim India. It provided the Muslim community a political voice and a religious movement. This organization later laid the foundations for the *Jamaʾat-i Islami*, founded in 1941.[105]

Mawdūdī transitioned from an ideologue to a politician along with the *Jamaʾat-i Islami*, changing their course from an Islamic movement into a political party and proposing an Islamic constitution in Pakistan.[106] His development of the party's program was interwoven with his political agenda, which was conceived in the Indian political and religious context of the time. At first, the party's orientation was primarily a cultural reassertion; later it became more politically and economically oriented in answer to the colonial usurpation and simultaneous rise of nationalistic tendencies in India. Mawdūdī's perception of colonialism and imperialism was at the beginning primarily a cultural concern against Western ideologies that influenced the political and socioeconomic makeup of India. At first, "he worried less

104 For more on Mawdūdī's political formulations and the state, see Irfan Ahmad, "Genealogy of the Islamic State: Reflections on Maududi's Political Thought and Islamism," *Journal of the Royal Anthropological Institute*, vol. 15 (2009): 145–162.

105 Jamaat-e-islami Pakistan, accessed May 17, 2017, http://jamaat.org/ur/jamaatOrDawat.php?cat_id=11; "The jamaʾat-i Islami was finally established in August 1941 in Lahore, and from the very beginning, it was the platform for Mawdudi's ideas. Especially after the founding of Pakistan six years later, Mawdudi's career as an ideologue ended. His most important and influential works had been published by this time (nineteen of his most noted works on *tabligh* – propagation of religious doctrine – were written between 1933 and 1941) and the years that followed would be dedicated to politics. By then his ideas had already found a niche in contemporary Islamic thought in South Asia and across the Muslim world." (Nasr, *Mawdudi and the Making of Islamic Revivalism*, 41).

106 Jamaat-e-islami Pakistan, accessed May 17, 2017, https://web.archive.org/web/20140418092730/http://jamaat.org/beta/site/page/3; "The Jamaʿat's ideas and policy positions defined the demands of the Islamic alliance and featured prominently in the debates between the government and the religious divines and parties from 1947 to 1956, when the country's first constitution was promulgated." (Nasr, *Mawdudi and the Making of Islamic Revivalism*, 41).

about economic liberation than about preserving dress, language, and customs, for they were essential to safeguarding Muslim culture. Mawdūdī's expositions on Islamic revolution, state, and economics attested to the central role played by the drive for cultural authenticity, what he termed 'intellectual independence'."[107] Some of Mawdūdī's key interpretations of Islamic religious concepts, such as *Sharīʿa*, Islamic state, *umma*, and *khilāfa* were utilized in intersection with modernity's political and cultural predicaments of a modern state. In this sense, his revivalism meant not only restructuring Muslim character but also establishing Islamic state institutions and economic programs.[108]

Mawdūdī was suspicious of democracy and Western political systems as well as simultaneously in favor of some of its ideas and mechanisms. He perceived the (Islamic) state in ahistorical terms as an ideal archetype, while pursuing the idea of a political entity that would include the Islamic fundamental tenets. On the one hand, he referred to a utopian Islamic state as a theo-democracy, based on the example of Medina, and, on the other, to the political order in Europe. This contradictory political ideology implied Western political ideas compounded with an Islamic religious worldview, which integrated Islamic vicegerency and the idea of state sovereignty.[109] The amalgamation of the philosophical foundations of Western democracy as the sovereignty of the people with the core ideas of Islam as a religious doctrine made him believe in a social order designated as theo-democracy:

> The philosophical foundation of Western democracy is the sovereignty of the people .... This is not the case in Islam .... Islam, as already explained, altogether repudiates the philosophy of popular sovereignty and rears its polity on the foundations of the sovereignty of God and vicegerency (*khilāfa*)

107 Nasr, *Mawdudi and the Making of Islamic Revivalism*, 49.

108 See e.g. Sayyid Abū al-Aʿlā Mawdūdī, *First Principles of the Islamic State* (Lahore: Islamic Publications, 1960); Sayyid Abū al-Aʿlā Mawdūdī, *Islamic Law and Constitution*, trans. Khurshid Ahmad (Lahore: Islamic Publications, 1960), chapter 4.

109 Mawdūdī, *Islamic Law and Constitution*, 2–3. Roughly stated, Mawdūdī sought to combine Islam as a social system with *dīn* as religion, which would give incentive for a creation of a state. "The problem with Mawdudi is that he does idealize the Islamic state and fails to take account of its social and cultural milieu and development. The very thought that Islam could have been influenced by something outside of Islam was inconceivable for Mawdudi." (Jackson, *Mawlana Mawdudi and Political Islam*, 86).

of man. A more apt name for the Islamic polity would be the "kingdom of God" which is described in English as a "theocracy." But Islamic theocracy is something altogether different from the theocracy of which Europe has had a bitter experience ... the theocracy built up by Islam is not ruled by any particular religious class but by the whole community of Muslims including the rank and file. The entire Muslim population runs the state in accordance with the Book of God and the practice of His Prophet. If I were permitted to coin a new term, I would describe this system of government as a "theo-democracy," that is to say a divine democratic government, because under it the Muslims have been given a limited popular sovereignty under the suzerainty of God.[110]

Mawdūdī's central aim was to develop a vision of a modern state enshrined in the Islamic narrative wherein the Qur'an and *ḥādīth* play a crucial role.[111] For him, the notion of an Islamic state was relevant to the idea of leading a moral and virtuous life,[112] whereby Islamic terminology was incorporated into the narrative of the modern nation-state based on *shūrā* (Islamic consultation).[113] Despite the fact that references to an Islamic state were generic in nature, given the absence of national boundaries and the reinforcement of the idea of the *umma* as Islamic community, the very idea of an Islamic state for Mawdūdī meant both a practical and an ideological (religious) entity. Even though he promoted an Islamic state as a universal and all-embracing entity, it exposes his methodological inconsistencies.[114]

According to Mawdūdī, the Islamic state would comprise of the legislature, the executive, and the judiciary branches, wherein the

110 Mawdūdī, *Islamic Law and Constitution*, 139–140.
111 Mawdūdī, *Islamic Law and Constitution*, 4–5.
112 "This is best expressed in Mawdūdī's 'trinity' of religion (*iqamat-i din*), virtuous leadership (*imamat-i salihah*) and divine government (*hukumat-i ilahiyah*). The continuity between Islam and politics was, for Mawdūdī, like the relation of 'roots with the trunk and the branches with the leaves [of a tree]', for, 'In Islam the religious, the political, the economic, and the social are not separate systems; they are different departments and parts of the same system'." (Mawdūdī, *Islamic Economic System*, 20, 21, in Jackson, *Mawlana Mawdudi and Political Islam*, 128).
113 This is based on the Qur'anic paradigm of "promoting the good and forbidding the evil." Mawdūdī, *First Principles of the Islamic State*, 30ff. On his critique of socialism and limited support of capitalists' idea of private property, see Sayyid Abū al-A'lā Mawdūdī, *Capitalism, Socialism, and Islam* (Kuwait: Islamic Book Publishers, 1977), 40.
114 Mawdūdī, *Islam: Its Meaning and Message*, 163–165.

ruler would be bound to the laws of God.[115] Yet his vision of the modern ruler would be incomparable to the role of the caliph, for the former was to be responsible to the state as well as to the nation.[116] Despite his criticism of nationalistic tendencies and his support for transnational Islamic unity and universal *umma*, his one-sided perception of twentieth-century sociopolitical and international contexts made him oblivious to the fact that the only possibility of conceiving an Islamic state in the modern period would be through the coercive power of state authority and its apparatus, which deviates from his idealistic vision of society. The idea of the Islamic state was henceforth in his mind not a utopian project but something tangible, wherein the modes of Islamic governance, law, and economics would flourish. Since Mawdūdī believed in a united form of Islamic nationalism, an Islamic state would function as a cultural, social, and religious entity. Its leadership would be elected, for him meaning a democratic government that was based on Islamic principles of political engagement. In this sense, the democratic process (of modernity) could be Islamized.

As such, Mawdūdī's Islamic revivalism was envisioned as a reaction and an adaptation to sociopolitical changes, incorporating political, cultural as well as economic predicaments of Islamic tradition. It endorsed modern social and political thought in order to achieve political and economic strength in Muslim society. Hence, Mawdūdī's assimilation of Western thought into Islamic intellectual discourse was crucial to conceiving the modernist trend of Islamic

115 Mawdūdī, *Islamic Law and Constitution*, 16–17; "Islamic theocracy is not controlled by a special religious group of people but by ordinary Muslims. They run it according to the Qur'an and Sunna. And if I am allowed to coin a new word, I would call it 'theodemocracy'. It would grant limited popular sovereignty to Muslims under the paramount sovereignty of God. In this [state], the executive and the legislature would be formed in consultation with the Muslims. Only Muslims would have the right to remove them. Administrative and other issues, regarding which there are no clear orders in the Shariah, would be settled only with the consensus of Muslims. If the law of God needs interpretation no special group or race but all those Muslims would be entitled to interpret (ijtihad) who have achieved the capability of interpretation." Sayyid Abū al-Aʿlā Mawdūdī, *Islami Riyasat* (Lahore: Islamic Publications, 1969), 130, in Jackson, *Mawlana Mawdudi and Political Islam*, 131. See also Farzin Vahdat, *Islamic Ethos and the Specter of Modernity* (London: Anthem Press, 2015).

116 Mawdūdī believed that the corrupt reign is the source of political destruction and social destitution. "Korrupte Führung ist die Ursache allen Elends auf dieser Welt." (Mawdūdī, *Als Muslim leben*, 158).

revivalism,[117] which became "a vehicle for modernization of Islam and in turn would bring about and sustain a new Islamic order."[118] This development to an extent prompted the process of Islamizing modern sciences,[119] which aimed not only to revive the religion of Islam but also to reinforce its political and economic teachings. Such an impetus of reinforcing a sociopolitical and spiritual revivalism aimed to restructure the individual and the community, whereby *dīn* as a religious reality was extended to sociopolitical and economic understanding, if it were to preserve and advance the well-being of the Islamic community.

1.4 Islam and the Economic System between the 1930s and the 1970s

1.4.1 South Asian Muslim Economists

The majority of modern Muslim economists were natives of South Asia, writing primarily in Urdu and English, while other proponents of Islamic economics could also be found in Southeast Asia, Iran, and Iraq. Abdul Azim Islahi notes that the first book on Islamic economics was the 1932 publication of Hifzur Rahman Seoharwi's *Islam ka Iqtisadi Nizam* (*The Economic System of Islam*), a critique of socialism and capitalism that advocated for an Islamic economic system. More than a decade later, the second most important book on the subject was published in 1945, *Islami Ma'shiyat* (*Islamic Economics*) by Manazir

117 Mawdūdī differentiated between the process of modernization, which he saw as a necessary component of Islamic revivalism, and westernization. "The approach of the Islamic movement is to ... modernize without compromising on Islamic principles and values." Khurshid Ahmad, "The Nature of Islamic Resurgence," in *Voices of Resurgent Islam*, ed. John L. Esposito (New York: Oxford University Press, 1983), 224.

118 Nasr, *Mawdudi and the Making of Islamic Revivalism*, 51.

119 "The rejection of Western culture while appropriating its tools of progress was the cornerstone of Islamic revival. He sought to appropriate modern scientific thought and Islamize it; they accepted modern scientific thought and attempted to interpret Islam according to it. The modernists wanted to modernize Islam whereas Mawdudi wanted to also Islamize modernity. The distinction was enough to permit Mawdudi to inveigh against his modernist rivals." (Nasr, *Mawdudi and the Making of Islamic Revivalism*, 52). See also Rahman, *Islam and Modernity*; Charles J. Adams, "The Ideology of Mawlana Mawdudi," in *South Asian Politics and Religion*, ed. Donald E. Smith (Princeton, NJ: Princeton University Press, 1966), 371–391.

Ahsan Gilani from Hyderabad.[120] There were also publications in English by Anwar Iqbal Qureshi, *Islam and the Theory of Interest*, in 1947, and by Shaikh Mahmud Ahmad, *Economics of Islam: A Comparative Study*, in 1938, which were followed by Muhammad Hamidullah's writings on similar topics in Urdu and in English.[121] Despite the relative importance of their works and the nuances in their writings, the scholarly corpus on Islamic economics was formed into a discipline only in the 1970s, manifest in an institutional, bureaucratic, and educational systematization of the discipline.[122] This further illustrates that it was not Mawdūdī who coined the term "Islamic economics" (what would in Urdu be translated as *Islāmī maʿāshīāt*), since he referred to *maʿāshī niẓām* as an "economic system." Moreover, it was certainly not only Mawdūdī who pursued the idea of Islamic economics as a distinct economic system.[123] Yet, as indicated above, he did establish the popular discourse of political and religious engagement with an Islamic vision of state and society. This ideological discourse also consisted of an economic philosophy that was pertinent to the lives of Indian Muslims at the time.[124] His theoretical writings were later developed by the following

120 Abdul Azim Islahi, "The Genesis of Islamic Economics," *Islamic Economic Studies*, vol. 23, no. 2, (2015): 15.

121 Islahi, "Genesis of Islamic Economics," 16.

122 Islahi, as a response to Timur Kuran's critique of Islamic economics being politically motivated, maintains that Islamic economics did not develop only to support political Islam (Islahi, "Genesis of Islamic Economics," 17).

123 See Arshad Zaman, "Mawlana Mawdudi and the Genesis of Islamic Economics," (paper presented at the Ninth International Conference on Islamic Economics and Finance, Istanbul, Turkey, November 9–11, 2013), 2. On the contrary, Rodney Wilson and Timur Kuran claim that it was Mawdūdī who coined the term Islamic economics. "Mawdūdī term 'Islamic economics'." Rodney Wilson, "The Development of Islamic Economics," in *Islamic Thought in the Twentieth Century*, ed. Suha Taji-Farouki and Basheer M. Nafi (London: I.b. Tauris, 2004), 197. "In addition to 'Islamic economics', Mawdudi coined or popularized many other terms that quickly became key elements of Islamist discourse, including 'Islamic ideology', 'Islamic politics', 'Islamic constitution', and 'Islamic way of life'." Timur Kuran, "The Genesis of Islamic Economics: A Chapter in the Politics of Muslim Identity," *Islam and Mammon* (Princeton, NJ: Princeton University Press, 2004), 84.

124 "Mawlāna Mawdūdī developed a unified political philosophy, and a practical programme of action." (Zaman, "Mawlana Mawdudi and the Genesis of Islamic Economics," 8).

generations of Muslim economists,[125] and they became applicable beyond the borders of Pakistan. Khurshid Ahmad, a respected Muslim economist and one of Mawdūdī's students, transmitted, edited, and published his teachings on Islamic economics.[126]

Muhammad Hamidullah, a Pakistani scholar who wrote in Urdu, Arabic, German, French, and English, began his writings on Islamic economics as early as the 1930s, and it was Hamidullah who coined the term "Islamic economics."[127] Originally from Hyderabad, Hamidullah stated that the region continuously had Islamic rule: "Dynasties changed and wars came, yet its independence was always preserved, until 1948."[128] The nationalization of currency and interest-free lending banks were long known to the region. In 1891, the first-known step was taken in this direction, when the *Mu'ayyid al-Ikhwān* society was founded by a local mystic, Sayyid 'Umar Qādirī. In 1902 another society, *Mu'īn al-Muslimīn*, was established, which organized interest-free deposits of money, on the basis that its members paid a certain amount in order to purchase shares.[129] This marks the beginning of how interest-free loans were issued in South Asia. In 1913, however, the Hyderabad government

125 "Mawdūdī's writings and speeches profoundly influenced a new generation of professional economists in the Indian sub-continent who sought to reconcile Islamic teachings with the ideas and concepts they had acquired through their economic training." (Wilson, "Development of Islamic Economics," 196).

126 Khurshid Ahmad also edited and compiled Mawdūdī's writings in English from the original 1969 Urdu compilation. In the introduction, he states that "It was in the 1960s that I felt the need to compile a book, which would bring together all his essential writings on Islamic economics, so as to make his thought available in one volume. This need had gained more urgency because of a national debate in Pakistan on the future shape of the economy in the country, which was caught between the conflicting demands of the emerging capitalist system in the country and its critique from writers on the left. It was in the context of this national debate that Islamic economics moved into the centre of the political discourse." (Mawdūdī, *First Principles of Islamic Economics*, xxxii). See also Khurshid Ahmad, *The Religion of Islam* (Lahore: Islamic Publication, 1960).

127 See "Islam's Solution of the Basic Economic Problems," in Abdul Azim Islahi, ed., *Muhammad Hamidullah and His Pioneering Works on Islamic Economics* (Jeddah: Islamic Economics Institute, King Abdulaziz University, 2014); "Hamidullah: Life and Works," in Islahi, ed., *Muhammad Hamidullah and His Pioneering Works*, 19.

128 Hamidullah, "Haidarabad's Contribution to Islamic Economic Thought and Practice," 73.

129 Hamidullah, "Haidarabad's Contribution to Islamic Economic Thought and Practice," 74.

instituted cooperative lending societies modeled according to a Western form, allowing interest-free societies to be registered at the department of state.[130] Thus, the Hyderabad *'ulamā'* had extensive experience with issuing inheritance laws, prohibition of interest, and commercial transactions. Hamidullah himself met with the Pakistani government in 1948 to draft a new constitution for the newly established state.[131] In 1949, he also participated in the Board of Islamic Education of Pakistan. Similar to other Muslim economists, he refers to the scriptural sources of Islam in stating that the theocratic fundaments of Muslim polity deny an absolute state ownership.[132] Hamidullah maintained that both laissez-faire and socialist economic systems are untenable extremes and that Islam offers an attainable solution since it eliminates economic fluctuations.[133]

In analyzing capitalist and communist systems and critiquing them for their materialist exposition of reality, Hamidullah maintains that no existing form of governance is particularly Islamic, and yet all of them could be regarded as such, if the protection of the state and its citizens would be guaranteed:

What form of government is truly Islamic? Republican, monarchic, elective, hereditary, universal, regional, unitary, composite, etc., etc. None and

130 Hamidullah, "Haidarabad's Contribution to Islamic Economic Thought and Practice," 75.

131 Islahi, ed., *Muhammad Hamidullah and His Pioneering Works*, 4.

132 "Unlike some other systems of law where the individual owns property in lands as a delegated authority or trustee, all land of a territory being vested in the State. Islamic jurists have opined that every individual owner has the same Divine authority, and the supervising authority of the State is only a symbol or a manifestation of the collective authority of the community . . .. All parts of the Muslim territory are under the authority of the Imam (Ruler) of the Muslims, and his authority is the authority of the community of the Muslims." (Islahi, ed., *Muhammad Hamidullah and His Pioneering Works*, 94). Maḥmūd Tāliqānī (1911–79), an Iranian cleric and reformer and a contemporary of the revolutionary leader Ayatollah Ruhollah Khomeini, also contested that unlimited freedom of individual ownership is not attainable in Islam and that material attachments are interrelated to the modes of man's thought. He further held that Islam has organized ownership around three components – individuals, laws, and state government. See Tāliqānī, *Islām va Mālkīyāt*.

133 "Another feature of Islamic Economics which goes to solve our problems is that it eliminates the central defect of laissez-faire Economics by prohibiting all economic practices which yield a 'private net product' at the cost of the 'social net product'." (Islahi, ed., *Muhammad Hamidullah and His Pioneering Works*, 70, 85).

practically everyone. I mean to say, Islam simply enjoins upon the Government the duty of protecting the State and its inhabitants and administering impartial justice, no matter what form of Government the Muslims of a time or country choose.[134]

Hamidullah reiterates that any form of government could be Islamic if it were only based on Islamic principles of governance. Even if there are certain similarities between Islam and communism,[135] the two are in essence incompatible. Since the notion of equality and pious behavior are some of the main Islamic principles, according to Hamidullah, Islam opposes class divisions and upholds the idea of unity. According to him, modern Muslim economists are not versed in *fiqh* studies, as much as *fiqh* scholars lack knowledge of economics.[136] The problem of such a reading is that it displays economic and financial science as interpreted by the dominant voices in Islamic economics. As will be shown in Chapter 2, literature on contemporary Islamic economics emphasizes ethical economic norms and an interest-free economic system[137] that is nonetheless theorized within the scope of modernity.

134 Hamidullah, "Islam and Communism," in Islahi, ed., *Muhammad Hamidullah and His Pioneering Works*, 135. First published at Hyderabad Deccan, 1981 in *The Islamic Review*, vol. 38 (March 1950): 11–15, revised in 1975.

135 Communism "nationalizes land and the more important means and instruments of production, with many exceptions, as seen above; and this includes also foreign trade as a Government monopoly. Islam does not enjoin this; yet if it is a temporary measure in the interest of the whole community, Islam will not prohibit it either, I suppose." Second, it "allows private property, of course restricted: and even then it includes house, garden, and small fields and farms, not to speak of the movable property and herds of animals. Regarding the permissions, there is nothing against Islam in them. As to the restrictions, if they are temporary and in the interest of the whole community, there will again be no clash with Islam." (Islahi, ed., *Muhammad Hamidullah and His Pioneering Works*, 146).

136 "Economists (in the modern sense) are not fuqahā‘, and fuqahā‘ have no knowledge of economics, in general. Without the combination of the two it is not possible to study Islamic economics. The university came to the help, where the faculty of Muslim Theology, and the School of Economics worked under the same roof (of course together with many other faculties necessary in modern universities.") (Hamidullah, "Haidarabad's Contribution to Islamic Economic Thought and Practice," 78).

137 Islahi, ed., *Muhammad Hamidullah and His Pioneering Works*, 141, 150; see also 181–196 ("The Economic System of Islam"). The article appeared as chapter 10 (pp. 121–133) of Hamidullah's book *Introduction to Islam* (Paris: Centre Culturel Islamique, 1957; second edition 1969).

1.4.2 *Mawdūdī's Economic System*

As is the case with many other modern Muslim scholars, Mawdūdī did not focus only on economics in his writings but on the wider socioeconomic and political propositions as an alternative economic system. He advanced the link between Islamic economics and the political-ideological spectrum of the modern Islamic nation-state. The need to modernize Islamic (economic) law due to the constant dynamism of *Sharī'a* was introduced as the prerequisite for the establishment of an Islamic state, which also involved recodifying bylaws. His writings on economics were not systematized in a field but rather scattered and closely related to the concepts of *dīn*: "The Pakistan movement was an expression of Muslim India's firm desire to establish an Islamic State. The movement was inspired by the ideology of Islam and the country was carved into existence solely to demonstrate the efficacy of the Islamic way of life."[138] Despite the distinct features of an Islamic economic system as an alternative model to both capitalism and socialism, its moral imprint, and *Sharī'a*-stipulated economic behavior, Mawdūdī's economic discourse remained confined to the mechanisms of economic science.

Still, his *Economic Problem of Man and Its Islamic Solution* has been cited as being the first book on Islamic economics – though, as previously mentioned, he never used the term "Islamic economics," but rather "economic system of Islam." Even though the book was published in 1955, there were several other texts on Islamic economics published before it.[139] Translated into English, it elaborated his theological, legal, social, and political opinions on an Islamic society and state, making him one of the most prominent representatives of Islamic economics. In it, Mawdūdī stresses that man is also a moral and spiritual being.[140] He rightly assessed that an economic problem is

[138] Mawdūdī, *Islamic Law and Constitution*, 11; "Mawdudi's position was based on classical sources, which he interpreted conservatively in keeping with the position of the ulama. Because the Islamic state was the panacea for all sociopolitical problems, all other movements were unnecessary and redundant. This conservatism, combined with his horror of socialism, shaped his response to all social and economic problems." (Nasr, *Mawdudi and the Making of Islamic Revivalism*, 105).

[139] Sayyid Abū al-A'lā Mawdūdī, *Economic Problem of Man and Its Islamic Solution* (Lahore: Markazi Maktaba Jama'at-e-islami Pakistan, 1955), 59, 60.

[140] Mawdūdī, *Economic Problem of Man and Its Islamic Solution*, 8.

hence not only economic in nature, but it is also relevant to morality, culture, and society,[141] for a human being's economic standpoint only reflects the (lack of) moral, spiritual, sociological, and political (dis) equilibrium. Humanity's economic problems originate from human selfishness, which "exceeds the limits of moderation"[142] and extends to the issue of wealth and ownership. Private ownership is licit when entangled with a political system that fosters human goodness and social justice. What remains responsible for the social malaise is, however, the degradation of humankind to selfish consumers who are centered in the material world.

Furthermore, *Economic Problem of Man and Its Islamic Solution* discusses his views on communism and capitalism. The former treats an economic problem as the central issue of human life and hence lacks an ethical attitude toward the economic problem of man.[143] As a centralized system of the means of production, it indicates that in practice a small executive body runs the collective ownership.[144] On the other hand, for Mawdūdī, capitalism encourages an illicit means of acquisition of wealth and stockpiling of money. The Islamic solution is incongruent to economic behavior alone and must be linked with the moral transformation of society.[145] The so-called "Islamic economic system" is based both on Qur'anic predicaments and on objectives such as personal freedom, moral and material progress, and justice.[146] Concerning those objectives, Islamic economic principles are preserved through the parameters of private ownership, the value of labor, the institution of *zakāt*, interest-free economy, and the interrelationship between economic, political, and social systems.[147]

[141] Mawdūdī, *Economic Problem of Man and Its Islamic Solution*, 11.
[142] Mawdūdī, *Economic Problem of Man and Its Islamic Solution*, 19–20; Mawdūdī, *First Principles of Islamic Economics*, 9.
[143] Mawdūdī, *Economic Problem of Man and Its Islamic Solution*, 43.
[144] Mawdūdī, *Economic Problem of Man and Its Islamic Solution*, 37–38.
[145] Mawdūdī, *Economic Problem of Man and Its Islamic Solution*, 46.
[146] Mawdūdī, *First Principles of Islamic Economics*, 88–90.
[147] "It is a system that evolves out of Faith in the Oneness of God and the Finality of Prophethood. It is out of this root that emerges the system of moral conduct, the system of Divine Worship, the economic system and the political system." (Mawdūdī, *First Principles of Islamic Economics*, 101; see also 91–102).

Mawdūdī stands against the delinking of economics from religion and morality.[148] Yet, his usage of Islamic order or economic system must be understood within the broader context of the Islamic vision of life, as inextricably related to broader social developments. Linking economic postulates with a sociopolitical vision not only generates a distinct ideological characteristic of such economics but also places it within secular methodology and a paradigm centered on the modern nation-state. He writes,

> In order to recodify the economic laws, we have to look first at the economic scenario of the modern world and carefully study the modern methods of economic and financial transactions. We have to understand the underlying forces governing economic activities, learn about the various concepts and principles at work and the practical shapes that they are taking. We then have to see how to categorize the changes that have taken place in the field of economy and finance from the Islamic legal perspective, and how to frame rules that can be applicable to these categories; all this time, we must also be in accord with the dictates of the *Sharīʿa*, its legal vision and its objectives.[149]

The discrepancies between Muslim religious scholars' and economists' theories of Islamic economics as being based on the moral predicaments of *Sharīʿa*, and the factual application of those theories within the dominant economic paradigm, exemplify the structural inconsistencies of merging religious ethics and modern economics. It also illustrates a process of a gradual yet forceful applicability of Islamic economic theories within the systemic confinements of the nation-state. Even though Mawdūdī states that capitalism and secular democracy are one of the biggest deceptions of modern times to which humanity is being subjected,[150] his vision of an Islamic society (in Pakistan), which also entails a developed economic system, would be structurally possible only within the modern Islamic nation-state. This entity would have all the corresponding systemic, bureaucratic, administrative, political, and economic configurations, while reappropriating the modern state conditions.[151]

148 Muslim economists highlighted, for instance, that the principle of money plays only an intermediary role, and is not an objective in itself as it is in capitalism. (Khurshid Ahmad in Mawdūdī, *First Principles of Islamic Economics*, xviii, xxix).

149 Mawdūdī, *First Principles of Islamic Economics*, 265; see also 260–262.

150 Mawdūdī, *First Principles of Islamic Economics*, 230.

151 What it will be evident in due time about Pakistan's Islamization process is also the restructuring of the juridical and economic systems, some of them also

1.5 Islamization of Knowledge Process and Contemporary Islamic Thought

The Islamization of knowledge (IOK) process shaped the understanding of some of the modern intellectual movements across Euro-America, the Middle East, and South Asia. Due to its intellectual impact on Muslim economists, it is pivotal to understanding the project of contemporary Islamic economics. The majority of Muslim economists that will be presented in Chapter 2 situate their theories within the framework of IOK. This book understands IOK as the epistemological, scientific, and educational field of study that emerged in the 1970s, with the aim to re-Islamize educational curriculums and human disciplines. In addition to Islamization efforts in the domain of economics, academically and intellectually, it is primarily associated with Isma'il al-Faruqi's and Muhammad Naquib al-Attas's conceptualizations of recuperating and reassessing the role of knowledge in contemporary period despite their methodological and epistemological differences.[152] Their works had an impact on the curriculum and methodology of Islamic educational institutions and centers, including Islamic economic institutions. One of the main aims of IOK was the epistemological reimagining of the Islamic legacy and reverting the lost knowledge according to an Islamic worldview.[153] This, as we shall see below, prompted the advancement of Islamic economic theories by scholars who were trained in economic sciences and hence could be regarded as economists with Muslim background, who were primarily based in Malaysia, Pakistan, Saudi Arabia, and in other postcolonial Muslim-majority countries. According to the cofounder of the International Institute of Islamic Thought (IIIT), Taha Jabir Al-Alwani, IOK is not to be considered as a set of axioms or an ideology

proposed by Mawdūdī. The measures to reform the country's economic system are to legally ban interest, carry out accountability for the rich in light of Islamic principles, abolish feudal landholdings, reduce ownership right of land to a certain limit, replace the banking system as the brainchild of capitalism with the Islamic foundations of *mushāraka*, organize the system of *zakāt*, and so forth. (Mawdūdī, *First Principles of Islamic Economics*, 249).

152 Isma'il al-Faruqi (1921–1986) was a prominent Palestinian-American scholar of Islam and the founder of the International Institute of Islamic Thought (IIIT) in Herndon, Virginia. Muhammad Naquib al-Attas (b. 1931) is a contemporary Muslim philosopher from Malaysia who pioneered the idea of Islamization of knowledge.

153 Al-Faruqi, *Islamization of Knowledge*, 39–47.

but rather as a methodology of knowledge, rooted in an Islamic worldview.[154] Proponents of the IOK perceive the spread of Western knowledge and secularism as the fundamental philosophy for Islamic sciences as one of the root causes for the malaise of modern Muslim societies. Some among them argue for a synthesis of Islamic heritage and knowledge as it emerged in modern Europe in order to achieve the scientific status of Islamic disciplines, such as Islamic economics.

The way society formulates and understands knowledge is inseparable from the usage of language and ideas expressed in that very language.[155] The concept of knowledge provides for the birth of different disciplines, educational philosophy, and institutions. In Islamic tradition, multiple types of *ʿilm* (loosely translated as knowledge) exist, including revealed knowledge (*al-waḥy*), derived or acquired knowledge,[156] and branches of knowledge based on both the divine knowledge and the human intellect. Many modern Muslim scholars refer to the principles of knowledge comprised of *tawḥīd* as unity of creation, *waḥy* as revelation, and *ʿaql* as human reason.[157] From such a perspective, knowledge is imbued with the construction of a personality or an agent (in economic terms, *homo Islamicus* as an opposition to *homo economicus*) within a particular worldview. According to the proponents of the IOK, this translates into a rejection of Western sciences due to the different conceptual and epistemological sources of knowledge that are to be found in Islamic tradition.[158]

154 See Ahmad S. Moussalli "Islamism: Modernization of Islam, or Islamization of Knowledge," in *Cosmopolitanism, Identity and Authenticity in the Middle East*, ed. Roel Meijer (London: Routledge, 1999).

155 See Seyyed Hossein Nasr, *Knowledge and the Sacred* (New York: State University of New York, 1989), 43; Hallaq, *Sharīʿa*, 1–6; Muhammad Naquib al-Attas, *Prolegomena to the Metaphysics of Islam* (Kuala Lumpur: ISTAC, 2001), 20.

156 On the notion of *ʿilm* and the history of knowledge and sciences in Islam, see Osman Bakar, *Classification of Knowledge in Islam* (Cambridge: Islamic Texts Society, 1998); Nasr, *Knowledge and the Sacred*.

157 For the classification of knowledge in the Islamic tradition see e.g. Bakar, *Classification of Knowledge in Islam*.

158 Apart from the different sources of knowledge, the objectives and branches of knowledge are also being discerned and appropriated in a distinct way in Islamic and Western epistemologies. Muhammad Amin, *An Analytical Appraisal of Islamization of Knowledge* (Lahore: Safa Educational Reforms Trust Pakistan, 2009), 17.

In what follows, I discuss how individual scholars like al-Faruqi and al-Attas envisioned correcting and implementing the Islamization process of scientific disciplines in order to reconcile Islamic tradition and modernity and to further the scientific method in a way that would be in accordance with Islamic normativity.

1.5.1 *Isma'il al-Faruqi's Division of Islamic Sciences*

Islamization of academic discourse in the twentieth century is in part linked to a particular intellectual orientation by Muslim reformists who espoused an antithetic vision of a modern Islamic nation-state. Much of the unease among the intelligentsia of the *umma* they claim, was because Muslims "were secularized, westernized, and de-Islamized by internal and external agents."[159] Contemporary Western-trained Muslim economists advanced the idea of an Islamic society and Islamic economic agents on the grounds of an Islamic, politically independent, and economically viable system.

Al-Faruqi, a Palestinian-American scholar on Islam, who with Taha Jabir Al-Alwani cofounded the IIIT in 1981 by securing $25 million from the Saudi Islamic Development Bank, was pivotal for the promotion and expansion of the IOK agenda. The far-reaching influence of al-Faruqi's ideas in the creation of the IIIT has had tremendous impact on the implementation of the IOK project by various scholars, institutes, and educational facilities in the West. His book, *Islamization of Knowledge* has become the manifesto for many Islamic universities that implemented their curriculum programs and designed their learning pedagogy according to its main framework.

Since contemporary knowledge has undergone a process of secularization and westernization, al-Faruqi, unlike al-Attas, sees IOK as a process that can contest the Eurocentric knowledge that has been universalized,[160] since, he argues, education is the cornerstone and a prerequisite of any state. Al-Faruqi defines the Islamization process as applying new knowledge to the Islamic intellectual corpus,[161] rooted in the *tawḥīd* epistemology. Yet IOK presents only one type of knowledge, and "a way and a method to formulate a methodological,

[159] Al-Faruqi, *Islamization of Knowledge*, 1.
[160] Al-Faruqi, *Islamization of Knowledge*, 36.
[161] Al-Faruqi, *Islamization of Knowledge*, 30.

scientific, mental approach to humanities, social sciences, and applied sciences."[162] One of its aims, which targets contemporary knowledge, is to expand the methodology due to the shortcomings of traditional Islamic sciences.[163] Al-Faruqi sets up the Islamization plan founded on several objectives, which include efforts to increase awareness among the *umma* of the crisis of ideas; to revive the lost ideology; to define the relationship between the failure of Islamic thought and its methodology; to adopt Islamic methodology in the field of social sciences; to master modern disciplines and Islamic history; to establish a bridge between Islamic and modern knowledge; and to launch a trajectory of knowledge that would fulfill the divine message.[164] In order to achieve those objectives of the IOK plan, certain steps should be taken: for instance, mastering and critically evaluating modern and classical disciplines; analyzing the current problems of the *umma*; disseminating Islamized knowledge;[165] and producing university-level texts books to recast the modern disciplines as imbued with Islamic vision.[166] A central task would be to integrate the two systems, instilling an Islamic vision through political, cultural, social, and educational platforms. Moreover, Islamic educational systems would be established, consisting of elementary and secondary schools, colleges, and universities,[167] which would be instrumental for the dissemination for the Islamization of Islamic economics.

Along with al-Faruqi, Muhammad Naquib al-Attas is the main representative of the IOK process in Malaysia, who espouses the theory

162 Al-Faruqi, *Islamization of Knowledge*, 85.

163 Al-Faruqi holds that the classical scholarship abandoned *ijtihād* since they perceived *Sharī'a* as being in a perfect state. Since *fiqh* as a closed system presented a stalemate, Muslims sought to overcame the difficulties through *teṣawwuf*. (Al-Faruqi, *Islamization of Knowledge*, 23–25).

164 Al-Faruqi, *Islamization of Knowledge*, 57–58.

165 Al-Faruqi, *Islamization of Knowledge*, 57–82.

166 By Islamic values, al-Faruqi means the usefulness of knowledge, nurturing the divine patterns, and building culture and civilization, based on virtues of piety and righteousness. The concepts and methodology used to disseminate the IOK consist of intellectual, academic, educational, cultural, administrative, and research-based preparations of the institute's cadres. (Al-Faruqi, *Islamization of Knowledge*, 19–20, 60–79). For the division of Islamized disciplines see a detailed study in 'Abdul Ḥamīd Abū Sulaymān, *Mafāhim fī I'ādat Binā' Manhajīyāt al-Fikr al-Islāmī al-Mu'āṣir*. (Concepts of Reconstruction: Methodology in Contemporary Muslim Thought) (Herndon, VA: IIIT, 1989); see also al-Faruqi, *Islamization of Knowledge*, 31–68.

167 Al-Faruqi, *Islamization of Knowledge*, 13–14.

of Islamization through the study of Islamic intellectual history and *taṣawwuf*.

1.5.2 *Muhammad Naquib al-Attas and the Metaphysics of Islam*

Al-Attas maintains that knowledge as such is never value-neutral, but rather it is influenced by the religious, moral, social, and cultural worldview of the society in which it emerges.[168] In spite of Western disciplines not accepting the Islamic sources or division of knowledge,[169] the IOK process has consequently meant assimilating Islamic knowledge from within its own epistemology into the modernist discourse, which has shaped in part the discipline of Islamic economics. As a result, in the modern period many Muslim scholars and economists amalgamated Western knowledge with their own tradition, procuring a Cartesian dualism embedded in different worldviews and ideologies.[170] According to al-Attas, Islamization involves the Islamization of language, since language is closely related to one's worldview. He maintains that IOK is the inclusion of knowledge from its interpretations based on secular logic.[171] The deletion from Islamic legacy of foreign concepts within the Western tradition – such as the philosophy of dualism and secular logic – is a precondition for a successful process of Islamization, whereby the category of knowledge becomes fundamental not only to the Islamic tradition but to any real modern education. In the traditional Islamic worldview, knowledge was encapsulated in the open-ended *farḍ kifāya* knowledge, which includes the natural, physical, and applied sciences and the *farḍ ʿayn*, the absolute nature of the knowledge pertaining to God and the spiritual realities and moral truths.[172] *Farḍ ʿayn* knowledge is dynamic, increasing in accordance with the spiritual and social responsibilities of a person. Contemporary modern knowledge is, however, delivered from its interpretations based on secular ideology, which requires

168 Amin, *Analytical Appraisal of Islamization of Knowledge*, 5.
169 Al-Attas, *Islam, Secularism and the Philosophy of Future*, 128.
170 Al-Attas, *Islam and Secularism*, 36 and 134–135.
171 Al-Attas, *Islam and Secularism*, 44.
172 Al-Attas, *Islam and Secularism*, 84.

a critical examination of the methods of modern science; its concepts, presuppositions, and symbols; its empirical and rational aspects, and those impinging upon values and ethics; its interpretations of origins; its theory of knowledge; its presuppositions on the existence of an external world, of the uniformity of nature and of the rationality of natural processes; its theory of the universe; its classification of the sciences; its limitations and interrelations with one another of the sciences, and its social relations.[173]

However, for al-Attas, *ma'rifa*[174] as a priori knowledge does not need to undergo an Islamization process since it is inherently Islamic; this is why al-Attas refers to the term "Islamization of present-day knowledge" as *aslamat 'ulūm al-mu'āṣirah* or *Islamīyatul 'ulūm al-mu'āṣirah*.[175] Science is hence regarded as a form of *ta'wīl* or allegorical interpretation of the empirical reality that constitutes the natural and cosmological world,[176] whereas religion is constituted as an established law (*Sharī'a*) and truth (*haqīqa*).[177]

Al-Attas expounded the notion of *adab*, which he translated as "right action," which became one of the central terms of his philosophy of Islamization. *Adab* is closely linked to *kashf* as a source of inner predisposition that springs from self-discipline and is intrinsically connected to knowledge, whereas *'adl* (justice) is the condition of things in their proper places that has been lost in the Muslim world as a result of neglecting *adab*.[178] In the context of disciplines and fields of scientific

173 Al-Attas, *Prolegomena to the Metaphysics of Islam*, 114.

174 "*Ma'rifah* as 'knowledge' is both right cognition (*'ilm*) and right feeling or spiritual mood (*ḥāl*); and the former, which marks the final stages of the spiritual 'stations' (*maqāmāt*), precedes the latter, which marks time beginning of the spiritual 'states' (*aḥwāl*). So *ma'rifah* marks the spiritual transition – point between the spiritual station and the spiritual state." (Al-Attas, *Islam and Secularism*, 71).

175 Al-Attas, *Islam, Secularism and the Philosophy of Future*, 127.

176 Muhammad Naquib al-Attas, *Islam and the Philosophy of Science* (Kuala Lumpur: ISTAC, 1989), 116.

177 Al-Attas argues that the constituent components of the fundaments of Islamic metaphysics are the primacy of the reality of existence; the dynamic nature of this reality; determination and individuation; the perpetual process of the new creation; the absence of a necessary relation between cause and effect and its explanation in the Divine causality; the third metaphysical category between existence and nonexistence (the realm of the permanent entities); and the metaphysics of change and permanence pertaining to the realities. It is within the framework of this metaphysics that the philosophy of science must be formulated. (Al-Attas, *Islam and the Philosophy of Science*, 35–36).

178 Al-Attas, *Islam and Secularism*, 105–110, 149–152. The first edition of the book was published in 1979.

inquiry, education is acquired knowledge only if it includes morality and moral purposes, also called *adab*.[179] Islamization is hence the recalibration and reintegration of *adab* into the Muslim social fabric. The disintegration of *adab* in Muslim societies occurred due to both the corruption of knowledge[180] and the blind adaptation of Western patterns of education, which impacted the theory of knowledge of sciences. This was inextricably related to the "secularization process" in Western societies, which disassociated moral postulates from scientific inquiries. Al-Attas has thus been advocating the process of purifying Islamic knowledge, its epistemology, and its sciences of Western concepts – which have been integrated into the very composition of the Muslim perception of the world. In order to reintegrate Islamic concepts into the Muslim worldview, one has to reexamine and analyze the fundamental terms within Islamic tradition as manifestations of theory and practice.[181] This entails isolating key Western concepts from a modern vocabulary – such as secularism, humanism, and dualism – and infusing them with an Islamic epistemology.[182]

Below, I analyze the case study of Pakistan and its Islamization processes with the aim to explain how the Islamization of its state economy was introduced and how Islamic finances were established in a modern Islamic nation-state.

1.6 Islamization of the Islamic Economy (1979–Present)

1.6.1 Islamization of Pakistan's Economy

The creation of Islamic finances and banking and the emergence of Islamic universities in Pakistan, Malaysia, and elsewhere, as well as the

179 "Education, then, is the absorption of *adab* in the self . . .. *Adab*, concisely defined, is the spectacle of justice (*'adl*) as it is reflected by wisdom (*ḥikmah*)." (Al-Attas, *Prolegomena to the Metaphysics of Islam*, 16, 17).

180 Al-Attas, *Prolegomena to the Metaphysics of Islam*, 19.

181 One example is the word *dīn* translated into English simply as "religion." Al-Attas contests that *dīn* connotes a much broader and more profound understanding of Islamic faith and can be translated as indebtedness, submissiveness, judicial power, and natural inclination or tendency. (Al-Attas, *Prolegomena to the Metaphysics of Islam*, 42; al-Attas, *Islam and Secularism*, 52).

182 Al-Attas, *Islam and Secularism*, 43, 130.

demand for educational curriculums and religious education, went hand in hand with the ideology of Islamic economics as part of the restructuring of modern Muslim societies. Islamization involved social, political, cultural, and economic reforms, encompassing finances and economic transactions. Islamic financial institutions were created across the Middle East, North Africa, and South(east) Asia. In many respects, the process of Islamization was easier to accommodate in economics than in other fields, providing an Islamic legitimacy to national economic and political decisions.[183]

The secular postcolonial states such as Pakistan and Malaysia adapted a unique path to the development of Islamic economics as a prerogative based on religious identity that was eventually incorporated as a state ideology during the transition from secular to Islamic state.[184] The institutional flourishing of Islamic economics occurred gradually and systematically. In the case of Pakistan, General Arif, a member of its military forces, stated that Pakistani state power and sovereignty ultimately had to be addressed within the parameters of God.[185] Eventually, the Islamic state of Pakistan[186] was at the forefront of opposition to the secular logic of the postcolonial state, when Muhammad Zia ul-Haq, a Pakistani four-star general and the sixth president of Pakistan, eliminated interest from three financial institutions in 1979. This was also an opposition move to his predecessor, Prime Minister Zulfikar Ali Bhutto, and his program of nationalization and land reform. The 1979 declaration of the Pakistani government transferred the country's economic system to an Islamic economy, which was the first attempt to put into practice "Islamic economic principles" through real economic policies, implementing an Islamic taxation system, the institution of *zakāt*, and the

183 Mahathir Muhammad, "Islamization of Knowledge and the Future of the Ummah," in *Toward Islamization of Disciplines* (Herndon, VA: IIIT, 1995), 9–12.

184 Vali Nasr, "Islamization, the State and Development," in *Islamization and the Pakistani Economy*, ed. Robert M. Hathaway and Wilson Lee (Washington, DC: Woodrow Wilson International Center for Scholars, 2004), 91–100.

185 Khalid Mahmud Arif, *Working with Zia: Pakistan's Power Politics, 1977–88* (Karachi: Oxford University Press, 1995), 79.

186 In 1979, the military regime of Pakistan promulgated corporal punishment in place of the British criminal code. The Islamization of the judiciary and state apparatus was designed to produce a legal system that would prompt political and economic reforms and replace the Anglo-Saxon codes and laws. See e.g. Iqbal, *Islamisation of Pakistan*.

elimination of *ribā*.[187] Modern and Islamic education systems would coexist as long as they were infused with Islamic values. The establishment of the International Islamic University of Islamabad and the International Islamic University in Kuala Lumpur sought to provide the state with modern, albeit religiously stipulated, knowledge and a workforce that would cope with the modern economy. As such, Pakistan's Islamization efforts were thorough on societal, juridical, and economic levels, assuring that a particular ideological strand met political ends. However, due to various historical factors, the Pakistani state was unable to assert the same level of political hegemony as that which was established in Malaysia.[188]

Pakistan turned to Islamization in order to consolidate political control and state formation.[189] In both Pakistan and Malaysia, when the establishment of the state apparatus and the national economy were still in their early stages, the process of Islamization, which happened in 1977 and 1981 respectively, enabled a political hegemony over national identity and economic development.[190] Pakistan continued the colonial project's governing systems, interweaving hegemonic policies, modernization process, and formations of

[187] Arif, *Working with Zia*; Khurshid Ahmad, "Islamizing the Economy: The Pakistan Experience," in Hathaway and Lee, *Islamization and the Pakistani Economy*, 40–42; Charles H. Kennedy, "Pakistan's Superior Courts and the Prohibition of Riba," in Hathaway and Lee, *Islamization and the Pakistani Economy*, 102.

[188] See e.g. Radia Abdul Kader and Mohamed Ariff, "The Political Economy of Islamic Finance: The Malaysian Experience," in *Islamic Political Economy in Capitalist Globalization: An Agenda for Change*, ed. Masudul Alam Choudhry, Abdad M. Z., and Muhammad Syukri Salleh (Kuala Lumpur: IPIPE, 1997).

[189] On the Islamization of the Pakistani economy see e.g. Ishrat Husain, "The Economy of Pakistan: Past, Present and Future," in Hathaway and Lee, *Islamization and the Pakistani Economy*, 11–36; "Islamization is a proactive rather than a reactive process, in which state interests serve as a causal factor." (Nasr, *Islamic Leviathan*, 6).

[190] The state in the Muslim world emerged not as an organic entity but rather as an inherently colonial project. For more, see Timothy Mitchell, "The Limits of the State: Beyond Statist Approaches and Their Critics," *American Political Science Review*, vol. 85, no. 1 (1991): 77–96; Sami Zubaida, "Islam, the State and Democracy: Contrasting Conceptions of Society in Egypt," *Middle East Report*, no. 179 (1992): 2–10; Lisa Anderson, "The State in the Middle East and North Africa," *Comparative Politics*, vol. 20, no. 1 (1987): 1–18; James C. Scott, *Political Ideology in Malaysia: Reality and the Beliefs of an Elite* (Kuala Lumpur: University of Malaya Press, 1968).

secular governments in accordance with the European notion of sovereignty, while implementing an Islamic economy; in brief, they replicated similar state operations. The political institutions and social structures inherited from colonial powers included a bureaucracy, a judiciary, and a military, ensuring the promulgation of political conditions that resembled the colonial situation. Furthermore, the propagation of religious, tribal, and ethnic affiliations by colonial states in the Muslim world facilitated national disunity in the 1970s and 1980s through the political assertion of Islamism, which was seen as a solution to the crisis of the secular state.[191] The Islamization of state politics in Pakistan demarcated the adaptation of the postcolonial state apparatus based on local cultural and social structures.[192] In this regard, Islamism and Islamization ought to be analyzed in light of modernity and secular ideologies. The secularization process in the Muslim world politicized religious tendencies that had an effect on the political landscape.[193] Because of this dichotomy, Pakistan, Malaysia, and other postcolonial countries experienced an inclusion of religious principles into domestic politics and a gradual decline of secular politics based on colonial administration. In Pakistan, the ruling regimes empowered an Islamic narrative as a political discourse by also drawing new constitutions and establishing state–society relations, which meant also Islamizing the economy. Interest-free banking became prominent in the 1980s,

[191] "At the critical juncture of 1977–80 in both Malaysia and Pakistan the postcolonial state faced a serious crisis. Its strategies of survival and efforts to shore up state authority and pursue economic development – NEP in Malaysia and the PPP's populism in Pakistan – had faced resistance. That resistance had parlayed into Islamist activism that threatened state authority and, in the case of Pakistan, came close to debunking the state altogether. State leaders were thus compelled to look for new ways in which to bolster state authority and augment its powers. The task of empowering the state would inevitably become anchored in the ideas and political tools of Islamism, for the decade of Islamist activism greatly affected social norms and values, and the relation of society to the state. (Nasr, *Islamic Leviathan*, 101). See also Kuran, *Islam and Mammon*, 1.

[192] See Mumtaz Ahmad, "Islamization and the Structural Crises of the State in Pakistan," *Issues in Islamic Thought*, vol. 12 (1993): 304–310.

[193] This view is shared by various scholars. For Reza Vali Nasr "Islamism is the product of this dialectic in the postcolonial Muslim world .... Islamism was opposed only to the secular ideology of the state, but not to state hegemony, its extensive intervention in the economy and society. Islamism at its core supports statism, provided that the state is 'Islamic'." (Nasr, *Islamic Leviathan*, 14).

especially in Pakistan.[194] Islamizing academic disciplines in order to make them compatible with Islamic teachings was designated as an effort to decolonize the society and Islamize the judiciary. This, however, also meant developing a modern Islamic theory of knowledge based on Western epistemologies such as phenomenology, historicity, and relativism, as well as Islamizing concepts such as state and democracy.[195]

The founding of other Islamic financial institutions throughout the Middle East and North Africa transformed Islamic economic teachings into concrete establishments, for example, the Mit-Ghamr Saving Bank in Egypt in 1963, the Islamic Development Bank (ISDB) in 1975, the Dubai Islamic Bank in 1975, Kuwait Finance House in 1977, Jordan's Islamic Bank for Finance and Investment in 1978, Bahrain's Islamic Bank in 1979, Iran's Islamic Bank in 1979, the Islamic Exchange and Investment Corporation in Qatar in 1979, International Islamic Bank in Bangladesh in 1983, Tadamon Islamic Bank in Sudan in 1983, Bank Islam Malaysia in 1983, a group of Faisal Islamic Banks in the 1970s and 1980s.[196]

1.6.2 *Intellectual and Institutional Efforts of Islamization*

The establishment of Islamic finances and banking has its origins in the theoretical, ideological, and institutional frameworks of ideologues,

194 In Pakistan, in the 1980s, interest-free banking dominated the financial sector but accounted for only a fraction of banking services, over 90 percent of which were carried out by foreign banks. (Nasr, *Islamic Leviathan*, 123). In Malaysia, for instance, Islamic finance and interest-free banking were introduced by the government in 1983, leading to the Islamization of educational curricula. See e.g. Rodney Wilson, "Islam and Malaysia's Economic Development," *Journal of Islamic Studies*, vol. 9, no. 2 (1998): 259–276; William R. Roff, "Patterns of Islamization in Malaysia, 1890s–1990s: Exemplars, Institutions, and Vectors," *Journal of Islamic Studies*, vol. 9, no. 2 (1998): 210–228.

195 For more on the state of knowledge in modernity, see e.g. Moussalli, "Islamism," 97–101; Bauer, *Die Kultur der Ambiguität*, 388; Fazlur Rahman, "Islamization of Knowledge: A Response," *Islamic Studies*, vol. 50, no. 3/4 (2011): 449–457; Seyyed Vali Reza Nasr, "Islamization of Knowledge: A Critical Overview," *Islamic Studies*, vol. 30, no. 3 (1991): 387–400.

196 El-Ashker, Wilson, *Islamic Economics: A Short History*, 336. The ISDB was established in 1975 by the Organization of Islamic Countries. It was devised as an intergovernmental bank with the primary aim to provide financial assistance (with no interest) in member countries. For more on the ISDB and the history of Islamic banking, see www.isdb.org.

scholars, and Muslim economists, a motley group who created and expanded the field of Islamic economics.[197] Islamic economics grew through the establishment of religious, social, educational, and economic organizations and institutions, such as the Organization of the Islamic Conference (1969); the Islamic Development Bank (1975), which was founded by the finance ministers at the Organization of the Islamic Conference and includes ten member states; the International Conference on Islamic Economics (1976); the International Centre for Research in Islamic Economics (1977); the International Islamic University in Islamabad (1980) and Malaysia (1983); the Islamic Research and Training Institute (1981); and the IIIT (1981), which directed the course of Islamizing knowledge processes, educational curriculums, and economic incentives of those countries, along with the establishment of Islamic financial institutions and business enterprises.[198] Hundreds of works on Islamic economics, finance, and banking appeared, predominantly in English, Arabic, and Urdu languages,[199] published primarily by Islamic Publications in Lahore, Pakistan; the International Islamic University in Kuala Lumpur, Malaysia; the Islamic Foundation in Leicester, UK; and the Islamic Economics Institute at King Abdul Aziz University in Jeddah, Saudi Arabia, in addition to the literature on IOK published by the IIIT in Herndon, USA. This literature commented on social justice, taxation, ownership, financial transactions, the legal system, banking, and more. Even though the literature produced by these centers and institutions was not meant to be political per se, it impacted some of the implementation policies on the ground, in that Muslim economists' writings on the Islamic economic ideas in the second half of the twentieth century were favored by the very academic institutions that published their work.

Despite the diverse body of literature on Islamic economics, early Muslim revivalists and Islamic ideologues of South Asia, as well as

[197] Timur Kuran states that Islamism blossomed primarily through economic and financial mechanisms and instruments (Kuran, *Islam and Mammon*, 64–66).

[198] See e.g. the Islamic Development Bank, accessed March 17, 2017, www.isdb.org/irj/portal/anonymous?NavigationTarget=navurl://8dfe53c09be96621aee748c849549322; El-Ashker, Wilson, *Islamic Economics: A Short History*, 329.

[199] See Mohammad Nejatullah Siddiqi, "Muslim Economic Thinking: A Survey of Contemporary Literature," in *Studies in Islamic Economics*, ed. Khurshid Ahmad (Leicester: Islamic Foundation, 1980).

Western-trained Muslim economists, give evidence of a particular intellectual lineage of Islamic economics. Islamic finance and banking are only by-products of a long stretch of intellectual, ideological, and political contestations and accommodations of Islamic teachings and Western-induced knowledge through epistemological tendencies. The Islamic financial system, however, would not be possible without the potential clientele who forms the majority of its markets.

Three methodological trends can be observed in the formation of contemporary Islamic economics and finance: first, the application of *uṣūl al-fiqh* methodology to Islamic economics; second, the utilization of various economic methodologies from Western and Islamic sources; and third, the inclusion of Islamic economic ethics into the episteme of conventional economics.[200] The notion of *dīn* as the central element of the Qurʾanic worldview plays a prominent role for the proponents of the Islamization of Islamic economics, as is found in the writings of Mawdūdī and al-Faruqi. The epistemology of Islamic economics is hence formed around the centrality of revelation in the pursuit of knowledge,[201] whereby Islamic methodology invokes the knowledge of *Sharīʿa* and other secondary sources.[202] Muslim economists are interested in both sources and methodologies.[203] For instance, Muḥammad Zarqa perceives Islam as a religion of guidance with normative statements, encouraging the analysis of normative hypotheses of economic thought in Islamic tradition and focusing on the relationship between

[200] Furqani and Haneef – who state that *fiqh* dominates the Islamic economic discourse – follow the Islamization of knowledge theory. Hafas Furqani and Muhammad Aslam Haneef, "Methodology of Islamic Economics: Typology of Current Practices, Evaluation and Way Forward," (paper presented at the Eighth International Conference on Islamic Economics and Finance, Doha Qatar, December 19–21, 2011), 2–8; Muhammad Aslam Haneef and Hafas Furqani, "Contemporary Islamic Economics: The Missing Dimension of Genuine Islamization," *Thoughts on Economics*, vol. 19, no. 4 (2004): 29–48.

[201] Muhammad Aslam Haneef, "Islam, the Islamic Worldview and Islamic Economics," IIUM Journal of Economics and Management, vol. 5, no. 1 (1997): 48.

[202] Mahmud Abu Saud, "The Methodology of the Islamic Behavioural Sciences," *American Journal of Islamic Social Sciences*, vol. 10, no. 3, (1993): 382–395.

[203] Muḥammad Zarqa, "Islamization of Economics: The Concept and Methodology," *Journal of King Abdul Aziz University: Islamic Economics*, vol. 16, no. 1 (2003): 12. See also the Arabic version of this article: Muḥammad Zarqa "Tahqiq Islamiyyat Ilm al Iqtisad: al Mahfum wa'l Manhaj," *Journal of King Abdul Aziz University: Islamic Economics*, vol. 2, 1990.

Islamic economics and jurisprudence.[204] The objective of Islamic economics is thus "to arrive at descriptive hypotheses or assumptions that diagnose reality and link the various economic phenomena."[205] Al-Faruqi's eight-step Islamization plan,[206] which reintegrates *Sharī'a* into the economic philosophy of Islam, has been referenced by Muslim economists such as Zarqa,[207] Monzer Kahf, Muhammad Haneef, and Mohammad Nejatullah Siddiqi.[208] The main representatives of contemporary Islamic economics, as presented in Chapter 2, despite their various methodologies, seem to follow the basic plan of the IOK.

Among the most prominent areas dominating IOK were Islamic economics and finance. Even though early discourse on Islam and economics commenced in the 1930s, and IOK only emerged in the 1970s, the Islamization of financial institutions and state economies, as well as more intellectual endeavors, such as al-Attas's conceptualization of Islam and secularism, and especially al-Faruqi's elaborated IOK plan, had repercussions on the blossoming of the Islamic economic project, in addition to the implementation practices by the aforementioned institutional and financial centers that produced or advocated for an inclusive model of Islamic economics and finances. As a discipline, Islamic economics was included in the Western and Islamic educational curricula through Islamic finance and banking,[209] and also became an academic field. Part of the credit for its development goes to the subsequent proponents of the IOK and to the global institutions that advanced their teachings in the United States, Pakistan, Indonesia, and Malaysia. The most known by-product of the Islamic economic project became its financial aspect – the creation of Islamic banks – which was product-focused, and not so much an

204 Zarqa, "Islamization of Economics," 22.

205 Zarqa, "Islamization of Economics," 22.

206 Al-Faruqi, *Islamization of Knowledge*, 57–58; see also 58–79.

207 Zarqa, "Islamization of Economics," 33–39.

208 Mohammad Nejatullah Siddiqi, "An Islamic Approach to Economics," in *Islam: Source and Purpose of Knowledge* (Herndon, VA: IIIT, 1988), 153–175; Mohammad Nejatullah Siddiqi, "Islamizing Economics," in *Toward Islamization of Disciplines* (Herndon, VA: IIIT, 1995), 253–264. See also Mahmud Abu Saud, "Toward Islamic Economics," in *Toward Islamization of Disciplines* (Herndon, VA: IIIT, 1995), 265–723.

209 Mohammad Nejatullah Siddiqi, "Islamization of Knowledge: Reflections and Priorities," *American Journal of Islamic Sciences*, vol. 28, no. 3 (2011): 25.

epistemological quest for theoretical and historical analysis of Islam's moral economy. Islamic banks also emerged across Europe, including the United Kingdom, Luxembourg, and Denmark.

1.7 Concluding Remarks

This chapter analyzed some of the epistemological contentions of Muslim reformists and modernists on economic thought within the broader frame of the historical, political, and socioeconomic realities of the late nineteenth and twentieth centuries. While the aforementioned Muslim reformists criticized socialism and capitalism, they focused on the theological and moral restructuring of the colonial Muslim subject; notably, they did not directly invoke an alternative economic system until the inception of the subject by South Asian scholars. Against the backdrop of colonial political struggles, especially in Pakistan, many Muslim scholars came to defend an Islamic economic system, for example, Mawdūdī, who was one of the most visible and vocal proponents of an Islamic society and state. His political economy and theory of an Islamic state, which was nonetheless anchored in the modernist paradigm, gave prominence to the flourishing of Islamic economics after the 1950s. The Islamization process, which swept through Malaysia, Indonesia, Pakistan, and other Muslim-majority countries, gradually forced the alteration of domestic juridical and economic systems and the inclusion of more religiously conservative political vision. Moreover, as an intellectual program, the IOK process in the 1970s influenced and furthered the Islamization of sciences and disciplines, including Islamic economics, despite the methodological and epistemological inconsistencies that appeared in the merging of two distinct paradigms – Islamic heritage and Western knowledge, especially in al-Faruqi's works.

Muslim economists drew on IOK ideas that advanced the development of Islamic economics, grounding it in an Islamic tradition of jurisprudence. While the disciplines of Islamic economics and Islamic jurisprudence differ methodologically, many Muslim economists (who will be presented in Chapter 2) intended to centralize *fiqh* in Islamic economics. This is highly problematic, since economic behavior discusses much broader fields than only legal postulates. The proponents of the Islamization of Islamic economics proposed multiple sources of knowledge, which entails in part Western epistemic knowledge of economic science and the division of disciplines. The Islamization also supports the integration of Islamic principles into the commercial economic system based on the unification methodology,[210] most visible in Islamic finance and banking, which become its torchbearer.

[210] See Monzer Kahf, "Islamic Economics: Notes on Definition and Methodology," *Review of Islamic Economics*, vol. 13 (2003): 23–47; Zarqa, "Islamization of Economics"; Haneef, "Islam, the Islamic Worldview and Islamic Economics."

2 The Present: Muslim Economists and the Constellation of Islamic Economics

While we agree that Islamic economics must proceed from the Islamic worldview and economic vision, utilizing an Islamic methodology founded upon the epistemology of Islam, we cannot be oblivious to developments in western economics.

Muhammad Aslam Haneef, "Islam, the Islamic Worldview and Islamic Economics," 53

By entering into arguments about the economy as a particular realm of human activity, many of the Muslim intellectuals seemed to accept – with various degrees of unease, some acknowledged, others not – that they were engaging with a discourse not of their own making. The struggle to make it theirs has been a constant and sometimes problematic one.

Charles Tripp, *Islam and the Moral Economy*, 105

2.1 Introductory Remarks

The subject of contemporary Islamic economics owes much of its discursive origins to the revivalist Islamic movements of the early to mid-twentieth century whose ideologues considered broader intellectual, theological, and social aspects of the colonial context; they henceforth laid the groundwork for the eventual Islamization process (of economics). Contemporary Islamic economics (in this chapter often referred to also as "Islamic economic doctrine," "Islamic economic system," and so forth) is not only the result of an attempt to revitalize the economic sources of Islam but also an outcome of the triumph of the global political-economic paradigm.[1] Despite the contemporary Islamic economic project's distinct ethical and ideological-religious characteristics,

[1] "Globalization is clearly the project of the rich and powerful states and the colossal corporations ostensibly regulated by them, a project largely imposed on weaker states. And it so happens that the political-economic paradigm of these powerful states is a liberal one." (Hallaq, *Impossible State*, 141).

it emerged within the economic, social, and political contestations of the early twentieth century, in parallel to attempts made to form an Islamic state and society. However, much of the discussion about its conceptualization and within the discipline itself does not consider the Islamic sciences of nature and their implications for the epistemological appraisal and moral restructuring of human economic behavior.

As explicated below, and especially in Chapter 4, modern Islamic economic theories contain many methodological and epistemological inconsistencies. In this chapter, I delve further into the concepts, contexts, and methods of contemporary Muslim economists and theoreticians, unpacking the birth and subsequent resonance of Islamic economics by investigating the dominant methodologies and philosophies associated with its naissance. This discussion will form the basis of the theoretical critique of contemporary Islamic economic doctrines that I provide in Chapter 4.

Even if some scholars, such as Haneef, who defines Islamization of Islamic economics as an intellectual endeavor, recast economic history from an Islamic point of view, they do not fully consider the terminological and epistemological issues of utilizing theoretical frameworks and scientific predispositions interpreted according to Western norms. As a result, many Muslim economists believe that Islamic economics became a distinct discipline with its own philosophy, methodology, and worldview; however, they overlooked the danger of being positioned as a subdiscipline of neoclassical conventional economics at worst or heterodox economics at best, which designates it as part of the modernist discourse. Hence, the question remains as to whether an Islamic economic ideology can escape the secular-liberal logic, resting upon the idea of a nation-state formation.

Soon after the mid-twentieth century, various Muslim scholars attempted to justify the need for a new economic system in order to oppose the philosophical shortcomings of capitalism and socialism.[2] Even though there is a loose consensus among Muslim economists on which principles constitute the discipline of Islamic economics, the nature of the subject matter and the epistemology of Islamic economics is far from determined.[3] Broadly speaking, four different groups of

[2] See e.g. Mawdūdī, *Capitalism, Socialism, and Islam.*

[3] M. Iqbal, S. Syed Ali, and D. Muljawan, "Advances in Islamic Economics and Finance," *Proceedings of 6th International Conference on Islamic Economics*

scholars write on the subject of Islamic economics, which are associated with four different dimensions of economic analysis. The first group consists of Muslim economists and scholars who believe that Islamic economics presents an alternative to the systems of capitalism and socialism. They favor altering the existing economic model and often invoke studies that relate to economic issues within the discipline of *tafsīr* (exegesis) as hermeneutics of the Qur'an and *fiqh* (Islamic jurisprudence), while addressing issues such as the prohibition of usury. This appears to be the dominant aspect of Islamic economics. The second group comprises scholars who believe that Islamic economics is a distinct science, yet is not ready to present itself as a complete system, and are also critical of its naissance. This group includes scholars such as Timur Kuran and Seyyed Reza Vali Nasr, who contend that Islamic economics is not a genuine answer to financial and economic postulates.[4] For the third group, there is no difference between Islamic and capitalist economics, since the system is based on rational principles that can be found in the Qur'an. The fourth group elaborates upon economic questions in light of classical Muslim theologians, Sufis, and philosophers from the perspective of Islamic ethics, as a response to the growing need of the time.[5] The fourth group is the least represented in the discipline. In relation to the four different elements within the field of Islamic economics, for Muhammad Akram Khan there are three categories of scholars who have contributed to Islamic economics, namely, *'ulamā'*,[6] modernists, and Western-educated economists, whereby the *'ulamā'* have been the main

and Finance, 4, in Necati Aydin, "Redefining Islamic Economics As a New Economic Paradigm," *Islamic Economic Studies*, vol. 21, no. 1 (2013): 24.

4 Similarly, Muhammad Akram Khan in his latest writings critically assesses numerous authors on Islamic economics and even repositions his own stance on Islamic economics in relation to his previous research. See Khan, *What Is Wrong with Islamic Economics?*

5 For more on the various divisions of Islamic economics and its approaches, see for instance, Aydin, "Redefining Islamic Economics As a New Economic Paradigm," 24; Abdul-Hasan Muhammad Sadeq and Aidit Ghazali, eds., *Pregled islamske ekonomske misli* (Sarajevo: El-Kalem, 1996), 12, 148; Sami Al-Daghistani, "Semiotics of Islamic Law, Maṣlaḥa, and Islamic Economic Thought," *International Journal of the Semiotics of Law*, vol. 29, no. 2 (2016): 394.

6 See also the works of 'Abdallah Bin Bayyah and 'Alī al-Quradāghī; Yūsuf al-Qaraḍāwī, *Economic Security in Islam*, trans. Muhammed Iqbal Siddiqi (New Delhi: Islamic Book Services, 1997).

contributors.[7] Modernists have been active in reinterpreting the traditional sources in contemporary context, while the experts in economic studies have expressed support of Islamic economics[8] by predominantly focusing on economic analysis and the financial and banking sectors. On the other hand, one of the main concerns for *ʿulamāʾ* was explaining economic teaching in Islamic tradition in contemporary terms, applying a rather traditional outlook onto the discipline, while relying on the major sources in Islamic tradition. The *ʿulamāʾ* have been predominantly interested in the legal aspect of economic conduct in Islam and in *Sharīʿa*-related questions.[9] The legal focus is dominant, and it presents the core of Islamic economics,[10] whereas modernists and Western-educated scholars are supportive of Islamization of knowledge in economics and their writings are mainly conceptual, since they analyze the basic teachings and principles of the discipline.

The majority of voices and proponents of the Islamization of knowledge come from specific centers, publishing houses, and economic institutions, largely consisting of the Islamic Foundation and its Economic Unit in Leicestershire in the United Kingdom;[11] the Islamic Development Bank and the Islamic Economics Institute, King Abdulaziz University in Jeddah, Saudi Arabia;[12] and the International Islamic University Malaysia, Kuala Lumpur,[13] to name a few. Despite their important work in the field, those institutions have pursued structural and educational development plans of Islamic economics as a discipline that are grounded in the Islamization process, generating a narrative of self-perpetuating views and beliefs of a contemporary

7 Muhammad Akram Khan, "Islamic Economics: The State of the Art," in *Toward Islamization of Disciplines* (Herndon, VA: IIIT, 1989), 274.

8 Khan, "Islamic Economics: The State of the Art," 274.

9 Most jurists "are not well-versed in economics they test at the mainstream concepts on the juristic touchstone for pronouncing judgment on their efficacy for Islamic economics . . .. A second route is taken by economists turned fuqaha. They have modified numerous mainstream concepts, theories, and models to make them look Islamic including: wants, utility, efficiency, entrepreneurship, marginal productivity, scarcity and so on." (Addas, *Methodology of Economics*, 98).

10 Khan, "Islamic Economics: The State of the Art," 274.

11 "Islamic Economics Unit," Islamic Foundation, accessed March 20, 2021, www.islamic-foundation.org.uk.

12 Islamic Economics Institute, last modified November 13, 2014, http://iei.kau.edu.sa/Pages-E-DirectorMessage.aspx.

13 Center for Islamic Economics, accessed March 20, 2021, www.iium.edu.my/centre/cie.

ethical economics rather than engaging with the epistemic knowledge of its science. As a distinct academic subject, despite Muslim economists' position against the economic-political fabric of capitalism, contemporary Islamic economics has appeared as a niche within the current global economic system.[14] As will be discussed below, Islamic economics proposed alternative economic norms but failed to deliver them on the ground. This discrepancy is clear when one reviews the nature of contemporary Islamic economics and its predicaments, the (absence of the) role of the nation-state, the concept of economic justice (as *maṣlaḥa*, *istiḥsan*, and *ʿadāla*), and the ontological position of Islamic economics in relation to other fields within Islamic studies.

The majority of contemporary Muslim scholars on Islamic economics are economists by training who laid the foundations of the subject, including Islamic finance. Thus far Muslim economists, albeit pioneers in the field who made seminal contributions to its methodology, its philosophy, and the field of Islamic banking, have made many claims about "the structure of what could be regarded as an Islamic economy rather than the discipline of economics as such,"[15] though offering little insight into the theoretical and genealogical conceptualization of the field. Despite the proliferation of monographs justifying the existence of Islamic economics as a "third way" and a unique economic system, such a system has yet to come into existence; rather, Islamic economics has been incorporated into conventional economic science and its apparatus, manifesting as a subeconomy, since there is no existing, fully operative "Islamic" economy in the Middle East or South Asia.[16] Islamic ethics and law were considered the backbone and foundation of Islamic economics, yet many authors combine theoretical propositions from conventional economics and social sciences, which presents a methodological stalemate, for Islamic economic norms were meant to be specific to entail the gist of the premodern understanding of the universe.[17] Moreover, contemporary

14 For a historical overview of contemporary Islamic economics, see Figure 1 in the Appendix.

15 Rauf Azhar, *Economics of an Islamic Economy* (Leiden: Brill, 2009), 4.

16 See the Organisation of Islamic Cooperation, which combines 49 predominantly Muslim states. For the economy of the Muslim member countries, see Islamic Development Bank report "Facts and Figures on IDB Member Countries 2017," accessed March 21, 2021, www.isdb.org/pub/fact-figures/2017/facts-and-figures-1438h-2017.

17 Wilson, however, notes that there are core distinctions between conventional and Muslim economists, such as the incorporation of ethical values, specific

Muslim economists reiterate that the conjunction between an Islamic paradigm and modern knowledge is necessary, while they too often narrowly link the discourse on Islamic economics with *fiqh*,[18] without critically assessing the nature and genealogy of that knowledge.

Chapter 2 takes this claim seriously, analyzing the intricate writings of some of the main representatives of Islamic economics, chiefly Masudul Alam Choudhury, Muhammad Umer Chapra, Syed Nawab Haider Naqvi, Mohammad Nejatullah Siddiqi, and Muhammad Akram Khan, by scrutinizing their original work, as well as ethical, legal, and theoretical extolments of the very subject matter against the backdrop of epistemic value of the discipline. Concomitantly, the literature of other contemporary Muslim economists will be addressed, such as Muhammad Fahim Khan, Monzer Kahf, and Rauf Azhar. By exploring the theory of knowledge on Islamic economics, especially concerning the key concepts and methodologies in their works, the validity of their theories, their opposing views, and the scope of their research, this chapter explores the theoretical justifications that distinguish the aforementioned authors' views on Islamic economics and sets the stage for the discussion in Chapter 3 of classical legal and economic thought in Islamic tradition – a body of work chronically omitted by contemporary scholars.

2.2 Theories and Definitions: Recent Developments and Contentions

Muslim revivalists of the nineteenth and early twentieth centuries did not employ terms such as "Islamic economics" or "Islamic finance," instead they discussed the sociopolitical realities of their societies by attempting to revive theological teachings in Islam. Nevertheless, religious scholars such as Abū al-Aʿlā Mawdūdī,[19] Muḥammad Bāqir al-Ṣadr,[20] Seyyed Maḥmūd Tāliqānī,[21] as well as Western-trained economists and proponents of the Islamization process, such as Muhammad

methodology laid down in Islam, and objectives based on the Divine revelation (El-Ashker, Wilson, *Islamic Economics: A Short History*, 379).

18 See Addas, *Methodology of Economics*, vii.

19 Mawdūdī, *Economic Problem of Man and Its Islamic Solution.*

20 Al-Ṣadr, *Iqtiṣādunā* (1982).

21 Seyyed Maḥmūd Tāliqānī, *Society and Economics in Islam*, trans. R. Campbell (Berkeley, CA: Mizan Press, 1982).

Abdul Mannan,[22] Kurshid Ahmad,[23] Mohammad Nejatullah Siddiqi, Umer Chapra, Muḥammad Anas Zarqa, Alam Choudhury, and others formed and expanded a new field of Islamic economics. Those and other scholars and economists are affiliated with a few specific academic centers, financial institutions, and publishing houses – such as the IIIT in Herndon, Virginia, the Islamic Economic Center at the King Abdulaziz University in Jeddah, Islamic Development Bank Jeddah, Saudi Arabia, International Islamic University Malaysia, and the Islamic Foundation in the UK, among others – all of which favor Islamization efforts. The majority of Muslim economists would agree on basic tenets of Islamic economic doctrine but nonetheless differ in their methodology, epistemology, and application. For instance, Siddiqi's ethical and moral considerations of economic problems differ from Choudhury's *tawḥīd* theological epistemology, or from Chapra's approach. Contemporary Islamic economics is motivated by the intellectual developments of the nineteenth-century and secular schools of thought, including the very study of basic economic tenets.[24] A swirling set of factors led to the rising interest in Islamic economics: dissatisfaction with the world economy; policy of the mainstream economic doctrine; the impact the world economy has had on indigenous cultures;[25] and the institutionalized

[22] See e.g. Mannan, *Islamic Economics*.

[23] Ahmad, *Studies in Islamic Economics*; Khurshid Ahmad, "Nature and Significance of Islamic Economics," in *Lectures on Islamic Economics*, ed. Ahmad Ausaf and Kazim R. Awan (Jeddah: IDB, 1992); Khurshid Ahmad, *Economic Development in an Islamic Framework* (Leicester: Islamic Foundations, 1979); Khurshid Ahmad, *Islamic Approach to Development: Some Policy Implications* (Islamabad: Institute of Policy Studies, 1994). For his more recent writings, see Khurshid Ahmad, "The Challenge of Global Capitalism: An Islamic Perspective," *Policy Perspectives*, vol. 1, no. 1 (2004): 1–29; Khurshid Ahmad, "Global Economic Crisis Need for a Paradigm Shift," *Policy Perspectives*, vol. 8, no. 2 (2011): 1–17; Khurshid Ahmad, "Western Philosophies of Research and Fundamentals of Islamic Paradigm," *Policy Perspectives*, vol. 10, no. 1 (2013): 45–62.

[24] An economic system is "an integral structure of a society characterized by a set of institutions established to enable it to accomplish the twin tasks of allocation of resources at its disposal, and distribution of the goods and services thus produced among its citizens." Rauf, *Economics of an Islamic Economy*, 45.

[25] "In a capitalistic system, the market is not only the major site for the exchange of commodities, but becomes the supreme institution and dominant metaphor for most social transactions .... This model of rationality colonises the ethical world, suggesting that it is the model for a universal rationality, its triumph evident in the ethnically sanctioned freeing of 'human nature' to become the

exploitation of developing countries.[26] By the second half of the twentieth century, the Islamic economic discipline had emerged as a distinct field of study,[27] and ever since, it has been credited as having a recognizably ethical dimension.[28] Rauf Azhar has advanced the idea that Islam has its own distinct economic system, whose rules and basic premise can be deduced from the scriptural sources, which also include viewing any form of interest as *ribā*.[29] From such a discussion, Islamic economics emerged as science, which was nonetheless rooted in the Islamization of knowledge process, with Islamic finance and banking[30] as its most noticeable subsidiary branch.

The turning point for the expansion of the discipline, according to Muhammad Akram Khan, whose works on economics will be scrutinized in the following paragraphs,[31] occurred with the establishment of the Centre for Research in Islamic Economics in 1976 at King Abdulaziz University in Jeddah, which produced theoretical material on the subject and also contributed to the development of Islamic

agent that will reproduce capitalist enterprise." (Tripp, *Islam and Moral Economy*, 5). See also R. Dilley, ed., *Contesting Markets* (Edinburgh: Edinburgh University Press, 1992).

26 Muhammad Akram Khan, "The Future of Islamic Economics," *Futures*, vol. 23, no. 3 (1991): 249.

27 See the survey made by Siddiqi: Mohammad Nejatullah Siddiqi, *Contemporary Literature on Islamic Economics* (Leicester: Islamic Foundation, 1978), 68.

28 Rodney Wilson, "Islamic Economics and Finances," *World Economics*, vol. 9, no. 1 (2008): 177.

29 "The writings on Islamic economics can be split into two distinct though related strands: First, following the Qur'ānic sanction against *ribā*, one strand of writings explores the various Islamic financing alternatives to interest on the presumption that interest is precisely the same thing as *ribā*. Some of these alternatives are based on the idea of variable returns on capital – and therefore stipulate some sort of profit sharing arrangements – while others, in sharp contrast allow fixed returns to capital that are supposed to be compatible with Islamic *Sharīʿa*. It is this strand of writings that, understandably, provided the initial impetus to the venture of Islamic economics." For more on the differentiation between *ribā* and usury see Azhar, *Economics of an Islamic Economy*, 4.

30 "The principles of Islamic finance are, however, based on Islamic economic theory, and to understand the former some knowledge of the latter is required." (Wilson, "Islamic Economics and Finances," 180).

31 It is important to note that there are at least two phases of Muhammad Akram Khan's writing – the earlier one, which reflects the ideas shared by most of the mainstream Muslim economists, and the later one, which displays departure from such a position.

finance and banking. Already in 2006, there were more than 6,484 publications available on the subject of Islamic economics and finance;[32] of these, the majority upheld the fields' main premise, and some of them will be studied in connection with the aforementioned Muslim economists.[33] Since the 1970s, theoreticians of Islamic economics have defined its origins not within the intellectual history of Islam but by distinguishing it from other economic systems.[34] It was therefore easy to define the discipline in terms of "what Islamic economics was not, rather than to find a positive content for it."[35] The approach to Islamic economics was often defined on the basis of differentiating it from other economic traditions, such as capitalism and socialism. Contemporary Muslim economists aimed at defining the Islamic worldview and its possible ramifications for economic behavior both by justifying its existence in social science as it emerged in the West and by basing it on a narrow understanding of Islamic jurisprudence. They predominantly relied on their own interpretations of the legal stipulations of the "Qurʾanic epistemology of unity,"[36] and on applying them to financial mechanisms. As interpreted by contemporary Muslim economists, economic ideas have throughout the history of Islam been regarded as an integral part of the legal framework. Hence,

32 Khan, *What Is Wrong with Islamic Economics?*, 5.

33 Several PhD theses have been written and numerous articles and books published on the field of Islamic economics. For the literature and surveys on Islamic economics, see Siddiqi, *Contemporary Literature on Islamic Economics*; Asad Zaman, *Islamic Economics: A Survey of the Literature* (Islamabad: International Islamic University of Islamabad, 2008).

34 As we shall see in Chapter 4, Muhammad Akram Khan suggests that Muslim scholars should stay within the parameters of already-existing economic knowledge and not resort to their own tradition. Such an assertion is, however, problematic, since Khan also seems not to realize that coupling Islamic economic knowledge with the current understanding of social sciences presupposes an adherence to already-existing epistemological and broader methodological parameters. Irrespective of that differentiation, the potential knowledge of Muslim scholars, who indeed could have collaborated with their counterparts in the West in order to, first, define the economic order in Islamic tradition and, second, set societal standards in order to enable the pursuit of a socioeconomic system, can be included only if the moral predicaments – grounded on the Islamic premodern understanding of the economic-moral-legal amalgam – would be placed at the core of their deliberations. Khan, *What Is Wrong with Islamic Economics?*, xiii.

35 See Thomas Philipp, "The Idea of Islamic Economics," *Die Welt des Islams*, new series, vol. 30, no. 1/4 (1990): 122.

36 See e.g. the writings of Alam Choudhury.

in the contemporary era, Islamic economic doctrine is often viewed as a subfield of Islamic legal principles and prescriptions, derived from the Qur'an and the Prophetic Tradition, perceived through *Sharīʿa* legislative regulations. The revival of Islamic economics hence by extension necessitated an approach that turned out to be detached from the reality on the ground.[37]

The literature on Islamic economics analyzes the teachings of Islam, but it is not related to real-life situations, which is why it is mostly conceptual and not theoretical.[38] Another conceptual mistake is that most analyses deal with an ideal Islamic society by applying Islamic jargon irrespective of the needs of a modern society. Khan observes that "The method of Islamic economics presumes a primary and binding role for the ideological content. The basic premises are defined by the Islamic law. The Muslims economists develop their analysis by employing reason and real life data to the divinely ordained content of Islam. Islamic economics cannot be conceived outside this basic framework."[39] He further argues that the academic tradition of Islamic economic thought builds upon the work of Muslim predecessors who made seminal contributions to economic thought in Islam,[40] including legal scholars, theologians, and reformists, relying on the scriptural sources of Islam. However, since there is no existing Islamic economy, there is no comprehensive theory that can be applied to it.[41]

Islamic economics has been defined in various ways, either categorized with "relative scarcity," "Islamic worldview," or with "*Sharīʿa*-concurred" injunctions, including the notions of resource allocation, production of *ḥalāl*-goods, and the concept

[37] Most proponents of Islamic economics resort to Islamic finances and banking as the only existing financial institutions in Muslim majority countries. See also Wilson, "Islamic Economics and Finances," 180.

[38] Khan also made similar claims in his book from 2013: Khan, *What Is Wrong with Islamic Economics?*, 15. See also Khan, "Islamic Economics: The State of the Art," 275.

[39] Muhammad Akram Khan, *An Introduction to Islamic Economics* (Islamabad: IIIT, 1994), 52.

[40] See Zubair Hasan, review of *An Introduction to Islamic Economics*, by Muhammad Akram Khan, *American Journal of Islamic Social Sciences*, vol. 13, no. 4, (1996): 583.

[41] Khan, *Introduction to Islamic Economics*, 74. See also Muhammad Akram Khan, "Methodology of Islamic Economics," *Journal of Islamic Economics*, vol. 1, no. 1 (1987): 17–33.

of justice.[42] Here are some examples of how Islamic economics is defined and how broadly the discipline has been conceptualized, pinpointing its often contradictory definitions due to the different training, orientation, and ideological premise the authors follow: "Islamic economics is the knowledge and application of injunctions and rules of the sharīʿah (Divine Islamic law) that prevents injustice in the acquisition and disposal of material resources in order to provide satisfaction of human beings and enable them to perform their obligations to Allah and the society";[43] it is the "study of how human achieve 'al-falah' by organizing the resources of earth on the basis of co-operation and participation";[44] it is "a social science which studies the economic problem of a people imbued with the values of Islam";[45] "Islamic economics is that which directs economic activity, and organizes it according to Islamic principles and their economic policy, as well as, Islamic economics is the knowledge of the principles of the practical law based on its detailed proofs, considering the acquisition of wealth, the expenditure, and the vision of its development";[46] it is a system "emanating from the Islamic worldview, dominated by revelation and having a flexible methodology which combines western neoclassical/Keynesian economics with fiqh";[47] it is "both a science and an art which deals with the daily routine of a Muslim's economic life i.e. how he earns his income and how he spends it. It is a science in the sense that it involves many scientific methods in the production of material goods, their distribution and consumption";[48] it is a discipline that "should not be separated from the general definition of economics. The laws of

[42] See e.g. Nagaoka Shinsuke, "Critical Overview of the History of Islamic Economics: Formation, Transformation, and New Horizons," *Asian and African Area Studies*, vol. 11, no. 2 (2012): 114–136; Ahmed, "Scientific Approach to Islamic Economics," 28.

[43] S. M. Hasanuzzaman, "Definition of Islamic Economics," *Journal of Research in Islamic Economics*, vol. 1, no. 2 (1984): 49–50.

[44] Khan, *Introduction to Islamic Economics*, 33.

[45] Mannan, *Islamic Economics*, 18.

[46] ʿAbdullāh bin ʿAbd al-Muḥsin al-Tirīqī, *Al-Iqtiṣād al-Islāmī: Usus wa Mabādī wa Ahdāf* (Riyad: Muʾasasat al-Jarīsī, 2009), 18; see also Muḥammad Shawqī al-Fanjarī, *Al-Madhab al-Iqtiṣādi fī al-Islām* (Cairo: al-Haiʾāt al-Miṣriyāt al-ʿAmmah li al-Kitāb, 1986).

[47] Siddiqi, "Islamic Approach to Economics."

[48] Abul Kalam, "The Basic Principles of Islamic Economics," *Journal of Islamic Banking and Finance*, vol. 8 (1991): 16–24.

Islamic economics remain the same";[49] it is "a nascent social discipline whose concern is to reformulate economic principles and prepositions in accordance with Islamic values and ideals";[50] it is a systematic effort that tries "to understand the human economic problem and his behavior in relation to that problem from an Islamic perspective";[51] it is "the study of a Muslim's behavior who organizes the resources which are a trust, to achieve *al-falah*";[52] it is "a study of human behaviour with regard to acquiring and using resources for the satisfaction of necessities, needs and other desires. This study is based on the assumption of the Islamic paradigm, i.e., the Islamic outlook on life and humanity," as well as "the study of the economic behaviour of men and women, as individual economic agents, and as communities and collective entities";[53] "It is a system that embodies Islamic norms in organizing economic life";[54] it is "an approach to interpreting and solving man's economic problems based on the values, norms, laws and institutions found in, and derived from, the sources of knowledge in Islam";[55] "It is that branch of knowledge which helps realize human well-being through an allocation and distribution of scarce resources that is in conformity with Islamic teaching without unduly curbing individual freedom or creating continued macroeconomic and ecological imbalance," as well as a body of knowledge that is about "the realization of human well-being through the actualization of the *maqasid* ... which helps realize human well-being through an allocation and distribution of scarce resources that is in conformity with Islamic teachings without unduly curbing individual freedom or creating continued macroeconomic and ecological imbalances";[56] and it is "the science that studies the best possible use of all available economic resources, endowed by Allah,

[49] Jafarhusein Laliwala, "Islamic Economics: Some Issues in Definition and Methodology," *Journal of King Abdulaziz University: Islamic Economics*, vol. 1 (1989): 129–131.

[50] Ahmad, *Studies in Islamic Economics*.

[51] Ahmad, "Nature and Significance of Islamic Economics."

[52] Mohammad Ariff, "Toward a Definition of Islamic Economics: Some Scientific Considerations," *Journal of Research in Islamic Economics*, vol. 2 (1985): 87–103.

[53] Kahf, "Islamic Economics," 24. [54] Al-Ṣadr, *Iqtiṣādunā* (1982).

[55] Haneef, "Islam, the Islamic Worldview, and Islamic Economics," 50.

[56] Muhammad Umer Chapra, *What Is Islamic Economics?* (Jeddah: Islamic Development Bank, Islamic Research and Training Institute, 1996), 30.

for the production of maximum possible output of halal goods and services that are needed for the community now and in the future and the just distribution of this output within the framework of *Shari'ah* and its intents."[57]

Despite the plentiful definitions and theories associated with the subject, as shown above, there is neither a clear indication nor a consensus of precisely what Islamic economics encompasses. Indeed, what was formulated as the Islamic economic position was simply the value system of Islam. Still, the majority of Muslim economists would tentatively agree that the study of Islamic economics revolves around concepts such as justice, equality, and the Prophetic message.[58] Yet similar could be said for any other discipline in Islamic studies. Naqvi and Siddiqi based their theories of Islamic economics predominantly on Islamic ethical and legal conceptions of economic thinking, as did many contemporary scholars, following the norm of "commanding the good and forbidding the evil," which includes forbiddance of hoarding and ethically stipulated means of provisions.[59] Some also believe that the science of Islamic economics emerged from Islamic economic knowledge, established by the *fuqahā'* and classical Muslim scholars[60] who analyzed economic problems of money, fiscal policy, trade, markets, and financial transactions. However, their methodologies differ substantially.

2.3 Methodologies of Contemporary Islamic Economics

Methodological formulations of contemporary Islamic economics speak about the nature of the subject and the position of the discipline within the broader spectrum of both religious and social sciences.

57 Abdulrahman Yousri Ahmed, "The Scientific Approach to Islamic Economics: Philosophy, Theoretical Construction and Applicability," *Theoretical Foundations of Islamic Economics*, ed. Habib Ahmed (Jeddah: Islamic Development Bank, Islamic Research and Training Institute, 2002), 28, 30.

58 See Abbas Mirakhor, *A Note on Islamic Economics* (Jeddah: Islamic Development Bank, Islamic Research and Training Institute, 2007), 10.

59 See Mohammad Nejatullah Siddiqi, *Economic Enterprise in Islam* (Delhi: Markazi Maktaba Islami; Lahore: Islamic Publications, 1972); Syed Nawab Haider Naqvi, *Ethics and Economics: An Islamic Synthesis* (Leicester: Islamic Foundation, 1981); Muhammad Umer Chapra, *Islam and the Economic Challenge* (Herndon, VA: IIIT, 1992).

60 Ahmed, "Scientific Approach to Islamic Economics," 21.

Though the topics, themes, and concepts of Islamic economics have been well studied, the new discipline was motivated also by intellectual progress in nineteenth-century secular economic thought,[61] which was allegedly based on two intertwined aspects: first, the historical underpinning of classical Muslim scholars, and, second, the urge to understand and tackle modern economic problems. Nonetheless, only a few contemporary Muslim scholars investigate classical Islamic scholarship on economic thought.[62] Whether or not the contemporary (Muslim) scholars' writings on economics are reflected in society at large remains an unanswered question.

2.3.1 *The Epistemology of* Tawḥīd *and the Religious Worldview*

Mainstream Muslim economists differ in how they apply their respective methodologies of an Islamic economic system. By referring to *Sharīʿa*, Choudhury, Siddiqi, and other scholars, given their training and association with the Islamization of knowledge project, justified the subject within religious terms.[63] For the majority of contemporary

61 "The emergence of Islamic economics as a new discipline was undoubtedly motivated by the intellectual progress in secular schools of economics during the 19th century. The new discipline resonated two attributes. On the one hand, it was an expression of the historic Islamic heritage and on the other hand, it was a reflection of a desire to understand economic issues and problems of the Muslim world on modern bases. In other words, Islamic economics attempts to analyze the causes of economic problems and issues and arrive at practical solutions that suit modern Islamic societies within the context of Islamic law and values. This development is part of modern Islamic movements aiming to revive Shariʿah in all walks of life and to preserve Islamic identity." (Ahmed, "Scientific Approach to Islamic Economics," 23).

62 See, for instance, Masudul Alam Choudhury, *The Principles of Islamic Political Economy: A Methodological Enquiry* (London: Palgrave Macmillan, 1992); Masudul Alam Choudhury, *Islamic Economics and Finance: An Epistemological Inquiry* (Bingley, UK: Emerald Group Publishing, 2011). Mirakhor affirms the generally held opinion that "there is no avoiding the fact that in Islam all behaviour is rules-based, that ethical values underline the rules, and that the sources of the rules is Allah," although the question as to what extent the discrepancy between the legal and the moral is reflected in contemporary Islamic economics is a disputable issue (Mirakhor, *Note on Islamic Economics*, 13).

63 See Mohammad Nejatullah Siddiqi, "Tawhid, the Concept and the Process," in *Islamic Perspectives: Studies in Honour of Mawlana Sayyid Abul Aʿla Mawdudi*, ed. Khurshid Ahmad and Zafar Ishaq Ansari (Leicester, UK: Islamic

Muslim economists who are the proponents of the Islamization of knowledge, the Islamic worldview builds upon the fundamental premise of *tawḥīd*[64] or the Divine Unity of God ("radical" or pure monotheism), encompassing ethical, aesthetical, scientific, economic, and sociopolitical domains. The epistemology of *tawḥīd* covers the following elements: *muḍāraba* (profit-sharing) and *mushāraka* (equity participation); joint ventures; prohibition of *ribā* (excessive) interest; the institution of *zakāt* (wealth tax); and avoidance of *isrāf* (wasteful behavior) in consumption and production. *Tawḥīd* epistemology, rooted in the Qur'an,[65] is indispensable for overall understanding of the Islamic sciences, including economic predicaments.

Choudhury integrates the moral law as the meta-epistemology into the subject of Islamic economics, in order to achieve an "equilibrium model" as opposed to a mainstream model.[66] This meta-epistemology is for Choudhury the extension of Divine laws and worldly terms of unity of knowledge that can extrapolate the worldview, which incorporates ethical considerations.[67] The result is the *tawḥīdi* phenomenological model, which can be further applied to the material and cognitive realities of Islamic political economy.[68] Islamic economics has relied on the mainstream theories of consumerism and neoclassical understanding of the allocation of resources, whereby Islamic values were implied only indirectly and thus ethical consideration remained exogenous.[69] The alternative is an Islamic political economy based upon and derived from the precepts (*aḥkām*) of the Qur'an.[70] By introducing Marxist, Keynesian, and liberal political economies,

Foundation, 1979), 17–33; Mawdūdī, *Economic Problem of Man and Its Islamic Solution.*

64 Masudul Alam Choudhury, *The Islamic World-System: A Study in Polity–Market Interaction* (New York: Routledge, 2004), 8.

65 Choudhury, *Islamic World-System*, 10.

66 Masudul Alam Choudhury, "A Critique of Economic Theory and Modeling: A Meta-epistemological General-System Model of Islamic Economics," *Social Epistemology: A Journal of Knowledge, Culture and Policy*, vol. 25, no. 4 (2011): 425.

67 Compare this approach to the one of al-Ṣadr and his differentiation between science and system almost 30 years earlier.

68 Choudhury, *Islamic Economics and Finance*, 2.

69 Masudul Alam Choudhury, "Islamic Political Economy: An Epistemological Approach," *Social Epistemology Review and Reply Collective*, vol. 3 no. 11 (2014): 53–103.

70 Masudul Alam Choudhury, "Critique of Current Thinking in Islamic Political and Economic Issues," *Islamic Quarterly*, vol. 42, no. 2 (1998): 126.

Choudhury distinguishes the Islamic economic model according to "the study of interactive relationships between polity (*Shūrā*) and the ecological order (market subsystem)."[71] Its epistemological foundations are rooted in *Sharīʿa*, through which the knowledge of God becomes integrated into the socioeconomic sphere. This is based on the theological understanding of fundamental concepts of morality and ethics, upon which the theoretical structure of an (Islamic) economic system is built. "Islamic political economy is an epistemological examination of socio-scientific phenomena"[72] based on the Qurʾanic *Weltanschauung*.[73] In his description, Islamic philosophy preceded the notion of utilitarianism in Islamic thought and extends to the field of Islamic law, specifically to the notion of *maṣlaha* and *istiḥsān*.[74] Since the scientific norms are interpreted as neutral, regardless of their religious, materialistic, or spiritual contexts,[75] Choudhury adheres to practices that are related to those contexts as well as their ethical framework, since, in absolute terms, a scientific activity does not engage with religious or any other ideological applications.

Similarly, Siddiqi's methodology to Islamic economics is contained in the Qurʾanic revelation,[76] whereby man is viewed as a whole, extending his existence above the bare fulfillment of (material) needs.[77] For Siddiqi,

71 Masudul Alam Choudhury, "Toward Islamic Political Economy at the Turn of the Century," *American Journal of Islamic Social Sciences*, vol. 13, no. 3 (1996): 370.

72 The epistemology of the Divine Unity is exogenous yet present in all the systems of human endeavor, including the socioeconomic domain. This epistemology is described "as the Stock of Knowledge by virtue of its completeness and absoluteness in the total creative frame of the universe." The methodological precepts for Islamic political economy are Shuratic process; the concept of value as it is known in economic theories; universal complementarity related to the unification of knowledge; and analysis and inference of this endogenous system. (Choudhury, "Islamic Political Economy," 50; see also 49–71).

73 See Masudul Alam Choudhury, "Islamic Political Economy: An Epistemological Approach," *Social Epistemology Review and Reply Collective*, vol. 2, no. 11 (2014): 53–103; Choudhury, "Islamic Political Economy," 51.

74 Masudul Alam Choudhury, "A Critique of Modernist Synthesis in Islamic Thought: Special Reference to Political Economy," *American Journal of Islamic Social Sciences*, vol. 11, no. 4 (1994): 477.

75 See Imas al-Din Khalili, *Islamization of Knowledge: A Methodology* (Herndon, VA: IIIT, 1991), 7–8.

76 Zubair Hasan, review of "Teaching Economics in Islamic Perspective," by Siddiqi, *Islamic Economic Studies*, vol. 6, no. 1 (1998): 118.

77 Mohammad Nejatullah Siddiqi, *Teaching Economics in Islamic Perspective* (Jeddah: Scientific Publishing Centre, King Abdulaziz University, 2005), 3–4.

"economics is not the science of market only. Its nature as a social science necessitates due attention to goals of society among which universal need-fulfillment is on top."[78] Under the institutional framework in which Islamic economic practice takes place, Siddiqi acknowledges the following categories of Islamic economics: double ownership (including private property), freedom of enterprise (entailing competition), mutual risk-sharing and consultation, and responsibility of the state to secure rights of individuals. The overall goal of Islamic economics is accordingly encapsulated in economic well-being[79] through the conception of *tawḥīd*, based on the sources of Islam, which ought to be coordinated with the higher spiritual objectives and moral values, encompassing fulfillment of basic needs, equality, prohibition of hoarding and concentration of wealth, freedom to obtain moral objectives, and economic growth accordingly.

Muhammad Akram Khan's outline of an Islamic worldview presupposes a methodology based on a theological belief system and social sciences, in that it stems from the religious script and justifies a religious reading of an economic worldview.[80] He studies notions of ownership, universalism, and equilibrium to warrant economic organization in Islam, which differs from market mechanism in that it aims to avoid accumulation of power and wealth. Despite his conviction that contemporary Islamic economics is a free-market economy,[81] interest and hoarding are prohibited. Khan does not differ from other contemporary Muslim economists, in that he maintains that "economics must be open to contributions from other disciplines"[82] in order to attain an Islamic vision of economic life. Islamic economics draws upon the Islamic legal literature since it studies the impact of various legal opinions on the (economic) behavior of people.[83] Moreover, Islamic economics includes the study of Islamic values, where the falsifiability criterion is applicable to theories that tackle the *how* and not the *why* of economic questions.[84] As such, Islamic economics is a normative

78 Siddiqi, *Teaching Economics in Islamic Perspective*, 4.

79 Siddiqi, *Teaching Economics in Islamic Perspective*, 6.

80 The Qur'anic verses provide basic principles on economic matters, whereas the Sunna contains traditions that provide insights into the economic life of how a pious Muslim ought to behave. Khan, *Introduction to Islamic Economics*, 49. See also the Qur'an, e.g. 2:276, 5:66, 6:44, 11:3, 11:52, 14:7, 20:124.

81 Khan, *Introduction to Islamic Economics*, 8.

82 Siddiqi, "Islamic Approach to Economics," 155.

83 Khan, *Introduction to Islamic Economics*, 51.

84 Khan, *Introduction to Islamic Economics*, 63.

discipline, since it not only addresses economic problems[85] but also aspires to translate economic problems with regards to legal and, more importantly, theological concerns.

2.3.2 Ethical Considerations of Islamic Economic Theories

With religion as its main source, the majority of Muslim economists point out that Islamic economic philosophy differs substantially from other mainstream economic systems.[86] The idea of ethics in economics does not mean, in reverse, that economics does not have an impact on human ethical behavior[87] but rather that ethically stipulated teachings play a pivotal role in economic matters in Islam, whereby individual happiness is measured by one's own welfare as well as the welfare of others – that is, especially that of the needy and the poor. As such, for many Muslim economists, Islamic economics does not deal with a utopian Islamic or Muslim society but addresses "falsifiable statements about the economic behaviour of 'representative' Muslims in a typical real-life Muslim society with reference to the ideals that impart a distinct 'personality'," [88] an account that in Naqvi's view diverges from the existing literature on Islamic economics.

The idea of a distinctively "Islamic individual," or the "Islamic personality" (*al-shakhṣiyāt al-islamiyyah*), was developed as an antidote to the secular-rational logic of economic science and as a control mechanism for society.[89] This so-called *homo islamicus* is the agent of the Islamic economic model in practice,[90] founded upon adherence to *Sharīʿa* regulations, by maintaining a distinctively Islamic character when dealing with socioeconomic issues. In this context, Islam rejects the notion of absolute ownership, either from a state or an individual,

[85] Khan, *Introduction to Islamic Economics*, 68.

[86] As pointed out by al-Ṣadr, this method might be problematic, namely, if economics deals only with ethical stipulations, while for its research applying moral values, it cannot be regarded as scientific. See al-Ṣadr, *Iqtiṣādunā* (1982), vol. 1, 89.

[87] Poverty and riches would have an impact on man's behavior. Further, Marxism considers ethics but it positions it on a lower level, since it confirms that economic conditions (relations of production) are primary concerns in societies. Syed Nawab Haider Naqvi, *Islam, Economics, and Society* (London: Kegan Paul International, 1994), xix.

[88] Naqvi, *Islam, Economics, and Society*, xix–xx.

[89] Tripp, *Islam and Moral Economy*, 112. [90] Al-Ṣadr, *Iqtiṣādunā* (1987), 260.

since the sole ownership of all possessions belongs to God.[91] This principle of ownership and trusteeship according to Islamic law "minimizes the consequence-insensitivity of the capitalistic conception of a relatively freer exercise of the right to private property,"[92] which is the element that prompts individuals who have wealth to give to those who have less. Drawing on Islamic law, he asserts that the institution of private property is attainable only through one's own labor.[93] Labor is the sole principle through which private property can be obtained, whereby the equilibrium axiom perpetuates the exercise of (social) justice.[94] Despite the fact that various Muslim scholars recognize multiple forms of ownership (consisting of state, individual, and dual ownership), given their training in Islamic studies, Siddiqi[95] and Ahmed Mannan[96] strongly support private ownership. Since Mannan wrote on Islamic economics in the time when it was devised as a third-way economic system, he rejected historical materialism due to economic determinism and stresses the ethical values of Islamic economics,[97] yet his methodological contradictions are apparent because he relies on the neoclassical economic rationale. As suggested, too, by al-Ṣadr (discussed below), the state should play a role in implementing policies of private property and ownership.[98] Similarly, for Chapra the role of the state is an interventionist, positive one, seen as a moral obligation, complying with the Divine laws.

The support for economic purchases is not derived from material conditions separate from spiritual ones, thus Islamic economic objectives are expressions of practice encapsulated in the scriptural sources of Islam and in the theories laid down by Islamic classical scholars. Al-Ṣadr, one of the forerunners of Islamic economics and a traditionally trained Shiʿi cleric from Iraq who wrote broadly on Islamic philosophy

91 This claim is based on the Qurʾanic principle indicating that God is the owner of the heavens and the earth, whereby man has been entrusted the role of the vicegerent on earth. See the Qurʾan 3:180.
92 Syed Nawab Haider Naqvi, "The Dimensions of an Islamic Economic Model," *Islamic Economic Studies*, vol. 4, no. 2 (1997): 6.
93 Naqvi, *Islam, Economics, and Society*, 100.
94 See also e.g. Tāliqānī, *Islām va Mālkīyāt*.
95 Mohammad Nejatullah Siddiqi, *Some Aspects of the Islamic Economy* (Lahore: Islamic Publications, 1978), 120–122.
96 Mannan, *Islamic Economics*, 332–334.
97 Mannan, *Islamic Economics*, 314–326.
98 See al-Ṣadr, *Iqtiṣādunā* (1982), vol. 2, part 2, chapter 3.

and economics as a distinct ideology, defines Islamic economics in light of justice as being the preferred way "to follow in the pursuit of its economic life and in the solution of its practical economic problems in line with its concept of justice."[99] Rodney Wilson has described al-Ṣadr's approach as "holistic, and it can be categorized as 'juristic-economic' with the moral valuation of economic actions playing the central role."[100] In this context, social justice is part of the economic doctrine of Islam with a defined meaning, and it pertains to two general principles: general reciprocal responsibility and social balance.[101] For scholars such as Mannan and al-Ṣadr, the normativity of Islamic economic science is not a "neutral" economic system but rather one that rests upon the intelligibility of moral and social justice, and thus requires taking efficient actions. Its normativity is reflected in the context-dependent and consequence-sensitive circumstances, whereby individual freedom meets social responsibility. Islamic economics has a specific social and ethical narrative that expands to the means of production, consumption, commercial exchange, and distribution, encompassing norms and rules; it therefore ought to be seen as a system.[102] As such, it manages a worldview "where the ontological and epistemological sources namely the Qur'an and *aḥādīth* determine the framework of the economic value system, the operational dimension of the economy and also the economic and financial behavioural norms of the individual Muslims."[103]

For Muslim economist Chapra, a proponent of the Islamization of knowledge project, Islamic economics is rooted in the worldview of Islamic ethics.[104] Islamic economics advances the idea of a specific doctrine based upon the Islamic worldview and strategy, encompassing the principles of unity (*tawḥīd*), vicegerency (*khilāfah*), justice (*ʿadl*), and *maqāṣid*, or higher objectives of law. These foundations, rooted in

99 Al-Ṣadr, *Iqtiṣādunā* (1982), vol. 2, 6.

100 Rodney Wilson, "The Contribution of Muhammad Baqir al-Sadr to Contemporary Islamic Economic Thought," *Journal of Islamic Studies*, vol. 9, no. 1 (1998): 47.

101 Al-Ṣadr, *Iqtiṣādunā* (1982), vol. 1, 51–60.

102 Farhad Nomani and Ali Rahnema, *Islamic Economic Systems* (London: Zed Books, 1994), 41.

103 Mehmet Asutay, "A Political Economy Approach to Islamic Economics," *Kyoto Bulletin of Islamic Area Studies*, 1–2 (2007): 10.

104 Muhammad Umer Chapra, "Ethics and Economics: An Islamic Perspective," *Islamic Economic Studies*, vol. 16, no. 1 & 2 (2008/9): 2.

the Qur'an,[105] are present in the theological concepts for explaining the Islamic economic worldview.[106] The importance of ethics, Chapra argues, is foundational to the economic theory of Islam.[107] If self-interest is overemphasized without any moral impediments, other institutions, such as family, society, and government, may disintegrate and turn corrupt.[108] Hence, one of the distinguishing features of Islamic economics is the attachment to moral values, providing spiritual and moral uplift for individuals and society in changing their (economic) behavior. This promotes changing one's moral compass before changing one's economic behavior, which in turn asserts that alteration of economic systems occurs only after the individual restructuring of the soul – something that has been theorized but not fully implemented in practice by modern Muslim economists.[109]

Chapra is the main proponent of the notion of the so-called moral filter,[110] or a moral code in Islam, which functions as an equilibrium between demand and supply for the purposes of defending the underprivileged. The Islamic market places a dual filter – a moral and a market one – on the agent or subject to attain a spiritual uplift, and in such a relationship, the state plays a dynamic role.[111] The first filter is related to the notion of *khalīfa* and *'adl*, and provides Divine sanctions and rules for behavior.[112] However, inequality is believed to be natural

105 See e.g. the Qur'an on *tawḥīd* 3:191, 38:27, 23:15, on *khalīfa* 2:30, 6:165, 35:39, 38:28, 57:7, and on *'adl* 5:8.

106 These four categories, as important as they are nowadays, can be in a different form traced back to the writings of al-Ghazālī and other prominent Muslim scholars on the concept of *maṣlaḥa*, which makes Chapra one of the few contemporary scholars on Islamic economics who links the classical period with modern developments (Chapra, *Islam and the Economic Challenge*, 210).

107 Chapra, "Ethics and Economics," 1.

108 Muhammad Umer Chapra, "Islamic Economics: What It Is and How It Developed." *EH.net Online Encyclopedia of Economics and Business History*. Available at http://eh.net/encyclopedia/islamic-economics-what-it-is-and-how-it-developed," 6.

109 See e.g. al-Ghazālī, *Iḥyā'* and his definition on the moral restructuring in Chapter 3.

110 Muhammad Umer Chapra, *The Future of Economics: An Islamic Perspective* (Leicester: Islamic Foundation, 2000); Chapra, "Ethics and Economics"; Khan, *What Is Wrong with Islamic Economics?*, 34.

111 Chapra, *Islam and the Economic Challenge*, 214.

112 "To accept what is and not to struggle for the realization of the vision or what ought to be is a vote in favour of the prevailing inequalities and of doing nothing to remove them. Such an attitude cannot be justifiable within the Islamic worldview. The mission of human being is not just to abide themselves

to society, irrespective of the worldview being religious or secular, since "in a free market there is [a] foolproof method of suppressing human desire."[113] Because the free market never restrains riches and comfort, Chapra believes that through government regulation and a proper education and upbringing,[114] human behavior can become its own arbiter.[115]

Scholars such as Siddiqi and Naqvi claim that Islam is primarily about a particular spiritual view of life and its moral approach to one's problems, including economic ones.[116] Such an approach is similar to Chapra's and hence based upon the elements of unity (*tawḥīd*), equilibrium (*ʿadl wa iḥsān*), free will (*ikhtiyār*), and social responsibility (*farḍ*).[117] The unity element presupposes that an individual's economic activities ought to be exercised through the ethical considerations of the Qurʾan, whereby equilibrium stands for righteous actions for humanity based on social rights and economic justice. These axioms present synthetic truths of a Muslim society, whereby the Islamic concept of freedom is distinct as it presupposes that one does not have absolute freedom, but it is relative in relation to God's will[118] – the law is not man-made but Divinely inspired and thus universal for all humankind.[119]

While Naqvi rejects the positivistic view that separates economics from ethics, he upholds a broader view on economics that employs value judgments as scientific statements and utilizes religious corpus as a textual source (of ethics).[120] This commitment, which breaks apart from purely material welfare, relates to the second characteristic of Islamic economic philosophy, namely, economic ethical philosophy.

by the Islamic values, but also to struggle for the reform of their societies in accordance with these." (Chapra, "Ethics and Economics," 13–14).

113 Khan, *What Is Wrong with Islamic Economics?*, 34.

114 Umer M. Chapra, "The Need for a New Economic System," *Review of Islamic Economics*, vol. 1, no. 1 (1991): 40–41; reproduced in Tim Niblock and Rodney Wilson, *The Political Economy of the Middle East* (Cheltenham, UK: Edward Elgar, 1999), vol. 3.

115 See Chapra, *Future of Economics*.

116 Siddiqi, keynote address to the Roundtable, in Mirakhor, *Note on Islamic Economics*, 10.

117 See Naqvi, *Islam, Economics, and Society*; Chapra, *Islam and the Economic Challenge*.

118 See the Qurʾan, 96:6.

119 Naqvi, "Dimensions of an Islamic Economic Model," 5.

120 Naqvi, *Islam, Economics, and Society*, xxii–xxiii.

Such an economic philosophy entails economic growth and efficiency that are aligned with the notion of equity and justice.[121] The Islamic maxim *al-ʿadl wa al-iḥsān* – or equilibrium – covers the mechanisms of consumption, production, and distribution-related activities, which stipulates the rights of the unprivileged in society, encourages the underclass to have a right (*haqq*) to socioeconomic prosperity, and prevents it from being subjected to prosperity only through charity.[122] By applying an axiological approach to Islamic economics and its ethical philosophy through the application of mathematics,[123] Naqvi advocates the parameters of social justice, which entails the study of moral philosophy[124] and repudiates poverty, inequality, and overconsumption.[125]

For proponents of the Islamization of knowledge process, material provision and resource allocation are beneficial for humankind, however, using them comes with certain responsibilities that must be observed, since a human being is seen as a vicegerent of God.[126] Drawing an image of human nature through Islam's recognition of humanity's dual nature – as selfish and altruistic – paints the idea of the Islamic economic paradigm as a voluntary approach to economic provisions. This is related to the concept of *falāḥ* – advocated by another mainstream Muslim economist Muhammad Akram Khan[127] – roughly

121 Naqvi, "Dimensions of an Islamic Economic Model," 8.

122 Naqvi, "Dimensions of an Islamic Economic Model," 9. Naqvi advances the "optimum regime" as the best economic system, which he follows by presenting mathematical formulas and explanations for them, advocating the idea that ethical economy is as efficient as value-free positivistic economics. The "mathematization" of Islamic economics is problematic for various reasons. First, economic formulas do not necessarily relate to the practice on the ground; second, most of the time, complex and scientific explanation of economic theories does not necessarily correspond to its theoretical base; third, mathematical formulas require certain knowledge that the majority of the theoreticians do not have; and fourth, combining Islamic ethical tenets on economic matters with Western-inspired mathematical formulas does not facilitate the desired epistemological result of the subject.

123 Naqvi, *Islam, Economics, and Society*, xiii.

124 Naqvi, *Islam, Economics, and Society*, xvii.

125 Naqvi, *Islam, Economics, and Society*, 87.

126 See the Qur'an, 7:31, 17:70; Khan, *Introduction to Islamic Economics*, 4.

127 *Falāḥ* is derived from the verb *aflaḥa, yufliḥu* – to thrive, achieve happiness, success etc. The Qur'an emphasizes that *falāḥ* (individual and common success or good) has to be achieved in worldly life, although the ultimate goal is the *falāḥ* in the Hereafter. The notion of *falāḥ* has to be categorized in spiritual, economic, cultural, and political domains and can be differentiated on the basis

translated as achieving happiness, that has been promoted in ethical economic teachings, whereby in order to attain *falāḥ* several conditions must be met. The spiritual conditions consist of humility in prayers (*khushū'*), consciousness of God (*taqwā*), remembrance of God (*dhikr*), repentance for sins (*tawba*), and inner purification (*tazkiyyah*).[128] This translates as, spending for others, meaning those who are in need of economic support, is a social and spiritual necessity. The economic conditions of *falāḥ* are categorized in five concepts, namely, *infāq*; prohibition of *ribā*; the notion of trust; justice; and enterprise. *Infāq* should be exercised only for the sake of God, and it means spending on other members of society out of one's surplus. This is distinguished from social charity as it includes *zakāt*, which is described as an obligation with a spiritual dimension, through which *falāḥ* can be achieved (in this context, *zakāt* would be considered as part of the *infāq*).

2.4 Islamic Economics and Forms of Conventional Knowledge

2.4.1 Islamic Economics versus Mainstream Economic Systems

Since the proponents of the Islamization of knowledge claim that faith and morality are intertwined in Islamic economics, both inductive and deductive methods of reasoning are used by contemporary Muslim economists, whereby the latter constitutes the majority,[129] presupposing an "Islamic position" on human development and humankind's socioeconomic situation. Even if the methodology of Islamic economics draws upon the Divine text, contemporary Muslim economists claim that it also prioritizes an inductive method associated with the theory of (scientific) falsification.[130]

of survival (physical health, economic base, social brotherhood, political participation, etc.) and freedom (self-reliance, respect, civil liberties, etc.). These two categories exist on the personal (micro) as well as state (macro) level (Khan, *Introduction to Islamic Economics*, 35–36).

128 Khan, *Introduction to Islamic Economics*, 36.

129 Khan, *Introduction to Islamic Economics*, 66.

130 See, for instance, al-Ṣadr's discussion on economic science and doctrine in *Iqtiṣādunā*, vol. 1, part 2, chapter 2.

Most Muslim economists have aimed to differentiate Islamic (political) economy from the mainstream economic system[131] and to extend the scientific analytical model to the realm of religion and Islamic ethos. The vast literature on Islamic finance gives an impression that one of the main differences between mainstream and Islamic economics lies in the application of economic instruments and not in its epistemology and economic philosophy.

Various epistemological positions and contradictory views on Islamic economics are best evidenced through the works of the aforementioned Muslim economists.[132] It has been argued that, in traditional economics, it is the individual who is the measure of its epistemology; by contrast, in Islamic tradition, the justice-driven concept of *maṣlaḥa* replaces social utility,[133] which, for contemporary economists, is based on ethical considerations. Islamic economic philosophy, they claim, is not driven by egoism and selfishness, as is found in neoclassical economics, but by the rule of commitment and welfare.[134] This presupposes a twofold, voluntarist motivation meant to attain higher spiritual truth.[135] Such an approach attempts to purify capitalism and is in favor of a strong state's presence,[136] while it challenges the neoclassical economic paradigm due to its lack of moral dimension.[137] The above-mentioned Muhammad Akram Khan – in addition to affirming the ethical base – favors studying

131 For further critique of defining Islamic economics in relation to capitalist and socialist systems, see e.g. Thomas Philipp: "The negative definition of what Islamic economics is not serves a very concrete purpose, namely, the attack on and the denouncement of secular, especially socialist and communist, forms of social and economic order. It is the first step toward asserting an own identity and toward developing a positive content for a specifically Islamic economic order." (Philipp, "Idea of Islamic Economics," 124).

132 See Mirakhor, *Note on Islamic Economics*, 12.

133 See e.g. Taha Egri and Necmettin Kizilkaya, eds., *Islamic Economics: Basic Concepts, New Thinking and Future Directions* (Cambridge: Cambridge Scholars Publishing, 2015).

134 "You will not attain unto piety until you spend of that which you love" (Qur'an 3:92).

135 For Naqvi's question about the aim of Islamic economic system, see Naqvi, "Dimensions of an Islamic Economic Model," 2. See also Kuran, "Islamic Economics and the Islamic Subeconomy."

136 Muhammad Aslam Haneef. *Contemporary Islamic Economic Thought: A Selected Comparative Analysis* (Kuala Lumpur: S. Abdul Majeed & Co, 1995), 6.

137 Naqvi, *Islam, Economics, and Society*, xiii.

Islamic economics from the point of view of modern economic mechanisms,[138] asserting that "the work done by the Western economists has a lot of useful material but it need to be reviewed in the light of Islamic teachings."[139] He is rather critical of the current state of affairs of neoclassical economics, due to unemployment, the even-bigger public debt, and the lack of economic development in Muslim-majority countries.

Nonetheless, the vast literature on Islamic economics dealing with basic concepts and principles lacks a comprehensive discussion of the basic beliefs of Muslim economists and the values shared across their work.[140] *ʿUlamāʾ* wrote on those issues using a theological jargon that differed significantly from the lexicon employed by economists. As a result, the discussion of the theoretical significance of Islamic economics has been generally discordant. The majority of Muslim economists assert that although market economy and socialism share a common worldview, their strategies of interpreting economic life differ among them as well as in relation to an Islamic standpoint. The capitalist worldview rests upon an essentially secularist worldview, rooted in Enlightenment philosophy, which spotlights the faculty of reason and undermines the role of religion in society.[141] In such a worldview, materialism and utilitarianism generated a rational economic individual. On the other hand, socialism realizes its economy at the expense of individual freedoms in the role and function of the state, while generating distrust among people regarding the management of private property.[142] In comparison to secularist economic systems, the proponents of Islamic economics claim that the Islamic worldview fuses the material and the spiritual realms,[143] in order to materialize the sociopolitical and spiritual faculties of individuals. Despite propagating market mechanisms,[144] it predicates that the market (economy) does not fulfill all human needs, since the excessive use of

138 Khan, *Introduction to Islamic Economics*, 54.

139 Khan, "Islamic Economics: The State of the Art," 283.

140 Khan, "Islamic Economics: The State of the Art," 284.

141 Fernand Braudel, *Civilization and Capitalism 15th–18th Century* (London: Commerce, 1983); Tripp, *Islam and the Moral Economy*, 2–4.

142 Chapra, "Need for a New Economic System," 19.

143 See Frithjof Schuon, *Understanding Islam*, trans. D. D. Matheson (London: Allen & Unwin, 1963); Fazlur Rahman, *Islam* (Chicago, IL: Chicago University Press, 2002); Chapra, "Islamic Economics"; see also Chapra, "Ethics and Economics."

144 See Chapra, "Islamic Economics," 7. For Chapra, conventional economics is neutral about ethics, whereby humans are deemed selfish and the free market is efficient in allocating the resources. Muhammad Umer Chapra, "Islamic

resources by the wealthy against the poorer segments of society is inevitable. In "contrast with the secularist worldview of the failed systems, the Islamic worldview is a balanced synthesis of both the material and the spiritual dimensions of life."[145] Hence Islamic economics – unlike the secular-based economic systems – never departed from its religious background and postulates.

Conversely, there are propositions to study Islamic economics as a behavioral science from a comparative perspective using conventional economics.[146] By applying methodological pluralism, Islamic economics becomes rather a subsystem of economic science, since its proponents believe that every discipline can ultimately be regarded as Islamic.[147] Iranian economist Sohrab Behdad is nevertheless certain that the economy will remain capitalistic since the interventionist role of the state in accommodating a social balance does not extract other pressing economic problems from the subject matter that is capitalistic in nature. According to al-Ṣadr, the capitalist economic system is based upon three specific elements: freedom of ownership, freedom of exploitation, and freedom of consumption.[148] Al-Ṣadr contends that despite the apparent difference between capitalist and Marxist economy in addressing the issue of private rights and ownership, both systems have in common an endorsement of individualistic-oriented perception of nature. He heavily criticizes not only the Marxist doctrine of economic supplication but also the capitalist doctrine in which the freedom of economic exploitation provides grounds, presumably, for provision of welfare in society and production growth.[149] Hence,

Economic Thought and the New Global Economy," *Islamic Economic Studies*, vol. 9, no. 1 (2001): 16–17.

145 Chapra, "Need for a New Economic System," 30. See also Schuon, *Understanding Islam*.

146 "The rebirth of Islamic economics in the early part of the twentieth century was dominated by scholars and writers with a background in Islamic sciences. This strongly influenced its scope and methodology, giving Islamic economics a *fiqhī* and common knowledge type of tendency. In the mid-1970s a new generation of trained economists started their research in Islamic economics. For many reasons, the tendency persists to overstate the differences between Islamic and conventional economics to the extent that some like to believe that Islamic economics is a distinct discipline, quite independent of conventional economics. The present paper does not take such a position." (Kahf, "Islamic Economics," 25).

147 Kahf, "Islamic Economics," 30. 148 Al-Ṣadr, *Iqtiṣādunā* (1982), vol. 1, 6.

149 Al-Ṣadr, *Iqtiṣādunā* (1982), vol. 1, 24.

al-Ṣadr argues that Islamic economics differs substantially from capitalist and socialist economics in three main ways: nature of ownership, economic freedom, and social balance.[150] Islamic doctrine differs from conventional economic systems on the question of private ownership as a fundamental principle, and it sets up different forms of ownership simultaneously – private, public, and state ownership. The right to private property and inheritance tends to be one of the main features of the capitalist system.[151] Theoretically, everyone has the right to acquire wealth and private property, who is economically, socially, or otherwise deprived; this inevitably generates social and economic inequalities. The system's mechanisms of production are neither owned by the state nor by the community but by individuals, which implies that the inner structure of capitalism does stifle economic gains and individuals' benefits rather than increasing them for the public good. A second important element is economic freedom, which is linked to the usage of contracts and private properties. The motive for profit and the absence of a mediator and/or systemic regulation of these uncontrolled gains for profits include risk, generating competition, and excluding other possible parties. It may seem that this arrangement in an Islamic society is capitalist in nature, but al-Ṣadr disagrees, arguing that it allows a number of seemingly capitalistic appropriations within the means of production, for this is a manifestation of an era and not an ethical prerogative.

2.4.2 Islamic Economics As Islamic and Social Science

As Pakistan was in a formative stage in introducing Islamic principles to economic systems,[152] Muhammad Abdul Mannan, a US-trained Pakistani economist, in 1970, published the seminal textbook entitled *Islamic Economics: Theory and Practice.*[153] At the time, Islamic economics was not yet widely taught at universities. In 1978, he joined the

[150] In Islam, for instance, the notion of double ownership is possible. Private ownership is not a general rule in an Islamic economy but it is in a capitalist economy, which does not recognize public ownership for the general good, whereas the opposite is the case in a socialist society. According to al-Ṣadr, common ownership is in Islam a general principle (al-Ṣadr, *Iqtiṣādunā* (1982), vol. 1, part 2, 5).

[151] Al-Ṣadr, *Iqtiṣādunā* (1982), vol. 1, part 2, 5–8.

[152] Haneef, *Contemporary Islamic Economic Thought*, 14.

[153] Mannan, *Islamic Economics*.

International Center for Research in Islamic Economics in Jeddah, and in 1984, he published two more books on the subject, *The Making of Islamic Economic Society* and *The Frontiers of Islamic Economics*.[154] Mannan defines Islamic economics as a dynamic social science,[155] seeing it neither as normative nor as a positive science limited only to Islamic economic agents.[156] Instead, he interlinks the two aspects,[157] and by integrating the social paradigm in the state formation, he focuses on the moral economic restructuring of the individual through social cohesion, which presupposes *Sharī'a* as the law of the state.[158] By rejecting the idea behind excessive consumerism and overproductivity, he proposes the idea of voluntary cooperation, based on the norms of *Sharī'a*, which would regulate both people's economic behavior and (state) supervision of markets.[159]

Further, al-Ṣadr proposes studying Islamic economics as part of the system as a whole.[160] The interconnectedness of the Islamic economy with the concept of Islamic belief relates to economic justice, ownership rights, and social responsibilities; hence it cannot be purely material accounting. Even though Islamic economics is for al-Ṣadr not a science, it can constitute a scientific inquiry through "comprehensive religious study." Elaborating further, he states that there is a difference between economic doctrine and economic science. The former presupposes an expression of the way of life society prefers to follow while the latter explains economic life. The line of distinction between what constitutes science and doctrine is the ideology of social justice. According to al-Ṣadr, "The economic doctrine consists of every basic rule of economic life connected with the ideology of social Justice. And the science (of economics) consists of every theory, which explains the reality of economic life apart from a prefixed ideology or an ideal

[154] See Muhammad Abdul Mannan, *The Making of Islamic Economic Society: Islamic Dimensions in Economic Analysis* (Cairo: International Association of Islamic Banks; Turkish Federated State of Kibris, Turkish Cyprus: International Institute for Islamic Banking and Economics, 1984); Muhammad Abdul Mannan, *The Frontiers of Islamic Economics* (Delhi: Idarah-i Adabiyat-i Delli, 1984).

[155] Mannan, *Making of Islamic Economic Society*, 9–12, 51.

[156] Mannan, *Making of Islamic Economic Society*, 24.

[157] Mannan, *Islamic Economics*, 9.

[158] Mannan, *Frontiers of Islamic Economics*, 42.

[159] Mannan, *Making of Islamic Economic Society*, 200.

[160] Al-Ṣadr, *Iqtiṣādunā* (1982), vol. 1, 64ff.

of Justice."[161] This view asserts that economic preservation and expropriation of social rights is intrinsically embedded in the doctrine of Islamic economic writings. He subscribed to the notion that economics is a neutral instrument of analysis with universal validity that is capable of explaining people's economic behavior. Moreover, Islamic economics is regarded as a doctrine for the *way* Muslims follow the pursuit of their economic gains. It is concerned with the distribution of wealth, whereas science tends to the laws of production.[162] If this view is to be attained, then every investigation into the production of goods is the subject of the science of economics and every acquisition of wealth or ownership is doctrinal.

On the other hand, for Siddiqi, an Indian-trained Muslim economist who advocates *fiqh*-based neoclassical economics,[163] economics reflects a worldview, and he is thus against the idea of economic (pre) determination.[164] He defines three distinct components of Islamic economics, which are encapsulated in the notions of social goals, social relations, and the ideal socioeconomic reality. In more elaborated terms, he perceives social goals and individual behavioral patterns as being reflective of the ends that are in accordance with the norms and values of Islam. This presents a point of convergence between legal specialists and economists, whereby "the economist – one who specializes in the knowledge of the economic problems and processes – [is also one] who can discern the relevance of particular Shariʿah rules or its general precepts for real life economic problems."[165] Siddiqi is certain that an economist can decipher the looming matters within the legal as well as the sociopolitical realm. The second component pertains "to the analysis of human behavior, social relations, processes and institutions which relate to production, distribution and consumption of wealth which fulfils needs"[166] in light of positive economics, coupled with *Sharīʿa*-stipulated norms. He warns that the prevalent methodology caters to "western modes of behaviour to have universal validity."[167]

161 Al-Ṣadr, *Iqtiṣādunā* (1982), vol. 2, 9.
162 Al-Ṣadr, *Iqtiṣādunā* (1982), vol. 2, 5.
163 Haneef, *Contemporary Islamic Economic Thought*, 6.
164 Siddiqi, *Some Aspects of the Islamic Economy*, 11–13.
165 Siddiqi, "Islamic Approach to Economics," 168.
166 Siddiqi, "Islamic Approach to Economics," 168.
167 Siddiqi does not conceal that his methodology is of the neoclassical-Keynesian school, coupled with Islamic moral and legal values. For more see Haneef, *Contemporary Islamic Economic Thought*.

In order to further the discipline of Islamic economic science and to define human motivation, an Islamic economist may resort to history, sociology, and other contingent fields. The third component relates to realizing the goals of *Sharīʿa*, rooted in the Qurʾan, in real-time economy. As such, Islamic economics is "both a science, analyzing its data, and an art, discussing ways of creating a new order."[168] Attempts to modify the existing economy thorough Islamization of economics by developing financial institutions, despite some being committed to the neoclassical-Keynesian economic model,[169] and social sciences[170] have dominated the discourse. From the very outset, the economic model should incorporate human behavior, yet "there is no way to verify claims for the superiority of the Islamic economic system,"[171] since no existing economic model has thus far fully implemented Islamic economic teachings. While some admit that Islamic economics builds upon a well-established tradition within Western economic history,[172] this does not automatically translate into establishing a moral economy by Islamizing economic institutions. Even though the Qurʾan provided the moral framework, it does not contain a distinctive paradigm for economic life,[173] which is why, for Siddiqi, economics will eventually turn into an interdisciplinary science.[174]

168 Siddiqi, "Islamic Approach to Economics," 169.

169 Hasan, review of *Teaching Economics in Islamic Perspective*, by Siddiqi, 113.

170 Nejatullah Siddiqi, *Riba, Bank Interest and the Rationale of its Prohibition* (Jeddah: Islamic Development Bank, Islamic Research & Training Institute, 2004); Siddiqi, *Teaching Economics in Islamic Perspective*.

171 Khan, *What Is Wrong with Islamic Economics?*, 33.

172 See Smith, *Wealth of Nations* and the theory of economics as part of a moral system. Smith's work has been interpreted in light of the moral predicaments by Philipp, "Idea of Islamic Economics," and by Mirakhor, *Note on Islamic Economics*, 15–17. "Careful reading of the *Theory of Moral Sentiments* and *The Wealth of Nations* seems to indicate that Smith's view are based and focused on two characteristics that he postulated for human nature: self-interest and the need for social cooperation, both of which he needs to explain the workings in the market. A 'pure selfishness' seems an unnecessarily strong assumption for a theorist like Adam Smith with a moral/ethical orientation, on the one hand, and belief in parsimony and Occam's Razor, on the other." (Mirakhor, *Note on Islamic Economics*, 17). See also David Lieberman, "Adam Smith on Justice, Rights, and Law" (UC Berkeley Public Law and Legal Theory Working Paper No. 13, December 1999), available at http://dx.doi.org/10.2139/ssrn.215213.

173 See Mohammad Nejatullah Siddiqi, *Muslim Economic Thinking: A Survey of Contemporary Literature* (Leicester: The Islamic Foundation, 1981).

174 Haneef, *Contemporary Islamic Economic Thought*, 32.

Naqvi affirms that Islamic economics as a distinct discipline does exist, and he divides the existing group of authors into two categories: the mono-economists, or the proponents of the neoclassical economics, and the critics of Islamic economics who reject its scientific teachings.[175] Unlike contemporary Muslim economists, many of whom have pushed for the shift toward the neoclassical economic paradigm, Islamic legal specialists have tried to deduce moral teachings of economics from the Islamic sources.[176] Both groups, however, as we shall see in detail in Chapter 4, tend to conflate the epistemological foundations of economic thought in Islam with the need for an Islamic state, which would rest upon Islamic jurisprudence.

2.5 Islamic Jurisprudential Economics and Islamic Law

Contemporary scholars on Islamic economics employ concepts such as *Sharīʿa*, Islamic law, moral law, ethics, and social justice when discussing the core norms of Islamic economics, justifying the existence of the discipline. In spite of numerous theories of and approaches to the Islamic economic subject, they base their arguments on the ethical values of the Qurʾan and the scriptural sources. Their epistemological justifications of the legal and the moral are, however, based on the modern understanding of seemingly uncontested views on Islamic tradition.

For many modern authors, Islamic economics is grounded in *fiqh* foundations.[177] The methodology of *fiqh* is, however, very different

175 Islamic society for Naqvi differs from Muslim societies, upon which the economic doctrine is drawn. Economic laws derive from society, and thus do not present the absolute truth, and since religious texts are perceived as sacred, entailing ethical stipulations, they are often utilized as the methodological starting point. This inevitably addresses the question of validity and objectivity of the subject matter. Naqvi navigates out of this dilemma by quoting Harsanyi, who upheld that value judgments can be proven to be "objectively invalid – if they are contrary to the facts or because they are based on the wrong value perspective" (Naqvi, *Islam, Economics, and Society*, 19). This indicates that Islamic economics, with its religious-ethical considerations, is only in theory a reflection of economies in Muslim societies, which further extrapolates the critique that will be analyzed in Chapters 4 and 5 of this book.

176 Khan, *Introduction to Islamic Economics*, v–vi.

177 "Roots of Islamic economics should, by definition, lie in *fiqh*." M. Fahim Khan, "*Fiqh* Foundations of the Theory of Islamic Economics: A Survey of Selected Contemporary Writings on Economics Relevant Subjects of *Fiqh*," in *Theoretical Foundations of Islamic Economics*, ed. Habib Ahmed, (Jeddah:

from the methodology of economic science and further from premodern Islamic reasoning, since *fiqh* rules contain technical and normative statements of value.[178] Contemporary economic policies are descriptive and do not decipher what is allowed or forbidden. On the other hand, since modern interpretations of *fiqh* align with the concept of the legal, they entail various rules on transactions, family matters, criminal law, and worship-related practices, yet they do not give precedence to the premodern composition of economic behavior and the moral self.

Siddiqi recommends considering the Qur'an and the Sunnah as the primary sources and the reality of the contemporary environment as secondary, whereas *fiqh* would provide an answer to how to apply Islamic legal precepts to economic values.[179] For al-Ṣadr, an Islamic economic doctrine is depicted as an ethical system since it deals with (economic) justice, correlating to Islamic legal precepts (*aḥkām*), which play certain roles in preserving economic justice and property rights.[180] The legal precepts extend to the distribution of wealth, including private, state, and public ownership; *umma*-ownership; people's ownership; and common ownership (state and public).[181] While Naqvi sees his approach as axiomatic and inductive, since he believes the workings of an Islamic economy can be seen in the behavior of Muslim society,[182] al-Ṣadr, on the other hand, deduces economic principles from Islamic law.[183]

Islamic Development Bank, Islamic Research and Training Institute, 2002), 62. See also e.g. al-Fanjarī, *Al-Madhab al-Iqtiṣādi fī al-Islām*; al-Tirīqī, *Al-Iqtiṣād al-Islāmī.*

178 Muhammad Yusuf Saleem distinguishes between *fiqh* methodology and economic methodology in Islam, yet he defines Islamic economics as a social science, which is problematic in itself. Muhammad Yusuf Saleem, "Methods and Methodologies in Fiqh and Islamic Economics," *Review of Islamic Economics*, vol. 14, no. 1 (2010): 112. For a detailed discussion on the different methodologies between conventional and Islamic economics see Addas, *Methodology of Economics.*

179 See Mirakhor, *Note on Islamic Economics*, 11.

180 Al-Ṣadr, *Iqtiṣādunā* (1982), vol. 1, 89–94; vol. 2, 5–15.

181 Al-Ṣadr, *Iqtiṣādunā* (1982), vol. 1, 64–72.

182 Naqvi, in Wilson, "Contribution of Muhammad Baqir al-Sadr to Contemporary Islamic Economic Thought," 48.

183 Al-Ṣadr, *Iqtiṣādunā* (1982), vol. 1, 57–58.

2.5.1 Muʿāmalāt *As Commercial Law and* Maqāṣid al-Sharīʿa

Commercial law or *muʿāmalāt* and the objectives of the law[184] are most dominant in the field of Islamic finances.[185] Historically, many jurists conceived the whole of Islamic law as falling into four major fields, referred to as the four quarters, including the rituals, sales, marriage, and injuries. The quarter of sales would encompass, among many other subjects and topics, partnerships, guaranty, gifts exchange, and bequests.[186] Islamic commercial law, or Islamic law of transactions, has been regarded as one of the most important mechanisms in the field of (contemporary) economic jurisprudence. *Muʿāmalāt*, as part of *fiqh*, discerns the lawful from the unlawful in the development of economics and finances. Most *muʿāmalāt* transactions and procedures are approached and conducted from the Islamic legal perspective, involving future contracts, sales and purchase of commodities, and others.[187]

The Qurʾanic text gives incentives to economic, financial, constitutional, and commercial matters that became confined within the spectrum of the higher objectives of Islamic law (*maqāṣid*), whereas transactions, deferred payments, (excessive) usury,[188] property rights,

184 *Maqāṣid* has been studied by various classical Muslim scholars, primarily from the moral perspective, and it is regarded by jurists as serving the interests of society, including socioeconomic well-being, and preventing people from any form of harm; e.g. al-Māturīdī (d. 945), al-Juwaynī (d. 1085), al-Ghazālī (d. 1111), Fakhr al-Dīn al-Rāzi (d. 1209), Ibn Taymiyya (d. 1327), al-Shāṭibi (d. 1388), Ibn ʿĀshūr (d. 1973). See Imran Ahsan Khan Nyazee, *Theories of Islamic Law* (Herndon, VA: IIIT, 1994); al-Ghazāli, *al-Mustaṣfāʾ*, vol. 1, 30, 116, 135, 155; Ibn ʿĀshūr, *Maqāṣid al-Sharīʿah al-Islāmiyyah*, ed. El-Tahir el-Mesawi (Kuala Lumpur: al-Fajr, 1999), 274. For the classical period, see Chapter 3.

185 For more on the legal aspects of contracts in Islamic law, see Mathias Rohe, *Das Islamische Recht* (München: C. H. Beck, 2011), part 5.

186 Wael Hallaq, *An Introduction to Islamic Law* (Cambridge: Cambridge University Press, 2009), 28.

187 On void sales and transactions (*bayʿ al-fasad*), see ʿAbd al-Raḥmān al-Jāzirī, *Islamic Jurisprudence According to the Four Sunni Schools*, trans. Nancy Roberts (Louisville, KY: Fons Vitae, 2009); on allowance of sales see al-Ghazālī, *Iḥyāʾ*; for more on the *muʿāmalāt* in Islamic finance, see Mohammad Hashim Kamali, *Islamic Commercial Law: An Analysis of Futures and Options* (Cambridge: I. B. Tauris in Association with the Islamic Texts Society, 1990); Mohammad Hashim Kamali, *Islamic Finance Law, Economics, and Practice* (Cambridge: Cambridge University Press, 2006).

188 "God has permitted sale and prohibited usury," Qurʾan, surah al-Baqarah (2:275). For more on *ribā*, see the fifth section of this very chapter.

prohibitions, and allowances all fall under general, broad principles,[189] and not to specific rulings or observations. Lawful and unlawful modes of trade, possession of property, and usurious transactions are matters not elaborated in the Qur'an but explained by *'ulamā'* according to the general principles of the *Sharī'a*.[190] Based on the scriptural sources and its regulations, classical Muslim jurists differentiated between five ethical categories of Islamic jurisprudence, namely, obligation (*farḍ*),[191] recommendation (*mustaḥab*), prohibition (*ḥarām*), proscription (*makrūh*), and allowance (*mubāḥ*).[192] One of the rights that is divulged is that objective law guarantees the subjective rights of individuals, yet

189 Kamali notes that of the two verses in the Qur'an on the subject of commercial contracts, one appears in the form of a command, the other in the form of a question: "O you believers, fulfill your contracts" (al-Ma'idah, 5:1) and "O you believers, why do you say things which you do not carry through?" (al-Saff, 61:2). In addition, in al-Nisa' (4:29, 58) proper conduct is foreseen: "God commands you to turn over trusts to those to whom they belong, and when you judge among people, judge righteously." This for Kamali stipulates that "Contracts must therefore not amount to a violation of justice, a breach of trust, or a departure from the moral ideals of the law." See Mohammad Hashim Kamali, *Principles of Islamic Jurisprudence* (Cambridge: Islamic Texts Society, 2005), 27.

190 "*Fiqh*'s norms on legal transactions confirm the legitimacy of the major institutions of Muslim society, organize their reproduction and discuss, on the basis of an immense wealth of information and systematic thought, social conflicts and social order in the Muslim political community. *Fiqh*, in this field, puts the social order of the community squarely into the center of law and religion. It is, the jurists say, the objective law, the *shari*, that determines what is forbidden and allowed. But if individuals acquire legal claims based on the norms of the objective law they may turn to the judiciary in order to see them protected as their subjective rights." Baber Johansen, "The Changing Limits of Contingency in the History of Muslim Law" (third Annual Levtzion Lecture, Nehemia Levtzion Center for Islamic Studies, Institute for Asian and African Studies, Hebrew University of Jerusalem, 2013), 39.

191 On the ethical category of obligation as *taklīf* in Islam in relation to its theological and legal dimension, see Nobert Oberauer, *Religiöse Verpflichtung im Islam. Ein ethischer Grundbegriff und seine theologische, rechtliche und sozialgeschichtliche Dimension* (Würzburg: Ergon, 2004).

192 The first category relates to compulsory commandments and it builds the basis of legal normativity. The recommended behavior concerns the noncompulsory commandments. The so-called non-allowed commandments pertain to prohibition, whereas noncompulsory commandments relate to that which is proscribed. Every other deed falls in the category of allowed. A commandment is binding when omission of a particular norm can potentially occur. In other words, if there is no rebuttal of the norm, then no omission is needed. In this case, the commandment is not compulsory, and a particular activity is regarded only as a recommended (and not compulsory) religious norm. See e.g.

this produces different rulings when it comes to *ʿibādāt* and *muʿāmalāt*.[193] Religious practices of the former are clearly specified according to *Sharīʿa* principles and hence validated. The latter follows the opposite principle, in which everything is permitted (*mubāḥ*) unless explicitly forbidden with a rule (*ḥukm*).[194] The mechanisms of trading in Islamic perspective arguably exclude two important operational tools, namely usury (*ribā*) and risk or uncertainty (*gharār*).[195] The basic stipulations of the *muʿāmalāt* are provided by *Sharīʿa* rules, yet the interpretation of these principles as applicable to different circumstances are regulated by the *fiqh al-muʿāmalāt*. Hence, new understandings and rulings can be reached by "understanding the effective cause (*ʿilla*) and rationale (*hikma*) of the original ruling and the importance of *maṣlaḥa* (benefit) under the changed circumstances."[196]

For Chapra, Islamic economics is organized around four elements within the broader frame of the objectives of Islamic law, which interprets Islamic economics according to higher values; these elements include social filter, motivation system, restructuring economic thought in light of *maqāṣid*, and the goal-oriented role of the state

Mouhanad Khorchide, *Scharia – der missverstandene Gott. Der Weg zu einer modernne islamischen Ethik* (Freiburg: Herder, 2013), 123.

193 For a long time Western scholarship has perceived the *Sharīʿa* legal domain as two separate parts, rituals and legal dealings – *ʿibādāt* and *muʿāmalāt* – and thus overlooking the moral gist of *Sharīʿa*. Yet, the two are intrinsically connected and intertwined. See Hallaq, *Sharīʿa*; Hallaq, *Impossible State*, 115–116; see also reference 73 on page 116.

194 "Everything is muṭlaq (unconditional), until a prohibition arrives concerning it." Ibn Taymiyya, *Majmūʿ Fatāwā Shaykh al-Islām Aḥmad Ibn Taymiyya* (Al-Riyāḍ: Matābiʾ al-Riyāḍ, 1963), vol. 21, 535.

195 For many contemporary Islamic economists, the prohibitions are clearly specified in Islamic law and one has to be careful not to expand them. As commercial activities fall under *muʿāmalāt*, the underlying principle related to commercial laws is that of permissibility (*ibaha*). In particular, *ribā* and *gharār* are prohibited in commercial transactions and in Islamic commercial law. On the prohibition of *gharār* (translated as risky, ambiguous, undefined, vague, uncertain, doubtful and/or concealed elements of the contract) see e.g. Khan, "*Fiqh* Foundations of the Theory of Islamic Economics," 77–78; Siddiq Al-Darir, *Al-Gharar in Contracts and its Effects on Contemporary Transaction* (IRTI, IDB, Eminent Scholars Lecture Series, no. 16, 1997); Abdul-Rahim al-Sāti, "The Permissible Gharar (Risk) in Classical Islamic Jurisprudence," *JKAU: Islamic Economics*, vol. 16, no. 2, (2003): 3–19; Mohammad Hashim Kamali, "Islamic Commercial Law: An Analysis of Options," *American Journal of Islamic Social Sciences*, vol. 14, no. 3 (2000): 17–37.

196 Kamali, *Islamic Commercial Law*, 78.

supported by an Islamic worldview.[197] For instance, *māl* or wealth is a God-given trust and thus equally important as the first four *maqāṣid* since all five are interconnected for achieving the well-being of man. Acquiring wealth is not prohibited as long as it is conducted lawfully.[198] Since wealth has to operate within the scope of ethical considerations, it is a means rather than an end in itself,[199] to be used for fulfilling one's needs, promoting equity, and diminishing injustice.[200] Wealth and faith are positioned on an equally important level, from which the responsible utilization of resources for the environment and human kind is foreseen.[201] Economic development and increasing wealth directly relate to the categories of education, security, good governance, freedom of enterprise, employment and self-employment opportunities, removal of poverty, equitable distribution of wealth, social solidarity and trust, saving and investment mechanisms, optimum growth rate, and social development.

All of these categories have a direct impact on the remaining four *maqāṣid* of enrichment of faith, self, intellect, and posterity, which in turn influence a person's general well-being. This presupposes the idea that one's basic socioeconomic needs have to be fulfilled in order for one to preserve the other *maqāṣid* postulates.[202] The development of wealth is therefore part and parcel of diminishing economic inequalities in society. The methodological stalemate, however, of merging the *maqāṣid* postulates within the conventional economic system remains.

197 For more see Muhammad Umer Chapra, *The Islamic Vision of Development in the Light of Maqasid al-Shari'a* (Herndon, VA: IIIT, 2008).

198 Prophet Muḥammad said, "There is nothing wrong in wealth for him who fears God [i.e. abstains from evil]," Sahih al-Bukhari, *Al-Adab al-Mufrad*, 113:301; Bab Tīb al-Nafs in Chapra, *Islamic Vision of Development*, 46.

199 See al-Ghazālī, *Iḥyā'*; Chapra, *Islamic Vision of Development*, 47. In addition, Siddiqi expounds analogical reasoning in light of *maṣlaḥa* as public good; see Siddiqi, "Islamic Approach to Economics," 167–168.

200 It is believed that the Prophet said, "Wretched is the slave of dinar, dirham and velvet," Sahih al-Bukhari, *Kitāb al-Jihād wa al-Siyar* in Chapra, *Islamic Vision of Development*, 47.

201 See Mouhanad Khorchide, *Islam ist Bahrherzichkeit* (Freiburg im Breisgau: Herder, 2012); Chapra, *Islamic Vision of Development*, 1.

202 Compare this approach to Marx's postulate of how social being determines consciousness. For Marx, individual consciousness cannot be separated from one's socioeconomic group, yet by invoking *maqāṣid* it appears that the two are mutually engaged and thus interdependent – one's consciousness (soul or even faith) does procure one's social being as much as one's social being impacts one's consciousness.

Contemporary Muslim legal specialists criticize traditional *maqāṣid* on various points:[203] first, they investigate the whole of Islamic law and yet fail to include specific purposes; second, the traditional *maqāṣid* is concerned more with the individual than with communities; third, for Jasser Auda, traditionally *maqāṣid* did not include the notion of justice and freedom; and fourth, they were relegated to the legal spectrum only.[204] Many economic instruments can be derived from the objectives of Islamic law, as was explored by al-Shāṭibī and al-Ghazālī.[205] In this regard, *maṣlaḥa* would determine whether an economic activity (like consumption or production of a good) should be pursued or not. If an activity has a beneficial implication that corresponds to al-Shāṭibī's framework of objectives of *Sharīʿa*, then that activity ought to be pursued.[206] Purely egoistical, individual-based interests and endeavors are, according to contemporary Muslim scholars, regarded as undesirable, unless fostering the concept of *maṣlaḥa*.

The concept of *maṣlaḥa mursala* (explained in more detail in Chapter 3), as unrestricted *maṣlaḥa*, allows for public policy to meet social needs. *Maṣlaḥa mursala* can be applicable only insofar as *maṣlaḥa* does not became an arbitrary mechanism that expounds a subjective bias in providing legal rulings. It also must be general in that its values extend to society at large, and lastly it must not conflict with the values upheld by the consensus or the scriptural sources.[207]

2.5.2 *The Conception of* Zakāt *and* Ribā *in Contemporary Islamic Economics*

Zakāt and *ribā* have been the most visible components of contemporary Islamic economics and finance, ascertained primarily as legal

203 Jasser Auda, *Maqāsid al-Sharīʿa: An Introductory Guide* (Herndon, VA: IIIT, 2008), 6–7.

204 As will be shown in Chapter 3 through the examples of *Sharīʿa* being utilized as an ethical conception in the deliberations and endeavors of the premodern Muslim scholars, this argument does not hold entirely true, since the individual was in the premodern period seen as part of the communitarian reality, whereby legal meant also moral. This can be expounded by analyzing medieval scholars and their economic ideas, which are, as will be indicated in Chapter 4, encapsulated within the theological realm, in order to achieve higher ends.

205 See Chapter 3.

206 Auda, *Maqāsid al-Sharīʿa*, 29.

207 See Muḥammad Abū Zahra, *Uṣūl al-Fiqh* (Cairo: Dār al-Fikr al-ʿArabī, 1958), 219.

conceptions. *Zakāt* as a general levy on the wealth of individuals is commanded by the Qur'an,[208] even though the fixed percentage has not been decreed.[209] As a reflection of human conduct, it restores human relations toward others, and tackles the misery of the poor and the equanimity of the rich. More important than its legal range is its role in a moral economy. *Zakāt* epitomizes several economic predispositions, such as the right to regulate property, the idea of utilizing property for higher ends, the idea of assisting the needy while ensuring their integration in society, and the proposition of cleansing one's own wealth in order to establish economic (and more broadly even ecological) balance. Islamic wealth tax or the institution of *zakāt* levied on savings and assets has been reserved precisely for the weak to balance out wealth and to increase social welfare among the population.[210] In this context, *zakāt* has not only legal but also socioeconomic and, even more importantly, moral aspects. *Zakāt* is mentioned in the Qur'ān 82 times in combination with Islamic prayer (*ṣalāt*), which shows the importance and interrelation between tax charity and spiritual endeavors. *Zakāt* is a clear indication that in Islamic tradition poverty is both a social problem and a spiritual phenomenon.[211] Even though it has been theorized by contemporary Muslim economists, it seems that their objective was to coalesce *zakāt* as an Islamic concept with the intention of treating it as a financial tool to bolster the provision of basic needs. As we shall see in Chapter 4, the critics of Islamic economics point out that throughout Islamic history *zakāt* has maintained a mere spiritual endeavor rather than an institutionalized social or economic character.[212] Conceptually, *zakāt*, as an obligatory levy on surplus wealth and income, has been a milestone in providing social

[208] See, for instance, "We made them leaders who guide by Our command and We inspired them to work good deeds, to observe the Salat and to give the Zakat, they were worshippers of Us." (Qur'an, 21:73); "Eat from their fruits when it blossoms, and give its decreed obligation on the day of its harvest." (Qur'an, 6:141); "They ask you what should they give: say, "The good that you give should be to the parents, the close ones, the orphans, the needy and the homeless, and any good that you do, God is Knowledgeable thereof." (Qur'an, 2:215); "Woe to the mushrikeen who do not give the Zakat and with regards to the Hereafter, they are disbelievers." (Qur'an, 41:6–7).

[209] See the Qur'an, 17:26–29. [210] Qur'an, 4:28; 100:8.

[211] Abdolkarim Soroush, *Reason, Freedom, and Democracy in Islam*, ed. Mahmoud Sadri and Ahmad Sadri (Oxford: Oxford University Press, 2000).

[212] *Zakāt* has in Muslim-majority countries remained a mere reflection of the ideal economic model and has not impacted the factual economies on the ground.

benefits and security, but it has not attained such a role in Muslim-majority countries.

The Arabic word *ribā* means excess or increase, which according to some scholars is categorically prohibited in the Qur'an. Its prohibition has been one of the most widely discussed concepts, maintaining a central place in the imagination of an Islamic economy. According to Muhammad Akram Khan, the modernists argued that *ribā* does not relate to the interest added by banks, whereas the current consensus states that *ribā* applies to all forms of interest. The abolition of *ribā* has been enacted on the legal basis, or prohibition of interest in economic activities. Naqvi, however, states that there is also an economic aspect to interest, not only a legal one.[213] In Islamic banking, which is not discussed directly in this book but deserves at least a brief mention since it has been presented as the subsystem of Islamic economics, *ribā* has thus far been researched in light of financial and transactional prohibitions. Even if *ribā* is a necessary mechanism of banking system, the economic consequences and impact have not yet been sufficiently implemented by either Islamic banks or other financial institutions, since the focus has been primarily its legal and not its economic position. Furthermore, some economists advocate for a state-wide implementation of *zakāt* and *ribā* as the pinnacle of Islamic economics.[214]

The prohibition of *ribā*,[215] or excessive interest, is also based on the Qur'ān, where it is first referenced through the term itself, but the recipient or payer is not specified.[216] Islamic tradition has distinguished commercial activity from profit and the prohibition of *ribā*.[217]

"In Pakistan zakat revenue was estimated to be no more than 0.2 per cent of GDP by 1994 and in Iran, where zakat has been collected by government agencies, it has had no measurable impact on the inequalities of power at the heart of the political economy." See Nasr, *Islamic Leviathan*, 122–124 and 144–146; Tripp, *Islam and the Moral Economy*, 125; Ishrat Hussein *Pakistan: The Economy of an Elitist State* (Karachi: Oxford University Press, 1999); Din Pal, *Pakistan, Islam and Economics* (Karachi: Oxford University Press, 1999).

213 See Naqvi, *Ethics and Economics*.

214 Mannan, *Making of Islamic Economic Society*, 334.

215 Interest on capital loan. See Khan, *Introduction to Islamic Economics*, 25.

216 *Ribā* was common among pre-Islamic Arabs. The Qur'an states, "And whatever you give for interest (*ribā*) to increase within the wealth of people will not increase with Allah. But what you give in *zakāt*, desiring the countenance of Allah – those are the multipliers." (Qur'an, 30:39).

217 Qur'an, 2:275; see also 2:276, 278; 3:130, 4:161, 30:39.

Nonetheless, not every excess or increase that occurs in economic transactions falls under the rubric of this proscription, hence *fiqh* scholars had the task to determine which increase ought not to be marked, indicating that the *ribā* verses were not so clear after all;[218] therefore, legal scholars took the role of interpreting the meaning of the word. Over the centuries, the consensus of the jurists has been that *ribā* should be understood as any interest charged on a loan, regardless of the willingness of the borrower to enter into an agreement by which he or she will have to repay interest as well as principal. This consensus was based on the authority of the received texts but also on a moral repugnance at a number of features associated with the charging of interest on capital.[219] Nevertheless, it was acknowledged by some of the most distinguished *fuqaha'* that the identification of *ribā* was not always straightforward.[220] The consensus of jurists is that *ribā* refers to all interest-bearing transactions;[221] they see *ribā* as equivalent to interest (*al-fa'idah*) on all kinds of loans, however large or small, whether these involve banks, government agencies, or individuals.

The modern economic debates on the subject of *ribā* do not address the matter of *ribā* in detail since the term was never clearly articulated.[222] For traditional *fiqh* scholars, interest does not

218 Rauf Azhar notes that there were many variations of the term *ribā* existing simultaneously, indicating that *fiqh* scholars interpreted the concept in various ways, while none of them appeared in the time of the Prophet. The number of *ribā* terms in the fiqh literature "is quite understandable in view of the differences between the perspective of the Qur'ān and that of the ḥadīth literature on the subject. At the fundamental level, there is the so called Qur'ānic ribā, which was originally known as ribā al-jāhiliyya (pre-Islamic ribā), and then there is what has been called ribā al-ḥadīth. This latter variety is given several names depending partly on the nature of transaction for which it is being defined, and partly upon the individual likings of the different fiqh scholars." This includes also *ribā al-faḍl* (on barter transactions), *ribā al-buyū'* (on barter transactions), *ribā al-dayn* or *duyūn* (transactions with debt, and *ribā al-nasī'a* (defined on barter transactions on deferred payment basis). (Azhar, *Economics of an Islamic Economy*, 281).

219 Tripp, *Islam and Moral Economy*, 126.

220 See Azhar, *Economics of an Islamic Economy*, 279–335 and 339–406; Khan, *What Is Wrong with Islamic Economics?*, 123–227.

221 Tantawi holds the opposite approach on the so-called "riba-by-analogy". See Muḥammad Sayyid Ṭanṭāwī, "'Asi'lah 'an al-ribā'," *Al-Ahram*, November 21, 1993.

222 According to Azhar, this is due to complications regarding how the term *ribā* was understood: "The main contours of this discourse can be summed up as follows: the dominant fiqh school has recognized the futility of asserting that

necessarily fall under the rubric of *ribā* prohibition in all cases, while Muslim economists claim that they follow the classical predisposition on *ribā*. They have still influenced the discourse, and further complicated it, by advocating "for an abolition of interest from the financial system through an administrative fiat."[223] The main reason *ribā* was put into force was to prevent accumulation of wealth and, thus, to diminish the economic differences between different layers of society and also to maintain some kind of equitable social fabric. Nowadays the prohibition of *ribā* is an essential factor in the Islamic economic and banking system. Muslim economists generally encourage market economy through the imposition of a certain degree of ethically driven regulations and government interventions that aim to disable the exploitation of economic power and the accumulation of wealth: "Islam envisages a world in which everyone with authority is accountable for his actions,"[224] aiming at establishing an economic order based upon the ethical regulations of *Sharīʿa*. An active role in economic activities in society is encouraged; however, the hoarding of wealth and food supplies is illicit according to many medieval Muslim scholars[225] as merchants should always sell their commodities at a fair value,[226] according to the regulations on the market (another form of hoarding is leaving a land uncultivated, as the production has to circulate to benefit society). What has been advocated by some contemporary Muslim economists and scholars, such as Azhar,[227] al-Ṣadr,[228] and Mirakhor,[229] is the reform of Islamic jurisprudence; this includes the abrogation of many of the *aḥādīth* and opinion by consensus or *ijmāʿ*. Al-Ṣadr's and other Muslims economists' theories, however, remain confined either to the positivist

the meaning of the term ribā was not clearly understood because of the unassailable evidence provided by the exegetical works. Its writers take their point of departure by asserting that the meaning of the term ribā was well understood at the time of the revelation – and it is here that they significantly differ from the classical fiqh expositions – but then they use the classical concept of ribā al-nasīʾa to establish an equality between ribā and interest, all along giving the false impression that they are presenting the classical fiqh position." (Azhar, *Economics of an Islamic Economy*, 284).

223 Azhar, *Economics of an Islamic Economy*, 284.

224 Khan, *Introduction to Islamic Economics*, 4.

225 See e.g. al-Ghazālī, *Iḥyāʾ*, vol. 2, 72.

226 Ibn Taymiyya, in Sohrab Behdad, "Property Rights in Contemporary Islamic Economic Thought," *Review of Social Economy*, vol. 47, no. 2 (1989): 194.

227 Azhar, *Economics of an Islamic Economy*.

228 See al-Ṣadr, *Iqtiṣādunā* (1982).

229 Mirakhor, *Note on Islamic Economics*.

methodology or to the efforts to Islamize a state's economy. The restructuring of methodological and legal teachings is possible if a consensus were formed among contemporary scholars, who would, among other mechanisms, readdress the institutions of *zakāt* and the prohibition of *ribā* in light of Islamic intellectual history.

2.6 Contemporary Muslim Economists' Views on Classical Muslim Scholars

The significance of the moral predicaments of economic teachings and the notion of the Hereafter in Islamic tradition, invoked by many classical Muslim scholars,[230] has been introduced only by few contemporary Islamic economists. Chapra and Siddiqi, among others, were largely concerned with economic teachings and the idea of justice. However, the majority of contemporary Muslim economists do not invoke classical scholars' economic views, despite their claim of moral economy, since they are more concerned with defining a new economic discipline that would be cast as scientific to compete with other mainstream economic systems.

Rationalizing economics is not the only goal of scientific process. Conventional or orthodox economics does not conceptualize rationality in terms of social justice and well-being but rather along the lines of utilitarianism and maximization of self-interest. This indicates a very different conception of economic knowledge in comparison to classical economic scholarship.[231] Nonetheless, contemporary Muslim economists maintain that the concept of rationality in Islamic economics pertains not only to the material world but also "to the Hereafter through the faithful compliance with moral values that help rein self-interest to promote social interest."[232] Chapra's argument for Islamic economics is only in small part based on the contribution of some of the classical Muslim scholars (see below), covering topics such as the division of labor, specialization, trade and exchange, and the utilization of money, making him rather an exception in analyzing the classical scholars on economics. The brief

230 On economic thought by Abū Yūsuf, al-Shaybānī, Abī al-Dunyā, al-Ghazālī, Ibn Taymiyya, al-Maqrīzi, etc., see Chapter 3.

231 For Chapra also, the core features of conventional economics are rational economic man, positivism, and laissez faire. Chapra, "Islamic Economics," 8.

232 Chapra, "Islamic Economics," 9.

inclusion of the great gap theory[233] and selected classical Muslim scholars, for example, Abū Yūsuf (d. 789), al-Mawārdī (d. 1058), Ibn Hazm (d. 1064), al-Sarakhsi (d. 1090), al-Ṭūsi (d. 1093), al-Ghazālī (d. 1111), al-Dimashqī (d. 1175), Ibn Rushd (d. 1187), Ibn Taymiyya (d. 1328), al-Maqrīzī (d. 1442), al-Dawwānī (d. 1501), and Shah Waliyullah (d. 1762),[234] whose economic ideas I present in a very different light and in depth in Chapter 3, indicates that the classical Muslim scholars approached economic thinking not only from a dynamic and cross-disciplinary angle but also primarily within a different epistemic background. They considered both individual and communal well-being, one's virtuous traits of character, and the sciences of nature. Even though Chapra acknowledges that the early Muslim scholars provided a starting point of economic thought in Islamic tradition, his focus on Ibn Khaldūn in discussing the socioeconomic ideas and analysis[235] narrows his excursion into classical Islamic economic thought, which seems to be a paradigmatic malaise for the majority of contemporary Muslim economists. Though Ibn Khaldūn aimed to define economics as a separate discipline, he was neither the first nor the only scholar who

233 The great gap theory presupposes that medieval Islamic scholarship did not offer any significant development in the domain of economic thought in the Middle Ages. For more on debunking the great gap theory see Islahi, *Contribution of Muslim Scholars to Economic Thought*; Mohammad Ghazanfar and Abdul Azim Islahi, *Economic Thought of al-Ghazali* (Jeddah: Scientific Publishing Centre King Abdulaziz Univesity, 1997); Ghazanfar, *Medieval Islamic Thought*.

234 For more by Siddiqi on the medieval Muslim scholars and their economic ideas, see a text that surveys the recent writings in Arabic, English, and Urdu of various classical Muslim scholars. Mohammad Nejatullah Siddiqi, *Recent Writings on History of Economic Thought in Islam* (Jeddah: International Centre for Research in Islamic Economics King Abdulaziz University, 1982). See also Abū Yūsuf. *Kitāb al-Kharaj*, trans. Abid Ahmad Ali (Lahore: Islamic Book Center, 1979).

235 Chapra, "Islamic Economics," 13–25. In the center of Ibn Khaldūn's economic analysis is the human being and his moral, social, and political well-being. This well-being does not rest only on economic variables but also on other social and political factors. See Chapra, *Future of Economics*. In short, Ibn Khaldūn's ideas on economics included studying the factors that are interrelated: norms (*Sharīʿa*), administration, populations, wealth, development, and justice. This is linked with other variables such as the feeling of belonging or *ʿaasabiyya*, education, etc. Khaldūn implies the importance of norms when discussing state and economic life. For more on the premodern contributions of Islamic economic teachings and their relevance for contemporary Islamic economic thought see Chapter 3 of this book.

analyzed economic predicaments in Islamic tradition as a moral endeavor, and he is usually regarded as the father of modern sociology, which might explain Muslim economists' focus on his work. He asserted and analyzed human nature and the rise and fall of empires through economic, social, political, and demographic factors. Since, as the prevalent and rather misleading assumption goes, Islamic civilization after the fourteenth century underwent an intellectual decline, there were historical, sociopolitical, and economic reasons why certain areas did not develop as a separate intellectual discipline but rather remained an integral part of the social and moral philosophy of Islam.

2.7 Concluding Remarks

The reason for different epistemological understandings by Muslim economists may rest in the fact that economics explores human behavior that is embedded in society and culture, which in turn is formed by belief system, morals, and values. Muslim societies differ from each other in their income, resources, adherence to ideology, and economic development. Given the specific nature of Islamic economics, many contemporary scholars contest that the subject of Islamic economics is multidisciplinary, relying on both Western economic tradition and Islamic tenets. Methodological pluralism, however, in this context does not indicate a vibrant discipline but, rather, a systemic and at times contradictory framework. Authors such as Choudhury, Naqvi, Siddiqi, and Chapra read Islamic economics not by invigorating classical theological, legal, or ethical standpoints but within the modern framework of Islamization of economics or as a social science. The most notable theoreticians of contemporary Islamic economics, despite the field's unique intellectual makeup, follow this pattern, applying Islamic tenets to the subject of Islamic economics. Since the current Islamization of knowledge is an inadequate model for the revitalization of economic thought in Islamic tradition, even though Muslim economists like Chapra question whether the revival of Islam brought about positive repercussions for the social well-being of humankind, the majority firmly believe that only this particular Islamic worldview has the capacity to alter prevalent economic system due to its value-based justice[236] and *maqāṣid*.[237]

[236] Chapra, "Ethics and Economics," 14.
[237] Chapra, *Islam and the Economic Challenge*, 251.

By criticizing capitalism while discussing a morally guided, ideal Islamic society, Muslim economists give an impression of an oversimplified hypothesis of the discipline. The question of how many Muslim states adhere to these very norms remains unanswered.[238] Since conventional economics recognizes the market as the only arbiter of resources,[239] in which capitalism does not necessitate material provisions based on the preservation of human dignity, equitable income, and the concept of justice,[240] Islamic economics was presented as an alternative system to capitalism and socialism. Yet, since conclusions based solely on Islamic ethical norms cannot be simply drawn from empirical evidence,[241] embedding those very conclusions and assumptions in economic analysis would mean analyzing the primary texts of Islam, including the intellectual history and the socioeconomic developments of the nineteenth and twentieth centuries across the Middle East and South Asia. Thus far, Muslim economists have attempted to establish Islamic economics either through Islamic ethics or as a social science, maintaining that Islamic economics is in part based on conventional understanding of economic postulates coupled with an Islamic worldview, which seems to be a marriage of convenience.[242]

Murad W. Hofmann depicted Chapra's approach "as a perfect example of real (not just methodological) 'Islamization of Knowledge'";[243] Chapra, like many other proponents, favors combining Islamic and Western economic configurations. This approach is operative and not analytical. A change of economic paradigm and

238 See Khan, *What Is Wrong with Islamic Economics?*

239 See Philip Mirowski, *Never Let a Serious Crisis Go to Waste: How Neoliberalism Survived the Financial Meltdown* (London: Verso, 2014).

240 Apart from contemporary Muslim scholars, see also Amartya Sen, who holds that self-interest, power system of values, and corresponding norms are crucial motives in capitalist society. On the other hand, social values, democratic policies, and civil and political rights ought to provide for the basic public good and for the – often neglected – underlying idea of justice. Since raising productivity is related to promoting capitalistic success, self-interest has to include others, the notion of sympathy, and the integration of social justice. Amartya Sen, *Development Is Freedom* (New York: Anchor, 2000), 261–262.

241 Khan, *What Is Wrong with Islamic Economics?*, 36.

242 See e.g. Muhammad Fahim Khan, *Essays in Islamic Economics* (Leicester, UK : Islamic Foundation, 1995).

243 Murad Hoffman, review of *The Future of Economics: An Islamic Perspective by Umer Chapra, Intellectual Discourse*, vol. 10, no. 1 (2002): 91.

a new economic system that would, in turn, reform Muslim societies can only materialize if the historic processes of economic, political, social, and epistemological contentions that were introduced in the Middle East in nineteenth and twentieth centuries are negotiated in light of premodern scholars' conceptualization of moral economics.

Muhammad Akram Khan is in his later writings concerned with a methodology that would critically investigate the terms, concepts, theoretical considerations, and principles pertinent to the subject matter of Islamic economics, since the existing methodologies are mostly related to mainstream economic theories, considering only economic variables, whereby the human is perceived from a self-interest point of view, with a tendency to maximize material welfare. The theoretical works have not yet been developed, due to the extant body of literature that is preoccupied with basic principles of an ideal Islamic society. Often the objectives of Islamic economics are read into the religious Qur'anic text and thus influenced by the interpretation of its subject matter. As al-Ṣadr indicates, the discipline of economics has the most extensive impact within the capitalist ideology of the West due to its origins and the culture in which it emerged.[244] Separating the doctrinal from the scientific realm of (Islamic) economics is doubtful, since all economics is ideological due to its pre-existing set of regulations, assumptions, and predispositions about the worldview, human nature, and functioning of the world.

Since the reality on the ground in Muslim-majority countries is dictated by domestic and global financial conglomerates, many theories might be rendered inapplicable. It is hence crucial to study the existing realities of the socioeconomic societies in the Middle East and South Asia, as well as the epistemological-philosophical landscape of ideas pertinent to those economic theories. The systematic omission of the classical postulates by contemporary Muslim economists made them oblivious to the epistemic fields, which has had profound reverberations for the development of the contemporary Islamic economic project in that it reflected and imitated Western economic theories. Instead of focusing on joining modern Islamic economic tenets with already existing economic systems, examining premodern economic thinking in Islamic tradition would do more justice to the field. Also, Islamic banking as a branch of Islamic economics has little in common

244 Al-Ṣadr, *Iqtiṣāduna* (1982), vol. 2, part 1, 22–23.

with premodern economic thinking in Islamic tradition, even though it was established based on financial examples from the past and their conceptual apparatus. In some respects, Islamic banking has proffered an image of an institution that facilitates the mechanisms of *zakāt* and *ribā*, which gained momentum during the 1970s as revenues increased in the Gulf States.[245]

As it will be evident in Chapter 3, despite a limited and regulated, profit-based economy that had developed in early Islam,[246] classical Muslim scholars nonetheless called for safeguarding of economic activities in conformity with *Sharīʿa*'s moral cosmology.[247]

245 "A History of Islamic Finance," Islamic Finance.com, last modified February 8, 2015, www.islamicfinance.com/2015/02/an-overview-of-the-history-of-islamic-finance; Tripp, *Islam and the Moral Economy*, 135.

246 For the proponent of an idea that early Islam has developed a market-driven economics, see e.g. Benedikt Koehler, *Early Islam and The Birth of Capitalism* (Lanham, MD: Lexington Books, 2014), 145–156.

247 See e.g. the writings of al-Shaybānī, al-Ghazālī, Ibn Taymiyya, and al-Maqrīzī, and their exposition of economic conduct within the notion of the Hereafter.

3 *The Past Perfect:* Sharīʿa *and the Intellectual History of Islamic Economic Teachings*

The essence of fiqh discussions has always been theological.

Waleed A. J. Addas, *Methodology of Economics: Secular vs. Islamic*, 98

If the "moral" as we understand it in modernity did not exist in premodern Islam, then the distinction between the "moral" and the "legal" could not have existed, either in the Sharīʿa at large or in the Qurʾān in particular.

Wael Hallaq, *The Impossible State*, 82

Fī al-kasb maʿnā al-muʿāwana ʿalā al-qurab (In acquiring a livelihood there is meaning of assistance in acts of devotion).

Al-Shaybānī, *Kitāb al-Kasb*, 136

Al-tājiru al-ṣadūq afḍalu ʿinda Allāhi min al-mutʾbid (The honest merchant is superior to the servant).

Al-Ghazālī, *Iḥyāʾ*, vol. 2, 74

3.1 Widening the Scope of Classical Economic and Legal Thought in Islam

This chapter inquires into classical economic thought and its relation to *Sharīʿa* in Islamic tradition. It consists primarily of two parts – the first part deals with the moral cosmology of *Sharīʿa*,[1] including *maqāṣid* and *siyāsa*, whereas the second addresses the economic thought of

[1] The term "moral cosmology" is coined separately from yet in proximity to Hallaq's concept of *mystical Shariʿsm*, for it shows a great degree of contextual similarity. Hallaq's term is clearly congruent with the parameters and the narrative of the "moral cosmology" of Islamic economics, not only in regard to the position of Islamic law but also in reference to Islamic economic teachings. This will be more evident through the analysis of the classical Islamic economic corpus, and also through proposing the epistemological value of Islamic economics (Chapter 5).

classical Muslim scholars. To study the genealogy of economic thought in Islamic tradition, one needs to provide a definition of terminologies of Islamic legal and economic teachings and to scrutinize the correlation between and among them.

The first part of the chapter does not study court proceedings or legal opinions but focuses on a twofold analysis of *Sharīʿa*: first, on the theoretical considerations of *Sharīʿa* as a primarily moral conception in that it maintains an epistemological difference from the ontology of *fiqh* and, second, on classical as well as contemporary authors who have defined and extrapolated the concept of *Sharīʿa* in connection to classical Islamic economic thought. By doing so, I demonstrate that economic behavior and economic processes are in accordance with *Sharīʿa* moral behavioral patterns rather than legal codifications. This approach repudiates the claim that contemporary Islamic economics is based on Islamic legal precepts or that it is enmeshed only in commercial transactions. Even though contemporary theoretical considerations of Islamic economics often invoke commercial laws and ethical postulates, derived from religious sources such as the Qurʾan, the Sunna and (legal) scholarship, contemporary Muslim economists have rarely made in-depth analyses of the classical approaches to economic thought by studying the legal, theological, and Sufi corpus. The pertinent questions, therefore, are these: Have economic ideas in Islamic history flourished semi-independently from the legal normativity[2] of *Sharīʿa*? What kind of epistemic consequences did classical jurisprudential, yet profoundly moral, stipulations have upon economic ideas in Islamic intellectual history? In other words, to what extent and on what grounds does *Sharīʿa* define and legitimize the subject matter of economic thought, given not only legal but primarily moral, theological, and Sufi postulates in classical Islamic milieu?[3]

The second section of this chapter interrogates economic thought in classical Islam. By Islamic economic thought, I refer to economic tradition, moral economy, classical economic thought, economic philosophy in Islamic tradition and so forth, which are profoundly related to the moral cosmology of *Sharīʿa* in how it shaped human conduct in

[2] By the term "normativity," I refer to a standard model to be followed in the view of norms as an authoritative and legally binding set of rules.

[3] The question pertaining to the aim of *Sharīʿa* was posed by, among others, al-Ghazālī (d. 1111) and al-Shāṭibī (d. 1388). See al-Ghazālī, *al-Mustaṣfāʾ*, vol. 1, 116ff; al-Shāṭibī, *al-Muwāfaqāt fī Uṣūl al-Sharīʿa*, ed. ʿAbdullāh al Darrāz (Cairo: n.d.).

economic affairs as pertaining to wider socio-ecologico-metaphysical advancements. Reading classical Muslim scholars, jurists, Sufis, and theologians (and not only *fiqh* manuals) reveals that their economic ideas were embedded in and deduced from the theological and metaphysical understanding of the universe that is closely linked with the social system. Since the pleiad of classical Muslim scholars cannot be introduced in one chapter, the following scholars, in many respects perceived as representatives of economic tradition, will be examined in chronological order according to their main themes and key economic concepts. These are Abū Yūsuf (d. 798), perceived as one of the earliest jurists who wrote on land tax (*kharaj*);[4] Muḥammad bin al-Ḥasan al-Shaybānī (d. 804), a colleague and a student of Abū Yūsuf, a cofounder of the Hanafi school of jurisprudence, the first scholar who treated earning as an wholesome subject, in *Kitāb al-Kasb*,[5] also known as *al-Iktisāb fī al-Rizq al-Mustaṭāb*, and wrote a book on economic provision and law in *Kitāb al-Sijar*; Abū ʿAbd Allāh al-Ḥārith al-Muḥāsibī (d. 857), a renowned theologian and Sufi scholar whose work discusss asceticism, economic contribution, and human welfare; Ibn Abī al-Dunyā (d. 894), a famous *imām*, jurist, and a Muslim scholar who collected ideas on economic behavior from more than 180 teachers in *Iṣlāḥ al-māl*;[6] Abū Ḥamid al-Ghazāli (d. 1111), a follower of the Shāfiʿī school as much as an adherent of the Sufi tradition whose *Kitāb Adāb al-Kasb wa al-Maʿāsh*[7] presents a culmination and a synthesis of economic provision and spiritual qualities; al-Dimashqī, a twelfth-century scholar and merchant from Damascus who wrote *Kitāb al-Isharāh ila Maḥāsin at-Tijārah*, in which he defined an early form of price theory and expressed support for acquiring wealth;[8]

4 Abū Yūsuf, *Kitāb al-Kharaj* (Beirut: Dār al-Maʿrifa, 1979).

5 Muḥammad bin al-Ḥasan al-Shaybānī, *al-Iktisāb fī al-Rizq al-Mustaṭāb* (Beirut: Dār al-Kutub al-ʿIlmiyyah, 1986).

6 Ibn Abī al-Dunyā, *Iṣlāḥ al-Māl* (Beirut: Muʾassasa al-Kutub al-Thaqāfiyya, 1993).

7 al-Ghazālī, *Iḥyāʾ ʿUlūm al-Dīn*; Abū Ḥamid al-Ghazālī, *Mizān al-ʿAmal* (Cairo: Dār al-Maʿārif, 1964); al-Ghazālī, *al-Mustaṣfāʾ*; Abū Ḥamid al-Ghazali, *Nasihat al-Muluk*, trans. F. R. Bagley as *The Book of Counsel for Kings* (Oxford: Oxford University Press, 1964); Abū Ḥamid al-Ghazali, *Kīmiyā-yi Saʿādat (Alchemy of Eternal Bliss)*, trans. Muhammad Asim Bilal (Lahore: Kazi, 2001).

8 Abū al-Faḍl Jaʿfar al-Dimashqī, *Al-Ishārah ilā Maḥāsin al-Tijāra* (Cairo: Maktaba al-Kulliyyat al-Azhariyyah, 1977).

Ibn Taymiyya (d. 1328), a member of the Ḥanbalī school and a source of inspiration for current Orthodox Salafism who wrote on economic provisions and advocated for fair price;[9] Ibn Qayyim al-Jawziyya (d. 1350), a pupil of Ibn Taymiyya who furthered his legal, theological, and economic ideas;[10] Ibn Khaldūn (d. 1404), who belonged to the Māliki school and is often regarded as the father of sociology and the tradition of social sciences;[11] and al-Maqrīzī (d. 1441), a Māliki scholar from Egypt who provided official advices to the Fatimid government.[12] Ideas from,[13] al-Makkī (d. 966),[14] al-Rāghib al-Iṣfahānī (d. 1108), al-Māwardī (d. 1058),[15] Ibn Hazm (d. 1064),[16] al-Shayzarī (d. 1193),[17] Ibn Rushd (d. 1198),[18] and other Muslim ethicists will often accompany the aforementioned scholars in order to substantiate the claim of this chapter.

These figures underwent different forms of training and lived in different eras and geographical regions, which indicates the multivalent legal, sociopolitical, and cultural landscape of these thinkers, as well as the complexity of Islamic economic history. The scholars' writings on ethics, law, and economic ideas will be presented within the context of how they theorized and perceived economic philosophy, its mechanisms, the function of money, the role of *ḥisba*, price control, the value of goods, barter exchange, and the role of governmental authority. While their works can be perceived as an ethical ideal on perfect economic life,

9 Ibn Taymiyya, *al-Ḥisba fī al-Islām* (Cairo: Dār al-Sha'b, 1976), translated into English by Muhtar Holland as *Public Duties in Islam: The Institution of the Hisbah* (Leicester: Islamic Foundation, 1982); Ibn Taymiyya, *Majmū' Fatāwā Shaykh al-Islām Ahmad Ibn Taymiyya* (Al-Riyad: Matabi` al-Riyad, 1963).

10 Ibn Qayyim al-Jawziyya, *Zād al-Ma'ād* (Beirut: Dār al-Kitāb al-'Arabī, 1982).

11 Ibn Khaldūn, *Muqaddima* (Beirut: Dār al-Fikr, 1967).

12 Muḥammad 'Alī al-Maqrīzī, *Ighāthah al-Ummah bi Kashf al-Ghummah* (Cairo: 'Ayn al-Dirāsāt al-Ba'ūth al-Insāniyya wa al-Ijtimā'iyya, 2007); Adel Allouche, *Mamluk Economics: A Translation and Study of al-Maqrizi's Ighāthah* (Salt Lake City: University of Utah Press, 1994); al-Maqrīzī, *Kitāb al-Sulūk* (Cairo: Lajna al-Ta'lif wa al-Tarjama, 1956).

13 Al-Muḥāsibī, *al-Makāsib wa al-Wara'* (Beirut: Mu'ssasa al-Kutub al-Thaqāfiyya, 1987).

14 Al-Makkī, *Qūt al-Qulūb* (Beirut: Daar al-Kutub al-'Ilmiyyah, 1997); Saeko Yazaki, *Islamic Mysticism and Abū Ṭālib al-Makkī* (New York: Routledge, 2013).

15 Al-Māwardī, *Al-Aḥkām al-Sulṭāniyyah* (Cairo: al-Bābī al-Ḥalabī, 1973).

16 Ibn Hazm, *Al-Muhalla* (Egypt: Matba'a al-Nahdah, 1928 [AH 1347]), vol. 2.

17 'Abd al-Raḥmān bin Naṣr al-Shayzarī, *Aḥkām al-Ḥisba* (Beirut: Dār al-Thaqāfa, n.d.).

18 Ibn Rushd, *Bidāyat al-Mujtahid* (Beirut: Dār al-Ma'rifa, 1988).

nonetheless they write about righteous economic behavior which can be read as espousing a subtle critique of governmental authority and the religious circles of the time. I will extrapolate their main ideas and concepts pertinent to the chapter's narrative, such as *Sharīʿa*, *akhlāq* (the role of ethical conduct in trading activity), *tasʿīr* (price control), *zuhd* (renunciation or abstinence), and *maṣlaḥa* (the concept of public good). Instead of focusing on individual authors, the chapter will be structured according to the main similarities, differences, and economic ideas those authors invoked in their works. By doing so, the chapter aims not only to show the interconnectedness and flow of economic ideas across time and space but also the intricate relation between *Sharīʿa*'s moral cosmology and economic activities. Despite the fact that classical scholars, given their various backgrounds, often invoked Islamic legal philosophy of the four major Sunni schools of law and applied different approaches to the same economic matters, I argue that the ethical intricacy rooted in *Sharīʿa's* moral cosmology reigned supreme.

3.2 *Sharīʿa*'s Legal Supremacy versus Moral Cosmology

The term *akhlāq*, translated nowadays as ethics, was associated with classical (Qurʾanic) exegesis and closely interwoven into the systematic theology or *kalām*.[19] The Qurʾan provided Muslim society with natural

[19] Islamic ethics is being defined as *akhlāq* (plural of *khuluq*), which would be translated as character or disposition. The word *akhlāq* has a very close relationship with the word *khāliq* (the Creator) and *makhlūq* (created). The term *khuluq* appears in the Qurʾanic verse (68:4) and it has been regarded as the predicament of the soul that determines human deeds and its consequences. *ʿIlm al-akhlāq* as the science of the human soul pertains to qualities and to methods of maintaining and nurturing them. The task of classical ethicists was to discern concepts such as good, bad, virtue, obligation, and responsibility through the idea of God, the Hereafter, and the Qurʾanic revelation. In this sense, Islamic ethics is not disassociated from Islamic metaphysics. See Abdul Haq Ansari, "Islamic Ethics: Concepts and Prospects," *American Journal of Islamic Social Sciences*, vol. 6, no. 1, (1989): 81–91. "What is 'legal' in the Qurʾān and in the Sharīʿa that was based on it is also equally 'moral' and vice versa. In fact, we might even reverse the modern bias and argue (conceding for the moment to modern vocabulary) that the legal was an organically derivative category of the moral, the latter being the archetype .... The Qurʾānic moral arsenal was thus embedded in a holistic system of belief, in a cosmology that *comprised* a metaphysic ... this cosmology was itself part of an enveloping moral system that transcended the categories of theology, theosophy, and metaphysics." (Hallaq, *Impossible State*, 83); see also Ibn Manẓūr, *Lisān al-ʿArab* (Qom: Adab al-Hawza, 1984), al-Ghazālī, *Iḥyāʾ* Vol. 3 and 4.

laws and a new cosmology enhancing a moral system that transcended purely legal categories, for it was "constructed out of the moral fiber."[20] The *Sharīʿa's* moral principles are not technical or legal in nature, "but hearken back to the epistemic and psychological technologies of the moral subject."[21] According to such an understanding, human deeds are carried out in accordance with a particular worldview,[22] and economic behavior should primarily have an ethical deliberation and consequence. Despite the fact that the subject of *fiqh* has always been *Sharīʿa*,[23] *fiqh* and *Sharīʿa* are nonequivalent, for the latter is as Divine law encapsulated in the Qurʾan,[24] while the former is the body of Islamic law extracted from detailed sources, which are studied and interpreted by learned men as the principles of Islamic jurisprudence. Economic activities in the works of the aforementioned scholars tend to surpass purely legal precepts, because they are as much theological in nature as they are moral. As we shall see in the following paragraphs, concepts such as common good (*maṣlaḥa*), charity (*ṣadaqa*), and alms-tax (*zakāt*), and institutions such as charitable trust funds (*waqf*), supervision of markets, purchases and commodities (*ḥisba*), fiscal policy (*bayt al-māl*), social benefits, and others, despite their legal effect, were also analyzed by classical Muslim scholars within the

20 Hallaq, "Groundwork of the Moral Law," 259.

21 Hallaq, *Impossible State*, 152.

22 For instance, according to Toshihiko Izutsu, the moral code is one component of the overall ideology, embedded into the linguistic system, and therefore represents a certain worldview (*Weltanschauung*) and interprets it accordingly. See Toshihiko Izutsu, *Ethico-Religious Concepts in the Qurʾan* (Montreal: McGill-Queen's University Press, 2002), 12, in Mohamed Aslam Haneef and Hafas Furqani, "Developing the Ethical Foundations of Islamic Economics: Benefitting from Toshihiko Izutsu," *Intellectual Discourse*, vol. 17, no. 2 (2009): 176.

23 According to Shalakany, Islamic law is *Sharīʿa* due to its own subject matter. See Amr. A. Shalakany, "Islamic Legal Histories," *Berkeley Journal of Middle Eastern & Islamic Law*, vol. 1 (2008): 5.

24 For more on the orientalist understanding of *Shariʿa* as being detached from *fiqh* rules, see the legal history of Islam: Joseph Schacht, *An Introduction to Islamic Law* (Oxford: Clarendon Press, 1982); N. J. Coulson, *A History of Islamic Law* (Chicago, IL: Aldine Transaction, 1994). On the overall moral character of *Sharīʿa*, see e.g. Hallaq, *Sharīʿa*. On the history of Islamic legal thought, see e.g. Wael Hallaq, "From Fatwas to Furu: Growth and Change in Islamic Substantive Law," *Islamic Law and Society*, vol. 1, no. 1 (1994): 29–65; Mohammad Fadel, "The Social Logic of Taqlīd and the Rise of the Mukhataṣar," *Islamic Law and Society*, vol. 3, no. 2 (1996): 193–233; ʿAli Jumʿa, *Al-Naskh ʿinda al-Uṣūliyyīn* (Cairo: Nahḍat Miṣr li al-Ṭibāʿa wa al-Nashr wa al-Tawzīʿ, 2004), 9–13, 23–37, 41–42, 45–46, 49–88.

fields of theology, philosophy, Islamic mysticism, policy-oriented governance (*siyāsa Sharʿiyā*), and moral cosmology embedded in the Qurʾanic conceptions of *ʿadl*, *ʿilm*, and *ʿamal* and their human exposition, and not exclusively via commercial laws or transactions (*muʿāmalāt*), or rather that commercial laws were ingrained in an ethical understanding of the economic world. Classical Muslim scholars would derive and deduce legal rulings on micro and macro levels on economic ideas. Hence translating *Sharīʿa* simply as Islamic law would be incorrect, since *Sharīʿa* encompasses more than only legal rulings.[25]

Many classical Muslim scholars, among others, al-Shaybānī, al-Rāghib al-Iṣfahānī, and al-Ghazālī, perceive *Sharīʿa* as the Divine code of conduct, often interpreted as a submission of oneself to the will of God by confirming the Divine Unity of existence. *Sharīʿa* in the Arabic language means "path to the well," or within the context of Islam, "path to God."[26] According to Frank Griffel, "Islamic religious law" is an approximate translation of the term *Sharīʿa*.[27] In classical Arabic the word *Sharīʿa* referred to the law of God obtained through revelation, and it evolved as a technical term in the early period of Islamic history, depicting the practical aspect of the religion of Islam.[28] Throughout the history of Islamic law, *Sharīʿa* has been central to understanding Islamic legal and religious principles.[29] The four basic Sunni Islamic schools of law – Ḥanafī, Mālikī, Shāfiʿī, and Ḥanbalī[30] –

25 Muhammad Khalid Masud, "Muslim Jurists' Quest for the Normative Basis of Shariʿa," inaugural lecture (Leiden, International Institute for the Study of Islam in the Modern World, 2001), 2; *Shariʿa* cannot be simply equated to a book of law; it is, rather, a highly complex system of norms, codes, ethical stipulations, and their interpretations, see Rohe, *Das Islamische Recht*, 15. In this light, epistemic is a priori moral in the context of *Shariʿa*. See also Wael Hallaq, "God's Word: Between the Intentional and the Political," lecture (Institute for Religion, Culture and Public Life, Columbia University, February 13, 2015). See also the Qurʾan, e.g. 42:13; 5:97; 45:1–7.

26 See e.g. Khorchide, *Scharia*, 72–81; al-Rāghib al-Iṣfahānī, *Kitāb al-Dharīʿa ilā Makārim al-Sharīʿa* (Cairo: Dār al-Salām, 2007).

27 Abbas Amanat and Frank Griffel, eds., *Shariʿa: Islamic Law in the Contemporary Context* (Stanford, CA: Stanford University Press, 2007), 2.

28 See the Qurʾan, 45:1.

29 See al-Ghazālī, *al-Mustaṣfāʾ*; Ibn ʿĀshūr, *Maqāṣid al-Sharīʿah al-Islāmiyyah*; Ibn ʿĀshūr, *Treatise on Maqāsid al-Sharīʿa*, trans. Muhammad al-Tahir el Mesawi (Washington, DC: IIIT, 2006).

30 Masud states that, according to Abu Zayd, al-Shāfiʿī's *Risāla* was primarily a treatise on epistemology and not the methodology of Islamic law. See Masud, "'Classical' Islamic Legal Theory As Ideology: Nasr Abu Zayd's Study of al-Shafiʿi's *Risala*," draft.

agree that the four fundamental sources of *Sharīʿa* are the Qurʾān, the Sunna, *ijmāʿ* or consensus, and *qiyās* or analogy.[31] This would indicate that Islamic economic thought is derived indirectly from the Qurʾan and the Sunna, as these texts present the basis of juridical literature. However, the *fuqahāʾ* (legal specialists) in the classical period mainly established the judicial system (social, financial, public, private, penal, matrimonial articles of law), reflecting the ethical teachings of the Qurʾan. The legal reading of economic postulates presumes that economic thought is one of the subsystems of *Sharīʿa* and, in consequence, partakes in the interaction of all the subsystems as well as in the main system of *tawḥīd*, being the core of the discourse.[32]

Sharīʿa as God's law relates to the Islamic law (*fiqh*) and legal stipulations (*aḥkām*). Nonetheless, legal theory did not designate law but rather how to carry out law, hence it was not only prescriptive but also descriptive, providing juristic methodology and a hermeneutics to utilize the four sources of *Sharīʿa*.[33] In this light, *Sharīʿa* is, rather, Divine assessments of human conduct (*ḥukm*) and deals with human conduct, but it was often misunderstood as legal injunction and does not necessarily rest upon one's appropriation of it.[34] Interpreting how

[31] *Qiyās* or analogy denotes something that has common characteristics or the same value. Literally, *qiyās* means measuring or ascertaining the physical shape of something. In Islamic law, technically it means an extension of a *Sharīʿa* value from an original example or situation to a new case. On the historical development of Islamic law, see Rohe, *Das Islamische Recht*, 43–72.

[32] "It is important to distinguish between the concept of Sharīʿa as the totality of the duty of Muslims and any particular perception of it through a specific human methodology of interpretation of the Qurʾān and Sunna .... It should also be emphasized that Sharʿī principles are always derived from human interpretation of the Qurʾān and Sunna; they are what human beings can comprehend and seek to obey within their own specific historical context. It was a pre-Islamic Arab practice to distribute any surplus of property (faḍl al-mal) for social and charitable purposes. The Prophet applied this principle, which the jurists later thought to be his practice. And inasmuch as it was considered a Prophetic Sunna, it became part of the Shariʿa." Wael Hallaq, *A History of Islamic Legal Theories* (Cambridge: Cambridge University Press, 1997), 13. See also Shelomo Dov Goitein, *Studies in Islamic History and Institutions* (Leiden: E. J. Brill, 1966), 92–94.

[33] Hallaq, *Sharīʿa*, 74.

[34] I discuss this correlation in Al-Daghistani, "Semiotics of Islamic Law, Maṣlaḥa, and Islamic Economic Thought," 401. Thomas Bauer states that classical Islamic works on Islamic law reveal a high level of probability theories (*Wahrscheinlichkeittheorie*) of the Divine law, aiming to frame the law within the parameters of *Sharīʿa*. According to Bauer, this attempt was not always

jurists came to deduce these *aḥkām* from the religious scripts has been the task of *uṣūl al-fiqh*, the roots of the law or rather legal hermeneutical methodology,[35] which is in essence an endeavor of the learned to understand and interpret the sources of the law.[36] For Hallaq, "*usūl al-fiqh*'s whole purpose is universally acknowledged to be the prescription/description of a methodology by means of which legal rulings can be derived from the sources."[37]

The science of applying *Sharī'a* was developed in the classical period and is called *fiqh*.[38] *Fiqh* is the legal and ethical system that measures and foresees relations between individuals in society whose "notion of legal capacity is based on the concept of the rational actor."[39] Al-Ghazālī already in the twelfth century stated that "Fiqh in its original linguistic usage, means knowledge and understanding .... But in the convention of the *'ulamā*, it has come to specifically express knowledge of the *Sharī'a* rules, which have been established for [qualifying] the acts of the loci of obligation."[40] He further emphasized that, in its early phase, *fiqh* constituted part of the science of the Hereafter (*'ilm ṭarīq al-ākhira*) as an ethical

successfully applied, because *fiqh* dealt predominantly with socioeconomic, political, and administrative issues, however, it always maintained its theological resonance (Bauer, *Die Kultur der Ambiguität*, 158).

35 Generally, on the legal science al-Ghazālī holds that "the universal science among the religious disciplines is theology. But other sciences, such as jurisprudence, its principles, hadith, and tafsir are particular sciences." Ahmad Zakī Mansūr Ḥammād, "Abu Hamid al-Ghazali's Juristic Doctrine in al-Mustasfa min 'ilm al'usūl" (PhD dissertation, vol. 2, University of Chicago, 1987), 310. See also al-Ghazālī, *Iḥyā'*, vol. 1, 12–40.

36 For more on ad hoc solutions to legal issues, legal transplants, and other legal modifications see Hallaq, "From Fatawas to Furu,"; E. Tyon, "Judicial Organization," in *Law in the Middle East*, ed. Majid Khadduri and H. J. Liebesny (Washington, DC: Middle East Institute, 1955), 236–278.

37 Wael Hallaq, "Was al-Shafi'i the Master Architect of Islamic Jurisprudence?," *International Journal of Middle East Studies*, vol. 25, no. 4 (1993): 592. See also al-Shāfi'ī, *al-Imām Muḥammad Idris al-Shāfi'ī's al-Risāla fī uṣūl al-fiqh: Treatise on the Foundations of Islamic Jurisprudence*, trans. Majid Khadduri (Cambridge, UK: Islamic Text Society, 1997).

38 See Harald Motzki, *Die Anfänge der islamischen Jurisprudenz: ihre Entwicklung in Mekka bis zur Mitte des 2./8. Jahrhunderts* (Stuttgart: Steiner, 1991); Hallaq, *Origins and Evolution of Islamic Law*; Mohammad Hashim Kamali, *Shari'ah Law: An Introduction* (Oxford: Oneworld, 2008).

39 Johansen, "Changing Limits of Contingency in the History of Muslim Law," 33. See also Baber Johansen, "Das islamische Recht," *Die islamische Welt*, vol. 1 (1984): 129–145.

40 Ḥammād, "Abu Hamid al-Ghazali's Juristic Doctrine in al-Mustasfa min 'ilm al'usūl," 307; al-Ghazālī, *Iḥyā'*, vol. 1, 32.

system, and that only later on has it become a specialized branch of legal opinions, exhibiting a technical aspect of legal rules. Specialists and legal authorities produced *fiqh* works concerned with moral behavior and legal practice in many Muslim lands in which *Sharīʿa* was considered the law until the collapse of the Ottoman Empire in the early twentieth century. Yet, law understood as binding rules of conduct would insufficiently describe *Sharīʿa*, since "there were no documents . . . and no commentaries that one could refer to as 'the law'. Rather, *Sharīʿa* was a practice and a process of deriving law and of adjudicating disputes."[41] It has been in this sense interconnected with moral behavior, encompassing various fields of human endeavors.[42]

Fiqh can be taken as understanding[43] the religion and its sources; hence *fiqh* law is not only legislated but first and foremost understood

41 "Law was established not by issuing legal codes or by the decision of principal authorities such as high courts or central administration, but rather by the rules of its legal discourse . . .. Before the nineteenth century *Shariʿa* was never understood as an abstract code, but rather as a series of commentaries on particular practices and of commentaries upon those commentaries." (Amanat and Griffel, eds., *Shariʿa*, 4). On the Sunni legal discourse and tradition, see Norman Calder, "The Limits of Islamic Orthodoxy," in *Intellectual Traditions in Islam*, ed. Farhad Daftary (London: I. B. Tauris, 2000), 66–68. On the absence of the term *Sharīʿa* in Islamic legal discourse, see Bauer, *Die Kultur der Ambiguität*, 185.

42 According to Griffel, who is not a legal specialist, *Sharīʿa* does not play an important role in the Qurʾan and it appears only three time in the Qurʾanic text. Griffel also maintains that *Sharīʿa* always distinguished law from morality: "In principle, at least, traditional Shariʿa always made a distinction between law and morality. Unlike European jurisprudence, however, where the law is taught in its own faculty and where morality is a branch of philosophy and the humanities, the practice of Shariʿa includes all branches of normative human behavior." (Amanat and Griffel, eds., *Shariʿa*, 8). On the other hand, Hallaq states that the legal and the moral realm in the classical period were intertwined and interconnected, and thus the two epistemic systems were not separated: "Neither Muslim jurists nor Muslim intellectuals at large have – until the twentieth century – made any distinction between the legal and moral components of Islamic law. The punitive character of the obligatory and forbidden and the absence of this characteristic from the other three categories failed to engender a distinction between the moral and strictly legal, a phenomenon that should prompt us to wonder why Muslim jurists failed (if indeed they did) to realize the typological significance of this fact. To answer this question we must first understand that, by its very nature, Islam – both as a worldview and as an intellectual system – made no real distinction between the legal and the moral on the grounds that morality and ethics were never perceived an anything less than integral to the law." (Hallaq, *Sharīʿa*, 85).

43 One of the earliest Islamic legal scholars, Abū Hanīfah (d. 767), stated that understanding (*fiqh*) of religion (*dīn*) is better than understanding customs

as the term itself indicates. A closer look at *fiqh* science makes clear that one cannot study Islamic law without engaging in Islamic theology and that Islamic law has to be studied also through its moral implications. Therefore, the correlation between the mundane and the Divine realm is managed by understanding (*fiqh*) rather than by actual statutes (*hudūd*). This further presupposes that economic (mis)behavior falls into the realm of ethical considerations and not necessarily under the category of legal prescriptions. If one defines one's relation to God based exclusively on juridical concepts, one will inevitably diminish the gist of that relation, namely the personal correlation to God.[44] A legal understanding of a rule can overshadow its spiritual, emotional, and intellectual conditionings. "If religiosity is defined as compliance to juridical assertions, then it pushes in the background not only the contemplative Heart, but also the human freedom and therefore genuine moral conduct, in which morality is affirmed as self-commitment from the inner-most."[45] This understanding diminishes the totality of Islamic tradition to its judicial interpretation, instead of nurturing the cosmological essence of human behavior that pertains also to economic matters. In this constellation, the God–human relation is of utmost significance and is divided into two categories. The first illustrates this relation along the line of a top-down approach, whereby the human being as recipient carries out commands and laws, whereas the second category describes the God–human relation according to spiritual devotion and emotional intelligence.[46]

Such a perspective indicates that classical economic philosophy was not regulated exclusively juridically but rather was understood metaphysically and cosmologically. As asserted by many contemporary

(*ʿUrf*) and legal statutes (*al-hadd*). See e.g. Abū Hanīfah, *Al-Fiqh al-Akbar*, trans. Ali Ghandour (Istanbul: Kalbi Kitaplar, 2009).

44 "Denn wenn man seine Beziehung zu Gott über juristische Kategorien definiert, braucht man zwangslöfig einen Juristen, der einen über die Urteile Gottes aufklärt. Dann ist es aber vorbein mit einer direkten persönlichen Beziehung zu Gott." (Khorchide, *Scharia*, 15).

45 "Wenn Religiosität aber als Befolgung von juristischen Aussagen definiert wird, rückt nicht nur das Herzin den Hintergrund, sondern auch die Freiheit des Menschen und damit eine aufrichtige moralische Haltung, in der Moralität von Innen als Selbstverpflichtung bestimmt wird." (Khorchide, *Scharia*, 17; my translation).

46 The two categories cannot be exclusive but are, understandably, intertwined and interdependent.

Muslim economists,[47] Islamic economics is ingrained within Islamic law, yet it appears that contemporary Muslim economists distinguish it from the epistemic value of the very moral cosmology, which deals with metaphysical as well as worldly matters. *Sharīʿa* moral guidelines undeniably form the gist of economic matters in Islamic tradition, covering issues related to food, clothing, money utilization, purchase of commodities, and many others, and also stem from Qurʾanic ethical teachings.[48] Invoking classical scholarship on economic teachings, philosophy, and behavior patterns signifies that it does not rest solely upon Islamic legal precepts, since economic problems are distinct and cannot be resolved only by *fiqh* rules.[49] In other words, despite the importance of legal norms when performing economic activities, which (in)directly relate to the corpus of Islamic law and thus clearly point to the spiritual character of such conduct, claiming the "legal supremacy" of Islamic economics, namely that it intrinsically maintains a legal character, might be misleading.[50] Legal systems are rational when they are not subservient to various social, political, or theological elements. Due to the moral predicates of Islamic law,[51] it has always maintained a rational character, in spite of being grounded in the religious and ethical values of the Qurʾan.[52] Only continuous and

[47] See Chapter 2 of this book and the works of e.g. Choudhury, Chapra, Siddiqi, M. A. Khan.

[48] "And [they are] those who, when they spend, do so not excessively or sparingly but are ever, between that, [justly] moderate" (Qurʾan, 25:67); "but Allah has permitted trade and forbidden usury," (Qurʾan, 2:275); "man is violent in the love of wealth" (Qurʾan, 100:8).

[49] Ahmed, "Scientific Approach to Islamic Economics," 19–58.

[50] It has been argued that only 80 out of 6,236 verses in the Qurʾan can be described as juridical assertions dealing with the social order. See Khorchide, *Scharia*, 83. The Qurʾan contains only 228 verses that deal with legal precepts. See N. J. Coulson *Introduction to Islamic Law* (Edinburgh: Edinburgh University Press, 1964), 34, in Hallaq "Groundwork of the Moral Law," 244.

[51] On the relation between theological and legal, see e.g. Rüdiger Lohlker, *Islamisches Recht* (Wien: Facultas wuv, 2011), 99–116; on the moral understanding of *fiqh*, see e.g. al-Ghazālī, *al-Mustaṣfā*, Vol. 1.; al-Ghazālī, *Iḥyāʾ*, Vol. 1, 32.

[52] John Walbridge, *God and Logic in Islam: The Caliphate of Reason* (Cambridge: Cambridge University Press, 2011), 3. Max Weber, for instance, stated that Islamic law can never attain full rationalization due to its link to sacred institutions. While the bourgeoisie and its interests were inextricably linked with the development of European laws, this connection cannot be traced in Islamic societies as Islamic law was bound to bourgeois elements only in terms of commerce and trading. Islamic law was thus for him inconducive to capitalism

constant reciprocity between Islam as a historic phenomenon and Muslim society as a living experience can reassess the legal superiority in Islamic tradition.[53]

3.3 *Maqāsid, Istiḥsān, Maṣlaḥa,* and Economic Preservation in *Sharīʿa*

In order to examine classical economic doctrine, the discourse on *maqāṣid al-Sharīʿa*, or the objectives of Islamic law – along with *istiḥsān*, translated as equity, *istiṣlāḥ*, and *maṣlaḥa*, as common or public good or general well-being – is of particular relevance. Concerning *Sharīʿa* discourse as a source of economic thought, those terms advocate, among other elements, economic preservation and can be used as a vehicle for a legal change.[54] *Maṣlaḥa* appears to be an important tool in achieving a higher degree of economic justice, in spite of the fact that it has been primarily discussed within the parameters of Islamic law and legal discourse. Research on economic preservation and *maṣlaḥa* raises the following questions: What type of economic ideas does *maṣlaḥa* propose and how has it been incorporated into economic reasoning? As the core of ethical teachings of *Sharīʿa*, how can it be utilized in contemporary Islamic economics and what type of reading does it propose? Furthermore, since Islamic economic thought cannot be equated only with legal maxims and juridical underpinnings, how can the preservation of wealth be applied in real-time society via ethical considerations?[55]

in that it protected the institution of contract, stipulated ethical economic conduct, and prescribed certain economic activities, despite the fact that premodern capitalistic endeavors, such as pursuing profit, did exist in medieval Islamic societies. See Patricia Crone, "Weber, Islamic Law, and the Rise of Capitalism," in *Max Weber and Islam*, ed. Toby E. Huff and Wolfgang Schluchter (New Brunswick, NJ: Transaction Publishers, 1999), 254.

53 A reform of Islamic law can enhance the life of Muslims according to the Qurʾan (Khorchide, *Scharia*, 125).

54 On *maṣlaḥa* as a legal change, see Opwis, Felicitas, "Maslaha in Contemporary Islamic Legal Theory," *Islamic Law and Society*, vol. 12, no. 2, (2005): 182–223.

55 Abdullah al-Naʾim, discussing the abstractness of the objectives of the law, observes that "A modified version of the same argument asserts that all that is required is to observe the basic objectives or purposes of *Sharīʿa* (*Maqāṣid al-Sharīʿa*), while *fiqh* principles are subject to change from one time or place to another. But the problem with this view is that the so-called basic objectives of *Shariʿa* are expressed at such a high level of abstraction that they are neither

3.3.1 Maqāṣid al-Sharī'a *and* Maṣlaḥa

Certain concepts that were used historically by the aforementioned classical Muslim scholars and that relate to public good and provision of wealth can assist us in understanding the relation between Islamic law and the (economic) well-being of society. Numerous classical Muslim scholars perceived economic ideas as part of the Islamic theology of *kalām*, and the Sufi tradition from which they derived juridical rules.[56] They invoked theological, philosophical, and Sufi sources of knowledge when discussing legal and economic precepts to tackle various *Sharī'a*-stipulated questions. *Maqāṣid al-Sharī'a* provides norms for legal rulings and social welfare and can be seen as Divine intents and moral concepts dealing with justice, social welfare, human dignity, and preservation.[57]

One of the aims of *maqāṣid* is that it yields what is desirable and good for the general public and aims to reduce what can potentially harm the society. The five categories or universals, which are interdependent and intertwined, present the moral law of *Sharī' a* because of an inductive reasoning: "The very principle of property rights and the acquisition, maintenance, and dispensation of wealth were all at once regulated by a dialectic of spiritual, metaphysical, and worldly considerations."[58] Scholars such as Ibn Qayyim al-Jawziyya claim that *maqāṣid* is the core of *Sharī'a*[59] and based upon its principles. The objectives of Islamic law evolved after the companion era, however, the meanings behind the objectives as we know them nowadays were introduced much later, during the eleventh–fifteenth centuries (AD). *Maqāṣid* literally means

distinctly Islamic nor sufficiently specific for the purposes of public policy and legislation. As soon as these principles are presented in more specific and concrete terms, they will be immediately implicated in the familiar controversies and limitations of *fiqh*." Abdullahi Ahmed An-Na'im, *Islam and the Secular State: Negotiating the Future of Shari'a* (Cambridge, MA: Harvard University Press, 2008). This holds true also for applying *maqasid* in economic domains. For more on the application of the objectives of the law to economic science, see Chapra, *Islamic Vision of Development in the Light of Maqasid al-Shari'a*; Khan, "Fiqh Foundations of the Theory of Islamic Economics."

56 Al-Ghazālī, *Iḥyā'*, vol. 2, 60.

57 For Jasser Auda, the objectives of the *Sharī'a* were presented by different Islamic scholars; traditionally, *maqāṣid* did not include the notion of justice. This concept was extracted from *fiqh* literature and was not deduced from studying the original sources, Jasser Auda, *Maqāsid al-Sharī'a: An Introductory Guide* (Herndon, VA: IIIT, 2008), 1, 4.

58 Hallaq, *Impossible State*, 148–149.

59 See Ibn Qayyim al-Jawziyya, *Zād al-Ma'ād* (1982).

purpose, objective, principle, or intent,[60] and pertains to the wisdom and ethical means of the rulings.[61] Anything that directly or indirectly implies the preservation of the five categories, namely of life, faith, intellect, preservation, and wealth, can be considered as *maṣlaḥa*.

The concept of *maṣlaḥa* as part of the higher objectives is important yet neglected[62] when discussing the nature of economic endeavors in contemporary Islamic economic thought. Despite the fact that it is certainly not the only tool in delineating economic behavior (in addition to *adab*, *kasb*, *zuhd*, and other conceptualizations), it does provide grounds for further research on the subject. Islamic ethical perception in economic thought advocates the idea of regulating wants as *maṣlaḥa* leads to the concept of fulfilling needs. *Maṣlaḥa* contains the immutable principles of *Sharīʿa* that are meant to levitate and enhance the public good, and because the principles of *Sharīʿa* are contained in *maṣlaḥa*, it does not restrict itself only to legal reasoning. The *Sharīʿa* principles reinforce *maṣlaḥa* as the overall benefit by balancing needs and wants, whereby *maṣlaḥa* as a core mechanism of *maqāṣid al-Sharīʿa* frames new rules.[63] Derived from the word *ṣalaḥ*, which means reform, it has been defined according to overall benefit to society. The concept of *maṣlaḥa* has been introduced to Islamic legal science, and it was laid down by al-Juwaynī, al-Ghazālī, al-Ṭūfī,[64] and Ibn al-Jawziyya, to name but a few scholars. The following thinkers,

60 Jasser Ouda, *Maqāsid al-Sharīʿa* (Herndon, VA: al-M'had al-ʿālami lil fikr al-islāmī, 2012); Auda, *Maqāsid al-Sharīʿa: An Introductory Guide.*

61 Ibn ʿĀshūr, *Maqāṣid al-Sharīʿah al-Islāmiyyah*, 182–183.

62 Only Chapra and Siddiqi briefly analyze *maṣlaḥa* in their works in relation to economic preservation.

63 Muhammad Khalid Masud, *Shatibi's Philosophy of Islamic Law* (Islamabad: Islamic Research Institute, International Islamic University, 1995), 120.

64 "Whereas the majority of jurists do not allow recourse to istislah in the presence of a textual ruling, a prominent Ḥanbalī jurist, Najm al-Din al-Ṭūfī, stands out for his view which authorises recourse to maslahah with or without the existence of nass. In a treatise entitled al-Masalih al-Mursalah, which is a commentary on the Hadith that 'no harm shall be inflicted or reciprocated in Islam', al-Ṭūfī argues that this Hadith provides a clear nass in favour of maslahah. It enshrines the first and most important principle of Shariʿah and enables maslahah to take precedence over all other considerations. Al-Ṭūfī precludes devotional matters, and specific injunctions such as the prescribed penalties, from the scope of maslahah. In regard to these matters, the law can only be established by the *naṣ* and *ijmāʿ*." (Najm al-Dīn al-Ṭūfī, *Risālat fī Riʿāyat al-Maṣlaḥah*, 139, in Kamali, *Principles of Islamic Jurisprudence*, 242). See also, Najm ad-Dīn Abū al-Rabīʿ Sulaimān ibn ʿAbd al-Qawī al-Ṭūfī, *Kitāb at-Taʿyīn fī Sharḥ al-Arbaʿīn* (Beirut: al-Rayyān, 1998).

who are perceived as representatives of Sunni schools of law, have made seminal contributions to the field of Islamic law and economics, and are in turn referred to by contemporary Muslim scholars, will be briefly studied here. Al-Juwaynī conceptualized the term *maṣlaḥa*; Abū Ḥamid al-Ghazālī was al-Juwaynī's pupil, a famous theologian, a Sufi, and a member of the Shāfiʿi school, who wrote on *maṣlaḥa* as well as economic activities; in addition, al-Shaybānī and al-Shāfiʿi appear of great relevance for their contributions not only to Islamic jurisprudence but also to economic conduct as it traditionally refers to common good or benefit. On the other hand, *maṣlaḥa mursala* refers to unrestricted public interest in the sense that it is not regulated by the jurist, unless textual sources stipulate otherwise.[65]

If *maqāṣid* entails the wisdom behind the legal rulings including social welfare and cohesion, it inevitably addresses one's innermost being – one's mental disposition and moral state that ideally transforms into action-driven conduct through the fulfillment of the ideals of justice, dignity, free will, and social welfare. Since *maṣlaḥa* is the epitome of the overall teachings of *Sharīʿa*, the conception of *maṣlaḥa* in economics and finances can be justified in terms of the protection of economic provision or *ḥifẓ al-māl*,[66] expounding an overall moral character of allocation of wealth, circulation of money, purchases, and so forth. If the objectives (*maqāṣid*) are permanent, the means (*wasāʾil*) to achieve them are changeable, dynamic, and contemporary. Al-Shāfiʿi for instance did not promulgate *maṣlaḥa* in the same way as he repudiated *istiḥsān*;[67] in spite of the fact that each norm has a corresponding purpose, traditionally in Islamic law the norms were not bound with the purpose itself but rather with their reason or inducement (*ʿilla*).[68] This further underlines that religious teachings ought to be in correlation with the social interest and corresponding metaphysical goals.[69] Ibn Qayyim observed that there are two types of *Sharīʿa* that correspond to time and to societal changes:

65 The *hadīth* that provides the material on the subject states, "No harm shall be inflicted or reciprocated to Islam" (Ibn Majah, *Sunan*, *ḥadīth* no. 2340, in Kamali, *Principles of Islamic Jurisprudence*, 235–236).

66 See for instance al-Ghazālī's categorization of *maqāṣid* also in relation to *kasb*: al-Ghazālī, *Iḥyāʾ*, Vol 2 and 4.

67 Khorchide, *Scharia*, 130–135, 137.

68 Khorchide, *Scharia*, 138.

69 For more, see Ibn ʿĀshūr, *Treatise on Maqāsid al-Sharīʿa*; Ahmad al-Raysuni, *Imam al-Shatibi's Theory of the Higher Objectives and Intents of Islamic Law* (Herndon, VA: IIIT, 2005).

Firstly, laws which do not change with the vicissitudes of time and place or the propensities of *ijtihād*, such as the obligatoriness of the *wājibāt* (pl. of *wājib*), or illegality of *muḥarramāt* (pl. of *ḥarām*), the fixed quantities of inheritance and the like. They do not change and no *ijtihād* may be advanced so as to violate the substance and character of the *Sharī'ah* in these areas. The second variety of laws are those which are susceptible to change in accordance with the requirements of public interest (*maṣlaḥah*) and prevailing circumstances, such as the quantum, type, and attribute of deterrent punishments (*al-ta'zīrāt*). The Lawgiver has permitted variation in these in accordance with the dictates and considerations of *maṣlaḥah*.[70]

On another occasion, Ibn Qayyim states that

fiqh is about wisdom and achieving social welfare in this and next life. It is about justice, mercy, wisdom, and that which is good. Hence, any ruling that substitutes justice with injustice, mercy with that which is opposite, wellbeing with mischief, or wisdom with nonsense, is foreign to *fiqh*, even if it is claimed to be its part according to some interpretations.[71]

This further indicates that the jurisprudence and its methodology is grounded on the notion of (social) welfare.

3.3.1.1 Development of *Maqāṣid*, al-Juwaynī, and al-Ghazālī

Al-Juwaynī in the eleventh century deployed *maqāṣid* for his theory on necessities and needs. He coined it by proposing five levels of *maqāṣid*: necessities (*ḍarūriyyāt*), public needs (*al-hājah al-'amah*), moral behavior (*al-makrumāt*), recommendations (*al-mandūbāt*), and specifics.[72] Al-Ghazālī was one of many premodern Muslim scholars who explored the fields of *kalām*, *fiqh*, and *taṣawwuf*, in order to dissect epistemological connotations between the metaphysical worldview and social obligations. He elaborated the *maqāṣid* further in order to provide provision for the well-being of Muslim community, by safeguarding the categories of faith (*dīn*), human self (*nafs*), intellect (*'aql*),

[70] See Ibn Qayyim al-Jawziyya, *Ighathah al-Lahfin*, vol. 1, 346, in Kamali, *Shari'ah Law*, 50.

[71] Ibn Qayyim al-Jawziyya, *I'lām al-Muwaqqi'īn* (Beirut: Dār al-Jīl, 1973), vol. 1, 333.

[72] Abū al-Ma'ālī al-Juwaynī, *Kitāb al-Irshād ilā Qawāṭi' al-Aadilla fī Uṣūl al-I'tiqād*. (Cairo: Maktaba al-Thaqāfiyya al-Dīnīyya, 2009); al-Juwayni, *A Guide to the Conclusive Proofs for the Principles of Belief*, trans. Paul E. Walker (Reading: Garnet, 2001); Ouda, *Maqāsid al-Sharī'a*, 17.

offspring (*nasl*), and wealth (*māl*).[73] It is believed that along with *Iḥyā' 'Ulūm al-Dīn*, al-Ghazālī's most influential book is *Mustaṣfā*, a text on Islamic law and jurisprudence. He is credited as being the first Muslim scholar who introduced the study of Aristotelian logic into the discourse of Islamic jurisprudence, and he furthered his teacher's – al-Juwaynī – contributions in this field. Although it is believed that he based his juridical arguments predominantly upon the Shāfi'ite tradition of Islamic law, composing new terminologies and shaping new discourse on legal matters, al-Ghazālī's writings surpassed the existing legal schools of the time.[74] The early al-Ghazālī differentiated between the overall cosmological nature of the field of theology, which is for him the most rational science, and its subsidiary particular fields of inquiry, such as *ḥadīth* science, exegesis, and law:[75]

> The universal discipline (*al-'ilm al-kullu*) – among the religious disciplines – is theology. The other disciplines such as *fiqh* and its [methodological] foundations, and the transmission from the Prophet, and the exegesis (of revealed texts) are particular, partial [forms of] knowledge .... The sacred law (*shar'*) here brings what reason by itself is unable to comprehend, as reason independently cannot comprehend that obedience [to God] is the cause for happiness in the world to come, and that disobedience is the cause of misery [in the Hereafter].[76]

Al-Ghazālī, although a jurist by traineeship, was theologian and a Sufi, who took a path that allowed him to deftly merge different segments of intellectual traditions with his own capacity to question the religious and political establishment. He initiated new channels of acquiring knowledge, while preserving the core of traditional principles.[77] On the science of *fiqh*, al-Ghazālī states that it constitutes part of the

[73] Al-Juwaynī, *Kitāb al-Irshād 'alā Qawāṭi' al-Adilla fī Uṣūl al-I'tiqād*, vol. 1, 286–287. Prior to al-Ghazālī and al-Juwaynī, al-'Āmirī presented the concepts with which the latter two operated.

[74] See Nakamura Kojiro, "Was Al-Ghazali an Ash'arite," *The Memories of the Toyo Bunko*, vol. 51 (1993): 1–24. Originally published as "Gazali and Ash'arite Theology" in *Isuramu Sekai* (The World of Islam).

[75] Ḥammād, "Abū Ḥāmid al-Ghazālī's Juristic Doctrine in al-Mustaṣfā' min 'Ilm al-usūl," 5.

[76] Ḥammād, "Abū Ḥāmid al-Ghazālī's Juristic Doctrine in al-Mustaṣfā' min 'Ilm al-usūl," 4.

[77] "In Ghazālī and in the entire premodern Islamic tradition, law is embedded in a dialectic not only with social and cultural norms but also, preeminently, with psychology as a mildly mystical realm." (Hallaq, *Impossible State*, 137).

sciences of the Hereafter (*'ilm ṭarīq al-ākhira*), in whose core is the notion of eternal happiness or *sa'āda*, and he warns that its meaning has changed over the centuries. He further notes that *fiqh*

> has become a specialized branch of *fatwas* and *waqfs*, on small details about them, and excessive debates surrounding them .... The meaning of *fiqh* in the first period was, however, undisputedly linked to the science of the path of the hereafter, knowledge of the details of harmful matters of the self, that which corrupts human action, understanding of indulging in the wickedness of the world, perseverance for reaching the grace of the hereafter, and [God's] fear's domination over the heart.[78]

Since the Shāfi'ī school of law also bases its legal reasoning not only on *qiyās*, as indicated in the Qur'an and the Prophetic tradition but on *munāsaba* (suitability), al-Ghazālī utilized this approach to tackle various legal questions in his writings.[79] The jurist has to engage directly with legal, social, and even economic affairs with their practical implications. Per al-Ghazālī's definition then, the science of *fiqh* requires ethical teachings.

For him, one of the overriding, *Sharī'a*-based concepts that includes economic behavior is *maṣlaḥa*, which promotes social welfare of the community.[80] All matters and activities of people have to be seen as a means to achieve goals toward increasing the social welfare. The institution of *maṣlaḥa* concerns individual as well as social needs.[81] Al-Ghazālī not only furthered al-Juwaynī's conception of *maṣlaḥa* but also coined the notion of preservation of the aforementioned five necessities

[78] Al-Ghazālī, *Iḥyā'*, vol. 1, 32, as quoted in Sami Al-Daghistani, *Ethical Teachings of Abū Ḥāmid al-Ghazālī: Economics of Happiness* (London: Anthem Press, 2021), 70.

[79] "No ratio legis may be deemed suitable without being relevant. Any irrelevant ratio becomes, ipso facto, unsuitable, and this precludes it from any further juristic consideration"; "the ultimate goal of suitability is thus the protection of public interest (*maṣlaḥa*) in accordance with the fundamental principles of the law. But in determining the *ratio legis* by the method of suitability, the jurist does not deal directly with the texts, since the ratio is not, strictly speaking, textual. Rather, he infers it through his rational faculty, though it must be in agreement with what may be called the spirit of the law." For more on the notion of *maqāṣid* and al-Ghazālī, see Wael Hallaq, "Maqāṣid and the Challenges of Modernity," *Al-Jāmi'ah*, vol. 49, no. 1 (2011): 5–6.

[80] al-Ghazālī, *Iḥyā'*, vol. 2, 109.

[81] (al-Ghazālī, *al-Mustaṣfā'*, vol. 1, 102; vol. 3, 212–213).

(*al-ḥifẓ*), while repudiating *maṣlaḥa mursala* with the argument that *maṣlaḥa* (as well as *istiḥsān*) cannot be derived from textual sources but rather originates in the discretion of the respective scholars.[82] Al-Ghazālī defined *maṣlaḥa* as observing objectives of the lawgiver and thus as an integral part of *maqāṣid,* which includes the aforementioned five elements.[83] *Maṣlaḥa* as "public good" is inextricably related to *Sharīʿa*, whose key objective is advocating what, according to the Qurʾan, is perceived as good in the mundane and in the Hereafter (*maṣlaḥa al-dīn wa al-dunyā*). According to al-Ghazālī, there are three stages of *maṣlaḥa*: *darūri* or essential, *haji* or complementary, and *taḥsīni* or amelioratory.[84] The basic level of *maṣlaḥa* incorporates five elements, aiming to preserve the dignity of human life or to prevent human beings from being harmed. The first level takes precedence over the second, and the second over the third. Since *maqāsid al-Sharīʿa* appears to be crucial in the development of Islamic law and economic thought, this indicates that an economic agent will try to seek *maṣlaḥa* instead of the notion of utility[85] in a conventional sense. Utility relates to the subjective conceptualization deriving from individual endeavors, whereas *maṣlaḥa* is more amenable to standard ethical verification and pertains also to society as a whole. Individual-based economic endeavors are regarded as undesirable for they do not correspond to the ethical concept of *maṣlaḥa*.[86] Since *maṣlaḥa* leads to fulfilling needs it supports the idea of regulating wants.

82 See al-Ghazālī, *al-Mustaṣfāʿ*, vol. 2, 306ff.
83 See al-Ghazālī, *al-Mustaṣfāʿ*, vol. 1. 84 Ouda, *Maqāsid al-Sharīʿa*, 7.
85 The concept of *falāḥ* can be translated as welfare and could roughly correspond to the Western construction of welfare, which, of course, is absent in *fiqh* literature. Jeremy Bentham (1748–1832) wrote on social utility, which comes from the Latin *utilis*, meaning useful. Bentham used it for utilitarian ethics or utilitarianism to argue that what is useful is good. For Azhar, there is a difference between the institutional mechanism through which Islamic law evolved and Bentham's thought. In Islam, *fiqh* has been an effort of private *fiqh* scholars, a living tradition, whereas for Bentham, it was the institution of government that supposedly performed this task. It appears, however, that the sphere of *fiqh* is much wider than the governmental legislation. The Western conceptualization of law would correspond to *qanūn*, which is only a part of the *fiqh* or rather *Sharīʿa*. (Azhar, *Economics of an Islamic Economy*, 147.) Concomitantly, for Mohammad Fadel, *maqāṣid*, translated as purposivism, has traditionally been devised to serve higher moral objectives (Mohammad Fadel, "Is Islamic Purposivism (*maqāṣid al-sharīʿa*) a Thinly-Disguised Form of Utilitarianism?," accessed on December 28, 2019, https://islamiclaw.blog/2019/09/05/is-islamic-purposivism-maqaṣid-al-shariʿa-a-thinly-disguised-form-of-utilitarianism).
86 Al-Ghazālī, *Iḥyāʾ*, vol. 3, 234; vol. 4, 101.

For al-Ghazālī, *maṣlaḥa* consists of considerations that would secure benefit or prevent harmful deed. Any mechanism that would preserve the values within the scope of *maṣlaḥa*, and anything that would violate those very values, which is considered as *mafsada* (evil), is also *maṣlaḥa*. His notion of *maṣlaḥa* "reconciled between two intellectual approaches in Islamic thought toward moral knowledge, the rationalist and subjectivist position."[87] And since human needs fluctuate, so do the normative patterns that ought to correspond to the former.[88]

3.3.1.2 Al-Shāṭibī, Human Well-Being, and the Flexibility of *Sharī'a*

Al-Shāṭibī advanced al-Juwaynī's and al-Ghazālī's theory and restored what he believed to be the essence of law by pointing to the epistemological principles of the law.[89] The so-called "universals," as five universal principles (*kuliyyāt*), exist in relation to particularities. The aim of the three legal categories relates to *maṣlaḥa*, whose primary aim should be the benefit of the people. "In light of this taxonomy of interests (*maṣālih*) placed in the service of the aims of the law (*maqāṣid*),"[90] as also indicated by al-Shāṭibī, who stated that the very *Shar'ī* rules have been devised to produce *maṣālih* and avoid *mafāsid*.[91] For analyzing legal normativity, al-Shāṭibī suggested the inductive method of approaching the textual sources, as he believed that the core of *Sharī'a* constituted principles of human good. *Maṣālih* encompass the preservation of human life or soul, and one's livelihood, intellectual qualities, religious expression, and procreation or

[87] According to the Mu'tazili school of thought, deeds are inherently good or bad and hence in conjugation with the concept of harm. Following this, a ruling will be legible and correct if and when it permits somethings that is beneficial to an individual or society, and incorrect when it encourages something that is harmful. On the other hand, theistic subjectivism and the Ash'arī school of thought advocated the idea that human intellect is not capable of deriving moral knowledge separately from the Divine commands of the scriptural sources, and thus requires a Divine intervention. Good and bad are hence dependent upon the notion of good and bad according to God alone, His command and prohibition. Despite the fact that theistic subjectivism became the mainstream position of Sunni Islam, it was appropriated with the rationalistic method of human reasoning, making the legal process more arbitrary. See Opwis, "Maslaha in Contemporary Islamic Legal Theory," 188–190.

[88] Khorchide, *Scharia*, 138.

[89] Hallaq, *History of Islamic Legal Theories*, 164–165.

[90] Hallaq, *History of Islamic Legal Theories*, 169.

[91] Al-Shāṭibī, *al-Muwāfaqāt fī Uṣūl al-Sharī' a*, vol. 1, 195.

descendants.[92] He also expounded three stages or rather circles of *maṣlaḥa*: *darūri* or essential, that is innermost, *haji* or complementary, pertaining to the public sphere, and *taḥsīni* or amelioratory, relevant to societal practices and conduct. It is important to note that since there is no *maṣlaḥa* as such, the definition and value of *maṣlaḥa* is based on the prevalence of benefit that results from it.[93] Al-Shāṭibī formed an important element, pertinent to the *maqāṣid*: since there is a danger of missing the objectives behind the interpreted texts if translated word for word, they have to be approached from an overall standpoint in regard to the objectives, for textual sources themselves do not provide rulings. If religious teachings serve the fulfillment of human necessities, classification of what is allowed or forbidden is always associated with the fulfillment of one's needs.[94] This indicates that *maṣlaḥa* does not exist on its own and that religious norms are never objectives of themselves but are in the service of fulfilling societal needs and achieving moral ends. When the Qur'an dispenses indications of rule or conduct, for al-Shāṭibī this suggests a quest for better understanding (*fiqh*) of the underlined religious propositions,[95] including sale contracts, prohibition of (excessive) usury, ownership rights, and other forms of contract. His approach to legal knowledge (*ʿilm Sharʿī*) asserts that licit *ʿilm* leads to *ʿamal*.

3.3.2 Istiḥsān *and* Istiṣlāḥ

Maṣlaḥa is closely associated with *istiḥsān* and *istiṣlāḥ*, too. *Istiḥsān* was developed by the Hanafī *maddhab*, while the concept of *istiṣlāḥ* is a Mālikī one. *Istiḥsān* is an important branch of *ijtihād* and has played a prominent role in the adaptation of Islamic law to the changing needs of society using human knowledge and has developed the principle of *istiṣlāḥ* on that premise. *Istiḥsān* is antithetic to *qiyās*, and, therefore, much closer to *ijtihād*.[96] *Istiḥsān* means to approve, or to deem something preferable. It is a derivation from the Arabic word *ḥasana*, which

92 Al-Shāṭibī, *al-Muwāfaqāt fī Uṣūl al-Sharīʿa*, vol. 1, 25.
93 Al-Shāṭibī, *al-Muwāfaqāt fī Uṣūl al-Sharīʿa*, vol. 2, 27.
94 Al-Shāṭibī, *al-Muwāfaqāt fī Uṣūl al-Sharīʿa* (Cairo, 1975), vol. 3, 154, 153; and vol. 2, 2, in Khorchide, *Scharia*, 142–143.
95 See al-Shāṭibī, *al-Muwāfaqāt fī Uṣūl al-Sharīʿa*, vol. 3, 217.
96 The concepts of *raʾy*, *ʿilm*, and *ijtihād* were intertwined and interrelated. "*Ijtihad*, from the very beginning, signified an intellectual quality supplementing *ʿilm*, namely, the knowledge of traditional practice and the ability to deduce

means good or beautiful, and in Islamic law it was inspired by the principle of fair conduct and conscience, diverging from the rule of positive law. Unlike the Western concept of equity, which relies on the philosophy of natural and common law,[97] *istiḥsān* points to the ethical principles of *Sharīʿa*.[98] As such, *istiḥsān* is flexible and utilized for various legal and economic mechanisms. Muslim jurists have historically disagreed on the validation of the term as a source of law.[99] The use of *istiḥsān* avoids rigid judgments and unfairness that might result from an enforcement of the existing law. *Istiḥsān* can be used to create new

from it, through *ra'y*, a solution. It is no coincidence therefore that the combination *ijtihad al-ra'y* was of frequent use, signaling the exertion of *ra'y* on the basis of *ʿilm*, knowledge of the authoritative past. Technically, *ʿilm*, *ra'y* and *ijtihad* were interconnected and at times overlapping. So were the concepts of *ra'y* and derivatives of *ijmaʿ*, consensus, a concept that was to acquire central importance in later legal thought. The notion of consensus met *ra'y* when the latter emanated from a group or from a collective tribal agreement. Consensual opinion of a group ... not only provided an authoritative basis for action but also for the creation of *sunan*. A new *sunna* might thus be introduced by a caliph on the basis of a unanimous resolution of a (usually influential) group of people. Other forms of consensus might reflect the common, unanimous practice of a community, originally of a tribe and later of a garrison town or a city." (Hallaq, *Origins and Evolution of Islamic Law*, 54). Hallaq attempts to explain these derivations in the meaning of *istiḥsān* by stating that "The broad outlines of the evolution of istihsan from the second/eighth-century arbitrary or semi-arbitrary mode of reasoning – severely attacked by Shafiʿi – to a coherent and systematic doctrine during the fifth/eleventh century and thereafter are well known," Wael B. Hallaq, "Usul Al-Fiqh: Beyond the Tradition," *Journal of Islamic Studies*, vol. 3, no. 2 (1992): 196. For more on *istiḥsān* and *istiṣlāḥ*, see Bernard G. Weiss, ed., *Studies in Islamic Legal Theory* (Leiden: Brill, 2002).

97 Equity, pertaining to natural law, signifies the moral law furnished by earlier Reformed and contemporary Puritan literature. Equity, as the righteousness of the moral law, is embodied in a natural law and scriptural sources. The Roman perception of the natural law, however, differs from today's understanding of the natural law. For more on equity and natural law, see e.g. Howard L. Oleck, "Historical Nature of Equity Jurisprudence," *Fordham Law Review*, vol. 20, no. 1 (1951): 23–44; Godfrey P. Schmidt, "An Approach to the Natural Law," *Fordham Law Review*, vol. 18, no. 1 (1950): 1–42, available at http://ir.lawnet.fordham.edu/flr/vol19/iss1/1.

98 "Unlike equity, which is founded in the recognition of a superior law, istiḥsān does not seek to constitute an independent authority beyond the Shariʿah. Istiḥsān, in other words, is an integral part of the Shariʿah, and differs with equity in that the latter recognises a natural law apart from, and essentially superior to, positive law." (Kamali, *Principles of Islamic Jurisprudence*, 217).

99 Proponents of Shafīʿi, Ẓāhirī, and Shiʿi doctrine have rejected it in their legal theory of *uṣūl al-fiqh*, while those of the Ḥanafī, Mālikī, and Ḥanbalī *ʿulamaʾ* have validated it. See Kamali, *Principles of Islamic Jurisprudence*, 248.

rulings in various contexts. Since *istiḥsān* is, in the juristic sense, related to a method of exercising personal opinion, it is closely associated with *ra'y*.[100] *Istiṣlāḥ* on the other hand is derived from the word *maṣlaḥa*, which can be translated as "common good." *Istiṣlāḥ* is defined as distinguished from the principle of the *maṣlaḥa* and it permits more flexibility of analogy as compared to *qiyās*.[101] *Istiṣlāḥ* can be derived and applied within the legal spectrum in order to protect the welfare (or well-being) of individuals and community by promoting what is beneficial and reducing harm, including advocating lawful economic trade agreements and avoiding investing in economic assets that would turn out to be harmful, such as alcohol or armaments. The *maṣāliḥ* can neither be calculated nor projected in advance because they are amenable to change according to time and circumstance.[102]

3.4 *Siyāsa Shar'iyya*: Between the Moral and Legal Realm

3.4.1 The Term and the Scope

If we take the proposition that the political and the legal were, in classical milieu interwoven on a moral level,[103] it is necessary to take a closer look at the historical notion of *siyāsa Shar'iyya* and its applicability to economic well-being. However, not everyone agrees with such statements. Scholars such as Joseph Schacht maintain that in the premodern period, given the emergence of early Islamic rule, the political and the legal were set apart.[104] Thus *siyāsa* and *Sharī'a*, despite a certain degree of intertwinement, would be mutually exclusive concepts. Yet, while Islamic law has been primarily

[100] *Ra'y* expresses personal opinion in both *qiyās* and *istiḥsān*. The latter two concepts have been criticized by al-Shāfi'ī, which contributed to the discussion of the validity of *istiḥsān*. See Miklós Maróth, "Qiyās", in *Encyclopedia of Arabic Language and Linguistics*, Managing Editors Online Edition: Lutz Edzard, Rudolf de Jong. Accessed 20 August 2021 <http://dx.doi.org/10.1163/1570-6699_eall_EALL_SIM_0114>.

[101] Imran Ahsan Khan Nyazee, *Theories of Islamic Jurisprudence* (Cambridge: Islamic Texts Society, 2003), chapter 12.

[102] Al-Shāṭibī, *al-Muwāfaqāt fī Uṣūl al-Sharī'a*, vol. 2, 2–3.

[103] See Hallaq, "Groundwork of the Moral Law," 256ff. See also Hallaq, *Impossible State*, 67. "In theory, and largely in practice, the powers conferred upon the ruler through *siyāsa Shar'iyya* were not only consistent with the dictates of religious law; they were, as we will soon see, an integral extension of this law."

[104] See Schacht, *Introduction to Islamic Law*, 302.

restricted to the study of *fiqh*, other domains, such as *siyāsa* or *maṣlaḥa*, have also remained in the backdrop of the legal terminology.[105]

Siyāsa Shar'iyya can be translated as government or political authority in accordance with the goals and objectives of *Sharī'a* and it is applicable to all government policies, be it in areas where the *Sharī'a* provides explicit guidelines or otherwise.[106] It can be also understood as a *Sharī'a*-oriented policy that is seen as a tool of flexibility, designed to serve the cause of justice and good government, especially when the rules of *Sharī'a* fall short of addressing certain situations or developments, that as a doctrine demands from the ruler engagement in worldly affairs and the upholding of the norm of *Sharī'a*. As the term suggests, policy measures that are taken in the name of *siyāsa Shar'iyya* must be *Sharī'a*-compliant,[107] as its purpose is generally to facilitate rather than circumvent the implementation of *Sharī'a*. Rules of procedure, policy decisions, and legislative and administrative measures that are laid down and taken for the purpose would thus fall within the ambit of *siyāsa Shar'iyya*. There is also an understanding that *siyāsa* only applies outside the substantive *Sharī'a*, whereas according to an opposite view, *Sharī'a* and *siyāsa* go hand in hand, indicating that the *Sharī'a* is deficient without *siyāsa*.[108]

Under the banner of Islamic law can be classified the study of legal opinions (*fatāwa*), legal and court rulings (*aḥkām*), and governance-oriented policy based on *Sharī'a* norms (*siyāsa*).[109] Yet *siyāsa* can be found in various texts and deliberations, not

105 *Siyāsa Shar'iyya* can be denoted as *Sharī'a*-compliant governance or the executive branch of Muslim government. For some Ḥanafī scholars, *siyāsa Shar'iyya* refers strictly to the extant regulatory instruments of a *Sharī'a* law-based government pertaining to punishment. The legal authority for *siyāsa Shar'iyya* is implied by Muslim theocracies as a necessary extension to their responsibilities to supplement the broad criminal law principles of the Qur'an and other Muslim legal texts of sacred origin, on points of detail, to make regulations or policy decisions. *Siyāsa* means politics, or in this context policy, and is distinguished from the literal content of the Qur'an.

106 Kamali, *Shari'ah Law*, 226; on the classical work, see e.g. al-Māwardī, *al-Aḥkām al-Sulṭāniyya* (Cairo: al-Bābī al-Ḥalabī, 1973).

107 There are dual, mixed, classical-*Sharī'a*-based, and secular legal systems. Nigeria and Kenya, for instance, have *Sharī'a* courts that rule on family law for Muslims. The application of *siyāsa* historically pertains to the discretionary power of the rule of judges, as well as to administration on public affairs.

108 Kamali, *Shari'ah Law*, 225.

109 Muhammad Khalid Masud, "The Doctrine of *Siyāsa* in Islamic Law," *Recht van de Islam*, vol. 18 (2001): 2.

only in *fiqh* literature.[110] The fact that appointing a ruler was not just discussed in *fiqh* manuals but also in texts dealing with broader sociopolitical and theological (*kalām*) issues under the subject of *imāma*[111], as well as in the literature entitled *al-Aḥkām al-Sulṭāniyya*,[112] says a great deal about how *siyāsa* was invoked in various fields of Islamic sciences. This applies to the administrative-related laws and financial matters that occupy a space also outside of *fiqh*.[113]

In the view of the marriage of the moral and the legal, the sociopolitical cannot be squared in the judicial prescriptions. Despite the fact that until the middle of the ninth century the Muslim community perceived caliphs as political and religious advocates,[114] caliphs in fact did not legislate. Rather, they held symbolic and political power over the *umma*. Later, at least from the tenth century onwards, the political authorities were no longer considered to be lawgivers.[115] In this regard,

> The ruler's *siyāsat*, then, is precisely the responsibility of making specific laws in accordance with the general principles of the *sharīʿat* by observation of the needs of the time and place .... And since the test of *siyāsat* as *sharīʿat* is *maṣlaḥat* (i.e., if the *siyāsat* delivers *māslaḥat* then it is self-evidently in accordance with health-giving *sharīʿat*), the reverse also applies: whenever a ruling entails *maṣlaḥat* as a source of jurist's law.[116]

110 See e.g. Muhammad Khalid Masud, Brinkly Messick and David Powers, eds., *Islamic Legal Interpretation: The Muftis and Their Fatwas* (Cambridge, MA: Harvard, 1996); George Makdisi, "The Shariʿa Court Records of Ottoman Cairo and Other Resources for the Study of Islamic Law," *American Research Center in Egypt Newsletter*, no. 114 (1982): 3–10; Fawzi M. Najjar, "Siyāsa in Islamic Political Philosophy," in *Islamic Theology and Philosophy. Studies in Honor of George F. Hourani*, ed. M. E. Marmura (Albany: State University of New York Press, 1984), 92–110.

111 See e.g. al-Māwardī, *al-Aḥkām al-Sulṭāniyya*; al-Ghazālī, *Iḥyāʾ* and *Naṣīḥat al-Mulūk*.

112 See *al-Aḥkām al-Sulṭāniyya* texts by al-Māwardī, Ibn al-Farrāʾ, Ibn Taymiyya, etc.

113 Masud, "Doctrine of *Siyāsa* in Islamic Law," 3. See e.g. Abū Yūsuf, *Kitāb al-Kharaj* (Beirut, 1979); Abū Yūsuf. *Kitāb al-Kharaj*, trans. Abid Ahmad Ali (Lahore: Islamic Book Center, 1979).

114 See Josef van Ess, *Theologie und Gesellschaft im 2. und 3. Jahrhundert Hidschra. Eine Geschichte des religiösen Denkens im frühen Islam* (Berlin: Walter de Gruyter, 1991–7), vol. 1; Patricia Crone and Martin Hinds, *God's Caliph: Religious Authority in the First Centuries of Islam* (Cambridge: Cambridge University Press, 1986), 5–15, 20–36; Roy P. Mottahedeh, *Loyalty and Leadership in an Early Islamic Society* (Princeton, NJ: Princeton University Press, 1980). With Abū Yūsuf's appointment as chief justice (*qāḍī al-quḍāt*) it was decided that rulers cover public legal acts but not *fiqh*, which was the domain of the *fuqahāʾ*.

115 Johansen, "Changing Limits of Contingency in the History of Muslim Law," 7.

116 Ahmed, *What Is Islam?*, 471.

3.4.2 Siyāsa *in Classical Islam As Law and Policy*

Siyāsa as a technical term denoting government-oriented policy predated *siyāsa* as a concept within Islamic law, which later came to mean rulers' discretional power in applying *fiqh* law. As indicated by al-Shāfi'ī, the notion of *siyāsa* targets ruler's discretion. Muhammad Khalid Masud notes that

> Neither the Caliphs were interested in adopting *fiqh* as law of the Caliphate, nor the jurists were writing *fiqh* texts for the caliphs to adopt them. The jurists were writing these books for the *qādis* as source books. They were never meant to be binding. It was left to the discretion of the *qādis* to accept, choose or refine the view given in those books. The *fiqh* books themselves preserved the proverbial diversity of views on legal issues that existed in the madhhab (law school) literature.[117]

For al-Shāfi'ī, society at large ought to be governed based on the wisdom of the Qur'an. For this reason, he refuted any form of *siyāsa* that did not accord with the Qur'anic and the Prophetic teachings.[118] Al-Māwardī's *al-Aḥkām al-Sulṭāniyya*[119] also explains political authority and its relation to the Islamic legal corpus, whereby the notion of religion is often confronted with the conception of governmental authority. For him, *siyāsa* refers to governmental ordinances, in the function of an *imām* who strives to preserve legal matters concerning this world and the Hereafter.[120] Al-Ghazālī's notion of *siyāsa* points to moral pragmatism, economic preservation, the ruler's control over it, and the role of the governmental authority, discussed in more detail later in the chapter.[121] Ibn Qayyim divides *siyāsa* into two types: oppressive policy (*siyāsa ẓālima*), which goes against the nature of *Sharī'a*, and just policy (*siyāsa 'ādila*), which is meant to be

117 Masud, "Doctrine of *Siyāsa* in Islamic Law," 5.

118 See al-Shāfi'ī, *Kitāb al-Umm* (Cairo: al-Dār al-Miṣrriyya, n.d.), vol. 1, 7. Al-Shāfi'ī preferred *qiyās* over *ra'y* also when it comes to ruling and governing.

119 Al-Māwardī, *Aḥkām al-Sulṭāniyya*, 3–4.

120 On this note al-Māwardī differs from al-Shāfi'ī on the notion of rights of God and the rights of man in how a Caliph should conduct his authority. The latter did not allow the Caliph to exercise his opinion with members of the community in the domain of the rights of God. The former, however, permits the Caliph as the political authority to do so, since it might pertain to the well-being of the community.

121 Al-Ghazālī, *Iḥyā'*, 10–11, 53, 55.

in the service of justice.[122] The main principles of just policy are justice (*'adl*) and good government, whereas oppressive policy expounds self-interest and unjust reign. Likewise, for Ibn Taymiyya, *siyāsa* is linked to punishment, and is grounded in the Qur'an and its promulgation of good faith and devotion. Government as such is a trustee and hence ought to perform justice for the subjects over which it reigns.[123] Just rule further pertains to the elimination of corruption, incompetency, and the encouragement of good character of the ruler. *Siyāsa* must be in accordance with norms and thus compatible with *Sharī'a* and pertains to the social and political realm. This extends to his conviction that governmental authority has to be formed on religious grounds, for *'adl* can be achieved also through the implementation of governmental policy.[124] These texts pinpoint to the diverse idea that governmental authority rests not only on legal and political but primarily on ethical and metaphysical foundations, sustained by the legal scholars and the community who – unlike the nation-state – does not possess political sovereignty.

Trusteeship facilitates a degree of discretional power in order to attain a certain level of justice, yet *Sharī'a* does not provide details on governance, rule, and political assertion of power in terms that correspond to modern standards. It instead offers broad and left-to-interpretation-based schemes for just policy, and it can be perceived as being tantamount to *maṣlaḥa* due to the aim of facilitating the well-being of society on matters that could not be found in the scriptural sources. In the context of those scholars' deliberations, *Siyāsa shar'iyya* aims at securing benefit for the people and ensuring efficient management of their affairs, even if the measures taken are not stipulated in the text.[125] In this regard not only legal regulations of punishment but primarily the Qur'anic ethos and the ruler's political decisions can constitute premise for (just) governance.

122 Ibn Qayyim al-Jawziyya, *Al-Ṭuruq al-Ḥukmiyyah fī al-Siyāsa al-Shar'iyya*, ed. Muḥammad Ḥāmid al-Fāqi (Cairo: Maṭba'āt al-Sunnah al-Muḥammadiyyah, 1993), 5.

123 "[L]aws made in consonance with and for the fulfillment of the universal principles of the *sharī'at* are expressions and specifications of *sharī'at*: as such, it is difficult to conceive of the ruler's *siyāsat* as anything other than an expression of *sharī'at* .... And *maṣlaḥat* is the proof of the *siyāsat-sharī'at* pudding." Ahmed, *What Is Islam?*, 471.

124 Ibn Taymiyya, *al-Siyāsah Shar'iyyah fī Iṣlāḥ al-Rā'ī wa al Ra'īya* (Cairo: al-Sha'b, 1971), 180–181.

125 Kamali, *Shari'ah Law*, 227; Mohammad Hashim Kamali, "Siyasa Shari'a or the Policies of Islamic Government," *American Journal of Islamic Social Sciences*, vol. 6, no. 1 (1989): 61.

Siyāsa shar'iyya hence denotes the administration of public affairs in an Islamic polity with the aim of realizing the interests of the people and safeguarding them against mischief, in harmony with the general principles of the moral law. Additionally, the term *'ilm tadbīr al-manzil*, which in classical period denoted the science of household management, is often used in parallel with *siyāsa*.[126] 'Abd Allāh Ibn al-Muqaffa' (d. 756) asserts that *siyāsa* means good governance, wherein the Caliph had to be obedient to *Sharī'a*. When the subject has to be obedient to the Caliph and where there is a clear divergence from *Sharī'a* norms, are for him both extreme cases. Ibn al-Muqaffa' hence encourages the Caliph to exercise *ra'y* and *ijtihād* but only in the absence of the text.[127] He saw religious and political duties of the Caliph as an extension of other regulations and affirmed that subsequent Caliphs could revise such regulations. No one had, however, the power to abrogate the major principles of *Sharī'a's* moral law. Ibn Khaldūn, whose ideas on political, social, and economic aspects of government will be presented below, also spoke of two types of *siyāsa*: *siyāsa 'aqlīyya*, or rational policy, and *siyāsa dinīyya*, or religious policy. The former is put forward by rulers who have the ability to govern justly, whereas the latter follows the already prescribed revealed text.[128]

3.5 Metaphysics and the History of Islam's Moral Economics

During the formative period when Islamic legal schools were established, many works on economic thought were produced.[129] During this

126 Hallaq notes that "the Shari'a . . . was suspicious of the ruler's executive power, and insisted on an economic and social system that served the interests of the communities of believers, not those of the ruler (or ruling class). That the general goal of Islamic law has always and everywhere been to maintain individuals – to the greatest extent possible – in their social positions, remains one of the most valid generalizations about legal system." (Hallaq, *Sharī'a*, 366). See also Wael Hallaq, "Qur'anic Constitutionalism and Moral Governmentality: Further Notes on the Founding Principles of Islamic Society and Polity," *Comparative Islamic Studies*, vol. 8, no. 1–2 (2012): 1–51.

127 See Ibn al-Muqaffa', *Athār Ibn al-Muqaff'* (Beirut: Dār al-Kutub al-'Ilmīyya, 1989).

128 Ibn Khaldūn, *Muqaddima*, vol. 1, 337.

129 According to Islahi, Muslim scholars' writings on economic ideas can be divided into three periods – the formation, the translation, and the transmission periods. The first phase can be described as the formation period, spanning from the commencement of the Qur'anic revelation to the end of the era of companions i.e. *ṣahāba* (AH 11–100/AD 632–718). The second phase is the translation period, marking the influx of foreign intellectual ideas into the

period, various foreign ideas and texts were incorporated and translated into Arabic and the Islamic tradition. Theologians or the so-called *mutakallimūn*; *falāsifa* or Islamic philosophers, who were deeply influenced by Greek philosophy; *fuqahā'* or Islamic legal scholars; and *ahl al-taṣawwuf* or Sufis, who incorporated mystic elements of Divine worship into an economic rationale founded upon religious sources wrote on economic thought, merging legal, moral, and political views. To the first circle belonged, for instance, Fakhr al-Dīn al-Rāzī,[130] to the second Abū 'Alī al-Ḥusayn ibn 'Abd Allāh Ibn Sīnā,[131] Ibn al-Haytham,[132] and Ibn Ṭufayl,[133] to the third Abū Yūsuf, Abū 'Ubayd al-Qāsim Ibn Sallām,[134] Kinānī,[135] Abū Ya'lā Muḥammad ibn al-Ḥusayn Ibn al-Farrā',[136] al-Sarakhsī,[137] and

Arab-Muslim cultural milieu (AH second–fifth century/AD eighth–eleventh century). The third phase is the transmission period, which witnessed the dissemination of translated texts from the hands of Muslim scholars, when Greco-Islamic ideas reached Europe (AH sixth–ninth century/AD twelfth–fifteenth century) (Islahi, *Contribution of Muslim Scholars to Economic Thought*, 11–18).

130 Fakhr al-Dīn al-Rāzī (d. 1209) was a judge, theologian, and historian. His commentaries on the Qur'an are of great interest also to economists.

131 Ibn Sīnā (d. 1037) wrote on logic, philosophy, and medicine. His *al-Qanūn* (The canon of medicine) and *al-Shifā'* (Healing, known in the West as the *Sanatio*) were utilized for teaching medicine in Europe until the seventeenth century.

132 Al-Ḥasan bin Ḥusayn Ibn al-Haytham (d. 1039) from Basra was an Arab mathematician and physicist.

133 Ibn Ṭufayl (d. 1182) was the first Andalusian thinker who utilized Ibn Sīnā's *al-Shifā'*. His thought represents a late continuation of Ibn Sīnā's philosophy, as well as the more Aristotelian line of reasoning that would later be represented by Latin scholasticism.

134 Abū 'Ubayd al-Qāsim Ibn Sallām was Abī al-Dunyā's teacher, who provides a record of legal precedents laid down in the first two centuries of Islam, in particular those pertaining to the sources of revenue and the avenues of public expenditure. Abū 'Ubayd al-Qāsim Ibn Sallām, *Kitāb al-Amwāl* (al-Manṣūrah: Dār al-Hadī al-Nabawī, 2007); for an English translation see Abū 'Ubayd al-Qāsim Ibn Sallām, *The Book of Revenue: Kitāb al-Amwāl*, trans. Imran Ahsan Khan Nyazee (Doha: Garnet Publishing, Center for Muslim Contribution to Civilization, 2005).

135 Abū Bakr Yaḥyā b. Umar al-Kinānī (d. 901) a Malikite jurist, who composed *Kitāb Aḥkām al-Sūq* (A book on rules of the market) in which he deals with issues related to market problems, price, supply and demand, and monopoly.

136 Abū Ya'lā Muḥammad ibn al-Ḥusayn Ibn al-Farrā' (d. 1066) addressed economic issues in *al-Aḥkām al-Sulṭāniyya* (The rules of government).

137 Abū Bakr Muḥammad bin Aḥmad al-Sarakhsī was a Ḥanafī jurist from Transoxania. His most important work is *al-Mabsūṭ*, which is a detailed commentary on *al-Sijār al-Kabīr* by Muḥammad al-Shaybānī.

al-Māwardī,[138] and to the fourth Naṣīr al-Dīn al-Ṭūsī,[139] Ibn Abī al-Dunyā, al-Muḥāsibī, al-Rāghib al-Iṣfahānī (d. 1108), and al-Ghazālī, among others. Classical scholars' writings can be roughly divided according to their contents, since many scholars who mastered various fields were polymaths and hence maintained a degree of overlap with other contingent fields. Texts which consisted of more legal-political content were equally ethical as they provided basic principles of conduct for rulers and the structures of power in economic behavior. For instance, texts that address economic thought in a more technical and systematized fashion, for example by al-Shaybāni, Ibn Taymiyya, Ibn Khaldūn, or al-Maqrīzī, were simultaneously concerned also with legal-ethical questions. In the transmission period, various Arabic texts were translated into European languages, such as the works of Ibn Sīnā, al-Farābi, Ibn Rushd, Ibn Ṭufayl, and others, and classical Islamic scholarship's influence on European scholasticism[140] has been well documented.[141]

Generally, at least three approaches to classical economic analysis can be detected, each corresponding to a different objective: studies on medieval economics that largely leave out the contribution made by Muslim scholars on economic analysis;[142] studies aiming to prove that

138 Ali b. Muḥammad al-Māwardī's (d. 1058) work *al-Aḥkām al-Sulṭāniyyah* (The ordinances of government) was commissioned by the Caliph in Baghdad, containing a wide range of subjects including market supervision and economic role of government. Thomas Bauer, however, notes that *al-Aḥkām al-Sulṭāniyyah* was not a book on state theory in Islam but a book on Islamic law. Bauer, *Die Kultur der Ambiguität*, 315–319.

139 Naṣīr al-Dīn Abū Jaʿfar al-Ṭūsi (d. 1274) was born in Ṭus and died in Baghdad. His writings on economic matters can be found in his treatises on finance – *Risālah Maliyyah* and *Akhlāq al-Nasiri*.

140 The term "scholastics" relates to the Christian philosophical approach that aimed to reconcile theology with philosophy, commencing with thinkers such as Thomas Aquinas (d. 1274). S. Mohammad Ghazanfar and Abdul Azim Islahi, "Economic Thought of an Arab Scholastic: Abu Hamid Al-Ghazali," *History of Political Economy*, vol. 22, no. 2 (1990): 381.

141 See e.g. Ahmed El-Ashker and Rodney Wilson, *Islamic Economics: A Short History* (Leiden: Brill, 2006); Ghazanfar, *Medieval Islamic Thought*.

142 Joseph Schumpeter discussed the evolution and history of economic thought in his famous *History of Economic Analysis*. Various scholars have commented on Schumpeter's book, in which he presented the early, classical, and modern history of economics in an elaborated fashion. Despite the importance of Schumpeter's analysis of the development of economic history, he left out an important part of this history, namely the contribution of Muslim scholars to

Muslim scholars had invented an early form of capitalism;[143] and studies expounding the idea of ethical and economic convergence in Islamic tradition. The last strand pertains to analysis of classical economic ideas within the context of broader theological, philosophical, legal, and ethical ideas.

Economic ideas predated Islam, including the economic philosophy of the Greeks, who are presumably considered as the forefathers of what is today known as Western economic thought.[144] Historically, the Muslim community was well versed in trade, barter exchange, and

the field. The Schumpeterian "great gap" has been questioned by several scholars (e.g. Ghazanfar, *Medieval Islamic Thought*; Abbas Mirakhor, "Muslim Scholars and the History of Economics: A Need for Consideration," *American Journal of Islamic Social Sciences*, vol. 4, no. 2 (1987): 249) due to the omission of Islamic economic history and the influence it had upon the ideas of European medieval scholars. The study of medieval Islamic economics and Arab scholastics reveals that the Muslim contribution to the subject bears a profound relevance for the overall development and perception of economic thought. The "great gap" in economic history, as well as the omission of major medieval Muslim scholars, shed light on how neglected the writings of Muslim contributors have been in the modern era. Schumpeter's primary aim was the analysis, not the theory, of economic thought (Ameer Ali and Herb Thompson, "The Schumpeterian Gap and Muslim Economic Thought," *Journal of Interdisciplinary Economics*, vol. 10 (1999): 31–49).

143 Benedikt Koehler maintains that the Prophet Muḥammad's approach toward economic matters and early Islamic trade arrangements were the first form of capitalism; Benedikt Koehler, *Early Islam and the Birth of Capitalism* (Lanham: Lexington Books, 2014). However, early modes of conduct that allowed profit, trade routes, and market-based prices (in a time of healthy economic production) mostly fit a description of capital and trade, and not capitalism as a system. Capitalism as an economic system and legal organization that benefited the market to exist was designated as market-capitalism by e.g. Marx, and later Weber, and was protected by law and violence by the state (see e.g. Huff and Schluchter, eds., *Max Weber and Islam*; Marx, *Das Kapital*). What capital demands in order to preserve its self-existence is a surplus value beyond the (morally) regulated trade agreements and the treatment of market as a competitive force of exploitation. Despite the fact that profit is licit in in classical texts, the existence of certain types of private property, and semi-regulated markets, classical Muslim scholars, based on the Qurʾanic design of ethical cosmology, upheld *Sharīʿa*-compliant, regulated and well-being-oriented, ethical policies for society at large. Further, even if the works in intellectual history point to a different reality than the matters on the ground concerning the limits of pursuit of a livelihood, this, however, does not negate the fact that classical Muslim scholars' warned against certain economic practices that were in opposition to the general ethos of *Sharīʿa*, which came to flourish under the aegis of certain Muslim administrations and rulers.

144 See e.g. Schumpeter, *History of Economic Analysis*.

supply and demand, and established various forms of taxation. The evolution of economic thought in Muslim societies can be traced back to the earliest period of Islam, as economic issues had been raised already by the Prophet Muḥammad and the Rashidun caliphate.[145] In the first centuries various economic issues were discussed in light of the Qur'an, such as the prohibition of usury, the institution of *zakāt*, and the encouragement of economic activities for human welfare, in line with the Divine law.[146] The Qur'an emphasizes the notion of *ʿadl* (justice) in all dimensions of one's life, including the economic.[147] Economic purchases are expected to be conducted in a fair and truthful manner, meaning securing channels of cooperation between a buyer and a seller with honest description of the product.[148] The maintenance of justice in economic affairs has also been upheld by the Qur'anic maxim *ʿamr bi al-maʿrūf wa al-naḥi ʿan al-munkar* (allowing what is right and forbidding what is wrong).[149] Yet, as important as the Qur'anic epistemology is as the origin and bedrock of Islamic economic thought, it is the human interpretation of the early jurists and scholars who attempted to produce, reflect, and apply economic thought in order to address appurtenant topics of the day. The establishment of more systematic intellectual underpinnings emerged in classical Muslim scholarship already in the ninth century, advancing ideas on economic philosophy as an integral component of *Sharīʿa's* righteous behavior. Economics as an independent discipline did not exist in the classical Muslim world (as a matter of fact, it did not exist in pre-Enlightenment Europe either). While early scholars, among other subjects, wrote on acquiring wealth, taxation, poverty, and the role of wealth in light of various theological and ethical predispositions, later scholars, such as Ibn Taymiyya, Ibn Khaldūn, and al-Maqrīzī during the fourteenth and fifteenth centuries, produced more systematic economic literature that was nonetheless imbued with ethical concerns. In spite of the flourishing of markets and trading activities, the subject of economy was not a distinct sphere but was addressed under the domains of law, theology, and moral epistemology. This, however,

[145] See El-Ashker and Wilson, *Islamic Economics*, 92–125.
[146] See the Qur'an, 7:10, 7:32, 34:15.
[147] See the Qur'an, e.g. 4:58, 11:84, 16:76, 43:15.
[148] See the Qur'an, e.g. 5:39, 6:152, 7:85, 11:84, etc.
[149] Qur'an, 7:152, 9:71.

does not indicate a religious economy per se but an economic discourse pertinent to the moral cosmology.

The Arabic term for household management was *tadbīr al-manzil*, [150] equivalent to the Greek concept of *oikonomia*,[151] which pertains to family-based management of a household. Some scholars claim that it was differentiated from the terms ethics (*tadbīr al-nafs*; *al-akhlāq*) and political management (*siyāsa*), since in a household, the primary concern was the provision of basic necessities for the needy.[152] Yet, for classical Muslim scholars, the term "economics" is equated with *kasb* or *al-iqtiṣād*[153] as the science of earning and provision (*'ilm al-iktisāb wa al-infāq*),[154] as understanding and analyzing how one acquires wealth and distributes it according to moral measures. *Iqtiṣād* is thus the activity of seeking and realizing what is judicious and sage.[155] Due to the judicious objectives of the term, the worldly and the material of *iqtiṣād* and *qaṣd* hence cannot be extrapolated from the transcendent and the moral.[156] As such, the economic (trading, acquiring wealth, consumption, and so forth) entails wider socio-ecological as well as moral derivations, for the judicious acquisition of wealth denotes one's spiritual well-being, something which was prudently analyzed by

150 "To pay attention to where things lead" (*an tazzura ila mā ta'ūlu ilayhi 'āqibatuhu*). Ibn Manẓūr, *Lisān al-'Arab* (Qom: Adab al-Hawza, 1984).

151 For more on different meanings of *oikonomia* by Plato and Aristotle, and the development of the concept in the Christian tradition, see Giorgio Agamben, *The Kindgdom and the Glory* (Stanford, CA: Stanford University Press, 2011), 17–52.

152 The household model can be applied to a community or a state, or globally speaking to earth, intertwining economic ideas with ecological and political one. Economy and ecology belong to the same root – the second pertains to management, the first to the study of the household. Economy and ecology are in this sense regarded as two corresponding domains of the extended household. "There is no tradeoff between economy and ecology, but rather, *economy must conform to ecology*." Adi Setia, "The Restoration of Wealth: Introducing Ibn Abī al-Dunyā's *Iṣlāḥ al-Māl*," *Islamic Sciences*, vol. 13, no. 2 (2015): 93.

153 *Iqtiṣād* from *qaṣada*, meaning "purpose," "justice," "aim," direction," "objective."

154 Setia, "Restoration of Wealth," 93.

155 Adi Setia, "The Meaning of 'Economy': *Qaṣd, Iqtiṣād, Tadbīr al-Manzil*," *Islamic Sciences*, vol. 14, no. 1 (2016): 120–121.

156 I.e. the material (worldly) is not sought on its own but rather as a moral endeavor of eschatological proportions. In this regard, the Qur'anic is per se theological, and moral and transcends the purely material and techno-pragmatic realm.

classical scholars. The economic, then, could be understood as the backbone of what constitutes being human.

Not only jurists[157] but also philosophers, theologians, and Sufis discussed essential issues of ethical economics, touching upon the epistemology of moral conduct and the role of human obligations and responsibilities. As we shall see below, for many classical Muslim scholars, the core understanding of economic life correlates to the material realm but without losing sight of the higher goals and objectives of the Hereafter.[158] By applying the theory of analogy, Muslim scholars established rules from *Sharīʿa* injunctions, in which economic ideas were only one component of the overall complexity of Islamic jurisprudential, theological, and Sufi writings. Many works on legal theory (*uṣūl al-fiqh*) and Sufism (*taṣawwuf*) brought forth ethical, theological, and metaphysical conceptualities of just governance (*aḥkām al-sulṭāniyya*) and public expenditures (*al-kharāj*), among numerous others, that entail a sociopolitical dimension and a notion of economic justice.[159] There was no epistemological distinction between ideal knowledge to be obtained through the highest order of contemplation and moral virtues as righteous conduct. Even though Sufis, for instance, sought to attain a higher level of knowledge through *kashf* (spiritual retreat) and the practice of *zuhd* (asceticism, renunciation, or extramundane detachment), they also exerted ideas in how to exercise actions that have a direct impact with the *dunyā*, such as by using both revelation and the faculty of reason to exercise moral conduct in attaining economic provision or wealth (*māl*).[160] As we shall see in the following paragraphs, terms such as ethics (*akhlāq*), household management (*tadbīr al-manzil*), governmental policy, and political science (*ʿilm al-madani*)[161] are to be perceived not only within the technical-legal but first and foremost within the cosmological-ethical domain extrapolated through their ethos of the universe and society. The classical Muslim scholars' ethico-juristic and spiritual-moral treatises on

157 E.g. Abū ʿUbayd also emphasized justice and fairness as the backbone of one's wealth and economic and financial composition.

158 Ali and Thompson, "Schumpeterian Gap and Muslim Economic Thought." See e.g. al-Muḥāsibī; al-Ghazālī.

159 Ansari, "Islamic Ethics," 81.

160 *Māl*, in Arabic "wealth" or "money," means to acquire or possess something. See Ibn Manẓūr, *Lisān al-ʿArab*, s.v. "māl."

161 Francis E. Peters, *Allah's Commonwealth* (New York: Simon and Schuster, 1973).

economic thought provide insight into the intricate correlation between worldly economy (*kasb*) and extramundane detachment (*zuhd*)[162] in how to acquire livelihood, pursue religious obligations, obtain licit goods, and redistribute wealth among the poor. They put forward an idea of spiritual significance of work and, even more importantly, of production processes – as organizational processes, facilities, and techniques that are utilized in order to convert raw materials into finished products. The spiritual significance of production processes does not only mean that any type of work can be spiritual in itself (as vocation), despite its dehumanizing conditions, but rather that the profession is integrated into higher orders of knowledge and that the very relations of production are not based on inherent antagonisms but communal recognition and value of labor.

Many classical Muslim scholars maintain that justice is an economic prerogative as an objective of *Sharīʿa*.[163] For instance, Abū Yūsuf, a pupil of Abū Ḥanīfa and a *qādi*, who was recommended to the Caliph Hārūn al-Rashīd for providing advice on legal opinions, held more traditional views on the methodology of law by following his predecessor. He believed that only through justice can overall development (of society) take place, for justice causes development and increases income. Divine favor is linked with the notion of justice and disappears with the practice of injustice.[164] Abū Yūsuf is also credited with restricting caliphal authority in regard to the implementation of his fiscal policy. Ibn Qayyim, trained as a jurist and a theologian, discussed economic philosophy, riches and poverty, the prohibition of *ribā*, and market mechanisms. He maintains that "anything contrary to the notion of justice that can turn the matter from blessing and welfare into a curse or destruction, and from wisdom into disutility has no correlation with the *Sharīʿa*."[165] Al-Shaybānī, who studied *fiqh* under the guidance of Abū Yūsuf, also dedicated his book on earning

162 For the *kasb–zuhd* amalgam under the banner of *tawakkul*, see Figure 2 in the Appendix. See also Adi Setia who theorizes texts penned by some of the classical Muslim scholars as an ethico-economic genre. Setia, "Restoration of Wealth," 82, 83.

163 Ibn Sallam, *Book of Revenue*.

164 Abū Yūsuf, *Kitāb al-Kharaj* (Cairo: Dār al-Matbaʿah al-Salafiyyah, 1972), 120, in Islahi, *Contribution of Muslim Scholars to Economic Thought*, 65.

165 Ibn Qayyim al-Jawziyya, *Zād al-Maʿād* (1982), 15; Islahi, "Linkages and Similarities between Economics Ideas of Muslim Scholars and Scholastics," *Wednesday Dialogue*, 2010–2011, 11.

and livelihood, *Kitāb al-Kasb*, to more traditional (*āthārī*) rather than legal (*fiqhī*) interpretation of the topic of economics.[166] Hence, his legal arguments are supported by numerous *aḥādīth* and Qurʾanic verses. Even though one would think that *Kitāb al-Kasb* is a book on Islamic jurisprudence, Imām al-Sarakhsī (d. 1090) informs us that it expounds the meaning of *zuhd* as detachment from worldly endeavors, merging Islamic mysticism with *Sharīʿa* injunctions.[167] *Zuhd*, together with *waraʿ* (prudence), is the subject of al-Shaybānī's analysis on safeguarding from corruption and maintaining an honest livelihood, which points to economic discipline imbued with spiritual qualities. For al-Shaybānī, earning a living ought to be a service to public good, by providing for one's own needs and the needs of one's family and also for the community, since he urges that only when one provides for the poor does life become truly wholesome. In other words, *ʿibādāt* does not suffice to lead a full life if *muʿāmalāt* as a transactional relationship is missing.[168] Sales, accumulation of wealth, and value of money are hence analyzed with the parameters of piety, renunciation, and asceticism. In addition, Ibn Abī al-Dunyā produced many works on various Islamic sciences, including on the Qurʾan, *ḥadīth*, and *fiqh*, predicating ethical subjects such as *zuhd*, *adab*, and *taqwā*. He has divided economic themes into several fields. *Iṣlāḥ al-māl* (The emendation of wealth) is concerned with licit acquisition and positive functions of wealth, acquiring money, securing a livelihood and savings, craftsmanship, ways of conducting commerce, securing high prices, land rights, handcrafts, and investments, whereas the second deals with saving money (*qaṣd al-māl*), foods and clothing, inheritance, surplus of money, and the notion of poverty. He has considered commerce and trading activities within the parameters of moral predicaments. His book invokes numerous scholars but also limits itself to Qurʾanic passages and *ḥadīth* narrations, designating licit acquisition of wealth, favorable functions of money, and benefits of spending and saving. Close reading of his work reveals the twofold perception of wealth – the

166 Al-Shaybānī, *Kitāb al-Kasb* (Ḥalab: Maktab al-Maṭbuʿāt al-Islāmiyya, 1997); Adi Setia, *The Book of Earning a Livelihood* (Kuala Lumpur: IBFIM, 2011).

167 Adi Setia, "Imam Muḥammad Ibn al-Ḥasan al-Shaybāni on Earning a Livelihood: Seven Excerpts from His Kitāb al-Kasb," *Islam and Science*, vol. 10, no. 2 (2012): 103.

168 Setia, "Imam Muḥammad Ibn al-Ḥasan al-Shaybāni on Earning a Livelihood," 105. See also Hallaq, *Impossible State*, 114–116.

material and the moral. *Iṣlāḥ al-māl* can be analyzed within the parameters of Sufi terminology, for it addresses spiritual reverberations of human behavior, a genre that was systematically commenced by al-Shaybānī's *Kitāb al-Kasb*.[169] The cultivation of the innermost goes hand in hand with the challenges of everyday life and earning a livelihood, whereby economic certitude is extrapolated in the name of spiritual uplift.[170]

3.6 The Nature of Markets, Price Control, and the Notion of Fair Price

Just or fair price and price regulation were two of the main tenets of economic philosophy addressed by classical Muslim scholars and later on in scholastics. In the period that became known in Europe as the Middle Ages, just price became one of the main topics of Muslim thinkers who discussed economic problems under the banner of moral law and Islamic theology. Fair price of a good is a price of that very object that is comparable to other similar objects, which was also called the price of the equivalent (*thaman al-mithl*).[171] Price control, governmental authority's intervention, and fair prices also invoked economic responsibilities of the rulers, which was a recurring topic in the classical period. As Abū Yūsuf was an Imām under the aegis of the Abbasid Caliph Hārūn al-Rashīd, his book *Kitāb al-Kharaj* is to a large extent advice on the Caliph's policies on the state's responsibility in regard to taxation, state administration, and public expenditure, and it can be perceived as a text on "good governance." Abū Yūsuf states that the leader of the righteous – the Caliph himself – asked him to compile a book on land taxes and revenues and to maintain public good.[172] In light of imperatives of social justice, Abū Yūsuf holds that public welfare has to be preserved and thus upholds proportional involvement of the governmental authority in agricultural policies, instead of imposing

169 Setia, "Restoration of Wealth," 82.

170 By enumerating those (and other) scholars and their relation between mystical concepts and economic ideas, I do not intend to position Sufism or major Sufi figures on a pedestal but rather to expound a dynamic and nuanced correlation between mystical, theological, legal, and economic ideas for the purposes of the argument of this book.

171 Ibn Nujayam, *al-Ashbāh wa al-Naẓā'ir* (Beirut: Dār al-Kutub al-'Ilmīyah, 1980), 362–363.

172 Abū Yūsuf, *Kitāb al-Kharaj* (Beirut: Dār al-Ma'rifa, 1979), 3.

a rent on the land. He was in favor of the idea of proportionality: "In my view the best system of taxation for generating more revenue for the treasury and the most adequate one to prevent injustice to the tax payers by tax collectors is the proportional agricultural tax."[173] He also discusses in detail the rules surrounding the revival of dead land, advocating the idea that one who revives it has the right to ownership and cultivation, insofar as he pays *ushr* levy or *kharaj* levy.[174]

On the nature of the market and price control, Abū Yūsuf observes that there is no definite limit of low or high prices that can be ascertained but rather that "it is a matter decided from heaven; the principle is unknown." The low and high levels of prices "are subject to the command and decision of Allah. Sometimes food is plentiful but still very dear and sometimes it is too little but cheap."[175] Although it seems that such a statement is in opposition to the belief that price does not depend solely on supply and that it further indicates the exclusive nature of markets and their invisible self-imposition of prices, this should not be mistakenly perceived as if there is no regulatory mechanism based on the ethical premise of economic behavior.

The irregularities and deficiencies in the market were already mended by the Prophet Muḥammad. After his death, Muslim jurists established mechanisms of intervention in the market from the principles laid down by the Prophet and the Rashidun Caliphs. The authoritative principles apropos fixing the price found in Islamic law are based on certain *aḥādīth*.[176] However, not all jurists advocated regulating prices. Imām al-Shāfiʿī and Imām Ibn Ḥanbal opposed price control in the market, indicating that the governmental authority only has the right to exercise price control in the case of abundance and scarcity of commodities. Prices are to rise naturally and as such belong to the Divine realm. Therefore, according to al-Shāfiʿī and Ibn Ḥanbal, imposing a fixed price would mean

173 Abū Yūsuf, *Kitāb al-Kharaj* (Beirut: Dār al-Maʿrifa, 1979) 50, in Nasir Nabi, "Islamic Economic Thought in the Medieval Times: Some Reflections," *Journal of Islamic Thought and Civilization*, vol. 3, no. 2 (2013): 25.

174 Abū Yūsuf, *Kitāb al-Kharaj* (Beirut: Dār al-Maʿrifa, 1979), 65, in Nabi, "Islamic Economic Thought in the Medieval Times."

175 Abū Yūsuf in Islahi, *Contribution of Muslim Scholars to Economic Thought*, 28.

176 There is also a report by Imām Malik's on Caliph Umar's intervention in the market by dismissing a seller for selling a commodity at a lower price.

injustice.[177] The notion of administrative fixation of price was known already in the time of the Prophet Muḥammad, who did not stipulate it, for he favored the determination of price by market forces, that is, according to supply and demand.[178] One of the earliest accounts of price variation came as a result of good or bad harvest, increase or decrease in the supply of agricultural goods, as stated by Ibn al-Muqaffaʿ.[179] The followers of Abū Ḥanīfa and Imām Mālik have expressed the same opinion regarding price control, namely that it is licit if it is in the interest of the common public.[180] The gist of the discussion is that the governmental authority will exercise price control if monopoly of market prices or goods occurs.

Ṣaḥīḥ Muslim reports that the Prophet said that hoarding is a practice done by a sinner. A hoarder purchases goods designated as necessities in order to earn profit, since the price of that good will rise. In case of such injustice (*ẓulm*), the authority has the right to remove the seller from the market. As will be evident from the analyzed texts below, according to *Sharīʿa*, prices are either valid or invalid. A valid price is a price established in a market, which is stipulated by legal precepts and does not include harmful actions such as cheating, fraud, or disguise of the true price. Even though this is perceived as a valid price, since justice is not entirely a juristic consideration, fair price is not only a legal but also a theological-ethical concept. On the other hand, an invalid price is one that opposes *Sharīʿa* requirements; it can occur through a deliberate violation of legal rules, or it may be an outcome of ignorance on a particular economic issue or activity.

[177] E.g. Shamsuddīn Ibn Qudāmah al-Maqdīsī, a Ḥanbalī jurist, argues that the authority of the state has no right to impose price control on goods in the market. This is associated with the fact that the Prophet equated price control with injustice (*ẓulm*). See Ibn Qudāmah al-Maqdīsī, *al-Sharḥ al-Kabīr* (Beirut: Dār al-Kitāb al-ʿArabī, 1972). On the contrary, for various Mālikī and Ḥanafī jurists price control is valid.

[178] Islahi, *Contribution of Muslim Scholars to Economic Thought*, 25. This, however, is disputable since despite some *aḥādīth* indicating that prices are set by the heavens and therefore left to the "invisible hand" of the market, an approach closely associated with Adam Smith, regulatory practices such as the *ḥisba* mechanism and moral predicaments based on *Sharīʿa*'s cosmology exist. Prophet Muḥammad as well as early Muslim companions and jurists aimed to end unregulated, excessive abuse of the market and prices.

[179] Islahi, *Contribution of Muslim Scholars to Economic Thought*, 27.

[180] Abdul Azim Islahi, *Economic Concepts of Ibn Taymiyyah* (Leicester, UK: Islamic Foundation, 1988), 95ff.

Ibn Abī al-Dunyā holds that maintaining high prices (of goods) at market conveys parsimony, therefore a seller or buyer is permitted to withdraw from a trading agreement if obliged to do so.[181] The rich are encouraged to redirect the surplus of their wealth into supporting the economic, social, and by extension also spiritual conditions of the poor.[182] In order to maintain a reasonable price for a commodity on the market, al-Ghazālī advocates for a moderate profit rate as a form of *iḥsān*. Fairness and equity are to be expected as social standards interrelated with market forces. If a spike in the prices of a commodity occurs, the authority can interfere in order to secure a just and equity-based distribution. Legitimate profits ought not to be obtained from goods regarded as necessities,[183] due to the human inclination to accumulate wealth,[184] distinguishing between two types of prices, the unjust and prohibited prices, and prices that are just and desired.

Ibn Taymiyya, writing extensively on *ḥadīth*, *tafsīr*, and *fiqh*, also made seminal contributions to economic thought. Ibn Taymiyya was a strong supporter of price control in case of any misuse at the market or if any harm or injury is foreseen to the public, for instance forcing sellers to sell at a higher price than normal, which is grounded on the prophetic *ḥadīth* stating that only God defines price control.[185] However, if price control itself involves an act of justice and preventing harm, it is obligatory in order to avoid suffering of people, for example when merchants have monopoly over prices at the market.[186] In relation to common good, Ibn Taymiyya proposes economic partnership based on equal shares.[187] He analyzed economic conduct under which regulated price control is licit and needed. If merchants are forced, due to price control, to sell their commodities for a different price than originally, it would be illicit. However, if price control upholds equity at the market and diminishes the misuse or the monopoly of markets,

181 Ibn Abī al-Dunyā, *Iṣlāḥ al-Māl*. 182 Setia, "Restoration of Wealth," 78.
183 Al-Ghazālī, *Iḥyā'*, vol. 2, 73. 184 Al-Ghazālī, *Iḥyā'*, vol. 2, 280.
185 "The market price rose in the time of the messenger of God, peace be upon him, and they said to him: Messenger of God if only you would provide price control. He replied: God is the Taker, the Disposer, the Winner and the Controller of prices." (Abū Dāwūd and al-Tirmidhī in Ibn Taymiyya, *Public Duties in Islam*, 35.). Yet, this apparent opposition to price control has to be viewed also in the context when there is no social-economic turmoil in society and when market functions well.
186 Ibn Taymiyya, *Public Duties in Islam*, 36.
187 Ibn Taymiyya, *Public Duties in Islam*, 40.

then it is obligatory to traders:[188] "When people's necessities cannot be safeguarded without a just price regulation, then a price regulation based on justice will be implemented."[189]

For Ibn Taymiyya, the so-called "price of the equivalent" is regarded as the just price.[190] Also the notion of just or fair compensation (*'iwaḍ al-mithl*) occurs in cases when one is responsible for causing injury to others' lives (*nufūs*), property (*amwāl*), or profit (*manāfi'*), when one has to pay reimbursement for caused injury *(ba'ḍ al-nufūs),* and when one has to arrange valid or invalid contracts (*al-'uqūd al-ṣaḥiḥa*) in relation to lives and property.[191] Ibn Taymiyya addressed the ethical and the legal aspects of fair price by using the terms "compensation of the equivalent" for the former and "price of the equivalent" for the latter: "Often it becomes ambiguous with experts in jurisprudence, and they argue against each other about the nature of the compensation of the equivalent – its kind (*jins*) and quantity (*miqdār*)."[192] In relation to purchases and commodities, he states, "If people are dealing with their goods as is it in their habit without any injustice and if the price rises either due to shortage of goods or due to increase in population, then it is sent by God. Then, to force the sellers to sell their goods at a particular price is a wrongful coercion (*ikrāh bi ghayr ḥaqq*)."[193] Ibn Taymiyya confirmed profit and the seller's appropriation of it by stipulating that the sellers can gain profit in what is known as an accepted manner (*al-ribḥ al-ma'rūf*)[194] without endangering their own interest or the interest of the consumers. From this, it stems that the fair or just profit is a profit obtained without exploiting the price, setting an abnormal rate of profit, or causing harm to others: "A person who acquired goods to earn income and to trade with them at a later date is permitted to do so but he is not allowed to charge from a needy person (*muḥtāj*) a higher profit than the customary one (*al-ribḥ al-mu'atād*), and he

188 Ibn Taymiyya, *Public Duties in Islam*, 15.
189 Ibn Taymiyya, *Public Duties in Islam*, 37.
190 Ibn Taymiyya, *Public Duties in Islam*, 24.
191 Ibn Taymiyya, *Majmū' Fatāwā Shaykh al-Islām*, vol. 29, 520, in Islahi, *Economic Concepts of Ibn Taymiyyah*, 81.
192 Ibn Taymiyya, *Majmū' Fatāwā Shaykh al-Islām*, 522, in Islahi, *Economic Concepts of Ibn Taymiyyah*, 82.
193 Ibn Taymiyya, *Public Duties in Islam*, 25.
194 Ibn Taymiyya, *Public Duties in Islam*, 37.

ought not to increase the price for him due to his need (*ḍarūrah*)."[195] One of the main objectives of the just price is to maintain justice on the market, especially between sellers and buyers, in addition to the fact that advice on just price turned out to be useful also for political authorities. Justice meant that goods are not sold at an abnormal price nor sellers coerced into illicit contracts, while injustice is equivalent with oppression (*ẓulm*).[196] The only time a seller can be coerced into a contract is when he has to sell his good at the price of the equivalent in order to protect the interests of other sellers,[197] while at the same time a consumer should also buy a commodity at the price of the equivalent.

3.7 The Value of Wealth (*Māl*) and the Hereafter

Money and wealth, including property, or *māl* in Arabic was in premodern scholarship considered as one of the key elements for attaining righteous economic conduct. It bears certain benefits as well as risks for an individual, and it can thus be rendered as a benefit as well as a detriment, depending on one's intentions (*niyya*).[198]

3.7.1 Kasb, Faqr, *and* Zuhd

It is believed that al-Shaybānī was the first scholar who treated the subject of earning as its own topic, in relation to reliance on God, lawful and unlawful means of earnings. Al-Shaybānī's methodology is based on the Qur'an, *ḥadīth* literature and Prophet's companions, as well as comprising his own views on the subject, addressing the notion of *kasb* within the material-legal and the ethical-moral framework.[199] The main theme of his book is the concept of earning in light of religious obligation, which is, however, among other

[195] Ibn Taymiyya, *Majmū' Fatāwā Shaykh al-Islām*, vol. 29, 501, in Islahi, *Economic Concepts of Ibn Taymiyyah*, 86.

[196] Ibn Taymiyya, *Public Duties in Islam*, 41–42.

[197] Ibn Taymiyya, *Public Duties in Islam*, 190.

[198] *Fainnahu yanfa'u min wajhi wa yadru min wajhi* (al -Ghazālī, *Mīzān al-'Amal*, 372).

[199] Mustafa Omar Mohammed, "Economic Consumption Model Revisited: *Infaq* Based on *Al-Shaybani's* Levels of *Al-Kasb*," *International Journal of Economics, Management and Accounting*, no. 19 (2011): 120.

subjects, expounded by espousing material abstinence and acts of charity, indicating that earning as a religious duty (law) ought to be seen within a theological-ethical context.

According to al-Shaybānī, *kasb* (earning a livelihood) is acquiring wealth by legal means (*taḥṣīlu al-māl bimā yaḥḥillu min al-asbāb*).[200] Al-Shaybānī states that earning (*makāsib*) a living (in a licit way) corresponds to expression of one's faith: "Permissible earning is in the category of cooperation in acts of devotion and obedience."[201] Earning, which is a licit means for obtaining money, can be divided into several levels. The first is indispensable for everyone and enables one to perform obligatory duties, to repay debt, and to provide for basic needs of one's family. Temperance (*muta'affifan*) is prompted in the sight of God,[202] as well as abstaining from amassing wealth,[203] since it is associated with the danger of committing unvirtuous deeds. Earning a living presupposes cooperating with others and is thus perceived as an economic behavior that pertains not only to economic and material preservation but primarily to spiritual purification (*ṭahāra*) and moral responsibility.[204] Earning a living is permissible according to the majority of *fuqahā'*, yet some Sufis and ascetics (*al-mutaqashshifa*) maintained that some types of earnings are regarded as lowly (*danā'a*) in the habits of people, unless one is in need of necessary provision.[205] *Kasb* is perceived as a necessary endeavor,[206] and one who refrains from it can be considered sinful, for it pertains to providing for one's basic needs such as food, clothing, and shelter, which in turn can

200 For al-Shaybānī, *al-kasb* can be obligatory (*farḍ al-'ayn*), recommended (*mandūb*), or permissible (*mubāḥ*) (Al-Shaybānī, *Kitāb al-Kasb*, 70).

201 Al-Shaybānī, *Kitāb al-Kasb*, 164, see also 136.

202 According to the prophetic *ḥadīth* narrated by Abū Nu'aym, see al-Shaybānī, *Kitāb al-Kasb*, 131.

203 This virtue is based on the *ḥadīth* expounding the dangers of wealth: perished be the owners of wealth who gain in excess, who treat wealth with disrespect, and those who worship wealth and hence do not give to charity. See al-Shaybānī, *Kitāb al-Kasb*, 135.

204 Al-Shaybānī, *Kitāb al-Kasb*, 136.

205 Setia, "Imam Muḥammad Ibn al-Ḥasan al-Shaybāni on Earning a Livelihood," 112. This presupposition is also based on *ḥadīth*, although there is no direct correlation between the nature of lowly earnings and the prohibition thereof. "Indeed, God the most Exalted likes noble things, and He dislikes inferior ones (*Inna Allaha ta'āla yuḥibu ma'ālīya al-umūr wa yubghiḍ safsāfahā*)," al-Shaybānī, *Kitāb al-Kasb*, 136–137.

206 "*Ṭalaba al-kasb farīḍa 'ala kulli muslim kama anna ṭalaba al-'ilm farīḍa*," al-Shaybānī, *Kitāb al-Kasb*, 71.

facilitate religious duty and spiritual uplift, such as performing prayer or giving *zakāt*. Since society at large can also benefit from one's *kasb*, it is generally considered beneficial. This, however, does not mean that *kasb* is a religious obligation per se, otherwise one would be invited to perform it incessantly. The first level of *kasb* encompasses basic needs for provision (such as food, clothing, and shelter), in order for one to come closer to the Divine.[207] Acquiring earnings to repay debt is also obligatory, as well as providing for one's family and food supplies. It is recommended to provide provisions for relatives and family members, guests, and companions, and accumulating wealth is permissible only with the aim of preserving dignity and moral stamina. It is clear that by stating *fiqh* maxims, such as whatever are the means to facilitate *wājib* is itself *wājib*, al-Shaybānī also gives precedence to moral uplift over purely jurisprudential decrees. Giving purchases a moral note, al-Shaybānī supposes preserving wealth to be a sacrifice for future generations. By situating acquisition against poverty, he advocates a stance against the accumulation of wealth beyond one's needs. Those who opposed acquisition of wealth are, in al-Shaybānī's view, ignorant and foolish Sufis: "*qawm min juhhāl ahl al-taqashshuf wa hamqa ahl al-taṣawwuf*."[208] In their view, gaining wealth is illicit since it corrupts the heart and diminishes reliance on God (*tawakkul*), and acquisition of wealth is permitted only when in dire need.

Hoarding wealth is illicit, yet being wealthy presents a moral liability to other members of society. According to al-Shaybānī, the notion of *kasb* is intrinsic to relying on God,[209] and it condemns "wastefulness, extravagance, haughtiness, boastfulness, and competitive accumulation (*al-isrāf wa al-saraf wa al-makhīla wa al-tafākhur wa al-*

[207] Al-Shaybānī, *Kitāb al-Kasb*, 63.

[208] Al-Shaybānī, *Kitāb al-Kasb*, 81, 99, 101. Further, for Michael Bonner, one of the main arguments of al-Shaybānī's adversaries is the Qur'anic verse "your sustenance and what you have been promised is in the heavens" (Qur'an, 51:22). Michael Bonner, "The Kitab al-Kasb Attributed to al-Shaybani: Poverty, Surplus, and the Circulation of Wealth," *Journal of the American Oriental Society*, vol. 121, no. 3 (2011): 410–427. Yet, to oppose this view, one does not need to look beyond the numerous passages from the Qur'an prompting economic provision, as well as Prophet Muḥammad's narrations, and early caliphs' endeavors on commerce and money. One of the Qur'anic verses that advocates *kasb* is, "Spend out [i.e. give charity and provide for your family] of the good things you have earned" (Qur'an, 2:267).

[209] Al-Shaybānī, *Kitāb al-Kasb*, 93.

takāthur)."[210] Since wasting food pertains to material and spiritual extravagance, al-Shaybānī holds that it is forbidden to waste food and that one's economic behavior should navigate between extravagance and miserliness. Stocking up food is permissible only in certain cases for which acceptable justification exists, otherwise one's own supplies become the right of someone else. Those who can afford to are obliged to spend on food for the poor and not lavishly spend on themselves,[211] however, one is also discouraged from purposefully starving[212] and must work first and foremost to sustain oneself.[213] Furthermore, one also has to give to those who are not able to work[214] and provide for one's family and relatives,[215] for giving is better than receiving,[216] although the one who receives does so obligatorily. Ultimately, a believer will be asked about his expenditure on the day of judgment.[217]

A similar approach is applied to other basic necessities, such as clothing. The necessity of *kasb* pertains also to the right as *al-haqq* to the less fortunate; providing for those who are incapable of providing (food) for themselves is the responsibility of others (society and governmental authority), and alms are given out of surplus and not out of one's basic provision. In such cases, those who are not capable of providing for themselves are permitted to beg.[218] When one has achieved enough for oneself and one's family (*ghinā*; nowadays *ghanī*, unlike in premodern *fiqh*, designates someone who is in possession of wealth, or a rich person), the attribute of poverty (*ṣifa al-faqr*), as a moral faculty, is regarded as higher than the quality of wealth: "If only people would be content with what suffices for them, and direct their attention to [their] surplus wealth, and direct [this surplus wealth] toward the matter of their eternal life, it would be better for them,"[219] for "no one is called to account for poverty."[220]

210 Bonner, "Kitab al-Kasb Attributed to al-Shaybani," 417; al-Shaybānī, *Kitāb al-Kasb*, 170.
211 Al-Shaybānī, *Kitāb al-Kasb*, 186.
212 Al-Shaybānī, *Kitāb al-Kasb*, 168–169.
213 Al-Shaybānī, *Kitāb al-Kasb*, 194.
214 Al-Shaybānī, *Kitāb al-Kasb*, 190.
215 Al-Shaybānī, *Kitāb al-Kasb*, 203.
216 Al-Shaybānī, *Kitāb al-Kasb*, 194.
217 Al-Shaybānī, *Kitāb al-Kasb*, 203–204.
218 Al-Shaybānī, *Kitāb al-Kasb*, 168.
219 Bonner, "Kitab al-Kasb Attributed to al-Shaybānī," 416.
220 Poverty is sounder than riches, since no poor man will be inspected because of being poor (al-Shaybānī, *Kitāb al-Kasb*, 106–107, 116).

If wealth is something that fluctuates and something that is owned by a person or community that is useful,[221] money can be designated as that which is beneficial. Earning a livelihood by ethical means translates into providing also for others, which is a form of *jihād*.[222]

Another important scholar who also wrote on abstinence, sustenance, and poverty from the perspective of retrieval from the mundane is al-Muḥāsibī, a Shāfiʿī jurist who thoroughly believed that the self needs constant examination and observation. He mastered dialectical theology, jurisprudence, and exegesis, incorporated views on *taṣawwuf*, and allegedly lived according to what he preached.[223] With his thought on Sufism, spiritual values, repentance (*tawba*), trust in God (*taqwā*), sincerity (*ikhlāṣ*), and other related concepts, al-Muḥāsibī influenced many prolific scholars of his time, including al-Ghazālī. Al-Muḥāsibī's book *al-Makāsib wa al-Waraʿ* elucidates human behavior and mannerisms in relation to the inward values and character traits in how people acquire wealth (the outward) and take care of daily obligations by addressing the notions of scrupulousness or prudence (*waraʿ*), abstinence (*zuhd*), reliance on the Divine (*tawakkul*), and introspection (*muḥāsaba*) in conjunction with legal and financial transactions (*muʿāmalāt*). By integrating theological, mystical, and economic ideas, he invokes the activity of working for a living also as a spiritual practice and a means for obtaining provision. One has to engage in praiseworthy economic activities by performing mindfulness, vigilance, remembrance (*dhikr*), dedication and closeness (*al-taqarrub*), and the purification of the heart (*ṭahārat al-qulūb*) in concordance with the moral premise of *Sharīʿa*.[224] Enacting those ethical dispositions enables one to avoid potential harms and vices, for benefits of any economic endeavor should outweigh possible harm and costs. In his view, people must rely for sustenance (*rizq*) solely on God,[225] while love for accumulation of

221 Saʿdī Abū Jayb, *Al-Qāmūs al-Fiqhī* (Damascus: Dār al-Fikr, 1982), 344.

222 Ibn Abī al-Dunyā, *Iṣlāḥ al-Māl*, 73.

223 Even in his name and appellation, al-Muḥāsibī points to one who examines his consciousness and purifies his soul of vice. See Adi Setia, "Al-Muḥāsibī: On Scrupulousness and the Pursuit of Livelihoods: Two Excerpts from His *al-Makāsib wa al-Waraʿ*," *Islamic Sciences*, vol. 14, no. 1 (2016): 69.

224 For the English translation, see Adi Setia, *Kitāb al-Makāsib (The Book of Earnings) by al-Ḥārith al-Muḥāsibī (751–857 CE)* (Kuala Lumpur: IBFIM, 2016).

225 Al-Muḥāsibī, *al-Makāsib wa al-Waraʿ* (Beirut: Muʾssasa al-Kutub al-Thaqāfiyya, 1987), 42.

wealth is due to one's doubt.[226] Al-Muḥāsibī articulates those concerns, especially the acquisition of wealth, in economic terms that further extend to virtuous behavior patterns and hence portray his moral economic ideas as an objective commitment to the Sufi-based principles and criteria. In *Kitāb Ta'dīb al-Murīd*, he further describes an ethical-educational scheme (*ta'dīb*) on how to govern oneself throughout the day, indicating that acquisition of wealth or *kasb* has to be obtained fairly. In *Kitāb al-Waṣāyā al-Naṣā'iḥ al-Dīniyya*[227] al-Muḥāsibī examines the so-called Islamic psychology (*'ilm al-nafs al-Islāmī*) and the impact deeds have on the soul, paying considerable attention to wealth. Since the origin of happiness is God-consciousness or *taqwā*, an idea that is shared also by al-Ghazālī, the source of one's discontent is love of the worldly life or *ḥubb al-dunyā*. Consequently, the accumulation of and desire for wealth goes against the idea of being careful and economical (*isrāf*) as well as miserly (*bakhīl*).

The ninth-century traditionalist from Baghdad Ibn Abī al-Dunyā in the introduction of *Iṣlāḥ al-Māl* invokes the *ḥadīth* narrated by Abū Bakr stating that one who acquires (*ya'khudh*) wealth in a righteous way/not more than they are entitled to (*bi haqq*), their money will be blessed, while one who acquires wealth in an unjust way (*bi ghayr haqq*) will always be complacent.[228] Also based on *ḥadīth* narration is the idea that if wealth gained in an illicit way remains with the person who acquired it, they will not be blessed but punished.[229] In relation to temptation and wasting money (*iḍā'at al-māl*), Ibn Abī al-Dunyā quotes the *ḥadīth* stating that "every *umma* has its *fiṭna* (tribulation), and the *fiṭna* of Muslims is wealth."[230] His second chapter addresses the beneficial functions of money or wealth, which is interrelated with honor (*ḥasab al-māl*) and exemplified through generosity as fear of God.[231] Hence, those who indulge in solitude and asceticism are denounced, for they neglect the mundane realm. Likewise, forsaking the afterlife due to worldly pleasures is also repudiated, that is why retaining faith for the Hereafter and wealth for this world is highly

226 Al-Muḥāsibī, *al-Makāsib wa al-Wara'*, 45.

227 Al-Muḥāsibī, *Kitāb al-Waṣāyā*, ed. 'Abd al-Qādir Aḥmad Aṭā (Beirut: Dār al-Kutub al-'Ilmiyya, 1986).

228 Ibn Abī al-Dunyā, *Iṣlāḥ al-Māl*, 13.

229 Ibn Abī al-Dunyā, *Iṣlāḥ al-Māl*, 18.

230 Ibn Abī al-Dunyā, *Iṣlāḥ al-Māl*, 18. See also the Qur'an, 16:97 on the notion of righteous or licit acquisitions (*kasb al-ṭayyib*).

231 Ibn Abī al-Dunyā, *Iṣlāḥ al-Māl*, 33.

encouraged.[232] Further, those who obtain money ought to consider giving to charity[233] and to utilize it as a means to attain God's bounties.[234] On the other hand, saving money (*qaṣd al-māl*) is a virtue, since the intention is to provide for others.[235] In light of moral integrity, Ibn Abī al-Dunyā holds that those who spend (*sarf*) will not value money less but will try to distribute it based on equity. Yet, those who spend on unnecessary matters (*al-infāq fī ghayr haqq*) have to be wary of their economic behavior.[236] Both wealth and poverty can become tribulations; the adversity of the first is in its insatiate appetite, while the woe of the second in its discontentment with one's status and can lead into further distress.

Abū Naṣr al-Sarrāj al-Ṭūsī (d. 988), one of the earliest authors of *taṣawwuf*, in the *Kitāb al-luma'*, which is considered an encyclopedia for the history of Sufism and has had relevance for introducing the science of *taṣawwuf* into mainstream Sunni Islam, introduces seven *maqāmāt* that play also into economic matters. They include *tawba* (repentance), which begins with the light of Divine recognition in *qalb* (heart) that realizes sin as antithetical to spiritual uplift and strives for spiritual purity, which also requires the faculties of *muḥāsaba* (self-examination) and *murāqaba* (introversion or meditation). The second is *warā'* (prudence), which translates into pious self-reflection and self-restraint. The third is *zuhd* (asceticism), in that it renounces worldly endeavors to the level of necessities. The fourth is *faqr* (poverty), in a spiritual and a material sense, as the denial of the self, in order to dedicate oneself to spiritual and communal obligations. The fifth is *ṣabr* (patience), whose characteristic is essential for spiritual endurance. The sixth is *tawakkul* (trust or confidence in God), as devoting oneself exclusively to the higher order, encompassing *ma'rifa* and *'amal*. The seventh and last is *riḍā'* (pure contentment), as submission to *qaḍā* (fate).[237] These *maqāmāt* are inveterated in the ethical-economic scholarship also in the works of al-Ghazālī.

Abū Ḥāmid al-Ghazālī, who discussed in detail the role of money from Sufi and jurisprudential points of view, is considered

232 Ibn Abī al-Dunyā, *Iṣlāḥ al-Māl*, 41.
233 Ibn Abī al-Dunyā, *Iṣlāḥ al-Māl*, 33.
234 Ibn Abī al-Dunyā, *Iṣlāḥ al-Māl*, 46, 48.
235 See the Qur'an, 25:67.
236 Ibn Abī al-Dunyā, *Iṣlāḥ al-Māl*, 100.
237 Abū Naṣr al-Sarrāj al-Ṭūsī, *Kitāb al-Luma' fī al-Taṣawwuf*, ed. Reynold Alleyne Nicholson (Leyden: Brill, 1914), 43–52.

one of the forerunners of economic thought in Islamic tradition.[238] His approach to economic affairs expounds ethical views embedded in the notion of *sa'āda* as eternal happiness, which is associated with the moral cosmology of *Sharī'a* in providing economic analysis as part of an all-encompassing socio-spiritual worldview. He produced neither a specific book dedicated to economics nor a book on economic jurisprudence, but like many other classical scholars his writing on economic thought can be found in various texts, dealing with *zakāt*, *adab* the role of governmental authority, and righteous behavior. He discussed economic matters, encompassing the nature of work and the means of earning a living, including the production processes; licit means of earning, concerning commerce and trade; justice, equity, and fairness in gaining a livelihood, with regard to, for example, counterfeiting, hoarding, and overpraising goods; and benevolence in trading.[239] The gist of his ideas on economics is to be found mostly in volume 2, book 3 of *Iḥyā' 'Ulūm al-Dīn* (Manners of earning a livelihood); volume 3, book 6 (Evils of wealth and miserliness); and volume 4, book 4 (Poverty and asceticism). According to Ghazanfar and Islahi, his contribution can be divided into four topics, covering various activities, such as voluntary exchange and evolution of markets; production activities and their hierarchy and stages; the barter system and the evolution of money; and the role of the governmental authority and public finances.[240] Al-Ghazālī's spiritual economics presents one component of the revival of Islamic sciences, whose ultimate aim is the alchemy of happiness extended to all human endeavors, based on the notions of justice and the Hereafter. It is well documented that al-Ghazālī was influenced by al-Muḥāsibī and al-Rāghib al-Iṣfahānī. Al-Iṣfahānī, an eleventh-century religious scholar and exegete, provided a psychological account on economic thought rooted in a religious ethic. He advocated for fair earnings for both men and women as a religious obligation. Work does not only bring about basic necessities and

238 On al-Ghazālī's economic thought and his notion of happiness, see Al-Daghistani, *Ethical Teachings of Abū Ḥāmid al-Ghazāli.*

239 On the rules of earnings, trade and commerce, lawful and unlawful issues, the rules of companionship and brotherhood, and the rules of enjoining good and forbidding evil, see al-Ghazālī, *Iḥyā'*, vol. 2.

240 Ghazanfar and Islahi, *Economic Thought of al-Ghazali*, 17.

wealth, which is beneficial for oneself and the community, but it also generates joy and allows one to be generous, since it is an expression of Divine qualities. Wealth is an external virtue linked to the idea of happiness. The remedy for both begging and overworking is frugality, which is the preferred path, since wealth is to be used for one to obtain basic necessities and not material desires. While moderation is the correct path, a believer should exercise effort to attain happiness in the Hereafter. All work is hence cooperative and integrative in that it brings people together, whose source is inspiration and human urge of restlessness (*iḍṭirāb*), in order to satisfy material and nonmaterial needs. In this regard, poverty is not only that which needs to be removed from society, but it also motivates one to be productive and/or to obtain wealth.[241] A similar account on economic philosophy is expounded by al-Ghazālī.

As I have discussed in detail elsewhere,[242] al-Ghazālī divides society into three different groups with regard to material gain: those who neglect the Hereafter and are occupied with worldly endeavors will perish; those whose aim in this life is the return to the Hereafter at the expense of the mundane will succeed; and those who are engaged in worldly (read economic) affairs and adhere to *Sharīʿa* will reach final salvation.[243] One can engage in economic activities by making a livelihood or by investing in one's wealth in order to increase it. Engagements pertaining to *maṣlaḥa* are praiseworthy objectives. Al-Ghazālī maintains that during commerce religious stipulations should not be neglected: "no one should forget his religion and the Hereafter during the course of one's trade and earning a livelihood," for those who do will perish in the afterlife. One's true capital is hence one's religion and matters pertaining to the Hereafter.[244] Since al-Ghazālī positions economic activity within the parameters of an ethical

[241] Yasien Mohamed, *The Path to Virtue: The Ethical Philosophy of al-Rāghib al-Iṣfahānī* (Kuala Lumpur: International Institute of Islamic Thought and Civilization, 2006), 375–414. Abū al-Ḳāsim al-Ḥusayn b. Muḥammad b. al-Mufaḍḍal al-Rāghib al-Iṣfahānī, *Kitāb al-Dharīʿa ilā Makārim al-Sharīʿa* (Cairo: Dār al-Salām, 2007).

[242] The following paragraphs on al-Ghazālī pertain to the ideas expressed in my book, Al-Daghistani, *Ethical Teachings of Abū Ḥāmid al-Ghazālī*. See also Sami Al-Daghistani, "Al-Ghazali and the Intellectual History of Islamic Economics," *ZIT Jahrbuch für Islamische Theologie und Religionspädagogik: Islamische Gelehrten neu gelesen*, vol. 3 (2014): 97–134.

[243] Al-Ghazālī, *Iḥyāʾ*, vol. 2, 62. [244] Al-Ghazālī, *Iḥyāʾ*, vol. 2, 62.

worldview, the Hereafter is seen as the ultimate goal. The middle path of al-Ghazālī's economic philosophy pins down a systematic, yet intuitively moral approach to one's contribution in the economic life of the *dunyā*, as well as one's own salvation, which is ultimately achieved in the afterlife. Righteous economic engagement might be a prerequisite for the latter, for earning is not an aim on its own.[245]

He criticized those who believe that economic activities are related only to the substance of survival or of living.[246] Al-Ghazālī has emphasized that money or wealth (*māl*) "is not a desire for its own sake,"[247] but it was invented only as a medium of exchange, since gold, due to outstanding qualities and high value, ought to be a common source for transactions. Therefore *fulūs* (cheap copper coins) are not to be mixed with silver and gold *dīnārs* and *dirhams*, for "dissemination of a single bad dirham is worse than stealing thousand dirhams," since stealing is a sinful act that ends once performed; yet, circulation of corrupt money stands as an innovation (*bid'a*) and has repercussions for many.[248] Since counterfeiting is penalized because it can affect the market rates, one should avoid selling broken coins and metals as *dīnārs* or *dirhams*.[249]

The level of consumption thus has to range between necessity and extravagance.[250] While necessity has to be met by the consumer, for it is perceived as a religious obligation, extravagance is forbidden (*ḥarām*). All economic activities that extend to meet human needs – food, clothing, and shelter[251] – are in accordance with *Sharī'a* law in that they improve one's (social) status. In *Mīzān al-'Amal*, a short work on ethics, al-Ghazālī mentions three levels of consumption: the lowest, the middle, and the highest,[252] corresponding to necessity, convenience, and luxury. Since acquiring wealth is intrinsic to human nature, "One loves to accumulate wealth and increases one's possessions of all types of property,"[253] due to the illusion that wealth is everlasting. This is the reason why goods ought not to be praised.[254] Money has been created for a particular purpose in order to fulfill human needs. On the other hand, miserliness means excessive restriction on expenditure,

245 Al-Ghazālī, *Iḥyā'*, vol. 2, 108. 246 Al-Ghazālī, *Iḥyā'*, vol. 2, 108.
247 Al-Ghazālī, *Iḥyā'*, vol. 4, 114–115.
248 Al-Ghazālī, *Iḥyā'*, vol. 2, 73–74; see also Ghazanfar and Islahi, *Economics of al-Ghazali*, 30.
249 Al-Ghazālī, *Iḥyā'*, vol. 2, 68. 250 Al-Ghazālī, *Iḥyā'*, vol. 2, 1.
251 Al-Ghazālī, *Mīzān al-'Amal*, 377. 252 Al-Ghazālī, *Mīzān al-'Amal*, 377.
253 Al-Ghazālī, *Iḥyā'*, vol. 3, 290. 254 Al-Ghazālī, *Iḥyā'*, vol. 2, 74.

while extravagance is excessive expenditure. Utilization of wealth must therefore be in accordance with Islamic jurisprudence, which is for al-Ghazālī embedded in his overall ethical system of the path of the Hereafter – whose teachings resonate with what I call the moral cosmology of *Sharīʿa* – in order to facilitate spending on lawful products in a righteous way. Yet, the ultimate aim is the remembrance and contemplation about the Hereafter.

Despite the fact that poverty countervails morally designed society,[255] the lust for money contravenes a righteous character. For al-Ghazālī, *māl* is one of the five necessities (*al-ḍarūriyyāt*) that *Sharīʿa* provides for safeguarding righteous conduct against any temptation (*fitna*), and no human being can survive without it.[256] To underpin the importance of the correct utilization of wealth, al-Ghazālī cites many Qurʾanic verses[257] and *ḥadīth*[258] that state that wealth should not be praised. Miserliness is condemned, for it leads to tyranny if not handled correctly; that is why spiritual predispositions or intentions (*niyya*) in the usage of wealth are a precondition. In order to distinguish the importance of *māl* from its sinful implications if utilized under certain conditions and manners, al-Ghazālī aims to provide a description of *māl* according to its social function, concerning not just ethical teachings within Islamic tradition but also its function in labor and production processes. *Māl* includes spiritual, bodily, and external benefits, nonetheless it is only a means and not an end of human endeavor in carrying out economic conduct. Wealth is the worst temptation,[259] and since extravagance in spending is undesirable, excessive expenditure also ought to be avoided. Extravagance means when money is spent on a good, at the time, and in the amount that it is not needed.[260] One of al-Ghazālī's most pertinent observations of *māl* is his analysis of human behavior toward it. *Māl* is praiseworthy only if exercising righteous objectives (*maqsūd*) and is thus divided into two categories – benefits of money related to the mundane and ones related to higher metaphysical objectives. Religious or metaphysical benefits are further subcategorized[261] as money that one can spend for the realization of religious endeavors as well as for other necessities that

[255] Poverty has to be abrogated, yet it is seen as a spiritual component over riches. Al-Ghazālī, *Iḥyāʾ*, vol. 3, 264–265.
[256] Al-Ghazālī, *Iḥyāʾ*, vol. 3, 231.
[257] Qurʾan, 62:9; 64:14; 96:6–7.
[258] Al-Ghazālī, *Iḥyāʾ*, vol. 3, 232.
[259] Al-Ghazālī, *Iḥyāʾ*, vol. 3, 234.
[260] Al-Ghazālī, *Mīzān al-ʿAmal*, 284.
[261] Al-Ghazālī, *Iḥyāʾ*, vol. 3, 235–236.

enable the performance of the first, such as pilgrimage to *hajj*, but also food, shelter, and clothing. In other words, money can be spent in relation to what is necessary for the accomplishment of that which is *wājib*.

In *Kīmiyā*, al-Ghazālī lays down the idea that gaining profit is licit but not at any cost; trading with illicit goods is also illicit, while one can trade only with what one owns.[262] Since possessing wealth facilitates the enjoyment of illicit pleasures, the more one has the more one might be prone to spending. Al-Ghazālī constantly draws attention to the fact that money does not possess an intrinsic value of its own, but its value is dependent upon trade and exchange of commodities.[263] Value is inextricably related to commodities and labor, as a means to achieve higher ends.[264]

Creation of dirhams and dīnārs is one of many bounties of God. Every aspect of economic activities relies on dealings with these two types of money. They are two metals that have no intrinsic benefit on their own, nonetheless, people need them, so that they can use them as [as a medium] for exchange for food, clothing, and other goods. Sometimes, one needs what one does not own and one owns what one does not need. For instance, if someone has saffron and needs a camel, and another person owns a camel but needs saffron, the two cannot carry out the exchange without using money [as a measure of goods], for the one who owns a camel does not need the same amount of saffron.[265]

As such trading in gold for gold and silver for silver for the purpose of making money is condemned, while selling gold for silver or vice versa is a licit economic transaction.[266] This means that money should not be spent in order to gain more money but rather to promote mutual cooperation between parties. An unjust person or merchant is thus the one who spends more than is needed and/or hoards money, while others are in need of money for religious (spiritual) purposes.[267] "Dirhams and dīnārs are not created for any specific person. They are

262 Al-Ghazālī, *Iḥyā'*, vol. 2; al-Ghazālī, *Kīmiyā*, 474.
263 This can be observed, centuries later, also in writings by Karl Marx and Friedrich Engels.
264 El-Ashker and Wilson, *Islamic Economics*, 248. Money should not be spent for its own sake. Al-Ghazālī, *Iḥyā'*, vol. 3, 278.
265 Al-Ghazālī, *Iḥyā'*, vol. 4, 91.
266 El-Ashker and Wilson, *Islamic Economics*, 248.
267 Al-Ghazālī, *Iḥyā'*, vol. 4, 95.

without value in themselves, and are like stones. Rather, they are created for circulation [from person to person], in order to promote transactions."[268] They are meant only as a value of goods, and whoever utilizes them simply as gold and silver is a transgressor.

On the other hand, al-Dimashqī, who was a Shafiʿī jurist and a businessperson, and dedicated a whole book to solving economic problems, stipulates accumulation of wealth, but by regulating the means.[269] Although a pious Muslim, he refrained from a theological discussion on the notion of fair price and believed that a merchant has to manipulate market forces in order to prosper. In his work, he analyzed the value of good in relation to its cost, the amount of work one puts in, and its demand. *Māl* as wealth or money[270] can be gained or inherited, and it is divided into four categories: coins as so-called "quiet wealth" (*al-ṣāmit*);[271] gifts, including clothing, jewelry, copper, and anything made out of it (*al-iʿrāḍ*);[272] property (*al-ʿaqār*);[273] and animals as "talking wealth" (*al-ḥaywān*).[274] Human needs are divided into two categories, namely basic necessities, such as food, clothing, and shelter, and supplemental necessities, such as armaments and medicine. Al-Dimashqī claims that all wealth is beneficial,[275] yet it depends on time, space, and other characteristics and should not be acquired as a means to deprive others.[276] Despite his support of wealth, he advocated a communal life, due to cooperation between industries and in order for a society to establish a stable price at the market, and opposed counterfeiting of coins. Accordingly, one can gain wealth either by intent or by chance, while a good merchant pursues a healthy measure of benefit and profit and possesses virtues such as honesty and fairness and does not engage in fraudulent behavior. Likewise, when purchasing, one has to avoid neglecting family relations, lust, overindulgence, boasting, and disproportional division of religious and social tasks.

[268] Al-Ghazālī, *Iḥyāʾ*, vol. 4, 91–92.
[269] Al-Dimashqī, *al-Ishāra ilā Maḥāsin al-Tijāra*, 54, 80–82.
[270] Al-Dimashqī, *al-Ishāra ilā Maḥāsin al-Tijāra*, 17–19.
[271] Al-Dimashqī, *al-Ishāra ilā Maḥāsin al-Tijāra*, 22–26.
[272] Al-Dimashqī, *al-Ishāra ilā Maḥāsin al-Tijāra*, 26–35.
[273] Al-Dimashqī, *al-Ishāra ilā Maḥāsin al-Tijāra*, 53–56.
[274] Al-Dimashqī, *al-Ishāra ilā Maḥāsin al-Tijāra*, 56–57.
[275] Al-Dimashqī, *al-Ishāra ilā Maḥāsin al-Tijāra*, 69.
[276] Al-Dimashqī, *al-Ishāra ilā Maḥāsin al-Tijāra*, 69, 85.

Ibn Taymiyya states that prices (*athmān*) "are meant to be a measurement of objects of value (*mi'yār al-amwāl*), through which the quantities of objects of value (*maqādir al-amwāl*) are known; and they are never meant to be consumed."[277] This indicates that the primary function of money is to measure value of goods and as a tool or medium of exchange. If goods are to be exchanged for money, the transactions have to be simultaneous. He also expressed concerns about the debasement of currency under the Mamluk reign, stating that the authority should mint coins (*fulūs*) according to the value of people's transactions, avoiding any possible harm or injustice. Coins should be minted according to real value without the motive of profit, for "trading in money means opening a great door of injustice for the people and of devouring their wealth by false pretences."[278] His disciple Ibn Qayyim also holds that money and coins are not meant for themselves but they are to be used for purchasing goods,[279] indicating that *fulūs* can be used only in order to exchange goods between people.

The idea that wealth has a complex nature, pertaining to both human benefit and detriment was held by Ibn Qayyim, a Ḥanbalī jurist with a great interest in Sufism, who affirmed that wealth is not meant only for pleasure. One of the main objectives of *Sharī'a* was for him, as for many other classical scholars, the conception of justice (*'adl*). As as a theologian and adherent of the Ḥanbalī *madhhab*, he believed that a person's piety is interrelated with their wealth, as well as that people should fulfill their social obligations by providing for others. In spite of the fact that wealth enables one to extend social and moral duties to other members of society, it is poverty and *zuhd*, as a means of purification from lusty endeavors, that are perceived as the most exalted. In his most developed spiritual treaties, Ibn Qayyim insists that *zuhd* does not mean the wholesale rejection of worldly endeavors, since even the most pious possess some sort of property. *Zuhd* is rather an approach, an attitude through which one purifies worldly excesses and lust for them.[280]

277 Ibn Taymiyya, *Majmū' Fatāwā Shaykh al-Islām*, vol. 29, 472, in Islahi, *Economic Concepts of Ibn Taymiyyah*, 140.

278 Ibn Taymiyya, *Majmū' Fatāwā Shaykh al-Islām*, vol. 29, 469, in Islahi, *Economic Concepts of Ibn Taymiyyah*, 140.

279 Ibn Qayyim al-Jawziyya, *I'lām al-Muwaqqi'īn* (1973).

280 See Ibn Qayyim al-Jawziyya, *Madārij al-Salikīn* (Cairo: al-Mu'asasa al-Mukhtār li al-Nashar wa al-Tawzīa', 2001), vol. 1, 437–438.

3.7.2 Zakāt *As Wealth and* Ribā *As an Illicit Use of Money*

Zakāt and *ribā* are not only legal or ritualistic in nature but have throughout Islamic history maintained a spiritual status of cleansing one's wealth and restoring balance. The dualistic moral-social value of *zakāt* has been an important mechanism of social justice in economic tradition and has often been addressed in relation to other ethical-economic tools.[281]

The prohibition against *ribā* is well known in economic history, and many scholars have forbidden it within trade activities. Exchange of goods is a necessary endeavor for any society, religious, or secular. *Ribā* (usury or excessive usurious practice) can be looked upon as a specific loan allocation; however, such a view indicates that money has value on its own. And since money only indicates the value of one's labor or traded commodity, it cannot be the measure of value.

In *Iḥyā' 'Ulūm al-Dīn*, al-Ghazālī does not tackle *ribā* in loans directly, but discusses nonmonetary transactions. He emphasized the subtle forms of *ribā*, when exchanging gold for gold, or any other good for the same good but with differences in quantity or time of delivery. In this case *ribā* may occur when the time of delivery is different from the arrangements (*ribā al nāṣi'ah*) or when the exchanged quantity of a good is not equal in value (*ribā al faḍl*).[282] Al-Ghazālī is thus criticizing the system of accumulation of money: when someone is trading in *dirhams* and *dīnārs* themselves, he is making them as his goal, which is contrary to their objectives. Money is not created to earn money and doing so would be a transgression.[283] Usurious practices refute ethical principles that are the core of al-Ghazālī's (and other classical scholars') understanding of economic behavior. Money was utilized as a measure or medium of exchange of commodities in order to ensure just transactions in terms of value and quantity.[284] Al-Ghazālī warns that *ribā* violates the very nature of the function of

[281] Hallaq, "Groundwork of the Moral Law," 268–269; Hallaq, *Impossible State*, 123.

[282] Al-Ghazāli, *Iḥyā'*, vol. 4, 192–193.

[283] Sadeq, "Ghazalijevi pogledi na ekonomske probleme i neka etičko-pravna pitanja značajna za ekonomsko ponašanje," in Sadeq and Ghazali, eds., *Pregled islamske ekonomske misli*, 31.

[284] Islahi, *Contribution of Muslim Scholars to Economic Thought*, 51. On the prohibition of *ribā*, see also the Qur'an, 2:275, 2:276, 2:278, 3:130, 4:161, 30:39.

money,[285] which is no more than a medium of exchange.[286] He concludes that the true gain is rather in "the market of the hereafter."[287]

Muslim philosopher and jurist Ibn Rushd based his views on money mostly on Aristotelian views. Ibn Rushd's prohibition of *ribā* is grounded in the conviction that *ribā* may involve cheating:

> It is clear from the *Sharīʿa* that the purpose of prohibiting *ribā* relates to the possibility of great cheating that exists therein. Justice in transactions lies in approximating equivalence. So, when realizing equivalence between different things was found to be almost impossible, *dīnār* and *dirham* were made to evaluate them, that is, measure them. As between different kind of commodities, I mean those which can neither be weighed nor measured, justice lies in their being proportionate. The ratio of the value of one thing to its kind should be equal to the ratio of the other things to that thing's kind.[288]

Furthermore, Ibn Taymiyya wrote on usury, upholding the prohibition thereof: "To exact a higher amount over and above the sum lent, on that conjectural basis is a kind of injustice and exploitation."[289] Yet, according to Ibn Taymiyya, despite the reason behind the prohibition of *ribā* being sometimes unclear, both types are prohibited as a precautionary measure, whereas loans without attached interest, *ṣadaqa*, and *zakāt*, are encouraged. His statement, "When Allah created two types of people – rich and poor – He made the *zakāt* obligatory for the rich as a right of the poor; and at the same time He forbade the rich from taking interest that harms people,"[290] promotes the removal of poverty from society, which can

285 Al-Ghazāli, vol. 4, 192–193.

286 Many other Muslim scholars have written on the notion of money usage and usury e.g. Ibn Taymiyya and Ibn Rushd. For the later, the main aim of the prohibition is to prevent misuse in the barter exchange of commodities, gold, and silver. Since *ribā* opens the door for cheating, the prohibition of it enforces a just transaction and equivalence. *Dīnārs* and *dirhams* were made for the sake of evaluation, thus the justice in the exchange between various commodities lies not in their weight or measurement but in their being proportioned. The ratio between two different kinds should be equal in respect to their kinds. See Ibn Rushd, *Bidāyat al-Mujtahid*, vol. 2, 135.

287 Al-Ghazāli, *Iḥyāʾ*, vol. 2, 75, 76, 84.

288 Ibn Rushd, *Bidāyat al-Mujtahid*, vol. 2, 135; in Islahi, *History of Islamic Economic Thought*, 42. Ibn Rushd, *The Distinguished Jurist Primer* (Doha: Garnet Publishing, 2000), vol. 2.

289 Ibn Taymiyya in Islahi, *Contribution of Muslim Scholars to Economic Thought*, 51.

290 Ibn Taymiyya, *Majmūʿ Fatāwā Shaykh al-Islām*, vol. 29, 346–347; Islahi, *Economic Concepts of Ibn Taymiyyah*, 138.

also be found in the Qur'an.[291] An alternative to *ribā*-based practices is the provision of profit- and loss-sharing, whereby the owner of a commodity and the buyer share the profit and loss.[292]

Ibn Qayyim took Ibn Taymiyya's notion on *ribā* further by developing two categories, *ribā al-jalī* and *ribā al-khafī*, or "open" and "disguised" interest. The former is explicitly illicit, whereas the latter is prohibited based on precautionary measures.[293] On *zakāt*, which accounts for at least 2.5 percent, he holds that it is imposed only on certain types of property, such as cattle, cultivated plants, gold and silver, and trading goods,[294] and should be given to the poor, those in need, prisoners, and travelers.

3.8 Productivity, Value of Labor, and Cooperation

As briefly mentioned above, Muslim scholars discussed in detail the division and value of labor, cooperation between various industries, distribution of goods, and levels of productivity, while also propounding the idea of production processes being part of wider ethical considerations based on Qur'anic metaphysics and a moral understanding of the universe.[295]

3.8.1 *Division of Labor and Mutual Cooperation*

For al-Shaybānī there are four types of earnings or ways of production: employment (*al-ijāra*), commerce or trading (*al-tijāra*), agriculture (*al-zirā'a*), and craftsmanship (*ṣinā'a*).[296] For him, agriculture supersedes other economic activities as the source of commerce.[297] Farming, along with handcraft, is a favorable activity also according to Ibn Abī al-Dunyā,[298] and since it depends on grazing, an owner of the land is

291 "Verily Allah abolishes *ribā* and increases charity" (Qur'an, 2:276).
292 Ibn Taymiyya *Majmū' Fatāwā Shaykh al-Islām*, 84, 108.
293 Ibn Qayyim al-Jawziyya, *I'lām al-Muwaqqi'īn* (Cairo: Maktaba al-Tijāriyah al-Kubrā, 1955), vol. 2, 135–142 in Islahi, *Economic Concepts of Ibn Taymiyyah*, 132.
294 Ibn Qayyim al-Jawziyya, *Zād al-Ma'ād* (1982), vol. 1, 222.
295 E.g. Qur'an, 62:10, 73:20.
296 Al-Shaybānī, *Kitāb al-Kasb*, 140.
297 Al-Shaybānī, *al-Iktisāb fī al-Rizq al-Mustaṭāb*, 41–42; al-Shaybānī, *Kitāb al-Kasb*, 131, 140, 146.
298 Ibn Abī al-Dunyā, *Iṣlāḥ al-Māl*, 94.

encouraged to preserve the land. Likewise, the owner will be rewarded from fertile land that is beneficial to a person or an animal.

Al-Ghazālī grouped economic activities into five categories, consisting of farming (producing food), grazing (producing food for animals), hunting (utilizing the natural environment), weaving (producing textiles), and building and construction (provision of shelter).[299] For al-Ghazālī, economic activity and production are part of his overall ethics of happiness (*sa ʿāda*), achieved on the path toward the Hereafter: "The highest aim of the science of unveiling (*ʿilm al-mukāshafa*) is the knowledge (*ma ʿrifa*) of God. This is the aim that is sought as an end in itself, for it is through it that happiness is achieved. Or rather it [knowledge of God] is itself happiness, even though in this world the heart may not feel so but will only feel this in the hereafter."[300] On the division of labor he states, "While the farmer produces grains, the miller then converts grains into flour, and the baker prepares bread from that flour."[301] Despite the fact that division of labor is evident, he recognizes the interdependence of economic activities[302] and, more importantly, that they constitute the higher order of knowledge. It is hence not only labor but also production processes (as a balance between natural resources and human labor, including science) that are enmeshed in a moral cosmological reasoning, since production is not only meant to provide utility but also to improve the physical and, more importantly, spiritual conditions of the moral self as the medium to achieve eternal happiness of the afterlife.

The value of labor was well known to classical scholars. Since human work is motivated by its usefulness or necessity for society at large, labor is not simply an instrument of production but a crucial part of one's daily religious (devotional) activity or *ʿibāda*. The ideal level of

[299] Al-Ghazālī, *Iḥyā ʾ*, vol. 4, 12; Ghazanfar and Islahi, *Economic Thought of al-Ghazali*, 24.

[300] Al-Ghazālī, *Iḥyā ʾ*, vol. 4, 137. See also an English translation in Abū Ḥāmid al-Ghazālī, *Mīzān al-ʿAmal*, translated by Muhammad Hozien, 180–181, available at http://ghazali.org/works/mizan-en.htm.

[301] Al-Ghazālī, *Iḥyā ʾ*, vol. 4, 137.

[302] "The blacksmith produces the tools so that a farmer can cultivate, and the carpenter produces the tools that are needed by the blacksmith. This is applicable for all who engage in the production of tools, that are needed for production of foodstuffs." Al-Ghazālī, *Iḥyā ʾ*, vol. 4, 12.

consumption and moderation has been promulgated by classical Muslim scholars according to basic human needs. The focal point of such an economic philosophy is thus inextricably related to the operation of trade agreements, market function, and, above all, the concept of equity and (social) responsibility. By providing for the poor, restricting extravagance, and prohibiting hoarding and interest, the idea is not only that work means provision or that it is spiritual in essence[303] but rather that it informs a spiritual understanding of production theory and production efficiency. In this context, production creates the usefulness of goods and the benefits of an object, in that produced goods must have a relationship with human needs. In other words, produced goods must meet human needs, including one's morality. Their function is directed not only toward the market but extends to human benefits.

For Ibn Taymiyya "People stand in need of trade, gift, hire and other practices in their economic life in the same way as they need food, drink and clothing. The Shariʿah has laid down proper guidelines for these practices. Thus it has forbidden such practices as are corrupt (fasid) and enjoined those that are desirable. It disapproves of the undesirable ones and prefers those in which there are great benefits."[304] It is apparent that Ibn Taymiyya bases his reasoning on the Divine authority, advocating its presence based on its rational faculties of justice and truth. "The Shariʿah has never prohibited a thing (whose prohibition) might create hindrance in economic life. It is against the spirit of Shariʿah."[305] All economic activities and transactions are, according to him, grouped in two categories – transactions based on justice and those that entail benevolent deeds.[306] The essential component of all transactions and

303 There are three purposes of work: to provide for necessary goods and services; to use gifts and goods; and to be in service with other individuals to liberate oneself from egocentricity. See Waleed El-Ansary, "Islamic Science and the Critique of Neoclassical Economic Theory," in *Contemporary Islamic finance: Innovations, Applications, and Best Practices*, ed. Karen Hunt-Ahmed (Hoboken, NJ: John Wiley & Sons, 2013), 75–101.

304 Ibn Taymiyya, *Majmūʿ Fatāwā Shaykh al-Islām*, vol. 19, 18, in Islahi, *Economic Concepts of Ibn Taymiyyah*, 152.

305 Ibn Taymiyya, *al-Qawāʾid al-Nurīniyah* (Cairo: Matbaʾah al-Sunnah al-Muḥammadiyah, 1951), 143, in Islahi, *Economic Concepts of Ibn Taymiyyah*, 168.

306 The justice-based transactions are further divided into two: transactions through exchange (*al-muāʿawamāt*) and transactions through partnership (*al-mushārakāt*). Examples of the first category are exchanges based on the same

contracts, in terms of labor and exchange of goods, is the notion of justice, which is applicable to all parties involved, advocating the sharing of losses and gains, for both invested money and one's labor are equally part of the production activity: "The basis of business and partnership is justice from both parties. Therefore, it is against justice that one party reserves the profit of some particular commodity or some specific quantity of profit to itself, or that only one party should bear the loss."[307] In this light, profit is to be obtained through the value of labor, and it thus ought to be divided among the participants.

3.8.2 *Ethical Principles of Trade Activities*

According to Ibn Abī al-Dunyā, if one seeks to attain a peaceful life, good social position, and sufficient food supplies, one can obtain them through seeking labor and licit acquisition of wealth (*al-rizq*), which is a form of *jihād* (*ṭala bi al-ḥalāl jihād*).[308] In view of valuing lawful provision, an honest merchant is positioned in the highest sphere[309] and trading of clothes and food is preferred,[310] while those who monopolize (goods or prices) are damned (*al-jālib marzūq wa al-muḥtakar mal'ūn*).[311] Ibn Abī al-Dunyā was also well aware of the concealed value of cheap goods at the market, which was the reason for his suggestion to purchase better and hence goods that are less expensive.[312]

In relation to mutual cooperation, a tradition of the Prophet Muḥammad advocated equity of barter exchange: forbidden was "the sale of gold by gold, and silver by silver, and wheat by wheat,

good or for money, or hire (*ijārah*) of goods, whereas partnership-based transactions are again divided into two: property partnership (*shirkah al-amlāk*) and contracts partnership (*shirkah al-'aqd*). Ibn Taymiyya, *Majmū' Fatāwā Shaykh al-Islām*, vol. 29, 99, in Islahi *Economic Concepts of Ibn Taymiyyah*, 168.

307 Ibn Taymiyya, *Majmū' Fatāwā Shaykh al-Islām*, 84, in Islahi, *Economic Concepts of Ibn Taymiyyah*, 157.

308 Ibn Abī al-Dunyā, *Iṣlāḥ al-Māl*, 71, 73.

309 "*Al-tājir al-sudūq al-amīn al-muslim ma'a shuhadā' fī yaum al-qiyāma*," Ibn Abī al-Dunyā, *Iṣlāḥ al-Māl*, 73.

310 Trading of slaves, however, is regarded as the lowest kind of trading activity. Ibn Abī al-Dunyā, *Iṣlāḥ al-Māl*, 81–82.

311 Ibn Abī al-Dunyā, *Iṣlāḥ al-Māl*, 84.

312 "I know that worthy goods are cheaper, and that the bad ones are expensive (*al-jayyid rakhīṣ wa al-radī'a ghālī*)." Ibn Abī al-Dunyā, *Iṣlāḥ al-Māl*, 86.

and barley by barley, and dates by dates, and salt by salt, except like for like and equal for equal. So he who made an addition or who accepted an addition (committed the sin of taking) interest."[313] According to profit- and loss-sharing endeavors, in *Kīmiyā-yi Sa'ādat* (*Alchemy of Happiness*), al-Ghazālī lays down ethical principles to be integrated into trade activities. Traders should be honest in their occupation, and one should earn one's living by offering one's labor, since labor is viewed upon as *tawakkul*.[314] In accordance with the ethical premise of *Sharī'a*, al-Ghazālī has analyzed three elements of trade: agreements between buyer and seller, commodities of the transaction, and contents of the agreement.[315] It is forbidden to sell goods to a minor, the mentally ill, a slave, a blind person, someone who will make unlawful profit, a tyrant, a usurer, a thief, or an unreliable person who engages in corruption.[316] Moreover, one should avoid fraud in weights of quantities in order to fix the price of a good,[317] for a fair price based on the principle of justice (*'adl*) is encouraged.[318] Based on this premise, if a buyer offers a higher price than the price currently on the market, the seller will not accept the offer, since an excess of profit might occur.[319]

In light of righteous trading activities and transactions, al-Ghazālī describes how trade should be conducted.[320] It is expected that one will refrain from harmful behavior, such as hoarding of foodstuff, counterfeiting coins, monopolizing a market, and praising a commodity, and attain to higher objectives, such as gaining enough profit as stipulated before the purchase, reducing the price of a commodity when selling to a poorer seller, extending the deadline of debt repayment, selling food supplies to the poor without any interest, and so forth.[321] Al-Ghazālī further discusses the development of marketplaces:

313 Saḥīh Muslim, book 10, chapter 37, *hadīth* number 3852. Accessible at www.sahihmuslim.com/sps/smm/sahihmuslim.cfm?scn=dspchaptersfull&BookID=10&ChapterID=629.

314 Al-Ghazālī, *Iḥyā'*, vol. 4, 265.

315 Sadeq, "Ghazalijevi pogledi na ekonomske probleme i neka etičko-pravna pitanja značajna za ekonomsko ponašanje" in Sadeq and Ghazali, *Pregled islamske ekonomske misli*, 150.

316 Al-Ghazālī, *Iḥyā'*, vol. 2, 64–65; al-Ghazālī, *Kīmiyā-yi Sa'ādat*, 471–472.

317 Al-Ghazālī, *Kīmiyā-yi Sa'ādat*, 355–356.

318 Al-Ghazālī, *Kīmiyā-yi Sa'ādat*, 356.

319 Al-Ghazālī, *Iḥyā'*, vol. 2, 79.

320 Muhammad Abdul Quasem, *The Ethics of Al-Ghazali* (Petaling Jaya, Selangor: Quasem, 1975), 223.

321 Al-Ghazālī, *Iḥyā'*, vol. 2, 75, 79-80. See also Quasem, *Ethics of Al-Ghazali*, 225.

It occurs that [sometimes] farmers live where tools are not available, and that blacksmiths and carpenters live where farming does not take place. Hence, the farmer needs blacksmiths and carpenters, and they are also in a need of farmers. By nature, each of them strives toward satisfying his own needs by giving away a certain amount of his possessions. However, it can also occur that when the carpenter needs food in exchange for tools, the farmer is not in need of the [offered] tools, or when the farmer needs tools from the carpenter, the carpenter is not in need of food. Since these kinds of occurrences create difficulties, this generates the creation of trading spaces where different kinds of tools are exchanged and of warehouses where farmers' products are stored. Customers can come to collect goods and [as a consequence] both markets and storehouses emerge. Farmers bring their products to the markets and in case they cannot sell or exchange it, they can sell them at a lower price to the merchants who in turn store the products and try to sell them to the buyers with a profit. This goes for all types of goods and services . . . . People's needs and their interests generate the need for collaboration and transfer of goods. After that stage, a group of professional traders who transport goods from a place to place comes into play. The reason for these activities is without a doubt the accumulation of profits.[322]

For al-Ghazālī, the process of mutual exchange and collaboration between industries is certainly motivated by profit, which is, nonetheless, guided by fair conduct.

Ibn Taymiyya asserts that certain goods are desired when they are scarce rather than when they are widely available,[323] since the sense of need revolves around those who demand them, as well as their economic circumstances.[324] Furthermore, Ibn Khaldūn considers agriculture an important activity, even though in *Muqqadima* he stated that sedentary people do not practice it,[325] while al-Dimashqī also warns that "Industries are interdependent on each other. The builder needs carpenter, while the carpenter needs blacksmith. The iron workers

322 Al-Ghazālī, *Iḥyā'*, vol. 3, 227, as quoted in Al-Daghistani, *Ethical Teachings of Abū Ḥamid al-Ghazālī*, 82–83; Ghazanfar and Islahi, *Economic Thought of al-Ghazali*, 24–25. The analysis of market developments by al-Ghazālī precedes many European classical economists. Al-Ghazālī's farmer–carpenter example is quite analogous to Adam Smith's illustration of "butcher–baker." See also Ghazanfar and Islahi, *Economic Thought of al-Ghazali*, 54 in reference.

323 Ibn Taymiyya, *Majmū' Fatāwā Shaykh al-Islām*, 523.

324 Abdul Azim Islahi, "Ibn Taymiyyah's Concept of Market Mechanism," *Journal of Research in Islamic Economics*, vol. 2, no. 2, (1985): 53.

325 Franz Rosenthal, *Muqaddimah of Ibn Khaldūn* (Princeton, NJ: Princeton University Press, 1967), vol. 2, 335; Ibn Khaldūn, *Muqaddima*.

need contribution by mine workers, and those are in a need of builders."[326]

3.8.3 Overall Well-Being and Development through Economic Provision

Along with al-Ghazālī and Ibn Taymiyya, Ibn Hazm is one of the many proponents of the imposition of extra taxes in times of state resource deficiencies.[327] He stressed not only the legal and juristic viewpoints of the *ʿulamāʾ* on economic matters but also the importance of their opinions and the rationale behind them. The provision of basic food, clothing, and shelter, which constitutes a basic standard of living, should come from governmental authority and from wealthy members of society. For him, poverty might occur due to the increased and disproportionate levels of needs in relation to the income that is needed to fulfill one's basic needs. Those who can afford are invited to pay *zakāt*, and if neglected it transforms into a debt to God (which again portrays the dual spiritual-material essence of *zakāt*). Al-Ghazālī foregrounded not only religious duty but also the material welfare encapsulated in spiritual well-being, based on the concepts of common good and the economics of *adab*. Al-Māwardī proposed justice (*ʿadl*), peace, religion, security, and proper education as the decisive components of overall human development in society.[328] Ibn Taymiyya furthermore, encouraged cooperation and interdependence between different fields and economic activities, in order to bring about welfare, which is based on benevolence and justice.

Ibn Khaldūn, in Western scholarship often labeled as the father of modern sociology, which insinuates a particular and rather Eurocentric reading of his work, whose thought was nonetheless also intricately bound to the mystical dimension in Islamic tradition, was one of the first scholars who conceptualized economic thought within historical analysis by looking also at social factors. Ibn Khaldūn invented a new discipline called *ʿilm al-ʿūmrān al-basharī wa al-ijtimāʿ al-insānī* (the science of the civilization of mankind and human socialization), by studying the nature of human society.[329] In *Muqaddima*, his political

326 Al-Dimashqī, *al-Ishāra ilā Maḥāsin al-Tijāra*, 21.

327 See Ibn Hazm, *al-Muhalla*, vols. 2 and 6.

328 Al-Māwardī, *Adab al-Wazir* (Egypt: Maktabah al-Khanji, 1929), 3–4, 20, in Islahi, *Contribution of Muslim Scholars to Economic Thought*, 66.

329 See Ibn Khaldūn, *Muqaddima*.

economy is less based on renunciation of worldly affairs and more on the theory of cycles and socioeconomic development, which goes hand in hand with the idea of just rule. His five-stage cycle[330] procures development of social cohesion of dynasties (societies). While the first phase is about establishment of the empire, in the second phase the ruler gains control over the people. During the third phase, economic prosperity is achieved and taxes collected, while in the fourth phase the ruler's successor steps in. It is the fifth phase that is the most devastating, by way of the elite's overindulgent and luscious life that leads into the shattering of the social system. Ibn Khaldūn's key concept of *ʿaṣabiyya* (social cohesion) provides stability and cooperation.[331] The cycle theory promulgates *Sharīʿa*-induced views on ruler's conduct, expenditure policy, tax returns, and social productivity being both socioeconomic and moral in essence.

3.9 Islamic Authority (*Wilāya*) and the Principle of Moral Integrity

From its early beginnings, the Islamic caliphate aimed at recognizing the legal execution of power and the political rule, linking them by way of moral norms. As shown by Hallaq, the state as we understand it in modern terms did not exist in Muslim societies, yet the role of the so-called state authority or government was discussed at length in many manuals on just governance, legal texts, and other treatise. Various scholars, such as Abū Yūsuf, al-Māwardī, al-Iṣfahānī, al-Ghazālī, Ibn Taymiyya, al-Maqrīzī, and so forth, discussed the ruler's role in facilitating fair economic policies. In spite of different geographical and political landscapes, many scholars raised similar concerns.

3.9.1 Ḥisba, Muḥtasib, *and the Supervision of Markets*

The state authority in Islamic tradition used to sanction false transactions, incorrect weights or illicit contracts, purchases of unlawful commodities,

330 Ibn Khaldūn divides society based on five distinct yet interrelated spheres: conquest and success; stability and self-exalting; economic expansion and enjoyment of the fruits of development; contentment and compromise; and extravagance, wastage, and decadence. Rosenthal, *Muqaddimah of Ibn Khaldūn*, vol. 1, 353.

331 Rosenthal, *Muqaddimah of Ibn Khaldūn*, vol. 2, 271–272.

and so forth. Marketplaces in the classical period in various parts of the Muslim world facilitated economic growth and contributed to the expansion of cities. The institution of (or rather concept) *ḥisba*, as part of the Islamic governmental authority, controlled market functioning. The nature of control differed due to geographical regions, political instabilities, and eras – it imposed judicial stipulations according to Islamic law, as well as aimed to preserve healthy economic growth.[332] The duties of *ḥisba* institutions encompassed both ethical and legal aspects of *Sharīʿa*. These state institutions were run by a *muḥtasib* (a public or market inspector or auditor), who regularly checked prices, false advertisements, incorrect weights, *ribā*-transactions, and illicit contracts. As such, the *sūq* was not only a marketplace but a space where juridical, ethical, economic, and spiritual aspects of the daily lives of Muslims were addressed.

The institution of *ḥisba* "led to the proliferation of a unique literature, the *ḥisba* handbooks."[333] The so-called *ḥisba* literature appertains to authority control as well as monitoring of prices, merchandise, and overall flow of trade, in order to facilitate just purchases and sales between buyers and merchants. Previously, Greek and Roman traditions knew *agoranomos*, or a market inspector who monitored the marketplace.[334] Islahi, for instance, points out that scholars such as al-Māwardī believed that the institution of *ḥisba* has its origins in the Qurʾan.[335] As much as the *muḥtasib*'s interventions can be invoked as legal rules, in that he prohibited sellers from inflating prices and/or monopolizing the market, as will be indicated below, they were also ethical in nature. The *ḥisba* institution was in this sense a mechanism to control the function of the market and morals in relation to public life.[336] Those who have written on

332 For more on the role of the *ḥisba*, see Yassine Essid, *A Critique of the Origins of Islamic Economic Thought* (Leiden: Brill, 1995); Ibn Taymiyya, *al-Ḥisba fī al-Islām*; al-Shayzarī, *The Book of the Islamic Market Inspector. Nihāyat al-Rutbah fī Ṭalab al-Ḥisba*, trans. R. P. Buckley (Oxford: Oxford University Press, 1999); Ibn al-Ukhūwwah, *Maʿālim al-Qūrbah fī Aḥkām al-Ḥisba*, ed. Reuben Levy (London: Luzac, 1938).

333 The institution of *ḥisba* played a different role under various rulers in the classical Islamic milieu. Ali and Thompson, "Schumpeterian Gap and Muslim Economic Thought."

334 Tripp, *Islam and the Moral Economy*, 106. For the history of Greek and Christian economic ideas see Leshem, *Origins of Neoliberalism*.

335 "Let there arise out of you a band of people inviting to all that is good, enjoining the right conduct and forbidding what is wrong. Such are they who are successful." (Qurʾan, 3:104).

336 Islahi, *Contribution of Muslim Scholars to Economic Thought*, 58–59.

ḥisba are, among others, Abū Yūsuf, al-Shayzarī,[337] al-Ghazālī, and Ibn Taymiyya. These authors describe the virtues and responsibilities of the *muḥtasib* and provide practical manuals for supervision of markets, administrative control, and industry,[338] including standardization of measures,[339] monitoring of harmful activities in markets such as forestalling and hoarding,[340] and fixing of prices in times of necessity.

The role of the *muḥtasib* was, in al-Ghazālī's view, to ensure "supply and provision of necessities"; his task was supervising market conduct, implementing the moral law and thereby mobilizing the religious sentiment it contained.[341] The *muḥtasib* promotes justice by preventing the abovementioned acts and is himself part of the institution.[342] One of his roles was to assure price control – believed to be set by market forces – which can be implemented in response to unlawful and undesirable activities by merchants. In this sense, the "natural regulation of the market corresponds to a cosmic regulation,"[343] which indicates restoring what is believed to be the normal price of commodities at the market. The criterion for a normal price is "the price people are used to paying for a given product under normal market circumstances."[344] Normal price is thus, as indicated in Chapter 2, market price. According to Ibn Taymiyya, *ḥisba*'s office ought to act in accordance with the Qur'anic statement of promoting the good and forbidding the harmful.[345] Ibn Taymiyya warns that a person's active

[337] al-Shayzarī, *Aḥkām al-Ḥisba*.

[338] Ibn Taymiyya, *al-Ḥisba fī al-Islām*, 21. See also the English translation by Holland, *Public Duties in Islam*.

[339] Ibn Taymiyya, *al-Ḥisba fī al-Islām*, 22.

[340] Ibn Taymiyya, *al-Ḥisba fī al-Islām*, 23.

[341] It has been documented that Caliph al-Ma'mūn (d. 833) was the first to replace the *sāhib al-sūq*, or market inspector, who controlled practical economic matters in Baghdad, with the official *muḥtasib*. The practical impact of the *sāhib al-sūq* still remained in place after the *muḥtasib* was introduced; however, the religious implications in inspecting moral behavior at the marketplace became much more frequent and permanent during the Abbasid reign, which can be perceived as an attempt to assure a more religious sentiment in the marketplace. Essid, *Critique of the Origins of Islamic Economic Thought*, 115, 118; Ira M. Lapidus, "The Separation of State and Religion in the Development of Early Islamic Society," *Journal of Middle East Studies*, vol. 6, no. 4 (1975): 376.

[342] Al-Ghazālī, *Iḥyā'*, vol. 2, 312.

[343] Essid, *Critique of the Origins of Islamic Economic Thought*, 153.

[344] Essid, *Critique of the Origins of Islamic Economic Thought*, 161.

[345] Ibn Taymiyya, *al-Ḥisba fī al-Islām*, 14.

role in economic life is desirable insofar as purchases and sales are strewn with various regulations, such as the prohibition against hoarding of wealth and food supplies,[346] as merchants should always seek to sell their commodities at a fair distributive price,[347] in accordance with the regulations set on markets, which are run by the market inspector, or *muḥtasib*.

3.9.2 *Advice for Rulers, Public Finances, and the Aims of Just Governance*

Abū Yūsuf stated that "The ruler is responsible for the welfare of the people and must do everything that he considers good for them"; he quoted Abū Mūsā al-Ash'arī, a companion of the Prophet: "The best of men in authority are those under whom people prosper and worst are those under whom people encounter hardship."[348] Most of al-Ghazālī's analysis on governmental authority and economic thought are to be found in *Iḥyā' 'Ulūm al-Dīn* and in *Naṣīḥat al-Mulūk*. The Saljūqs, who ruled the Middle East during the eleventh and twelfth centuries, marked a new era with their political institutions. The Saljūq-led government attempted to cultivate the Islamic identity by recognizing the legitimacy of the caliphate and its Divine descent.[349] Al-Ghazālī lived in the Saljūq period, which established the relation between governmental authority and society based upon religious grounds. Nevertheless, the political and religious branches of governance were distinct.[350] For al-Ghazālī, governmental authority (*dawla*) is a necessary institution for promoting just economic activities and exercising *Sharī'a*-mandated social obligations: "The governmental authority and religion are indivisible foundations of a law-abiding society. Religion is the foundation and the ruler, who represents the governmental authority, is its promoter and protector; if either pillar is

[346] Al-Ghazālī, *Iḥyā'*, 72. [347] Ibn Taymiyya, *Public Duties in Islam*, 32–33.

[348] Abū Yūsuf, *Kitāb al-Kharaj*, 16, 129, in Islahi, *Contribution of Muslim Scholars to Economic Thought*, 60.

[349] "They enforced Islamic law, patronized the pilgrimage, endowed colleges of learning and religious activity, and sometimes waged jihad against non-Muslim populations in Anatolia and Central Asia. None the less, these states were not considered inherently Islamic." Ira M. Lapidus, "State and Religion in Islamic Societies" *Past & Present*, no. 151 (1996): 13.

[350] Lapidus, " Separation of State and Religion in the Development of Early Islamic Society," 376.

weak, society will crumble."[351] Al-Ghazālī stipulates that the ideal government in the Islamic community bases its rules upon Islamic jurisprudence and ethical teachings.

Kitāb Naṣīḥat al-Mulūk,[352] or the Book of Counsel for Kings is a so-called Mirror for Princes, a genre of political writing and a distinctive form of literature known in the early Islamic world, especially in the Arab and Persian world.[353] In *Naṣīḥat*, al-Ghazālī's views of livelihood and politics are expressed,[354] discussing the inner dimensions of a ruler and merging political (and legal) with spiritual. The ruler is to obtain prosperity for his people and should cooperate with *'ulamā'*. The authority should keep all subjects satisfied and pleased with the rule. In regard to fair economic development, certain conditions are to be met: "Efforts of those Kings to develop the world were undertaken because they knew that the greater the prosperity, the longer would be their rule and more numerous their subjects. They also knew that the religion depends on the authority, the authority on the army, and the army on the supplies, supplies and prosperity on justice."[355] Various principles of just approach that pertain to all people within a state are explained:[356] the ruler ought to comprehend the responsibility of the role; never tolerate injustice; rule without

[351] Al-Ghazālī, *Iḥyā'*, vol. 1, 17, also vol. 2, 312–315, 338; al-Ghazāli *Naṣīḥat al-Mulūk*, 59.

[352] On the question of the authorship of *Naṣīḥat al-Mulūk*, see e.g. Patricia Crone, "Did al-Ghazālī Write a Mirror for Princes? On the Authorship of Nasīḥat al-Mulūk," *Jerusalem Studies of Arabic and Islam*, vol. 10 (1987): 167–197; Carole Hillenbrand, "A Little-Known Mirror for Princes by al-Ghazālī," in Gerhard Endress, Arnzen Rüdiger, and J. Thielmann, eds., *Words, Texts, and Concepts Cruising the Mediterranean Sea: Studies on the Sources, Contents and Influences of Islamic Civilization and Arabic Philosophy and Science: Dedicated to Gerhard Endress on His Sixty-Fifth Birthday* (Leuven: Peeters, 2004); Ann K. S. Lambton, "The Theory of Kingship in the Nasīḥat al-Mulūk," *The Islamic Quarterly*, vol. 1 (1954): 47–55.

[353] *Naṣīḥat al-Mulūk* was composed in al-Ghazali's birth town of Tūs upon his return from Nīshāpūr, after 1109, as a response to the criticism he received from a Ḥanafite *'ulamā* and as a gift to the Ṣultān Muḥammad ibn Malikshāh (d. 1092). The book is divided into two parts with related themes. The first part addresses rulership as a bestowed position which expounds one's accountability. The ruler does not possess ultimate power and is responsible for the just reign for his subjects. The second part addresses the virtues of a state-appointed ruler (al-Ghazālī, *Counsel for Kings*, ix, xviii).

[354] Al-Ghazālī, *Counsel for Kings*, xxxviii.

[355] Al-Ghazālī, *Counsel for Kings*, 56.

[356] Al-Ghazālī, *Counsel for Kings*, 13–31.

pride, since this might invoke revenge and turmoil; not indulge in lust; avoid harsh governing; and keep his subjects pleased. The responsibility of the ruler and the intervention of the state authority are grounded on the basis of also regulating economic conduct and facilitating secure conditions for trading:

> when injustice and oppression are present, the people have no foothold, the cities and localities go to ruin, the inhabitants flee and move to other territories, the cultivated lands are abandoned, the kingdom falls into decay, the revenue diminishes, the treasury becomes empty, and happiness fades among the people. The subjects do not love the unjust king, but always pray that evil may befall him.[357]

Among others, al-Ghazālī, Ibn Taymiyya, and Ibn Khaldūn believed that governmental authority is indispensable and its principal aim is to provide for its subjects. Ibn Khaldūn distinguished two types of authority, one based on reason (*ʿaqlīyya*) and one on Divine law with *Sharīʿa*-compliant higher values. While the first guards against injustice, the second provides for the positive enforcement of law and justice.[358] Unlike mercantilism, the notion of *wilāya* depends on the facilitation of mutual cooperation between people and the governmental authority, aiming at achieving trust and overall prosperity grounded in the moral values of *Sharīʿa*,[359] while not presupposing absolute power by the ruler. The above-mentioned classical Muslim scholars did not necessarily analyze the genealogy of the concept of governance or authority in Islam, however, they asserted that one of their crucial aims is the notion of justice and prevention of harm,[360] in order to secure the well-being of its members, including socioeconomic provision. Likewise, Islamic governance should strive to eradicate (material) poverty, provide equal opportunity, prevent exploitation, and guarantee the betterment of its subjects, for governmental influence extends also to the market. The twofold perspective of the state authority hinges upon the provision of both material welfare and moral well-being.

357 Al-Ghazālī, *Counsel for Kings*, 55. 358 Ibn Khaldūn, *Muqaddima*, 150.

359 Hallaq, "Groundwork of the Moral Law," 248; Hallaq, *Impossible State*, 10. "In the *Sharīʿa*, the legal is the instrument of the moral, not the other way around."

360 Ibn Taymiyya, *al-Siyāsa al-Sharʿiyya*, 90.

Analyzing the economic reasons for the demise of the Fatimid financial policy, and its political and spiritual remedies, cultivates a discussion on economic history that stretched over the medieval Mediterranean world and its possible ramifications for the analogous debates across the Muslim lands. Al-Maqrīzī, a historian who was trained as a theologian and jurist, also held a position as a public inspector. Even though al-Maqrīzī addressed monetary history and financial policies, his texts excoriate Mamluk officials and authorities by analyzing the reasons for the economic downfall, including agricultural production, and possible solutions for it. Three main reasons for the economic crisis were political corruption, the rise of land prices and associated agriculture activities, and the widespread circulation of copper money.[361]

> Three causes, and only three, contributed to this situation: the first cause, the source of this decay, is the holding of administrative and religious positions such as the vizirate, judgeships, provincial governorships, the hisbah, and other functions through bribery, to the point that it has become impossible for anyone to secure any of these positions without paying large amounts of money .... The second cause is the high cost of land: a number of persons were promoted to the service of the commanders, whose friendship they were seeking through money that they collected as taxes, to the point that they became their masters .... The third cause [of this situation] is the circulation of the *fulus*.[362]

Since copper coins functioned as a basic currency, it has become widely accepted that the overproduction and overcirculation of *fulūs* resulted in the debasement of gold. He held the Sultan Barqūq (r. 1399–1412) responsible for the inflation, the mismanagement of the treasury, the over-minting of copper coins (*fulūs*), and the monetary harm that struck Egypt, and believed that economic problems can be addressed through monetary policy that has to be communicated to the highest office:

361 Hiroshi Kato, "Reconsidering al-Maqrīzī's View on Money in Medieval Egypt," *Mediterranean World*, vol. 21 (2012): 36.

362 Muḥammad ʿAlī al-Maqrīzī, *Ighātha al-Ummah bi Kashf al-Ghummah* (Cairo: ʿAyn al-Dirāsāt al-Baʿūth al-Insāniyya wa al-Ijtimāʿiyya, 2007); Adel Allouche, *Mamluk Economics: A Translation and Study of al-Maqrizi's Ighāthah* (Salt Lake City: University of Utah Press, 1994), 52–55.

> Increases in the prices of those few exceptions would be caused by either of the following: first, the poor judgment and ignorance of the officials vested with the supervision of [economic] matters; this is the likeliest [cause]. Second, a disaster that strikes a natural product and causes its scarcity .... Nevertheless, had there been officials who were bestowed with [Divine] guidance and inspired with reason, the situation would have been different from that of the present ordeals. The money that anyone now receives from land tax or any other source consists instead of [copper] fulus, which are, as already mentioned, weighed by the ratl, while gold, silver, and all goods such as foodstuffs, clothing, and the like have become luxuries .... Had God guided those whom He entrusted with the welfare of [His] servants to restore the currency to what it was formerly, anyone who would receive these 10 dirhams would receive them in silver and would know that even at current prices they would be sufficient [not only] to meet his needs but even to exceed them.[363]

Al-Maqrīzī affirmed that the cause of the economic crisis and the subsequent famine was human action,[364] and would have to be addressed through a set of legal and economic policies, often linked to religious corpus: "the situation became critical; conditions became perilous, disaster was widespread and calamity universal, to the degree that more than one-half of the population of the land [of Egypt] died of hunger and cold. Death was so prevalent that even the animals perished in the years 806/1403–4 and 807/1404–5."[365] He was interested in knowing how the currency had been utilized, for determining "prices of goods and costs of labor consists only of gold and silver,"[366] since gold has traditionally been used in Egypt. Since inflation caused the dearth of economic stability, its main cause was the usage of copper coins as a main currency, which resulted in higher levels of corruption, and most importantly copper coins were utilized to make more money, which consequently also impacted the debasement of currency. Therefore, he advocated for a supervised minting of coins (since such an approach in his view departs from *Sharīʿa*) and a return to a monetary policy based on gold and silver as a measure of value in finances, trade, and economy as a whole,[367] for the inflation

363 Allouche, *Mamluk Economics*, 83–85.

364 John L. Meloy, "The Merits of Economic History: Re-reading al-Maqrīzī Ighāthah and Shudhūr," *Mamlūk Studies Review*, vol. 7, no. 2 (2003): 189.

365 Allouche, *Mamluk Economics*, 51.

366 Allouche, *Mamluk Economics*, 55.

367 Al-Maqrīzī, *Ighātha al-Ummah bi Kashf al-Ghummah*; Allouche, *Mamluk Economics*, 77–78.

(*ghalāʾ*)[368] occurred due to the over-proliferation of coins and the gradual disappearance of *dirham*. The quantity of copper coins circulated should be sufficient only to the needs of the economy and not to boost personal greed. The primary purpose of coins being as a store of value and a medium of exchange.[369]

In respect to economic theory, al-Maqrīzī discussed the effect of the economic crisis that swept through Egypt in the fifteenth century and classified social classes into seven groups: those who hold power, wealthy merchants, small-business merchants, farmers, scholars, skilled workers, and the poor.[370] He managed to analyze the monetary economy that influenced those social classes as an independent mechanism. Al-Maqrīzī's vivid descriptions of the conflict between the social classes insinuates that the ruling elite controlled the grain market, the middle and small businesses aimed to maximize their profits, while the common people (*ʿāmma*) sought to protect their livelihood, indicating that the governmental authority was only one of the participants in this competition. After analyzing the effects of the crisis, he concludes that a return to the monetary system based on gold and silver is necessary and in accordance with moral value, for copper coins were never meant to be a standardized currency, but *dirham* as an ideal account. Consequently, also goods would be linked to gold as a more stable currency. He proposes "to issue a whole decree to our masters the chief judges – God strengthen their religion – that they require the notaries to write land registers, building contracts, marriage contracts, and loan documents only in dirhams," as well as that judges should be directed to enforce market inspectors to assure *dirham*-based transactions.[371]

Even though al-Maqrizi does not directly address concepts related to Sufi or philosophical discourse, his critique of governmental policy on economic management in essence pertains to the ethical argument in delinking copper money from gold and silver in order to eradicate political corruption and reestablish a healthy economy. His advice designates a particular policy to the ruling class on monetary affairs

368 Allouche, *Mamluk Economics*, 27, 40, 50.

369 Warren C. Schultz, "Mamluk Monetary History: A Review Essay," *Mamlūk Studies Review*, vol. 3 (1999): 183.

370 Kato, "Reconsidering al-Maqrīzī's View on Money in Medieval Egypt," 36.

371 Al-Maqrīzī, *Shudhūr*, 35–36, in John L. Meloy, "The Merits of Economic History: Re-reading al-Maqrīzī Ighāthah and Shudhūr," *Mamlūk Studies Review*, vol. 7, no. 2 (2003): 200.

as to how to refurbish a healthy economy based on legal injunctions and sound ethical teachings.

3.10 Concluding Remarks

Classical Muslim society was not familiar with the concept of economics or the field of political economy as it is defined and extrapolated in the modern period. Hence, economic thought in Islamic tradition has to be approached via the epistemic route that would give precedence to moral understanding of the economic behavior, including the emergence of production processes in accordance with human needs. In light of the above-mentioned classical Muslim scholars, the focus of economic ideas was not to maximize profit but to construct a responsible and all-encompassing *modus operandi* to attain higher objectives, conducted with moral agency as a technology of the self.

The individual in those works was comprehended also as part of a communal reality. Even though commercial laws (*muʿāmalāt*) and judges' decisions indicate that it is always an individual that is addressed and remitted, given the essence of *Sharīʿa*, this is equally significant for the community at large. The individual's heart, salvation, and righteous behavior are henceforth made contingent upon the actions in relation to the communal reality, which is why so many scholars discuss the role of the heart (*qalb*), renunciation of the world (*zuhd*), and poverty (*faqr*) in conjunction. In consideration of a moral understanding of economic life, an individual is a microcosmos of society, in which there is a dialectical relation between the two. The ultimate duty of an individual is to be an operative part of the moral cosmology of *Sharīʿa*, in which one forms "individual communitarianism." *Sharīʿa* as Divine law does not address only the institutions of *zakāt*, *ribā*, *kasb*, *maṣlaḥa*, *ḥisba*, and other conceptualities in light of legal understanding but primarily as profoundly relevant mechanisms, as matters of the heart, which entails moral connotations and self-regulation. Therefore, it seems appropriate that the moral cosmology of economic thought in those texts looms large over legal normativity. In view of this distinction, Islamic economics ought to be studied through the theoretical corpus of Islamic intellectual history and virtuous traits of character.

The aim of classical scholars' writing was not necessarily to eradicate poverty but to refrain from riches. The *kasb–zuhd* amalgam imparts the idea that the poor do not need to contest the rich, while simultaneously the rich do not need to despise the poor, yet the motive of the rich has to change in order to facilitate the needs of the poor. Classical thought, encapsulated in the theological, philosophical, legal, and Sufi sources, conveys the importance of virtuous economic faculties. For many classical scholars, the market was something that evolved naturally according to society's needs and wants. Yet, this should not be mistakenly interpreted to mean that the early Muslim scholars advocated or anticipated a modern conception of the free market, for it was heavily regulated by ethical-legal mechanisms. Despite the fact that authority was exercised through the institution of *ḥisba*, which was responsible for market activities, it was not the final denominator. Markets were effective in the sense that they established a proposed scheme of measurements and needs, accordingly; scholars' texts, ideas, and advice were often taken into account, if not incorporated, into the governments' policies.

The so-called ethical-economic literature and the *kasb–zuhd* texts from the classical period are about everyday economics and economic behavior as well as about the spiritual qualities of man, whereby the material, however indispensable, is in service of the moral. As such, the economic postulates' final denominator is congruous with one's self-examination in order to achieve the ethical cognizance of the afterlife.

While Chapter 2 presented the bulk of contemporary Muslim economists, Chapter 4 critically examines contemporary Islamic economic theories and the indigenization of social sciences, which was manifested through the methodological confinement and epistemological contestation of contemporary Islamic economics vis-à-vis modernity's economic positivism.

4 *The Appraisal: Contemporary Islamic Economics and the Entrenchment of Modernity*

First, we must examine our own Islamic tradition in the light of these criteria and principles and then critically study the body of knowledge created by modernity.

Fazlur Rahman, "Islamization of Knowledge: A Response," 457

To rid myself of fear, or love, or the desire to conform is to liberate myself from the despotism of something which I cannot control.

Isaiah Berlin, *Liberty*, 185

4.1 Introductory Remarks

Apropos the analysis of the revivalists' ideas on socioeconomic developments in the Middle East and South Asia in Chapter 1, the study of contemporary Muslim economists in Chapter 2, and the theoretical examination of classical economic thought in Chapter 3, this fourth chapter interrogates and critiques the inner structure – that is the epistemology and methodology – of contemporary Islamic economics in relation to *Sharīʿa*'s moral predicaments.

The first part of the chapter discusses the intricate relation between *Sharīʿa* and the field of economics in Islamic tradition by critiquing the legal premise of contemporary Islamic economics. I do not provide a critique of *Sharīʿa* but rather of the understanding of *Sharīʿa* in its role in establishing the legal methodology of the subject of Islamic economics. Since part of the methodology of Islamic economics is based on the application of juristic principles and ethical norms to mainstream economic science, I argue that the classical perception of *Sharīʿa* as a moral institution has been lost in contemporary Islamic economics due to its adaptation of modern social sciences and its principles. Furthermore, expounding the inconsistencies of contemporary Islamic economics asserts that the notion of *Sharīʿa* as primarily a moral category is essential to understating broader economic behavior in classical Islamic tradition.

The second part of this chapter critically examines the Islamic economic project's epistemology and methodology and the amalgamation of two epistemic systems: Islamic conceptual history and Western economic tradition. This composition provided Islamic economics with a hybrid framework, consisting of Islamic ethics and neoclassical economic outlook. This section analyzes this subject also in relation to the secondary literature and the following scholars who have raised concerns and critiqued the nature of Islamic economics: Muhammad A. Khan and his later writings on Islamic economic science; Rauf Azhar, who rearticulated the role of *ribā* in Islamic history; Sohrab Behdad and Abbas Mirakhor, who elaborated on the epistemology of Islamic economics; Thomas Phillipp, Volker Nienhaus, Shinsuke Nagaoka, and Timur Kuran, who analyzed the subject from its very emergence; Seyyed Vali Reza Nasr, who addressed the lack of consistency of Islamic economic philosophy; and Syed Farid Alatas, who has voiced criticism over the construction of social sciences in the West and Muslim economists' blind following of its paradigm.

Contemporary Islamic economics did not evolve from the classical Islamic tradition and its association with the Islamic sciences of nature and the idea of production of work as a human process. Certain economic institutions and moral practices within the market existed in premodern milieu[1] yet were based on a different epistemic tradition. When classical Muslim scholars discussed traditional concepts of price regulations, market mechanisms, expenditures, and so forth, they did so in view of ethical-legal theories based on metaphysical considerations and a particular perception of the universe as a moral entity. However, contemporary Islamic economics is largely grounded in liberal philosophy or positivist economics and the very concept of economics as a predetermined science based on preexisting conditions.[2] It is a modern project, created within the philosophical structures of

[1] See e.g. Abdullah Alwi bin Haji Hassan, "Al-Mudarabah and Its Identical Islamic Partnership in Early Islam," *Hamdard Islamicus*, vol. 12, no. 2 (1989): 11–38.

[2] In spite of the fact that mainstream economics is diverse and that various views also exist within contemporary Islamic economics, the majority of Muslim economists resort to basic economic postulates found in the Western economic tradition. Alatas states that both Marxist-inspired and neoclassical theories are informed by that very discourse and the ideas of development of nineteenth-century liberal philosophy. See Syed Farid Alatas, "The Sacralization of the Social

modernity. In this context, modernity refers to the end result of the scientific, social, economic, and political process of modernization that began in Europe in the eighteenth century.[3] Modernist discourse (or modernism) was informed by the principles of nineteenth-century liberal philosophy and its outlook on scientific, social, legal, and economic life, including the process of democratization, economic development, scientific progress, and evolutionary theory.[4]

The process of modernization, encompassing modern scientific knowledge, including processes of rationalization of economic life, urbanization, and industrialization, spread beyond Europe and altered social structures in Muslim societies.[5] This shift in non-Western societies also meant academic dependency on social sciences, linking advancement of the industrialization process with a particular economic outlook. At the same time, Islamic economics was conceived as a reaction to materialism and capitalism.[6] In order to establish "Islamic" economic science, the majority of contemporary Muslim economists either proposed to Islamize the discipline of economics or suggested integrating Islamic economic and ethical concepts into the existing economic theories. It appears that the structural challenge the Muslim countries faced in the nineteenth and twentieth centuries coincided not only with militarism and cultural intrusion but also with a forceful economic restructuring.[7] Contesting capitalism and

Sciences: A Critique of an Emerging Theme in Academic Discourse," *Archives de sciences sociales des religions*, vol. 91 (1995): 92.

3 Syed Farid Alatas, "Islam and Modernization," in *Islam in Southeast Asia: Political, social and strategic challenges for the 21st century*, ed. K. S. Nathan and Mohammad Hashim Kamali (Singapore: ISEAS, 2005), 209.

4 See Kate Manzo, "Modernist Discourse and the Crisis of Development Theory," *Studies in Comparative International Development*, vol. 26, no. 2 (1991): 3–36.

5 For more on the concept of modernization in relation to colonialism and Arab nationalism, see e.g. Bassam Tibi, *Arab Nationalism: Between Islam and Nation-State* (London: Palgrave Macmillan, 1997), 46–47.

6 See Seyyed Vali Reza Nasr, "Toward a Philosophy of Islamic Economics," *Muslim World*, vol. 77, no. 3–4 (1987): 175–196; Muhammad Bāqir al-Ṣadr, *Towards an Islamic Economy* (Tehran: Bonyad Be'that, 1984); Alatas, "Islam and Modernization," 210.

7 Shahab Ahmed claims that the revivalist discourse of modernity addressed the conceptions of Islamic state and law, not other discursive fields of Islam, such as theology, philosophy, ethics, poetics, and, we could add, moral cosmology of economics. "It is striking that so much of the discourse of modern reformist Muslims – who have, for the most part, received the norms of modernity second-hand and by the force of arms and coercive administrations of European

socialism was part of the methodological blueprint of Islamic economic theories, aligned with the prevalent economic order, despite Islamic economics' distinct characteristics. This entailed negotiating over Islamic law and its legal aspects.

4.2 Modern Divergence of *Sharīʿa*'s Moral Principles

As demonstrated in Chapter 2, the majority of contemporary Muslim economists maintain that the Islamic economic project is part of Islamic law and jurisprudence, since Islamic economics builds upon knowledge established by Muslim scholars and jurists.[8] This would indicate that key terms that also have economic significance, such as *ribā*, *zakāt*, the utilization of money, *maṣlaḥa*, and commercial and legal transactions, would fall primarily under the category of *fiqh*.[9] However, since the gist of the classical *fiqh* discourse was from the very outset theological and metaphysical in nature,[10] the moral premise of *Sharīʿa* lies at the core of economic endeavors.

colonialisms – about what is Islam has been about rethinking the Islamic state by rethinking law, and *not* about rethinking theology, philosophy, ethics, poetics, and Sufism as a hermeneutical means to modern Islamic norms. The relative lack of concern on the part of even the most self-consciously critical modern Muslims to re-think or reform normative Islam in terms of theology, philosophy and ethics – let alone Sufism and poetics – is one of the most peculiar, but also symptomatic, elements of Muslim modernity as *modernity*." (Ahmed, *What Is Islam?*, 125–126). See also Hallaq, *Impossible State*, 152.

8 Waleed Addas's comparison of conventional and Islamic economics' methodologies indicate that the latter is based on *fiqh* and *usul*: "Islamic economics is in a measure generated through the application of Islamic *fiqh*." (Addas, *Methodology of Economics*, 97).

9 "For example, a person may claim that the prohibition of riba is decreed by Shariʿa, but this claim cannot be meaningful without a clear definition and application of this term, which is the subject of fiqh. Since human interpretation of relevant texts of the Qurʾan and Sunna is unavoidable in both aspects of this issue, it is difficult to distinguish between the two." (An-Naʾim, *Islam and the Secular State*, 35).

10 "The essence of fiqh discussions has always been theological; it is only of late that jurists tend to focus attention on economic matters in two directions. Since most of them are not well-versed in economics they test at the mainstream concepts on the juristic touchstone for pronouncing judgment on their efficacy for Islamic economics. Since jurisprudence is for most part micro in character they miss at times the macro implications of their opinion." (Addas, *Methodology of Economics*, 98).

Islamic law (*fiqh*) has always been perceived as religious law with a Divine character; however, this Divine aspect was made absolute,[11] which in the modern period also reinforced a legal supremacy. *Sharīʿa*, however, was not separated from the conception of Qurʾanic morality in the premodern era, therefore the dichotomy between the two epistemic systems did not exist.[12] The presupposition of viewing economic thought in Islamic history as part of *fiqh* rests upon the idea that modern Islamic economic thought was conceived within the mechanisms of the modern state and consequently as a legal devise, unlike classical economic philosophy by the aformentioned Muslim scholars, which was embedded predominately within the values of the moral self, including its metaphysics.[13] One of the main differences between classical and contemporary scholars of Islamic economics is that the former based their arguments on theological and broader cosmological foundations, whereas the latter based theirs on legal positivism and modernist discourse, extending it also to Islamic finances and banking. The majority of

[11] Bauer defined Islam as a culture of ambiguity also within the realm of Islamic law, by extrapolating legal terms in Islamic intellectual history; see Bauer, *Die Kultur der Ambiguität*. For the critique of Bauer not defining but rather presupposing the already established categories of "religious" and "secular," see Ahmed, *What Is Islam?*, 210, 409: "Invaluably, Bauer documents and describes a great deal of ambiguity in, especially, the Arabic-language discourse of premodern Muslims prior and adjacent to the Balkans-to-Bengal complex. However, he does not interrogate the categories of 'religious' and 'secular,' nor of 'culture,' but rather treats ambiguity in terms of these categories, which he evidently regards as inherently valid and with which he operates. In his conceptualization and analysis of the significance and meaning of ambiguity he thus falls into many of the deficiencies consequent upon the application of these categories that have been diagnosed above." (p. 210, footnote 73).

[12] For more on merging *taṣawwuf* with *Sharīʿa*, see e.g. al-Ghazālī, *Iḥyāʾ*; al-Ghazālī, *al-Mustaṣfāʾ*; see also Hallaq, "Groundwork of the Moral Law," 256; Hallaq, *Impossible State*, 111: "Islamic governance was productive of subjectivities that were paradigmatically Sharʿī based .... Their distinction between – and the segregation of – the legal and the moral indeed constituted the first act in the emergence in nineteenth century colonial Europe of the academic subject of 'Islamic law'."

[13] "Ultimately law was the systemic hallmark of submission to the Lord of the World, Rabb al-ʿAlamin, who literally owns everything – everything being, after all, created by Him. Technically, therefore, law becomes subservient to, and dependent on, the mother science of theology which established not only the existence, unity and attributes of God, but also the 'proof' of prophecies, revelation, and all the fundaments of religion." (Hallaq, *Sharīʿa*, 79); see also Al-Daghistani, "Semiotics of Islamic Law, Maṣlaḥa, and Islamic Economic Thought," 401.

classical Muslim scholars, many of whom were jurists themselves, positioned their ideas and theories on economic conduct in relation to the fields of theology, Sufism, and overall Qur'anic epistemology. For them, *fiqh* was not separate from the moral values of the Qur'an.[14]

The epistemological differences between premodern and modern conceptualizations of *Sharī'a* (which also affected the nature of economic thought in Islamic tradition) occurred in the colonial period in the Middle East region during the nineteenth century, which had a direct impact on governmentality and reforming of Muslim societies[15] in how forces within those countries reformulated legal and economic structures by proposing Islamic solutions. Unlike military interventions, the economic-political reshaping of colonized societies generated an epistemological rupture in the social order, in education, and in knowledge production, for it reimagined and reinvented a bygone Islamic society, while reconstitutionalizing subjects as citizens. The nineteenth century was transformative for the sociology of knowledge of those societies, since the reshaping of society meant a form of forced "progress," especially in the domain of politics, law, and sciences.[16] In order to reassess the genealogy of modern economic thought in Islamic tradition and the kind of role that morality plays in it, the nature of *Sharī'a* has to be ascertained, since in the premodern period *Sharī'a* not only regulated its subjects but also determined specific behavioral patterns of economic postulates. If *Sharī'a* is nowadays defunct, since it has been replaced by Western codes and laws, it serves only as a "moral resource." Yet, unlike Western laws, which are coercive systems, *Sharī'a* in the classical context of economic ideas was primarily a moral project from the very outset, drawing upon metaphysical sources of unity and historical precedence in Muslim societies. While law as understood in modern times contains systematic rules as something that is external to it, *Sharī'a* in its core encapsulated moral primacy as something that

14 See the classical scholars presented in Chapter 3. In this regard, Hallaq states that "economic life, however messy, was regulated not only by technical *Sharī'a* rules but also by a pervasive *Sharī'a* ethic." (Hallaq, *Impossible State*, 10).

15 For some of the writings, see Jamāl al-Dīn al-Afghānī, *Al-'Amal al-Kāmilah*; Muhammad 'Abduh, *Risālat al-Tawḥīd*; for examples of Malaya, Egypt, and British India, see Hussin, *Politics of Islamic Law*, 151–153.

16 For more on those processes, see Christopher Dawson, *The Making of Europe* (New York: Meridian Books, 1956); Hussin, *Politics of Islamic Law*, 209–235; Taylor, *Secular Age*, 235.

is inherent and achieved through the technologies of the self.[17] As such, *Sharīʿa* not only "regulates" human behavior and deeds but is first and foremost inextricably linked to one's *niyya* as intention, striving, intent, and predisposition. The differentiation between *is* and *ought* that is evident on the epistemological level in mainstream economics in the West pertains to the rise of the legal and the political.[18] "The scholars who created the knowledge that is 'Islamic law' and whose measure of legal culture is one imbued with the intrusive and ubiquitous agency of the state found incomprehensibly deficient a 'law' that not only seamlessly meshed with morality but depended on morality for enforcement."[19] Infusing religion, which was viewed as a theological and moral force, with the force of law foreclosed the perception that religion was based on moral terms.

4.2.1 Islamic Conceptions of the Modern State

Sharīʿa has often been conflated with the law of the Ottoman Muslim lands, known as *qanūn*.[20] According to Frank Griffel, many perceive

[17] On the concept, see Michel Foucault, "Technologies of the Self," in *Ethics, Subjectivity, and Truth*, ed. P. Rabinow (New York: The New Press, 1994), 223–251; Hallaq, *Impossible State*, 110: "Islamic governance was squarely the product of Islamdom, of the total historical experience of Islamic culture, values, and weltanschauung, however varied within the tradition these experiences may have been. Constitutive of the difference is the absence from the Islamic paradigm of a monarch or state that controlled legislation. The 'legislative' in Islam did account for the ruler and for a certain reality of politics, but it was not the product of politics or the political." On the development and nurture of character traits, see classical Muslim scholars, e.g. al-Muḥāsibī, al-Ghazālī, ʿAbd Allāh ibn al-Mubārak (*Kitāb al-Zuhd wa al-Rāqaʾiq*), etc.

[18] Taylor, *Secular Age*; Hallaq, "Groundwork of the Moral Law," 247; Hallaq, *Impossible State*, 75, 80–82, 90. "The political is not a distinct field of power relations, nor is it just a matter of politics, economy, ethics, or science. The political is an all-encompassing, pervasive phenomenon that intrudes upon all fields, upon existence itself." (Hallaq, *Impossible State*, 90).

[19] Hallaq, *Impossible State*, 112.

[20] "Islamic law, on the other hand, runs counter to the great majority of the code's attributes. First, Islamic law did not lay any claim to exclusive authority. In fact, it depended on the cooperation of customary and royal law (*siyāsa sharʿiyya*), the former being the systemic prop upon which morality meshed into law as a 'rational' system. Nowhere did Islamic law operate exclusively, and everywhere customary law was entwined with it in the realm of practice. Nor, in this connection, was Islamic law declaratory, in that it never pronounced itself as the bearer of exclusive authority, as having come to replace others in the field. By its hermeneutic and highly individualistic nature, Islamic law was not systematic

Sharīʿa as a canonized code of law, similar to Western laws,[21] which is, as Charles Taylor puts it, only one part of modernity's definition of legal culture.

Needless to remind ourselves, modernity didn't stop at the ethic of rational control. This is just one of the burning points of dissatisfaction with this reading of the modern identity, which was taken up in that broad stream of thought and sensibility sometimes called "Romanticism". The very idea that feeling could be stripped of all aura came to seem not only erroneous, but terribly impoverishing, a denial of our humanity. But within this identity of disengaged reason, disenchantment and instrumental control go closely together. And it was this which helped prepare the ground for the new option of exclusive humanism.[22]

In the context of modernity, Hallaq further observes that the modern term "law" is

charged with Foucauldian notions of surveillance, inconspicuous punishment, and hegemony over and subordination of the docile subject, all of which mechanisms of control (at the very least) make our modern notion of law, and therefore of morality, quite different from any earlier legal system and therefore from earlier notions of "law" – those of pre-sixteenth century Europe included. What is "legal"' in the Qurʾān and in the *Sharīʿa* that was based on it is also equally "moral" and vice versa.[23]

New interpretations of *Sharīʿa* by Muslim scholars and activists such as Ḥasan al-Bannā, Sayyid Quṭb, Abū al-Aʿlā Mawdūdī,[24] and others called for the integration of *Sharīʿa* into state institutions within

according to the European perception of the world, although an expert in it might have viewed the matter entirely otherwise. Similarly, from a modern perspective, Islamic law has been described as obscure and complex, unlike the 'clear and accessible' code. While the code is clearly more accessible than treatises of *fiqh*, the argument of clarity is no more than a relative one. An expert in *fiqh* may find it as clear as the modern lawyer finds the code. Admittedly, however, Islamic law cannot be said to have internal uniformity, since plurality of opinion – the so-called *ijtihādic* pluralism – is its defining feature par excellence." (Hallaq, "Maqāṣid and the Challenges of Modernity," 24).

21 On the modernization of traditional religious learning and its transformation of Islamic law, see Aria Nakissa, "An Epistemic Shift in Islamic Law: Educational Reform at al-Azhar and Dār al-ʿUlūm," *Islamic Law and Society*, vol. 21 (2014): 209–251. On the modernizing of the Middle East, the role of *Shariʿa* therein and islamists' turn, see Hallaq, *Introduction to Islamic Law*, part 2.

22 Taylor, *Secular Age*, 136.

23 Hallaq, *Impossible State*, 83, 113.

24 See Mawdūdī, *Islamic Law and Constitution*, 40ff.

Muslim countries. Along with the revivalist movement, which advocated the inclusion of *Sharī'a* into the daily lives of Muslims, their sociopolitical struggle consequently encouraged the reevaluation of the economic life of Muslims, which was nonetheless aligned with the modernist tradition.[25] The idea of the caliphate was reinterpreted as the supreme instance of policymaking – central to Islamic community, yet compatible with the nation-state. Politically, legally, and structurally, this culminated in a hybrid system of a utopian Islamic society.

The ubiquitous perception of Islamic law as *Sharī'a* stems from the dichotomization of the concept of law from morality. The problem of reading *Sharī'a* as both Islamic law derived from Qur'anic morality and a separate entity emanates from Western intellectual discussions and, later, Muslim and Orientalists' appropriation of such binaries and paradigms.[26] As shown by numerous examples, in premodern tradition, however, the moral and the legal (and, as their extension, the economic) were not dichotomized and were interwoven into the Qur'anic fabric of a worldview that put forward a distinct economic paradigm. It has been well documented that with the onslaught of colonialism, the institution of *Sharī'a* was marginalized and gradually diminished due to its importance as one of the central paradigms in Islamic tradition. This has resulted in the replacement of *Sharī'a*-related laws with European statutory laws.[27] The conceptual transformation of knowledge that occurred within the Enlightenment

[25] "The three key authors in the autochthonous making of a 'generic Islam' of reform, al-Afghani, 'Abduh and Rida, were all active in restating motifs of the Enlightenment, Romanticism and Positivism." (Salvatore, *Islam and the Political Discourse of Modernity*, 85–87).

[26] The culture in which this dichotomy is embedded has been generated through certain philosophical discourse. See René Descartes, *Discours de la méthode et essais*, 3 vols, ed. Marie Beyssade and Denis Kambouchner (Paris: Gallimard, 2009); Carl J. Friedrich, *The Philosophy of Law in Historical Perspective* (Chicago, IL: University of Chicago Press, 1963); Alasdair MacIntyre, *A Short History of Ethics* (London: Routledge, 1998). On the critique of the dualism *is/ought*, see Friedrich Nietzsche, *Sämtliche Werke*, ed. Giorgio Colli and Mazzino Montinari (Berlin : de Gruyter, 1967). Conversely, on the notion of the Qur'an as the primary structure for moral law in Islamic history, see Hallaq, "Groundwork of the Moral Law."

[27] Kamali, *Shariah Law*, 233; Hallaq further states that "Islamic law and the nation-state operated in two opposing directions, the latter compelling and pushing towards an exclusive and ultimate center, and the former demonstrably centrifugal. As typical of Islamic structures (evident in social organization, urban and rural economic organization, mosque architecture, and premodern

was to some extent replicated a century later with *modernized* Islam,[28] which extended also to the domain of economics.

Moreover, the idea of Islamic state reemerged, along with the discourse on the revival of political Islam and Islamic economics, and it was seen as the alternative to the abolished caliphate.[29] If the modern nation-state is seen as an antigonistic problematic for the Muslim realization of their societies, then the concept of an Islamic state is a fallacy and impossibility. While al-Naʾim distinguishes between state and politics and claims that the ultimate neutrality of the state is impossible, he calls for a secular state and not for secularizing society.[30] Even if some scholars claim that Islamic law is compatible

dynastic bureaucracies), the law operated horizontally, so to speak. Aside from judicial appointments which were nominally, if not symbolically, hierarchical, the administration of justice was largely, if not exclusively, limited to the self-structured legal profession." (Hallaq, "Maqāṣid and the Challenges of Modernity," 19).

28 Hallaq, "Groundwork of the Moral Law," 257; see also Thomas Bauer and his theory of Islam as a culture of ambiguity in relation to how Cartesian philosophy and worldview, via colonization, shaped a modern Islamic vision in various fields of knowledge, including law; Bauer, *Die Kultur der Ambiguität.*

29 Rulers of the Islamic nations have always promulgated statutory laws and regulations based on their prerogative of *siyāsa*, since after colonialism *Sharīʿa* left a legal void. However, it was argued that the practice of *siyāsa* was, by consequence, in accordance with *Sharīʿa* and could hence be considered "Islamic." See e.g. Ottoman penal code from the beginning of the twentieth century. John A Strachey Bucknill, trans., *The Imperial Ottoman Penal Code* (Oxford: Oxford University Press, 1913).

30 Despite al-Naʾim's defense of a secular state, he does have reservations about secularism: "Secularism does not mean the exclusion of religion from the public life of a society, though the misconception that it does is one of the reasons many Muslims tend to be hostile to the concept" (p. 36). Further, "It is true that secularism is not morally neutral, as it must encourage a certain civic ethos to achieve its own objective of separation of religion and state" (p. 37). "Secularism, defined to mean only the separation of religion and state, is therefore incapable of meeting the collective requirements of public policy. Moreover, such separation by itself cannot provide sufficient guidance for individual citizens in making important personal choices in their private lives or public political participation. In addition, secularism as simply the separation of religion and state is not sufficient for addressing any objections or reservations believers may have about specific constitutional norms and human rights standards" (p. 38). "The principle of secularism, as I am defining it here, includes a public role for religion in influencing public policy and legislation, subject to the requirement of civic reason" (p. 38). In one of his key statements, in which he conceives an already predefined notion of secularism, al-Naʾim proposes a subservient and subjugating role of religion-based civic reasoning in

with the modern state,[31] as long as the preservation of *adab* and *maṣlaḥa* exists,[32] the restructuring of the moral fiber of an individual inevitably involves rethinking the concept of the state itself. Legal scholars asserted that, the Islamic authority did not produce *Sharīʿa* legal norms (the law), but private specialists did who were seen as part of the larger community and not an elite.[33] The mufti or legal authority was a private legal specialist, who was in theory indebted to the society in which he lived, not to the Muslim ruler and his alleged political agenda.[34]

4.2.2 *Contemporary Convergences of* Siyāsa *As Politics*

The integrationist view maintains that *Sharīʿa* and *siyāsa* cannot be separated completely, and the *maṣlaḥa* and *maqāṣid al-Sharīʿa* are upheld through policy measures. Since *maṣlaḥa* and *maqāṣid* are not confined only to temporal affairs, it follows that *siyāsa sharʿiyya* also extends to both temporal and religious matters. As we have seen, *siyāsa sharʿiyya* was in premodern times regularly equated with laws and associated with religious norms and values. Once it became delinked from criminal laws – after the 1900s – it was disassociated from penalties and began playing a stronger role in public administration and the economic realm. This prompted the idea of applying the concept of

relation to the state. However, in defense of religion-based reasoning, the secular state can be neither Christian nor Muslim, and by the same token it ought to be neither Marxist nor utilitarian, for instance. See An-Naʾim, *Islam and the Secular State*. For a critique of the pervasive understanding of secularism and the secular project see Saba Mahmood, *Religious Difference in a Secular Age: A Minority Report* (Princeton, NJ: Princeton University Press, 2015); Saba Mahmood, "Secularism, Hermeneutics, and Empire: The Politics of Islamic Reformation," *Public Culture*, vol. 18, no. 2 (2006): 323–347; Taylor, *Secular Age*.

31 See e.g. An-Naʾim, *Islam and the Secular State*, 84–85, 112.

32 On the notion of *maṣlaḥa* in economic thought, see below and also Ṣubḥī Rajab Maḥmaṣānī, *Falsafat al-Tashrīʿ fī al-Islām* (Beirut: Dār al-ʿIlm li al-Malāyīn, 1961).

33 In this view, the "Islamic governance (that which stands parallel to what we call "state" today) rest on moral, legal, political, social, and metaphysical foundations that are dramatically different from those sustaining the modern state. In Islam, it is the Community (Umma) that displaces the nation of modern state. The Community is both abstract and concrete, but in either case it is governed by the same moral rules." (Hallaq, *Impossible State*, 49).

34 Knut S. Vikør, *Between God and the Sultan: A History of Islamic Law* (Oxford: Oxford University Press, 2005), 140ff.

siyāsa in the political domain in general, while it was often analyzed together with *maṣlaḥa*. In many cases, the modern nation-states substituted *Sharīʿa* law with European-inspired penal codes and laws and replaced the personal concept of governance with the institution of state sovereignty.[35] This led to questions concerning the legality and authority of governance.[36] Muslim revivalists also addressed the relation between *siyāsa* and *Sharīʿa*, and at the turn of the century, they became interested in the political leadership of the colonial states.[37]

Sharīʿa is flexible when it comes to governmental policy, taxation, and economic activities. Since it provides broad guidelines, it largely depended on scholars' discretion in exercising *ijtihād*.[38] The rationale behind the Islamic economic system is for many contemporary scholars in the value of the scriptural sources and in modern economic theories. Yet, since Muslim societies (with the help of the local elites and *ʿulamāʾ*) inherited and/or

35 This was evident in revivalists' usage of *Sharīʿa* by integrating Islamic tenets with their politics. Several decades later, the Islamization of politics and law in Muslim societies occurred both from the top down (Iran, Pakistan) and from the bottom up (Egypt). See e.g. the Constitution of the Islamic Republic of Iran from 1979, often labeled as a hybrid with theocratic and democratic elements. Available at www.constituteproject.org/constitution/Iran_1989.pdf?lang=en.

36 In the premodern period, the legality of the ruler was often based on the notion of *maṣlaḥa* as public good, while in the modern period it is conducted through the state as a law-induced entity. "The victory of the nation-state was not only one of displacing Islamic law, but also one which entailed the 'reordering' of Muslim social structures. The Muslim believer had to be converted into the 'good national citizen.' The rest is legal history. The nation-state's jural modus vivendi was codification, a method that entails a conscious harnessing of a particular tool of governance .... Codification is a deliberate choice in the exercise of legal and political power, a choice that at once accomplishes a multitude of tasks. The most essential feature of the code is the production of order, clarity, concision and authority." (Hallaq, "Maqāṣid and the Challenges of Modernity," 22–23).

37 See e.g. Mawdūdī's definition of *Sharīʿa*. For a comparative analysis of several postcolonial states, see Iza Hussin: "Whereas in the 1880s, the term 'shariʿa' tended to refer to an Islamic way of life, rather than positive law or the work of legislation, by the last years of the nineteenth century the focus had shifted to explicit criticism of the encroachment of European law within the Egyptian legal system. By the 1930s, shariʿa had become symbolically central to the political platforms of Muslim reformists, anticolonialists, and many Muslims within the state structure, in Egypt, India, and the Malay States. With the establishment of the nation-state in the postindependence period, shariʿa had become transformed – siyasa sharʿiyya, as state shariʿa politics – as codified law in a limited but symbolically central domain." (Hussin, *Politics of Islamic Law*, 177).

38 Johansen, "Changing Limits of Contingency in the History of Muslim Law," 3.

adapted an already established economic knowledge, they constructed their economic narrative in line with the idea of a modern "Islamic nation-state." The modern European nation-state is, however, grounded in the idea of secularism as a separation of church from state, in the political philosophy of liberalism, and in legal monism.[39] The latter perceives law as a product of coercive powers of the state. Therefore, a modern Islamic nation-state is a contradiction in terms.[40] Precolonial, that is premodern, Islamic legal tradition, nurtured legal pluralism, allocating both "state-like" and non-state laws that worked interdependently, including *siyāsa* and *fiqh* under the banner of *Sharīʿa*'. Traditionally, *siyāsa* was enacted to at times to enforce punishments, but also to both further and improve social relations in light of the notion of the public good – including issues crucial to the modern understanding of economics, taxes, market inspection, and other mechanisms, whereby through *maẓālim* courts rulers adjudicated various disputes. Theoretically, *siyāsa* and *fiqh*, or the collective enterprise of *Sharīʿa*, aimed to protect members of society from rulers' misconduct, coercing rulers to act in accordance with the structure of the Divine law. Contemporary Muslim economists believed it was necessary to discredit the classical views on market mechanisms and other institutions. This created a vacuum that needed to be filled by either an overwhelming reliance on the technologies of the modern nation-state or an Islamic economic agent, who is supposed to be "perfectly imbued" with the values

39 "[M]odern secularism emerged in the seventeenth century as a political solution intended to end the European Wars of Religion by establishing a lowest common denominator among the doctrines of conflicting Christian sects and by defining a political ethic altogether independent of religious doctrines .... In this narrative, both the ethics of religious tolerance and freedom of conscience are considered to be goods internal to the doctrinal separation that secularism institutes between operations of the state and church, between politics and religion. The assumption is that the state, by virtue of its declared neutrality toward specific religious truth claims, makes religious goals indifferent to the exercise of politics and, in doing so, ensures that religion is practiced without coercion, out of individual choice and personal assent .... Insomuch as liberalism is about the regulation of individual and collective liberties, it is the principle of freedom of conscience that makes secularism central to liberal political philosophy in this account." (Mahmood, "Secularism, Hermeneutics, and Empire," 324); see also Charles Taylor, "Modes of Secularism," in *Secularism and Its Critics*, ed. Rajeev Bhargava (New Delhi: Oxford University Press, 1998), 31–53; on the modern binary of secular vs. religious, see Armando Salvatore, *The Sociology of Islam* (Chichester, UK: Wiley Blackwell, 2016), 8; on the emergence of the nation-state and the adoption of Islamic law as the state law, see Ahmad, *What Is Islam?*, 530–531.

40 See Hallaq, *Sharīʿa*, 360.

of Islam (Islamizing economic discipline). However, the modern Islamic states, which includes Indonesia, Pakistan, Iran, and others, when deliberating economic philosophy, rarely implement the historic understanding of *siyāsa* and *fiqh* as coterminous to moral cosmology and not through the concept of the state. For many Muslim economists, "in their zeal to advance this hypothesis – of an all-pervading state – as a fundamental ingredient of an Islamic economy, some of the writers do not even feel it necessary to draw a distinction between the state and economy. For them, an Islamic economy is simply an extension of the Islamic state."[41] Establishing economic and financial systems on the conditions of a nation-state presupposes an approach that Muslim economists initially contested in their writings as being based on Western predicaments.

In relation to state policy, political economy, as the study of state–economy relations, is practically nonexistent in contemporary Islamic economics. This says a great deal about the stalemate facing Muslim scholars and countries with the functioning of their economic theories and policies, respectively. State power, international relations, and the global economic paradigm of neoliberal capitalism continue to carry profound consequences for the reimagining of economic development in Muslim countries. Pakistan, Iran, Saudi Arabia, and other Muslim majority countries are directly involved in the process of acquisition of capital through business enterprises and corporations that are not regulated by the economic principles found in classical Islamic discourse.

Scholars analyzed in Chapter 3 advocate that *Sharīʿa* begins with self-realization[42] and self-determination on the path to achieve higher ends. As such, it expounds and overcomes the egoistic self and prompts the devout good[43] that corresponds with one's inner strivings. *Sharīʿa* therefore extends beyond the legal limits of economic contracts and concentrates around the enmeshed behavior of the morality of selfhood and the broader cosmological principles. As an ethical method it can enhance an understanding of human relations and advances proclivity toward well-being. However, this cannot take place through modernity's encroachment on the

[41] Azhar, *Economics of an Islamic Economy*, 8.
[42] Khorchide, *Scharia*, 195–197.
[43] See the Qur'an e.g. 2:57; 2:272; 3:104; 5:88; 7:50; 9:67, 67:2; Izutsu, *Ethico-Religious Concepts in the Qur'an*; on performing good or *al-ṣāliḥāt* (though there are also other corresponding terms, such as *aslaḥa*, *fasad*, *taqwa*, and *imān*), see the Qur'an, e.g. 2:25, 62, 277; 3:57; 4:57, 122; 5:9; 10:4; 11:11, 23; 13:29; 16:97; 18:30, 88; 20:75; 30:44; 45:15.

state, since "by its nature and purpose, *Sharīʿa* can only be freely observed by believers; its principles lose their religious authority and value when enforced by the state. From this fundamental religious perspective, the state must not be allowed to claim the authority of implementing *Sharīʿa* as such."[44] *Fiqh* rules cannot address all economic issues. Even if Islamic jurisprudence regulates the practices of Muslims in how they perform their economic conduct, it ought to allow for the reapplication of the theoretical framework and ethical patterns provided by the generation of early and classical Muslim scholars to be implemented in the process.[45]

4.3 Critiquing the Discipline of Islamic Economics

The revivalists promoted the call of Islam in light of modernism by accepting European notions of socioeconomic and political development.[46] The making and discovery of Islamic economics occurred through envisioning Islamic society within the parameters of an emerging Islamic state rooted in historical modernization processes. It is therefore not a coincidence that the foremost Muslims economists were found primarily in Pakistan and other postcolonial states. The making of Islamic economics, however, was founded on the epistemological predicaments of positivist sociology and science,[47] for the design of Islamic economics was seemingly based on Islamic identity – that would challenge the materialist philosophy of socialism – which, paradoxically, enhanced the materialist philosophy of capitalism.[48]

44 An-Naʾim, *Islam and the Secular State*, 4.

45 Hence, "it is not enough for jurisprudence to seek Qurʾanic judgements and solutions to new problems, it must also seek to understand the deepest foundations of these judgements and solutions. This perpendicular search is as much of the jurist's task as the horizontal search. The Muslim jurist has a duty to do what is in his utmost human capacity to 'make the Qurʾan speak' on an ever-wider level, and an ever-deeper level. This duty can be fulfilled through the use of unitary interpretation." Muḥammad Bāqir al-Ṣadr, *Durūs fī ʿIlm Uṣūl al-Fiqh* (Beirut: Dār al-Kitāb al-Lubnānī, 1978), 29–33, in Aref Ali Nayed, "The Unitary Qurʾānic Hermeneutics of Muhammad Baqir al-Sadr," *Islamic Studies*, vol. 31, no. 4 (1992): 446.

46 Alatas, "Islam and Modernization," 215.

47 For more on positivist sociology and economics, see Lionel Robbins, *An Essay on the Nature and Significance of Economic Science* (New York: St. Martin's Press, 1962).

48 Even though Timur Kuran provides many valid points of critique, in my opinion he unjustifiably designates Islamic economics as a fundamentalist doctrine, due to its reliance on traditional sources. See Kuran, *Islam and Mammon*, 4–5.

Islamic economics as a discipline combines positive and normative economics,[49] but its teachings rarely reflected economic reality in the Muslim-majority countries, despite the fact that Islamic law was to accommodate various economic instruments such as property rights and other institutional changes from the nineteenth century onwards.[50] What is presented as Islamic economics is in essence a set of ethical theories related to modern economics, mechanisms, and concepts such as production, distribution of wealth, and demand and supply. It has drawn on abstract models of economic development, disconnected from real-life societies. Although appearing as an alternative system to the discourse of modernity according to its textual and religious sources (albeit concerning its economic philosophy), arguably it still follows neoclassical, Keynesian economics, while national economies in the Arab world range from centralized socialist to free market.[51] Moreover, the initial focus on the development of Islamic economics has shifted toward Islamic finance and banking and its *Sharīʿa*-compliant engineering. It appears that the Islamic finance industry dictates the discourse on economic teachings in Islam and not the other way around. Hence, questions on human development, economic prosperity, distribution of income, unemployment, and environmental sustainability, among many others, remain unaddressed in the field.

4.3.1 Amalgamation of Religious and Mainstream Economic Systems

One of the consequences of generating Islamic economics within the confinements of the economic science is the growth of Islamic economic and financial centers in industrialized capitalist societies across the

[49] By positive economics, I refer to "the forces that regulate the economy. It raises such questions as how the economy works, what factors determine the distribution of wealth, and so on," whereas normative economics "is suggestive; it explicitly concerns with what ought to be" and integrates also ethical considerations (Addas, *Methodology of Economics*, 110).

[50] Muslim economists based their theories on apologetic delineations of social theory and financial institutions. Seyyed Vali Reza Nasr, "Islamic Economics: Novel Perspectives," *Middle Eastern Studies*, vol. 25, no. 4 (1989): 517.

[51] See e.g. Alatas, "Islam and Modernization," 216; Alatas, "Sacralization of the Social Sciences," 94–95. See e.g. "Regional Economic Outlook: Middle East and Central Asia," International Monetary Fund, 2019, accessed April 4, 2021, available at www.imf.org/en/Publications/REO/MECA/Issues/2019/10/19/reo-menap-cca-1019.

contemporary Muslim world. In theory, anti-Western, anti-capitalist, and anti-materialist Islamic economic philosophy was co-opted by the very narrative it allegedly fought against several decades ago. According to El-Ansary, "Muslim economists eloquently critique greed and consumerism to distinguish between spiritual values and egoistic preferences, but this does not by itself address the distinction between Islamic and neoclassical economic theories."[52] The methodology of contemporary Muslim economists was not clear, since they defined Islamic economics as a *Sharīʿa* based, *fiqh*-stipulated discipline,[53] conceived within social sciences, which was "about a model economy that did not exist in the real world."[54] And because of a preponderance of *fiqh*, the enterprise of Islamic economics has been viewed as an internal, that is Islamic, affair.[55] Hence, Muslim economists found themselves primarily engaging with an undefined discipline. Coupling Islamic economics with Islamic law did not yield long-term or epistemologically sound results in that it would meticulously analyze the classical Muslim scholars and their economic teachings. The insufficient theoretical contribution of modern Islamic economics is perhaps a result of an intellectual trauma of Muslim communities, which was exacerbated by the political domination of colonization and its destruction of educational and other institutional centers. Muslim economists rarely explained and analyzed the discipline of Islamic economics in relation to the epistemic value and the meaning behind *Sharīʿa*'s moral outlook. Their methodology is at times tedious and presumptuous, for it presupposes the existing structure of conventional economics.[56]

[52] El-Ansary, "Quantum Enigma and Islamic Sciences of Nature," 169.

[53] For various definitions, see e.g. Zarqa, Khan, Siddiqi, Naqvi, Chapra.

[54] Khan, *What Is Wrong with Islamic Economics?*, 4.

[55] Azhar, *Economics of an Islamic Economy*, 2.

[56] "Great expectations were attached to the idea of 'Islamic economics' by its exponents at the time the venture was launched some four decades ago. They thought of themselves as embarking on an intellectual endeavor that aimed at nothing short of presenting an entirely new paradigm in the field of economic thought, and they were quite convinced that once the new paradigm established its roots, it would usher in a Kuhnian paradigm shift in the existing discipline of economics. And, regardless of how it might be received in the established circles of economics, it was at any rate supposed to represent an unparalleled development in the Islamic sciences, for hitherto these did not possess a distinct and well articulated body of economic thought at par with the contemporary Western economic literature." (Azhar, *Economics of an Islamic Economy*, 1).

Attempting to counter colonial structures and dominant economic discourse, Muslim economists of the twentieth century confined Islamic economics to legal terminology and political specificity, while in practice it has been gradually implemented into a global economic paradigm of lucrative market-economy, in part through Islamic finances and banking. Analyzing the Islamic economic system according to the criteria of any other secular economic system raises the question of how it is possible to separate its role as a functioning economic system from its role as the reinforcer of a distinctively Islamic ethos.[57] The vision of a just and effective alternative to capitalism, whether presented as secular or Islamic socialism, appeared to be wearing thin, both in the Islamic world and beyond, throwing into doubt many of the assumptions upon which an alternative global economic order had been based. For many Muslim economists, the new economic system became a discipline to counter the existing world order and imagine an alternative narrative.

The concern of Islamic economics as being encumbered with the growth of the mainstream economic narrative[58] across the Middle East (and South Asia) is accompanied by the political developments in the region. Imitation of the so-called Western industrialized societies and their economic and scientific criteria appears to be a structural pattern. What is missing is a moral refashioning and restructuring of a worldview, since economic ideas do not flourish independently from the social, cultural, and broader historical structures in which they are embedded. This suggests understanding it as a distinctively economic development that is influenced by the discourse of mainstream economics and by the historical trajectory of the industrialized countries.[59] By

Tripp maintains that an empirical claim has been made suggesting the equation of the Islamic and the capitalist economic system: "This terrain was not marked out by any of the individual writers or by a distinctively Islamic tradition. On the contrary, it is defined by the dominant discourse of the discipline of economics as it emerged in Europe. It is against this that the singularity and superiority of the Islamic economy is being asserted. Regardless of possible quantifiable comparisons which may not favour the Islamic alternative, this argumentative strategy runs the danger once again of dissolving the specificity of 'Islamic economics'." (Tripp, *Islam and Moral Economy*, 116).

57 See Nasr, "Islamic Economics"; Nasr, "Toward a Philosophy of Islamic Economics."

58 Mirakhor, *Note on Islamic Economics*, 7; Alatas, "Islam and Modernization," 94.

59 See Rashid al-Barrawi, *Al-Iqtiṣād al-Islāmi* (Cairo: Kitāb al-Ḥurriyyah, 1986).

the 1990s, this had developed into the justification of Islamic economic theories that were unmistakably neoliberal in their underlying rationale[60] – this includes the functioning of Islamic financial centers and the argument that free competition and the prohibition of monopoly are central to any truly Islamic economy. Religious scholars and Muslim economists, in spite of their differences, sought the opportunity to create a distinct field of economic knowledge, while engaging with the already established discourse of secular economics. The very concepts and methods utilized by Muslim economists were, apart from the Islamic terminology and religious sources, incorporated into the emerging scheme of economics as a particularly European experience – as was the modern nation-state.

For Timur Kuran, what distinguishes Islamic economics from mainstream economic systems is a severalfold perspective based upon prohibition of interest, *zakāt* as a redistribution system, and Islamic moral values based on the sources of Islam.[61] Yet, for Kuran the Islamic economy was established on shaky grounds, to "defend Islamic civilization against foreign cultural influences"[62] and not necessarily to provide social benefit for society as a whole or to tackle economic injustices.[63] Either Islamic financial institutions became the institutions of national economies, such as the banking system of Iran and Pakistan, or they developed as private financial and banking institutions in the 1970s.[64] Al-Ṣadr's book on Islamic banking proposed the idea that the foundation of Islamic economics is the individual Muslim, as a moral and an economic agent,[65] which with interest-free banking assisted in creating an image of an Islamic personality. Since the understanding of Islamic economics as an alternative economic system was about a moral struggle, the individual of an idealized Islamic order becomes a focus of the economy. The (theoretical) rejection of capitalism

60 Tripp, *Islam and Moral Economy*, 115.
61 Kuran, "Islamic Economics and the Islamic Subeconomy," 156–157.
62 Kuran, "Islamic Economics and the Islamic Subeconomy," 156.
63 See Timur Kuran, "The Discontents of Islamic Economic Morality," *American Economic Review*, vol. 86, no. 2 (1996): 438–443; Timur Kuran, "Further Reflections on the Behavioral Norms of Islamic Economics," *Journal of Economic Behavior and Organization*, vol. 27 (1995): 159–163.
64 For more on the social significance on Islamic banking and finance, see Kuran, *Islam and Mammon*, 56–58.
65 Muḥammad Bāqir al-Ṣadr, *Al-Bank al-la-Ribāwi fī al-Islām* (Kuwait: Jami' al-Naqi,1970).

became for some Muslim scholars a rejection of market economy because capitalism was equated with the market system.[66] Conventionally, economics has not thought to explicate the distinction between capitalism and market economy, as Islamic economists discredited the market economy and filled the vacuum with state government intervention to achieve the Islamic economic agent.[67] However, the so-called Islamic economic agent of *homo islamicus* became an ideal construct that would affirm the application of distinct characteristics of Islamic economy within a given social order of a nation-state. The Islamic personality, however, cannot be attained within the web of economic parameters that are factually neoclassical.[68]

4.3.2 Methodological Flaws and Epistemological Inconsistencies

Since the majority of Muslim scholars on Islamic economics invoke religious methodology and conceptions from the secular economic systems, their writings are rarely critically contextualized within the broader disciplines of humanities and religious studies. The fact that Muslim intellectuals had to adapt to existing economic ideas obliged them to engage with the discipline of economics itself. Those concepts and theoretical frameworks were closely related to the changes in early modern Europe brought about by intellectual movements and industrial revolution. Whether Muslim intellectuals were critical or not of the impacts and values of these processes, classical economists had

66 Muḥammad al-Ghazzālī, *Al-Islām wa al-Manāhij al-Ishtirākiyya* (Cairo: Dār al-Kitāb al-ʿArabī, 1954), 92; al-Ṣadr, *Iqtiṣādunā* (1982), vol. 1, part 2, 5–7, 21. "It was for Islam to remind people of the spiritual aspect of existence, filling the void left by these two materialist philosophies. Such a position was also important as a means of asserting that Islam was of relevance to the situation of contemporary society and was therefore capable of engaging with – and of refuting – the dominant ideologies that so marked the world of the late twentieth century." (Tripp, *Islam and Moral Economy*, 98–99).

67 Azhar, *Economics of an Islamic Economy*, 7.

68 The Islamic personality "is a projection onto the abstracted individual of the qualities of that order, its values and its characteristics .... In fact, the notion of the 'Islamic personality' is an ideal construct, an argumentative device to allow the reconciling of apparently contrary currents. It was bound to reflect the preoccupations of those concerned about capitalism and socialism." (Tripp, *Islam and Moral Economy*, 122).

developed a particular language corresponding to the emerging needs and ideas of the field of economy.

Many renowned contemporary Muslim economists share comparable views on ethically imbued economic philosophy, yet they hold very different stances on the methodology of an Islamic economic project. The *tawḥīd* epistemology, supported by Choudhury and reflected also in other scholars' writings, summons a twofold concern. Any human activity can be justified as rooted in the so-called *tawḥīdi* or Qurʾanic epistemology, since the Qurʾan stands as the ultimate and most important textual source of Islam. For Choudhury, the Qurʾanic epistemology is encapsulated in the Divine Law, and reflected, too, in economic Islam and financial matters concerning issues of inheritance, purchasing commodities, buying and selling. Since the "epistemology of Unity" entails all branches of human knowledge because of the Qurʾanic premise of a multifaceted and complete worldview, it presupposes the application of an economic model in an ideal and not real-time Islamic society. Thus far, Islamic political economy has been used as a tool to critique the mainstream economic system and not to provide all-embracing, epistemological, and theoretical considerations within the Islamic tradition.[69] Choudhury critiques the synthesis of modernist epistemology and Islamic thought[70] and argues that the authentic Qurʾanic epistemology has been neglected.[71] However, rooting the Islamic economic project solely on the *tawḥīd* argument is circular. Further, the mathematization of economic theories is flawed not only in

69 Such a theory deals predominately with the Islamic view of human nature and not specifically with Islamic legal postulates that would explain the former. James Midgeley, review of The *Principles of Islamic Political Economy*, and *Comparative Development Studies: In Search of the World View*, by Masudul Alam Choudhury, *Journal of Sociology and Social Welfare*, vol. 21, no.3 (2015): 229.

70 Choudhury, "Critique of Modernist Synthesis in Islamic Thought," 475.

71 According to Choudhury, Qurʾanic epistemology differs from the pursuits by Muslim scholars, since the latter referred in their works to Hellenic philosophy, Persian, and even Indian thought, whereas the former is premised upon the ethical rules (*aḥkām*) from the Qurʾanic text itself, incorporating the faculty of reason in the Revelation. Nonetheless, reading the Qurʾanic text and its epistemology separately from scholarly consideration, their contributions, and the development of historical intellectual movements would mean reading this epistemology in a vacuum, separated from the social reality in Muslim countries. For his argument, see Choudhury, "Critique of Modernist Synthesis in Islamic Thought," 476.

social sciences[72] but also in Islamic economics since it does not reflect the social and cultural aspects and practices in modern Middle Eastern and South Asian societies. Islamic economics contains many theoretical, philosophical, and epistemological concerns that cannot be addressed with mathematical or neoclassical models, since mathematization presupposes a highly skilled language that is accessible only to certain segment of scholars, predominantly those in the natural sciences.[73] This would further set apart mathematical data from epistemological and theoretical analysis.

Even though the discipline of Islamic economics has been approached from an Islamic viewpoint embedded in ontological and epistemological presupposition,[74] there is an influx of concepts and ideas that contribute to the confusion in the field. Despite the fact that markets in the Muslim lands were historically organized uniformly to achieve economic efficiency and control of goods, their quantity and their quality, Islamic economy is not a free market economy, since markets were structured to accommodate the enforcement of legal precepts with underlying ethical postulates. For Volker Nienhaus, however, the methodology of Islamic economics is comparable to a social market economy, which rests upon the following points:[75] people only have the right to utilize worldly possessions; wealth can be acquired only through licit means of work and inheritance, for which prescriptions exist; and the poor and the needy are taken care of through the institution of *zakāt*, which corresponds to social welfare.[76] Islamic economics implies that certain institutions could increase economic development in the Middle East, yet those institutions and mechanisms (such as capital markets, labor laws, and so forth) did not exist or were ineffective, since their structure was adjusted to the policy reform of the International Monetary Fund. Part of this failure lies in the fact that previously the Ottoman Empire, which reigned throughout the Middle East, was not successful in preserving sufficient institutions to accommodate social and

[72] Smith, *Cosmos and Transcendence*, 19.

[73] Choudhury, "Critique of Economic Theory and Modeling," 429.

[74] See Mirakhor, *Note on Islamic Economics*, 9.

[75] Volker Nienhaus, "Islamic Economic System: A Threat to Development?," (2006), 1–2, available at www.iefpedia.com/english/wp-content/uploads/2009/09/Islamic-Economic-System-%E2%80%93-A-Threat-to-Development.pdf.

[76] *Zakāt* is in theory "a compulsory levy of 2.5% on assets and 5% or 10% on agricultural produce" (Nienhaus, "Islamic Economic System," 2).

economic prosperity, in addition to the fact that *zakāt* was never structurally implemented within an economic system.[77] Another factor, vital in Islamic economic thinking, is *ribā*, which has been contested by critics of Islamic economics. The economic and legal setup is supportive of implementing the prohibition of *ribā*, or excessive usury of a loan. *Ribā* is rendered illicit only for loan (financial) transactions and not for trade or goods transactions resulting in profit. Since trade has always been deeply rooted in Islamic tradition, it required financial structure, therefore also Muslim legal specialists. Yet, skepticism remains whether legal justification of Islamic economics and finances addresses societal needs and aspirations, since there is no existing Islamic economy in the Middle East.[78]

4.3.3 The Erroneous Coupling of Islamic Economics with the Social Sciences

Coupling a religious worldview with the Western division of sciences and the predefined conceptualizations borrowed from social sciences in

77 Compare this with Kuran's claim that Islamic culture failed to produce an institution of cooperation due to the rigidity of Islamic law; Timur Kuran, *The Long Divergence: How Islamic Law Held Back the Middle East* (Princeton, NJ: Princeton University Press, 2010). Such an approach raises numerous concerns, for the gist of Islamic law was moral essence, based on cosmological and theological structures. The so-called rigidity of Islamic law did not prevent the blossoming of economy in Islam, whereas Kuran aims to prove the opposite. For Nienhaus, there are other more pertinent reasons, such as tax farming that was obtained by the Ottoman rulers, which "undermined private property and made it irrational to build-up immobile real assets"; Nienhaus, "Islamic Economic System," 3. Furthermore, the primary concern of Islamic law was not an early form of capital-oriented engagement but rather the moral fundaments of human conduct. For the latter, see Wael Hallaq's critique of Kuran as a flawed analytical project, in Hallaq, *Impossible State*, 212, reference 69. For a similar argument, see also Volker Nienhaus, "Der Beitrag des Islam zur ethnischen Fundierung einer Wirtschaftsordnung," in *Wirtschaft und Fundamentalismus*, ed. Gerhard Schich (Berlin: Stiftung Marktwirtschaft, 2003).

78 "Eine islamische Wirtschaftordnung ist in keinem modernen Staat der muslimischen Welt praktisch implementiert worder, vielleicht mit Ausnahme von Sudan und Iran. Die heute existierenden Wirtschaftsordnungen sind mehr oder weniger sistematische Fortentwicklungen von Systemen, die unter säkularen Vorzeichen nach Erlangung der Unabhängigkeit in Fortsetzung oder (revolutionärer) Überwindung der Systeme der kolonialzeit installiert wurden." Volker Nienhaus, "Grundzüge einer islamischen Wirtschaftsordnung im Vergleich zur sozialen Marktwirtschaft," *Kas Auslandsinformationen*, vol. 11 (2010): 81.

general and economic science in particular is one of the most fundamental problems of the discipline of Islamic economics. Since the social sciences perceive religion as an intellectually regressive endeavor, Muslim economists have tried to prove the scientific component of Islamic economics by adapting to Western theories of scientific knowledge, including the very term "economics."[79] This, however, has not been done without impacting the epistemic value and the ontological status of the discipline of Islamic economics, since both approaches – coupling Islamic economics with mainstream scientific ideas and concepts and resorting to the innovation of establishing Islamic economics as a separate domain – share a systemic drawback of splitting the moral norms (the moral) of economic thought from the legal value (the legal) and its metaphysical foundation. This split has been the result of theories that emerged as a response and opposition to the colonization and westernization processes. Muslim revivalists and scholars in the early twentieth century aimed to generate an ideal economic worldview, while simultaneously following political liberalism in order to justify the existence of the discipline. By building an Islamic economic doctrine on the division of knowledge and disciplines that is prevalent in the West and on the European experience of nation-state formations, such theories – while claiming Islamic character – stripped away the possibility of generating a profound analysis and critique of the subject. It is no wonder then that contemporary Islamic economics was epistemologically impaired by positivist sociology, which brought with it many of the assumptions of individual and society, as well as of the inner composition of the material world, that buttress the very ethos of capitalist existence.

Discursively, economics generated a distinct social and scientific universe that draws upon economic agents to act in accordance with its principles and rational character, such as accumulation of material goods.[80] Economic ideas, behavior, and institutions are hence socially

[79] For more, see Mohsin S. Khan and Abbas Mirakhor, "The Framework and Practice of Islamic Banking," *Finance and Development*, vol. 23, no. 3 (1986): 32ff; for the analytically faulty claim that the guidelines of Islamic economics are incompatible with modern times, see Rainer Hermann, "Islamisches Recht und Seine wirtschaftspolitischen Implikationen," in *Wirtschaft und Fundamentalismus*, ed. Gerhard Schich (Berlin: Stiftung Marktwirtschaft, 2003), 75–83.

[80] Polanyi, *Great Transformation*, 257–258.

constructed, which might explain why Muslim economists devised a hybrid field.

> There was nothing natural about laissez-faire; free markets could never have come into being merely by allowing things to take their course . . . laissez-faire itself was enforced by the state. The thirties and forties saw not only an outburst of legislation repealing restrictive regulations, but also an enormous increase in the administrative functions of the state, which was now being endowed with a central bureaucracy able to fulfil the tasks set by the adherents of liberalism. To the typical utilitarian, economic liberalism was a social project which should be put into effect for the greatest happiness of the greatest number; laissez-faire was not a method to achieve a thing, it was the thing to be achieved . . .. Benthamite liberalism meant the replacing of parliamentary action by action through administrative organs . . .. While laissez-faire economy was the product of deliberate State action, subsequent restrictions on laissez-faire started in a spontaneous way. Laissez-faire was planned; planning was not.[81]

Conventional economics as a social science draws upon human nature and social imaginary, deriving its epistemology and ontology, which are associated with a particular economic outlook, industrialization, and free market economy. The mainstream economic system, in spite of multiple economic theories, created its own set of criteria and understanding of human nature, according to which it expressed a particular system of values as it emerged in early modern Europe. Perceiving Islamic economics as economic science with Islamic terminological apparatus is indicative of thinking within the set of the existing disciplines, for the concepts and economic principles are already predefined. Even though this disciplinary hybridity was devised to be in theory independent from the neoclassical economic paradigm, it has proven the opposite, due to the absence of the ideal Islamic personality and economic model in real-time Muslim societies. Furthermore, the positivist logic of economics and the discipline of sociology shaped Muslim economists' views on society to the degree of meshing Islam's core ethical values and *Sharīʿa* norms with the prevalent socioeconomic structures of state formation.

For Muhammad Akram Khan, who clearly sought to revitalize economic thought,[82] Islamic economics is a mainstream economics,

[81] Polanyi, *Great Transformation*, 145–147.

[82] "I have been actively involved in thinking about, writing about and advocating Islamic economics as a distinct branch of knowledge for over four decades. However, over the last decade, my thinking had gradually moved away from

embellished with Qur'anic and *ḥadīth* terminology.[83] In this sense, Islamic economics is a "type of capitalism with a spiritual dimension,"[84] which positions the institution of *ribā* in its core.[85] Khan contends that religious scholars from the nineteenth and early twentieth centuries have addressed economic teachings in Islam within the scope of theological discourse. Since this failed to establish a solid theoretical ground for the emerging discipline of Islamic economics, he proposes studying the subject matter within the field of social sciences[86] and thus annexing it to the mainstream economic narrative. For him, one of the main obstacles is its theological reference and the lack of social scientific component. If Islamic economic teachings remain predominantly attached to their theological base, they cannot be formulated, verified, or delineated sufficiently. The early religious scholars and proponents of the Islamization process tried to develop Islamic economics based on a theological worldview, discussing inheritance law, *zakāt*, and conventional economics, yet the scope and the subject matter were neither clear nor theoretically sound.

Although Khan acknowledges the insufficiency of the contemporary Islamic economic project, he blames the theological framework for it and not the legal straitjacket and the dominant discourse of modernity in which the discipline of Islamic economics emerged. His method of positioning Islamic economics solely within the parameters of the social sciences remains highly problematic, since it refuses to consider epistemological, historic, theological, moral, and mystical entanglements of economic teachings in Islamic tradition that deploy a different hermeneutical field from mainstream social sciences and from the Islamization process.

mainstream thinking on the subject." (Khan, *What Is Wrong with Islamic Economics?*, xiv).

83 Khan, *What Is Wrong with Islamic Economics?*, xiv.

84 Khan, *What Is Wrong with Islamic Economics?*, xv.

85 There is a consensus among Muslims on the prohibition on *ribā*, yet there is no definite definition and description of what exactly this prohibition entails, and on this prohibition the modern institutions of Islamic finance are based. This leads Khan further to prove that all forms of interest are not *ribā*, even though the Islamic financial institutions have rendered them illicit, despite the fact that various forms of interest, such as double payment, profit gains, and others can be found in Islamic finances. On the concept of *ribā* and its historical and legal perspectives, see Azhar, *Economics of an Islamic Economy*.

86 Khan, *What Is Wrong with Islamic Economics?*, xiii, 27ff.

4.4 The Islamization of Economics

4.4.1 Islamizing Knowledge

The process of secularism compelled many Muslim scholars to grapple with the Western notion of knowledge and the division of disciplines, in general, and the social sciences, in particular. In the 1970s, Muslim scholars witnessed the materialization of the Islamization of knowledge process, which defined Islamic science according to its Islamic worldview and revealed knowledge paradigms.[87] Analogously, however, Muslim scholars also experienced the process of indigenism or nativism as orientalism in reverse.[88] Some of the traits of nativism are the repudiation of Western social sciences, the superficial critique of Western theories, and a lack of attention to the classical Islamic intellectual tradition.[89] This modernity-confined discourse of Western knowledge and sciences had a profound impact on the structural and imaginative nature of Islamic sciences in general and of Islamic economics in particular.

For Thomas Bauer, the Islamization of Islam is constructed around the following components. "Islamic" as used to indicate distinct fields of human endeavors (e.g. Islamic art, Islamic medicine, Islamic economics, etc.) suggests a religious identity, whereas nonreligious discourses are consequently being labeled as unimportant. In the case of multiple discourses, the one that corresponds most closely to the widespread perception of religion in the West is appropriated, and religious discourse is given precedence over a nonreligious one. In the case of multiple discourses, the one that will be accepted as the orthodox norm

[87] See Seyyed Hossein Nasr, *Islamic Science: An Illustrated Study* (London: World of Islam Festival Trust, 1976); Seyyed Hossein Nasr, "Reflections on Methodology in the Islamic Sciences," *Hamdard Islamicus*, vol. 3, no. 3 (1980): 3–13; Seyyed Hossein Nasr, *The Need for a Sacred Science: The Gifford Lectures* (Edinburgh: Edinburgh University Press, 1981).

[88] See e.g. Mona Abaza, "Some Reflections on the Question of Islam and Social Sciences in the Contemporary Muslim World," *Social Compass*, vol. 40, no. 2 (1993): 301–321; Mona Abaza and Georg Stauth, "Occidental Reason, Orientalism, Islamic Fundamentalism: A Critique," in *Globalization, Knowledge and Society: Readings from International Sociology*, ed. Martin Albrow and Elizabeth King (London: Sage Publications, 1990), 209–230; Sadiq Jalal al-ʿAzm, "Orientalism and Orientalism in Reverse," in *Forbidden Agendas: Intolerance and Defiance in the Middle East*, ed. John Rothschild (London: Al-Saqi Books, 1984), 349–376.

[89] Alatas, "Sacralization of the Social Sciences," 98.

relating to the essence of Islam is the one that corresponds the most to Western standards of "conservativism."[90] Such a mechanical process repudiates Islamic tradition's culture of ambiguity and sets the norm for a monolithic religion of Islam, which appears to Western culture as something alien and even contradictory. These political, economic, and cultural ramifications of European colonialism of the late nineteenth century paved the road to a selective public image of Islam. Consequently, various Islamist movements resorted to conservative (and some to Ḥanbalī) tradition[91] and – like their Western liberal counterparts – negated the multifaceted traditions of Islam.

Moreover, the fact that Islamization of Islam (and Islamic economics) is a relatively modern phenomenon is indicative of the level of usage of certain terminology and concepts. Terms like *niẓām* (system) and *manhaj* (method) incorporate a Cartesian worldview that was unknown to classical Islam.[92] The classical Islamic sciences offered a plural approach to the study of sciences of nature wherein theology, Islamic law, and *taṣawwuf* gave different answers to sometimes similar questions, whereas modern Islamic interpretation forms various fields of knowledge with the same method and principles. In turn, the Islamization process Islamizes science by utilizing Western concepts and placing them in an Islamic milieu, merging Islamic and non-Islamic thought.[93] The Islamization of knowledge has accommodated the teachings of *Sharīʿa* on a variety of topics; however, rather than contributing to the theory of knowledge, the Islamization of disciplines has generated a paradigmatic disjunction between faith and knowledge in Islam.[94] Both al-Faruqi and al-Attas refer to the modern worldview within which contemporary knowledge is interpreted.[95] While they consider *tawḥīd* as the basic principle of Islam, al-Attas espouses

90 Bauer, *Die Kultur der Ambiguität*, 222–223.

91 See for instance Ayatollah Ruhollah Khomeini's concept of *velāyat-e faqīh*: Ruhollah Khomeini. *Islamic Government*, trans. Joint Publications Research Service (Dublin: Manor Books, 1979); Sayyid Quṭb, *Maʿālīm fī al-Tarīq* (Beirut: Dār al-Shurūq, 1979); Sayyid Quṭb, *Milestones* (Birmingham: Maktabah, 2006); Salvatore, *Islam and the Political Discourse of Modernity*, 87.

92 Bauer, *Die Kultur der Ambiguität*, 387–388.

93 See Moussalli, "Islamism," 97–101.

94 Nasr, "Islamization of Knowledge," 387.

95 "It seems to me important to emphasize that knowledge is not neutral, and can indeed be infused with a nature and content which masquerades as knowledge. Yet it is in fact, taken as a whole, not true knowledge, hut its interpretation through the prism, as it were, the worldview, the intellectual 'vision and

metaphysical Islam as a synthesis of classical theologians, philosophers, and Sufis,[96] deriving its sources from the revelation and intellectual history. For him, knowledge is never pure but presents an intricate relation between revealed knowledge and human reasoning. Al-Attas's conception of Islamization is a form of liberation from secularism and from secular control of reason and language,[97] and focuses on Islamizing the inner self – the individual personality. *Taṣawwuf* formulates basic predicaments and concepts for all branches of knowledge.[98]

On the other hand, al-Faruqi's plan is to Islamize classical and modern disciplines by producing educational curricula based on Islamization methodology. Similar to other Muslim revivalists of the early twentieth century who censure *taṣawwuf,* al-Faruqi emphasizes the socioeconomic values and processes of Islamization that were later extended to the field of Islamic economics. Al-Faruqi's Islamization of knowledge appears more mechanical and is associated with the positivist approach, whereas al-Attas's method is rooted in Sufism and deals primarily with Islamizing ideas and concepts.

The critics of Islamization of knowledge have also voiced their concerns. Fazlur Rahman states that one has to critically analyze the worldview of classical Islam and not simply apply the Islamization process to modern sciences.[99] *'Ilm* as knowledge is in itself something that should be upheld, yet it is human (mis)appropriation of knowledge that can be irresponsible. Pertinent to such an approach is the integration of Islamic and modern disciplines of knowledge. Moreover, Ziauddin Sardar, one of the main critics of the Islamization process, believes that al-Faruqi's conception of the Unity of Truth and Unity of *'Ilm* is inconsistent and without any substance. Al-Faruqi's Islamization plan is directed mainly at the social sciences. Yet, it is impossible to perceive the Islamization of modern sciences as an end solution because they are rooted in the Western epistemological

psychological perception of the civilization that now plays the key role in is formulation and dissemination." (Al-Attas, *Islam and Secularism*, 133–134).

96 Rosnani Hashim and Imron Rossidy, "Islamization of Knowledge: A Comparative Analysis of the Conceptions of Al-Attas and Al-Fārūqī," *Intellectual Discourse*, vol. 8, no. 1 (2000): 24.

97 Al-Attas, *Islam and Secularism*, 42.

98 Al-Attas, *Islam and Secularism*, 121–123.

99 Rahman, *Islam and Modernity*, 134.

paradigm[100] and that pertains to particular theories, concepts, imaginaries, and practices of knowledge and the world. It would be therefore impossible to merge two distinct epistemological systems in the field of economics, since each has produced a specific worldview and a set of requirements that correspond to social world and its specificities.

The proponents of Islamization of knowledge should not uncritically accept the modern divisions of disciplines per se and should instead focus on the fundamental norms of what constitutes the theory of knowledge in Islamic tradition. Even if modern knowledge is relevant for the Islamic perception of knowledge and sciences, it must be made relevant through understanding of Islam's traditional framework. If science is "westernized" it means that it is not neutral,[101] and it is consequently bound to a cultural milieu. Since traditional knowledge was perceived to be derived from the theological sources, the Islamization process as understood in the twentieth century by al-Faruqi is not. The divorcing of the moral from the epistemological in early modern Europe generated a body of knowledge that was foreign to the Islamic understanding of key concerns of manifestations (and not only concepts) such as mutual cooperation, social justice, sacredness of nature, and so forth.[102] Muslim economists were too busy applying Western economic techniques and methods to Islamic economics. Instead of Islamizing disciplines, Muslim scholars can Islamize the philosophy of those disciplines, employing an Islamic outlook and the spirit of revelation.[103] Even if Islamization of knowledge commences with *Sharīʿa* as a legal term, it does not end with it, for such a process entails implementing a religious worldview, restructuring the moral fiber, and critiquing existing definitions and divisions of (social) sciences.

4.4.2 *Islamizing Economics*

Modern Islamic economic thought reinforced itself against the backdrop of Islamization of knowledge, which, despite its discontent with

[100] See Ziauddin Sardar, *Islamic Futures* (Kuala Lumpur: Pelanduk Publications, 1988). First published 1986.

[101] Nasr maintains that knowledge has become desacralized (Nasr, *Knowledge and the Sacred*, 10).

[102] See e.g. Sardar, *Islamic Futures*, 103–105; Seyyed Hossein Nasr, "Islam and the Problem of Modern Sciences," *Islam and Science*, vol. 8, no. 1 (2010): 63–74.

[103] Nasr, "Islamization of Knowledge," 393.

and opposition to the Western colonial project and its economic, political, and cultural implications, materialized within the preestablished order of the nation-state. In the twentieth century, the Islamists' envisioning of an Islamic state and society gave precedence to Islamizing national economies, which served as a mechanism for asserting religious ideas into state politics.[104] The development of Islamic economics as a distinct science occurred more in name than in substance, since the neorevivalists embarked upon the Islamic version of knowledge with economics as its subparadigm. By delineating a field of knowledge known by the common denominator as economics, contemporary Muslim scholars and economists were compelled to attune and harmonize the criteria and conventionalities of that very field, despite their Islamic standpoint. By preserving the imaginative sphere of scientific knowledge, the concepts and terminologies, and the scientific language of the modernist discourse, modern Muslim economists defiled their own project, which was initially seen as an alternative economic system.[105]

All of this is to say that the contemporary Islamic economic project has been devoid of traditional epistemic value. Contemporary Muslim reactions to economic problems in the twentieth century have sprouted first from the revivalists' project and second from the Islamization process, which have not developed a coherent program for rethinking the nature of economics and the role of its main components such as production processes, the role of money, developmental well-being, and moral and social consciousness in contemporary Muslim societies. Their offering of an exclusively religious outline of Islamic political economy has assumed a tautological and self-fulfilling narrative of economic doctrine. Furthermore, Islamizing a national economy indicates that it is Islam (or Islamic ethics) rather than the government that is responsible for the social equilibrium and economic performance of the economy.[106] Consequently, the religious worldview of Islamic economics was explicit, primarily in the creation of interest-free banking and financial institutions.[107] Their rise and success have

104 On the Islamization of Pakistani economy, see e.g. Hathaway and Lee, *Islamization and the Pakistani Economy*; Nasr, "Islamic Economics," 525.

105 On the pro-market economy, despite his critique of capitalism, see Azhar, *Economics of an Islamic Economy*.

106 Nasr, "Islamic Economics," 526; Nasr, "Islamization of Knowledge," 390.

107 See e.g. Yildiz Atasoy, *Islam's Marriage with Neoliberalism: State Transformation in Turkey* (London: Palgrave Macmillan, 2009).

compensated for the absence of a coherent philosophy in Islamic economic thought, since it appears to be inoperable, despite its intellectual potential.

4.5 Concluding Remarks

Given the lack of knowledge and the discursive formation of Islamic tradition by Muslim economists, Islamic economics will remain ill-equipped to deal not only with the language of *fiqh*[108] but also with the intricate historical, social, and cultural patterns of premodern Muslim societies and their perceptions of what constituted the economic. Such an approach to the field of economy has excluded the practice of economics and has led to a certain dogmatism in the subject. The example of Islamic economics indicates that it differs from conventional economics in its ethical considerations. However, the distinction between *homo islamicus* and *homo economicus* has no equivalent in any existing political economy.

Islamic culture did not encounter the onslaught of modernity and its colonial restructuring only through military occupation but also through bureaucratic-administrative, legal, political, and economic incursions. Muslim countries have undergone restructuring of their legal systems and have had to replace the institution of *Sharīʿa* with European laws. As a response, simply put, civil society and legal specialists called for a reintegration of Islamic law, coinciding with Islamists' call to create Islamic nation-states and society.[109]

Yet without the reexamination of historic analysis of economic thought in Islamic tradition, the modern project of Islamic economics (and finances) is doomed to only one feature – its own distinctive narrative. This perpetuates skepticism about the contemporary Islamic economic

108 "[T]he *fiqh* scholars were equally ill-prepared to deal with the discipline of economics and the working of the modern economy; indeed most of the *fiqh* scholars have lacked even an elementary knowledge of economics as well as the issues that it deems important. It is thus that those few who could occupy the middle ground – at the confluence of *fiqh* and economics – were able to set a course of their own liking for a discourse that was to be known as Islamic economics." (Azhar, *Economics of an Islamic Economy*, 3).

109 See the writings of al-Mawdūdī, Sayyid Quṭb, and other revivalists. "Calls to return to the application of Islamic law emerged into prominence during the 1970s." Frank E. Vogel and Samuel L. Hayes, *Islamic Law and Finance* (The Hague: Kluwer Law International, 1998), 20

project since it is ontologically based on the conditions of the liberal philosophy and the modern state. Reconstructing the Islamic economic (and legal) paradigm within the nation-state has to be addressed in relation to the moral metamorphosis. As such, the contemporary Islamic economic project is deprived of both methodological consideration and moral context and is either inauthentic or doomed to fail.

Islamists see *Sharī'a* primarily as legal and sociopolitical enforcement due to its Divine origin – an approach that can be compared with legal positivism.[110] Neither mimicking the mainstream economic system nor glorifying the self-perpetuated image of Islamization will do justice to the subject, since both approaches address the issues at stake only in part. Contemporary Islamic economic theories did not provide an overall economic system detached from the "centripetal pull of western economic thought."[111] Since "the political discourses of modernity have intervened in the construction of Islam," and "the definitions of Islam have contributed to shape political discourse of modernity, both in the West and in the 'Arab-Islamic' world,"[112] a particular hermeneutic field of political Islam manifested. This hermeneutical field owes its existence in part to the all-embracing discourse of modernity (and the construction of modern disciplines) that claims universal validity and even affects the indigenous interpretations of Islam.

Epistemology, as the study of theory of knowledge, is not confined to one particular realm of investigation, and hence it is not separated or isolated from other realms of knowledge. The twentieth-century definitions of Islamic economics are embedded in a particular social context and a religious ideology that are, however, concerned with the indigenization of social sciences. Islamic social, political, and economic history has been essentially explained in religious terms, and "the Muslim intellectual history is thus essentially a sociopolitical history."[113]

110 For M. K. Masud, the problem lies with secularists and Islamists, since the former try to diminish and the latter seek to overemphasize *Sharī'a's* legal positivism, and "None of them accepts the possibility that the normative basis of shari'a may lie elsewhere." (Masud, "Muslim Jurists' Quest for the Normative Basis of Shari'a," 5–6). Compare this view with Bauer's theory of cultural ambiguity.

111 Aydin, "Redefining Islamic Economics As a New Economic Paradigm," 2.

112 Salvatore, *Islam and the Political Discourse of Modernity*, xiv, xv, xxi, 23.

113 See Muhammad Khalid Masud's draft "'Classical' Islamic Legal Theory as Ideology: Nasr Abu Zayd's Study of al-Shafi'i's Risala," 11.

Regardless of whether Islamic economics is defined as science or dogma, as we have seen from the examples within the Islamic intellectual tradition, classical Muslim scholars encouraged moral economic behavior in light of broad epistemological contexts.[114] The majority of Muslim economists have largely disregarded the sociopolitical contestations that contributed to the establishment of economic ideas and by extension the historical underpinnings by premodern Muslim scholars who addressed economic subjects as part of the all-embracing cosmology rooted in the moral self.

Furthermore, at present, many Muslim organizations and networks have turned to the Islamic banking and finance industry in order, presumably, to restore and further the commercial life of the twenty-first century, while invoking the institution of *Sharīʿa*. On the ground, however, Islamic banks did not pose a threat to commercial finances and capital markets,[115] which are encapsulated in global capitalism, but instead they "have attracted those who felt morally uneasy about conventional, interest-based banking and whose sense of propriety in economic transactions has been better catered for by institutions which avoid interest and invest in activities that are *ḥalāl* under Islamic law."[116] While it can be a positive contributor to economic growth, this is often hindered by underdeveloped institutional frameworks in the Muslim-majority countries.[117] It is in this regard that Islamic finance in banking has created its own niche and become part of the global economic system, and since its conceptual frame is enfeeble, it remains within the fold of modernist discourse and its epistemological contentions.

Islamic banking and finance, as the most developed subfield within Islamic economics, deals also with commercial and contract laws. As

[114] For the moral self and the encouragement of economic stipulations, consult the works of al-Shaybānī, al-Muḥāsibī, Ibn Abī al-Dunyā, and al-Ghazālī discussed in Chapter 3.

[115] Islamic banks, despite progress and development, have had only a marginal impact on global financial markets, and their representatives have often resorted to their Western right-leaning colleagues and economists to steer their domestic projects.

[116] Tripp, *Islam and Moral Economy*, 146; Timur Kuran, "The Economic System in Contemporary Islamic Thought: Interpretations and Assessment," *International Journal for Middle East Studies*, vol. 18, (1986): 135–164.

[117] Jamel Boukhatem and Fatma Ben Moussa, "The Effect of Islamic Banks on GDP Growth: Some Evidence from Selected MENA Countries," *Borsa Istanbul Review*, vol. 18, no. 3 (2018): 231–247.

such, it is perceived as a subgenre of Islamic law, often coupled with mainstream financial terminologies and operational systems, whose methods present neither historical accuracy of the field nor theoretical definition of the subject matter. In Pakistan, Malaysia, Iran, and other countries, the process of Islamization has also penetrated the legal and political realms, yet Islamic banking in general does not impinge upon international policies to the degree of changing the economic paradigm. If Islamic banking and finance would seek to apply Islamic religious law (*Sharīʿa*) to a sector of modern trading and commerce,[118] which has much stronger precedence than politics or theology, it ought not to preclude only a positive economics but also the qualities of virtue. The objectives to be pursued should be, as one of the proponents of the Islamization process once stated, to "[minimize] cost in production (instead of maximizing profit) and maximizing *maṣlaḥa* in consumption (instead of maximizing utility)."[119]

In the final chapter, this book turns to the proposition of approaching economic thought in Islamic tradition from a pluralistic and polyvalent epistemology of moral and cosmological hermeneutics.

118 Vogel and Hayes, *Islamic Law and Finance*, 21.
119 Khan, "*Fiqh* Foundations of the Theory of Islamic Economics," 76.

5 *Pluralistic Epistemology of Islam's Moral Economics*

The social world, in all its aspects, turns upon human practice, the primary explanandum of social enquiry. And, whatever the practices of interest, amongst the explanans of social explanations are structures, positions, mechanisms, processes and the like. In other words, there is no obvious basis for distinguishing economics according to the nature of its object, i.e. as a separate science. Nor does it have its own domain.

Tony Lawson, *Reorienting Economics*, 162

The more man makes himself at home in the heart of the world, the further he advances in his possession of nature, the more strongly also does he feel the pressure of his finitude, and the closer he comes to his own death. History does not allow man to escape from his initial limitations – except in appearance, and if we take the word limitation in its superficial sense; but if we consider the fundamental finitude of man, we perceive that his anthropological situation never ceases its progressive dramatization of his History, never ceases to render it more perilous, and to bring it closer, as it were, to its own impossibility.

Michel Foucault, *The Order of Things*, 259

Earning is not the aim of human life but it is a means to an end.

Al-Ghazālī, *Iḥyā'*, vol. 2, 62

5.1 Introductory Remarks

This chapter does not exhaust the study of new approaches to economic teachings in Islamic tradition.[1] Instead, it analyzes how to study economic teachings in Islam as a multifaceted, polyvalent, and pluralistic

[1] Islamic economics can be perceived also as part of heterodox economics, which, in a way, opposes the mainstream economic project's concept of truth. On heterodox economics, see e.g. Lawson, *Reorienting Economics*; Lawson, *Economics and Reality*.

epistemological tradition[2] within a cross-disciplinary conceptual framework centered on the moral self. I argue for a particular epistemological conception, and through demonstrating the sustainability of this particular conception, I will introduce how to approach the study of economic thought and its intricacies.

In order to recover the economic teachings in the Islamic heritage, it is crucial to analyze multiple angles within the Islamic intellectual tradition, as well as the difference between the ontology of science and knowledge in premodern and modern traditions. Given, first, the formation of economics in the eighteenth century as a rational and objective science – an attitude that was also adopted by neoclassical economics – and, second, the epistemological ruptures that occurred in the eighteenth and nineteenth centuries with the introduction and expansion of scientific disciplines in early modern Europe, economic teachings in intellectual tradition cannot be studied simply as a combination of Islamic idioms and the prevalent neoclassical ideas. Analyzing the field of economics by itself is an impossible endeavor if any serious analysis is to be done on the project of Islamic studies in general, and economic tradition in particular, for economic matters in classical Islamic scholarship were conceptualized within a polyvalent methodological framework, often seen as part of moral conduct and broader ethical systems. The Qur'an has had an active and dialectic interaction with every major cosmological idea of its time, including human behavior as it pertains to economic activities, since its cosmology in its entirety is based on moral law.[3] As discussed in Chapter 3, the moral cosmology in analyzed classical texts translates human behavior into a morally driven engagement in light of higher metaphysical ends that surpass purely worldly or material aspirations. In this manner, the moral self is perhaps expressed most often through the dominion of *Sharīʿa*, yet there are other discursive traditions outside of it that refer to its moral cosmology.[4]

[2] By epistemological tradition in this case, I mean a theory of knowledge that was produced by the premodern hermeneutical field in Islamic tradition.

[3] For more, see e.g. Ibn Hazm, *Al-Iḥkām fī Uṣūl al-Aḥkām* (Damascus: al-Maktaba al-Islāmiyya, 1981); al-Ghazālī, *al-Mustaṣfā'*; Anver M. Emon, *Islamic Natural Law Theories* (Oxford: Oxford University Press); Hallaq, "Groundwork of the Moral Law," 273–274.

[4] See Shahab Ahmed's hermeneutical engagement of the Pre-Text, Text, and Con-Text in Ahmed, *What Is Islam?*, chapters 4, 5 and 6; and Talal Asad's notion of discursive tradition in Talal Asad, "The Idea of an Anthropology of Islam"

The concept of *Sharīʿa* inevitably leads us to reassess the notions of "Islam" and "Islamic." Namely, the first is "Islam" proper, usually identified as Islamic law as a historical, authentic phenomenon maintaining the position of explaining the orthodoxy, which is in Shahab Ahmed's view a restricted and selective definition. Ahmed's conceptualization of Islam "in terms of an expansion of phenomena without concern to pin down a focal point"[5] indicates the multiplicity of "Islam," or rather "Islams," that cannot be traced to the essence of Islamic law.[6] The second axis conceptualizes Islam in the category of "religion" or "religious," exposing its historical and human phenomenon as in opposition to "secular/secularism" or "culture/cultural."[7] Claiming that Islamic law is the final legitimizer of the conceptualization of Islam and that it exemplifies the core of the historical phenomenon of Islam undermines and marginalizes other human historical realms, such as *kalām*, Islamic philosophy, Sufism, and other fields that are intertwined with, yet separated from, the concept of Islamic law. For Islamic legal studies, Islamic law was by default the epitome of the historic phenomenon of Islam.[8] Yet, reform of economic thought in

(paper presented at the Annual Distinguished Lecture in Arab Studies, Center for Contemporary Arab Studies, Georgetown University, Washington DC, March 1986).

5 Ahmed, *What Is Islam?*, 115.

6 In regard to distinguishing the cultural patterns from the religious ones, some scholars convey the differentiation between "Islamic" and "Islamicate": the first pertains to Islam in the proper, religious sense, while the latter encompasses "the social and cultural complex historically associated with Islam and Muslims." If we were to affirm this distinction in regard to "Islamic economics," then with the formal term we refer to the theoretical corpus of Islam as a theologically driven enterprise. This theoretical compilation excludes the cultural practices of Muslims in the premodern era as well as the conceptual discrepancies between the economic theories and their applicability in Muslim-majority countries, which indicates the shortcomings of such a distinction. On the notion of "Islamicate," see Marshall Hodgson in A. K. Reinhart, "Islamic Law As Islamic Ethics," *Journal of Religious Ethics*, vol. 11, no. 2 (1983): 186.

7 The conceptualization of Islam and Islamic is explained in more elaborated fashion in Chapter 4; suffice to say here that the overall complexity and multiplicity of Islam should not be equated with the notion of Islamic law as a human historical phenomenon.

8 *Fiqh* as understanding the *Sharīʿa* also had social implications. This also entails the notion of *ikhtilāf* as diversity within *fiqh*. *Ikhtilāf* suggests that *fiqh* is human interpretation of Qur'anic injunctions and that legal interpretation is a continuous process in order to enable legal norms to change along with the needs and ends of societal norms. On the other hand, *ikhtilāf* also caused ruptures to emerge between legal schools, invigorating the authority of one's own school in

Islamic intellectual tradition can occur only through transformation of human understanding of different epistemic systems. The theory of moral cosmology can help shape human development on the microlevel as well as political economy on the macrolevel.

5.2 Moral Cosmology and Pluralistic Epistemology in Islamic Tradition

5.2.1 Moral Cosmology of Economics

Milton Friedman's economic theory of the Chicago school plays out in affirming the position of a natural human being as a rational, self-centered, and autonomous subject. Economic man seeks the maximization of production and an optimal state of affairs. Such theory relates to the so-called holy trinity of mainstream economics – the notions of rationality, greed, and equilibrium.[9] The Enlightenment, its predicaments of self-legislative reasoning, and utilitarian philosophy profoundly and collectively shaped the science of economics, as we know it nowadays. These are some of the core components of mainstream Western economic ideas, reflected in the canonical literature on economics, which further reflects scientific theories of physics[10] and evolutionary biology.[11] The adaptation of economic theory to natural

relation to the rest. For more on the notion of diversity in Islamic jurisprudence and social construction, see Muhammad Khalid Masud, "Ikhtilaf al-Fuqaha: Diversity in Fiqh as a Social Construction," in *Wanted: Equality and Justice in the Muslim Family*, ed. Zainah Anwar (Selangor, Malaysia: Musawah, 2009), 66–92.

9 Friedman, *Essays in Positive Economics*; David Colander et al., *The Changing Face of Economics* (Ann Arbor: University of Michigan Press, 2004). On the other hand, gratefulness is part of *Sharīʿa*'s conception of social responsibility. See al-Ghazālī, *Iḥyāʾ*, vol. 1; Hallaq, *Impossible State*, 150–151.

10 Pioneering economists William Stanley Jevons and Léon Walras drew their economic diagrams in accordance with Newton's theory of physics. Jevons's approach to the natural sciences was based on a belief in the mechanical constitution of the universe and scientific knowledge. For more, see Maas, *William Stanley Jevons and the Making of Modern Economics*. Walras provided the general equilibrium theory and amoral definition of economic utility, wherein value is independent of the common meaning of utility. See Léon Walras, *Éléments d'économie politique pure, ou théorie de la richesse sociale* (Paris, 1926).

11 John Searle argues that the epistemic and ontological level of economics can be either subjective or objective. Science is epistemically regarded as objective, but

sciences has been framed within the terms of individual self-assertion and competition, which modeled the existence of (socioeconomic) equilibrium, found also in (neo)classical economic theories.[12] The Western economic worldview as we know it nowadays has been informed by the scientific developments within a particular hermenutic thereby also espousing its biases, miscomprehensions, and errors.[13] Mainstream economics is represented by economic orthodoxy, which consists also of methods of mathematical-deductivist modeling.[14] In addition to its multiple subdivisions, it grounds its analysis and economic outlook in a particular experience of history and societies. These models provide a notion of an individual economic agent and particular economic pursuits.

While the term cosmology includes "cosmos" as a universe and "logos" as an account of knowledge and has its equivalent in the *ilm al-kawniyya* as the science of the Creation/Existence, including the Unseen Universe (*ʿālam al-ghayb*) and the Observable Universe (*ʿālam al-shahūd*), I refer to *Sharīʿa*'s moral cosmology as pertaining to humanistic ethical outlook toward economy, society, and their structures. The Qurʾanic notion of the universe is semantically and logically bound with the concept of God,

it can still study ontologically subjective realms. Conscious is ontologically subjective, however, there is no reason for not having an epistemically objective science of the domain that is ontologically subjective. Economics, on the other hand, is a domain created by a human ontological subjectivity that includes money, markets, and other mechanisms, whereby it is an epistemically objective science. John Searle, *Social Construction of Reality* (New York: The Free Press, 1995); John Searle, *Making the Social World* (Oxford: Oxford University Press, 2010); see also Lawson, *Reorienting Economics*, 110–123.

12 The invisible hand of the market, which raises the question of individual pursuits and the lack of moral limitations, is one of the most important components of Western cosmological economics. See Smith, *Wealth of Nations*; Robbins, *Essay on the Nature and Significance of Economic Science.*

13 As an example, neoclassical economic science studies utility in a mechanical manner, while reducing needs to wants. See e.g. Ezra J. Mishan, *Economic Myths and the Mythology of Economics* (Atlantic Highlands, NJ: Humanities Press International, 1986); Mark Lutz and Kenneth Lux, *Humanistic Economics: The New Challenge* (New York: Bootstrap Press, 1988). See also Diana Strassmann, who states, "To a mainstream economist, theory means model, and model means ideas expressed in mathematical form." Diana Strassmann, "Feminist Thought and Economics; or, What do the Visigoths Know?" *American Economic Review*, vol. 84, no. 2 (1994): 153; Syed Farid Alatas, *Alternative Discourses in Asian Social Science: Responses to Eurocentrism* (London: Sage, 2006).

14 Lawson, *Reorienting Economics*, 3, 54–55, 73.

linked with the general principle of creation (*haqq*). The three levels that can be found in Qur'anic discourse – the metaphysical, the human, and the material – constitute the cosmological realm. At the individual level, this presupposes a particular attitude toward the acquisition of wealth and production processes. A cosmological order that addressed material and spiritual reverberations of economic conduct/activities was well known in the classical Islamic orbit. The connection between spiritual qualities and economic practices is also noticeable in Islamic mysticism.[15] Such an epistemological approach neither discerns the substance of *'ilm* from the consequences of *'amal*, nor the moral cosmology of *Sharī'a* from practical economics, and is a spiritual-material acquisition based on conceptualizations such as *kasb*, *zuhd*, *faqr*, *tazkiyya*, *maṣlaḥa*, and *'adl*. *Faqr*, as spiritual poverty of detachment from worldly endeavors, also implies socioeconomic engagement that battles egocentricity and greed.[16] The definition of *'adl* (justice) pertains to terms such as *mizān*, *qast*, *haqq*, and beneficence, or *'adl wa al-iḥsān*. The acquisition of wealth fulfills not only material provision but is, in actuality, also contingent upon the social factors of cohesion, spiritual well-being, and the notion of *'adl*. *'Adl*, as part of morality's meta-narrative, fulfills basic needs while eliminating structural inequity.[17] As indicated in the writings of the classical scholars, the concept of livelihood was concerned with realizing moral goals, which encompasses the economic behavior of humankind.[18] In a similar manner, law was embedded in the dialectical relation with theology, mysticism, and ethics, whereby moral concerns and objectives were not coincidental but rather paradigmatic.[19] It is

[15] In opposition to the findings in Chapter 3, Hamid Hossein, in my opinion incorrectly, states that economic activities were not considered part of the Sufi narrative. See Hamid Hossein, "Understanding the Market Mechanism before Adam Smith: Economic Thought in Medieval Islam," in *Medieval Islamic Economic Thought*, ed. S. M. Ghazanfar (London: Routledge, 2003), 95; Hamid Hossein, "Inaccuracy of the Schumpeterian 'Great Gap' Thesis: Economic Thought in Medieval Iran (Persia)," in *Medieval Islamic Economic Thought*, ed. S. M. Ghazanfar (London: Routledge, 2003), 117.

[16] See e.g. al-Shaybānī, *Kitāb al-Kasb*; see also Rene Guenon, "Al-Faqr or 'Spiritual Poverty'", *Studies in Comparative Religion*, vol. 7, no. 1 (1973): 16–20.

[17] Soroush, *Reason, Freedom, and Democracy in Islam*, 132.

[18] For example, al-Ghazālī, *Iḥyā'*; al-Dunyā, *Iṣlāḥ al-Māl*; al-Muḥāsibī, *al-Makāsib wa al-Wara*.

[19] Hallaq, *Impossible State*, 137, 150.

conventionally understood that metaphysical concerns were not measured in Western economic terms,[20] which is why classical Muslim scholars treated economic gains as means to higher ends. In this manner, the *muʿāmalāt* is conducted in conjunction with *ʿibādāt*, hence despite Vali Reza Nasr's thorough critique of contemporary Islamic economics, economic engagements in the classical scholarship indeed prepared one to expand one's spiritual properties.[21]

Contemporary Muslim economists' enactment of a neoclassical economic philosophy negates the premodern body of knowledge and its economic cosmology that integrated theological, juridical, and mystical forms of knowledge subsumed in the moral universe. As indicated in Chapter 4, the early modern philosophical tradition of economics contributed to dismantling the epistemological basis and ontological status of ethical values, moral predicaments, and cosmological categories of economic thought that used to be prevalent in pre-Enlightenment Europe but also in Islamic tradition. The moral cosmology of economic thought is based on metaphysical understanding of the universe and its material aspects[22] and theorizes social, political, ecological, and legal policies rooted in a moral worldview,[23] and as such it stands for an unconventional methodological strategy. The virtuous fiber of the Qurʾan was embedded in both a holistic system of belief and a cosmology, which was itself part of the system "that transcended the categories of theology, theosophy, and metaphysics."[24] This all-embracing cosmology accounts for restructuring

20 Nasr, "Islamization of Knowledge," 398.

21 Vali Reza Nasr states that "Economics in Islam merely prepares man's social setting in such manner as to accommodate his spiritual satisfaction. It is based on the premise that Islamic economics, in practice, tends toward greater concern for society than is the case in Western economics." (Nasr, "Islamization of Knowledge," 398).

22 See the writings of e.g. Ibn Hazm, al-Muḥāsibī, al-Ghazālī, and other classical scholars discussed in Chapter 3, who put forward a comprehensive framework of economic behavior as traits of character, by drawing on various disciplines and sources.

23 See Figure 3 in the Appendix.

24 Hallaq, "Groundwork of the Moral Law," 259. "I contend that the Qurʾan has, ab initio, provided Muslim believers with a cosmology entirely grounded in moral natural laws, a cosmology with perhaps far more persuasive power than any of its Enlightenment metaphysical counterparts, and one that had powerful and deep psychological effects." (Hallaq, "Groundwork of the Moral Law," 259)."The Qurʾānic narrative of creation, which bears upon the modes of human action and behaviour, is single-mindedly geared toward laying down the foundations of moral cosmology." (Hallaq, *Impossible State*, 83).

individual character and social groups. Unlike conventional economics, economic teaching of cosmological proportions does not address utility but *maṣlaḥa* as an instrument of social, public, and common good, and welfare.[25] Given the multifaceted and cross-disciplinary foundation of economics in human life in relation to society, culture, politics, and law, it cannot be solely based on (modern Western) economic principles but must be informed by an intricate and complex web of various bodies of knowledge, exemplified in the nonmaterial predisposition of the self. This further indicates that the neoclassical understanding of economic man as an atomistic and self-interested agent opposes the notion of common good, as one of the key concepts in classical intellectual tradition. Examining the theory of moral cosmology of economic teachings in the works of classical Muslim scholars as a pluralistic epistemology assists in reevaluating and refashioning controversies and epistemological inconsistencies that have raged in neoclassical and contemporary Islamic economics.

5.2.2 The Theory of Pluralistic Epistemology

The theory of pluralistic epistemology[26] invokes the hermeneutical field wherein economic thought is studied from multiple angles and perspectives, unlike the linear, unidimensional hermeneutics that is primarily centered on an essentialized view of economics and/or Islam.[27] The relationship between Islamic intellectual history and social sciences is one of knowledge and power. Even though all human knowledge has a material foundation and involves the use of economic conditions, identifying those economic conditions, which concern the idea of well-being, is not the final determinant of what constitutes economic philosophy Muslim society. In consideration of modern interpretations of Islamic economics and the philosophical narrative of modernity, applying Abu Zayd's theory,[28] which

[25] On *maṣlaḥa* in Islamic economics, see e.g. Waleed El-Ansary, "The Spiritual Significance of *Jihād* in the Islamic Approach to Markets and the Environment," (PhD diss., George Washington University, 2006).

[26] See Figure 4 in the Appendix.

[27] For more on the mono and multidimensional hermeneutical field in Islam, see Salvatore, *Islam and the Political Discourse of Modernity*, 117.

[28] See Muhammad Khalid Masud's draft "'Classical' Islamic Legal Theory As Ideology," 13. See also Muhammad A. Khan's concern over the lack of critique of the contemporary Islamic economics and institutions that disallow such criticism.

distinguishes between (sacred) Text and the Authority of that Text, would be helpful to comprehend the discrepancy between Muslim economists' interpretations of the field of economics and the classical economic teachings. The former are not authoritative per se, since their authority stems from the so-called "epistemology of authority," that is, the community (*ʿulamāʾ*) that formulates and designates the Text as authoritative. Any rupture from that authority does not necessarily mean freedom from the Text(s) but rather from the authority, which claims the interpretative supremacy. This further indicates that the conflict and tension do not emerge between the Text and reason – or in the case of contemporary Islamic economics, between modern economic literature and the argumentations of the foremost Muslim economists – but between reason and the very authority (read dominant economic discourse) that interprets and/or omits the textual tradition.

Establishing an Islamic epistemology that would explain the intricate nature of social sciences is a valid claim in its own right. The process of indigenization questions and counters the claim of the positivist universality of social sciences. The call for indigenization can be interpreted as the "critique of modernist discourses of man and society, and the rejection of the universality of social scientific concepts that originated in the West."[29] This indigenization does not imply a wholesale rejection of Western sciences due to its Western origin but a process of accounting for epistemological, methodological, and historical assumptions and encounters. Such an attempt considers historical knowledge, theories, local worldviews, and cultural practices of indigenous cultures. For Syed Farid Alatas, the process of indigenization of social sciences is about internationalizing social sciences, which entails decolonization of knowledge and removal of ethnocentric bias,[30] and not simply applying methods of *fiqh*, *taṣawwuf*, and/or *tafṣīr*, if creating indigenous Islamic economic science is a prerogative. The

[29] Alatas, "Sacralization of the Social Sciences," 89. The idea of indigenization implies the creation of theories of social sciences as derived from histories, concepts, and experiences from non-Western societies. See also Fahim Hussein and Katherine Helmer, "Indigenous Anthropology in Non-Western Countries: A Further Elaboration," *Current Anthropology*, vol. 21, no. 5 (1980): 644–650; Syed Farid Alatas, "Reflections on the Idea of Islamic Social Science," *Comparative Civilizations Review*, vol. 17, no. 17 (1987): 60–86.

[30] Alatas, "Sacralization of the Social Sciences," 91.

internationalization of social sciences, however, would make sense only if we assume that the social sciences are not Eurocentric.

The interactions between cultures are often multiple, yet they usually contain a power relation. Muslim scholars borrowed from other cultures throughout the history of Islam, as is true for any other culture. Yet, the distinction between classical and modern Islamic modes of borrowings (or transplants) is apparent on various levels. Until the sixteenth century, Islamic culture borrowed from a position of strength, whereas in the modern period, it has been borrowing from a subordinate position in that it assimilated much of Western cultural, political, economic, and social values. If proponents of the Islamization process claim that classical Muslim scholars also incorporated ancient Greek, Iranian, and Indian philosophy, which could be nowadays equated with the process of Islamizing disciplines, the claim would be incorrect for several reasons. Classical Muslim philosophers did not Islamize knowledge (or disciplines for that matter) but rather translated various concepts that corresponded to the Islamic paradigm of thought,[31] while defining knowledge according to various categories. For instance, according to Ibn Khaldūn's classification, there are two categories of knowledge – *al-ʿulūm al-naqlīyya*, or traditional sciences, and *al-ʿulūm al-ʿaqlīyya*, or rational sciences.[32] The former is learned only by transmission, while religious sciences refer to the revelation, which includes the Qurʾan, its interpretation and recitation, *ḥadīth*, jurisprudence, *kalām*, *taṣawwuf*, and the linguistic sciences of grammar, lexicography, and literature. The latter sciences can be learned by people naturally through the use of their reason and intelligence and include logic, natural sciences or physics, medicine, agriculture, sciences that surpass the natural world such as metaphysics, and sciences dealing with quantity such as geometry, arithmetic, music, and astronomy. Studying classical scholars and their articulation and understanding of cosmology, such as Ibn Khaldūn and his theory of knowledge, is one example of indigenizing knowledge processes of Islamic heritage,[33]

31 Majid Fakhry, *History of Islamic Philosophy* (New York: Columbia University Press, 2004), 79, 91.

32 Ibn Khaldūn, *Muqaddima* (1967). See also Rosenthal, *Muqaddimah of Ibn Khaldūn*, vol. 2, 419–424.

33 See Syed Farid Alatas, *Ibn Khaldun* (Oxford: Oxford University Press, 2013); Syed Farid Alatas, *Applying Ibn Khaldun: The Recovery of a Lost Tradition in Sociology* (Abingdon, UK: Routledge, 2014).

which nonetheless posits a dichotomy between reason and traditional sciences.

In the modern period, however, "the quantitative and mathematical sciences in the modern sense refer not to the essence but to the material or material substratum of things."[34] The methodological unity of natural and social sciences, as exposed, for instance, by John Stewart Mill in the eighteenth century, had fundamental repercussions for the scientific and disciplinary outlook in the following decades and even centuries. Mill's enactment of Newtonian mechanics in economics speaks of a science based on "causes in which the order does not matter to predict the effect, e.g. the effect is the same whether the causes occur simultaneously or sequentially .... The resulting aggregate is quantitative and reducible to a sum of parts, an object for 'analysis' in which no *a priori* vision of the whole is necessary, for there are no qualitative differences to integrate."[35] This distinction between the physical and the corporeal had a profound impact on the analytical tools and the nature of neoclassical economics in delineating the mechanics of economics as opposed to the moral paradigm that was to be found in classical Islamic thought. Classical economics provided the material for what neoclassical economists would turn into a science on its own, importing the mono-utility function.[36] This quality to quantity reduction applies neither to the natural world nor to the human domain.[37] The solution, according to Wolfgang Smith, is the rebuttal of this bifurcation, which is the

> Cartesian tenet which affirms that the perceptual object is private or merely subjective. The idea of bifurcation goes hand-in-hand with the assumption that the external world is characterized exclusively by quantities and

34 Seyyed Hossein Nasr, "Perennial Ontology and Quantum Mechanics: A Review Essay of Wolfgang Smith's *The Quantum Enigma: Finding the Hidden Key*," *Sophia: A Journal of Traditional Studies*, vol. 3, no. 1 (1997): 151.

35 El-Ansary, "Quantum Enigma and Islamic Sciences of Nature," 160. See also El-Ansary, "Islamic Science and the Critique of Neoclassical Economic Theory," 88; Waleed El-Ansary, "Recovering the Islamic Economic Intellectual Heritage," in *Proceedings of the Third Harvard University Forum on Islamic Finance: Local Challenges, Global Opportunities* (Cambridge: Cambridge University Press, 1999), 9.

36 See the writings of e.g. Thorstein Veblen, Léon Walras, and Alfred Marshall; see also El-Ansary, "Quantum Enigma and Islamic Sciences of Nature," 161.

37 "[Q]uantity is the only thing that has objective reality, and that the modus operandi of empirical science constitute the only valid means for the acquisition of knowledge" (Smith, *Cosmos and Transcendence*, 145).

mathematical structure. According to this view, all qualities (such as color) exist only in the mind of the percipient.[38]

This lack of pluralistic epistemology endorses a monolithic understanding of the physical realm – or a mono-utility approach – and cannot accommodate qualitatively different ends that would include categories of spirituality and morality, which were regarded as "unscientific" and "irrational."[39] Consequently, spiritual and moral values lost their objective meaning and were degraded to mere subjectivity, which further problematized the loss of moral agency in economic science.[40]

As for the study of Islam and modernity, two different systems appear to be at stake: "the plural hermeneutics of a complex civilization and the flexible medium of a collective identity centered on one Koranic keyword (Islam), while modernity is conceived as the sort of politically relevant discourse mediated by intellectuals once the idea of rationality is recognized as embodied in society, no longer confined to a transcendent logos."[41] Within the larger context, developing a new epistemological base and a metanarrative for economic teachings and Islamic sciences takes the form of indigenizing knowledge by decolonizing social sciences, which allows for a more critical overview of emerging sciences. Epistemologically speaking, one has to affirm multiple sources of knowledge if justice is to be done to Islamic intellectual history, despite, or rather because of, the colonial processes that altered the very sociology of knowledge of the colonized societies. Applying ethics to science is a process that has to occur through technical and methodic transformations that are in close alignment with classical Islamic knowledge, invoked by jurists and Sufis alike. Instead of Islamizing, Muslim economists should critically engage with the sources of intellectual traditions in order to point out the different formation of knowledge and concepts.

38 Smith, *Quantum Enigma*, 137.

39 El-Ansary, "Recovering the Islamic Economic Intellectual Heritage," 9.

40 As shown in the Introduction and in Chapter 4, the Enlightenment and modernity differentiated the moral from the scientific. John S. Mill and David Hume, among many other philosophers, deprived ethics of intellectual foundations based on the reduction of quality to quantity, a path that the neoclassical economists also adhered to. For more on Hume's ethics, see Henry Veatch, *For an Ontology of Morals* (Evanston, IL: Northwestern University Press, 1971).

41 Salvatore, *Islam and the Political Discourse of Modernity*, xiii.

Indigenization as pluralistic epistemology of Islamic cultures, and not nativism as reverse orientalism, provides the framework that allows for applying multiple epistemologies to a particular domain of knowledge. A critical approach to reasserting economic teachings in the Islamic tradition would be neither to blindly adopt Western models, concepts, and theories of economic and political development nor to completely reject Western knowledge but to systemically formulate political economy as a study of relations between governmentality and society in Islamic tradition that is cognizant of moral qualities and its own epistemological specificities. Exactly in this light, such a theory would address not only the spiritual significance of labor – by which I do not mean an alignment with the capitalist mode of production, whereby work is seen through enslavement of human capital and as a liberating factor for those who do not own the means of production, which is a common "misconception" of spiritual economics – but also the ethical emergence of production processes and their functionality. It is in this sense that the reading of pluralistic epistemology as a polyvalent hermeneutical field that contains (*Sharīʿa*'s) moral archetypes in its core predicates, produces, and maintains theoretical reverberations of once acquired yet neglected knowledge of the classical schools of thought. Those theories are conducive to Muslim and non-Muslim societies alike. Studying Islamic economics cannot be developed owing to economic science alone, due to its cross-disciplinary and epistemologically pluralistic foundations. Rebranding Islamic economics in the twentieth century to fit the mainstream economic paradigm does a historical injustice to the idea of economic preservations and its moral archetypes. Both exclusionist approaches of modernists and of Islamists alike would be incorrect,[42] as they disregard *Sharīʿa*'s moral cosmology and the multivalent hermeneutical approach to economic reasoning. Endorsing the legal aspect of *Sharīʿa* as one of the central paradigms only through other peripheral paradigms can sufficiently explain the centrality of *Sharīʿa* moral cosmology, which is only partially reflected in legal norms of *fiqh*.

[42] Compare with Thomas Bauer's critique of the Islamists and liberal Muslims – the former strive for "authentic" Islam based on the scriptural sources, the latter on the modernization process under the aegis of their Western counterparts. In this sense, both groups are incorrect as they expound one "correct" view of interpreting Islam and thus neglect the multifaceted, pluralistic, and polyvalent culture of Islam.

5.3 Economic Development in Light of Spiritual Prosperity

Since economics cannot be established on its own terms,[43] it must be incorporated in other domains of human knowledge. This proposition does not translate into viewing ethical considerations as the final determinant of economic reality but, rather, stipulates that economics has to be in service of humanity and not the other way around. As such, ethical provisions ought to surpass or rather embody any legal configuration of one's economic endeavors.[44] Such theory is derived from a hermeneutical reading that pluralizes ethics of personal responsibility with sociopolitical deliberations, instead of solely embedding economics in the political and materialist discourses of modernity.

The Islamization of knowledge, even if perceived as a dewesternization of (neo)classical cosmological economics and its metaphysics, failed in attaining an authentic image and a reconciliatory approach to the study of economic thought, for it politicized Islamic studies. Despite their theoretical stance, paradoxically, Muslim economists pursued the inclusion of the Islamic economic project within the paradigms of conventional economics. In order to de-essentialize the contemporary Islamic economic project and its political economy, economic ideas in Islamic tradition should be delinked from monolithic postulates and analyzed in light of the malleability of the moral self.[45] Such an approach does not aim to compartmentalize disciplines based on positivist logic or to square its economic philosophy within the

[43] Lawson, *Economics and Reality*, 32, 121, 296.

[44] Ahmed, *What Is Islam?*, 126; for the argument on the centrality of Islamic law see e.g. Khaled Abu El Fadl, *Speaking in God's Name: Islamic Law, Authority and Women* (Oxford: Oneworld, 2001).

[45] The notion of the *self* as personal fulfillment, development, and endorsement of worldly existence can be found in Islamic tradition, expressed in various disciplines and registers. See e.g. al-Ghazālī's theory on happiness, al-Ghazālī, *Alchemy of Happiness*; see also Ahmed, *What Is Islam?*, 329–330; "Happiness is, therefore, an effect which constantly accompanies virtue, and is not a motivating cause alone like truth. Consequently, there is an intrinsic connection between the 'right' and the 'good,' between spiritual 'needs' and corresponding 'duties' as two sides of the same coin. Thus, the Islamic view of welfare requires that the satisfaction of desires be based on true beliefs and happiness be based on reality to count towards well-being. From this perspective, psychological hedonism rationalizes the sacrifice of spiritual and other needs for false happiness based on inferior intentions, providing a theory of choice and welfare of the 'lower soul' (the nafs al-ammārah in Qur'anic terms)." (El-Ansary, "Quantum Enigma and Islamic Sciences of Nature," 158).

global market economy. Currently, there is no existing political economy of Islamic economics that could analyze state–economy relations according to a specific set of Islamic principles. A solution is neither the political Islamization of religious texts nor a modernist vision of Islamic economics as pure social science but rather the transdisciplinary, pluralistic epistemology of moral considerations that feeds into the narrative of an economy that is an integrative part of an overall human knowledge and cosmological order.

The Islamic ideal of economic (and human development, which pertains to both work and production processes, cannot be expressed solely in the concept of *iqtiṣād*, which is translated as economics. The term *iqtiṣād*, derived from the root *iqtaṣada*, implies the process of economizing, moderation, and frugality,[46] which are essentially spiritual characteristics. Therefore, *iqtiṣād* cannot mean only economy from a dominant modern understanding in its technical sense as a rational, accumulation-based, and profit-oriented process but as a human behavior of providence, structured around the principles of moral uplift.[47] Similarly, the Islamic concept of development cannot be read as purely economic development but should be understood as a combination of material and nonmaterial aspects that pertain to the *here* and the *Hereafter*, embodied in the concept of *tazkiyya* as psycho-spiritual purification as well as growth.[48] The *maqāmāt* of *tazkiyya*, as a process of both learning and applying, means maximizing social welfare and inner restoration in developing political, socioeconomic, and technological factors based on *akhlāq* as moral conditions. Thus the conception of *iqtiṣād*, first, has to be re-evaluated in its connection with conventional economic theory and philosophy; second, it must be

[46] Ibn Manẓūr, *Lisān al-ʿArab*, 3642–3644; Alatas, "Islam and Modernization," 212; Baqir Al-Hasani, "The Concept of *iqtiṣād*," in *Essays on Iqtiṣād: The Islamic Approach to Economic Problems*, ed. Baqir Al-Hasani and Abbas Mirakhor (Silver Spring, MD: Nur Corporations, 1989), 24; see also Rafīq Yūsuf al-Maṣry, *Uṣūl al-Iqtiṣād al-Islāmi* (Damascus: Dār al-Qalam, 1987).

[47] Similarities can be drawn also to early Christian theology and the concept of *oikonomia* as providence, in that the economic and the providential paradigms are interconnected. See Clement of Alexandria, *The Stromata, or Miscellanies*, book VI, chapter XV, in A. Roberts and J. Donaldson, eds., *The Ante-Nicene Fathers*, vol. 2 (Grand Rapids, MI: Wm. B. Eerdmans Publishing, 1962).

[48] See the writings of e.g. Bisṭāmī (d. 874), Qushayrī (d. 1072–3), and Sulamī (d. 1106); see also Khurshid Ahmad, "Economic Development in an Islamic Framework," in *Studies in Islamic Development*, ed. Khurshid Ahmad (Jeddah: International Centre for Research in Islamic Economics, 1980), 179.

the basis of reassessing the ontological foundation of economic science and the roots of the modern nation-state; and last, it has to reach beyond the legal/financial confinements of contemporary Islamic economics.[49] The vision, philosophy, ontology, methodology, and epistemology of *iqtiṣād* (or *kasb*) would have to affirm a moral character since it deals with behaviorial analysis and not a scientific framework, as it was conceived in seventeenth-century Europe.

It is clear that the principles of economic and spiritual development are composed of precepts of ethics of science and prosperity. Many classical Muslim thinkers believed that riches trigger carnal desires.[50] Choosing spiritual poverty instead of material excess is a well-intended (ascetic) prescription for achieving redemption. For many classical Muslim scholars, choosing poverty and deprivation over wealth was a Sufi prescription intended to increase one's well-being,[51] for "poverty is better and safer than affluence because the poor have less of an interest in the worldly affairs and to that extent, they will be more inclined to prayer and pious reflection," and "in the majority of cases the danger of poverty is less than that of affluence, because the temptations of wealth are greater than those of poverty."[52] On the other hand, for instance, the Iranian poet Saadī (d. 1292), sought the superiority of wealth over poverty,[53] since for him financial provision meant spiritual security.[54]

[49] Haneef and Furqani, who adhere to Islamization of economics, rightly assert that *uṣūl al-iqtiṣād* would have to involve epistemology and methodology beyond the scope of *uṣūl al-fiqh*. Mohamed Aslam Haneef and Hafas Furqani, "Usul al-Iqtisad: The Missing Dimension in Contemporary Islamic Economics and Finance," in *Readings in Islamic Economics and Finance*, ed. Nur Azura Sanusi et al. (Sintok: Universiti Utara Malaysia Press 2007), 8–9.

[50] Al-Ghazālī, *Iḥyā'*, vol. 2, 83, and vol. 3, 227.

[51] See e.g. al-Shaybānī, *Kitāb al-Kasb*, 106–107; Al-Muḥāsibī, *al-Makāsib wa al-Wara'*, 14f; Allāh ibn al-Mubārak, *Kitāb al-Zuhd wa al-Rāqa'iq* (Riyāḍ: Dār al-Mu'rāj al-Dawlīyya li Nashr, 1990), 38–39; Abū Bakr al-Kalābādhī, *The Doctrine of the Sufis*, trans. Arthur John Arberry (Cambridge: Cambridge University Press, 1977), 86–87.

[52] Soroush, *Reason, Freedom, and Democracy in Islam*, 19–20.

[53] "On the contrary, if the virtues of poverty and those of wealth are properly observed, they would be morally equivalent. If the modern way of life is somehow flawed, it is not because it fails to be poor and patient, but because it fails to be rich and grateful." (Soroush, *Reason, Freedom, and Democracy in Islam*, 25).

[54] Poverty as a technology of the (moral) self is related also to the concept of positive liberty as an anti-Berlinian outlook, whereby it is – unlike the negative or coercive freedom – described as a liberty that "derives from the wish on the part of the individual to be his own master." Free action (also to devote oneself

A hermeneutical reading that studies economic thought as "the process of extracting economic meaning from the first order interpretation"[55] which is classical intellectual thought, would reinvigorate processes of knowledge that were displaced through the application of the utilitarian philosophy of economics in the modern era. Unlike Western classical economic thought, Islamic intellectual history reveals the intricate relation between means and ends, while combining metaphysical imaginary with worldly deeds.[56] In this respect, the perception of nature and sciences of nature correspond to the cosmological understanding of social organization of human productivity. Unlike conventional economics, which are governed by their own logic, the analyzed texts reveal that all endeavors have an inner dimension (*bāṭin*) that constitutes part of the *absolute*, including the acquisition of work and production processes.[57] A minimal division of labor as specialized work is, according to various classical scholars, necessary only to assert the objective of work and the maintenance of each profession in society, and as such is perceived as part of the collective obligations (*farḍ al-kifāya*). The minimal division of labor is hence a duty and a right.[58] The interconnectedness between economic activities and *Sharīʿa*'s moral predicaments highlights an overall development of an economic-moral equilibrium, which renders lucrative market economy and industrial norms of production as devoid of inner quality.[59] In relation to pluralistic epistemology, work requires "a *multiple* utility approach in which each type of value combines an essentially useful object with the corresponding capacity to use it .... The

to spiritual poverty) is neither limited by law (Isaiah Berlin) nor by the carnal desires of the self (al-Ghazālī) but derives directly from views of what constitutes a (moral) self. See Berlin, *Liberty*, 166–217.

55 Mirakhor, *Note on Islamic Economics*, 18.

56 See e.g. Titus Burckhardt, *Alchemy: Science of the Cosmos, Science of the Soul* (Louisville, KY: Fons Vitae, 1997).

57 For more on the traditional economic account on work, see Ernst F. Schumacher, *Good Work* (New York: Harper & Row, 1979), 3–4.

58 Waleed El-Ansary, "Linking Ethics and Economics for Integral Development: The Need for a New Economic Paradigm and the Three Dimensions of Islam," (Al-Alwani Lectures, Washington Theological Consortium), 2.

59 "The basic aim of modern industrialism is not to make work satisfying but to raise productivity; its proudest achievement is labor saving, whereby labor is stamped with the mark of undesirability." (Schumacher, *Good Work*, 28).

solution from the Islamic point of view is therefore *multiple* use values on one hand and a spiritual end on the other hand."[60]

The true relevance of economic design in Islamic tradition is its attachment to higher imperatives, which should be conceived in a social milieu whose politics and legal practices are subordinated to those very principles. (Muslim) economists should not take for granted the entities of acquisition of nation-state, modern technocracy and scientific economic theories. Given that money has no inherent value,[61] it is about the exchanges and transactions between people; it is not an objective but, rather, a collective story. Money became innately libertarian in that it has a value because members of society agreed upon such an arrangement. The obsoleteness of money is related to the swift development of technology, which is already picking up work that is being produced by humans.[62] This also means that the acquisition of wealth will not be the driving force of humanity, while in the post-scarcity world of cashless societies, human beings will become more dependent on renewable energy surplus as a resource-based economy. The convoluted relations among economic gains, acquisition of wealth, and social responsibility are evident in the socioeconomic history of Muslim societies, whereby forms of asceticism were accompanied by economic gains. Instead of following the laws of physics and secular economic theories, the future of (Islamic) economic thought ought to follow the laws of nature and moral predispositions.

60 El-Ansary, "Linking Ethics and Economics for Integral Development," 12; see also Naṣīr al-Dīn Ṭūsī, *The Nasirean Ethics*, trans. G. M. Wickens (London: G. Allen & Unwin, 1964).

61 For example, al-Ghazālī, *Mizān al-'Amal*, 372; al-Ghazālī, *Iḥyā'*, vol. 3, 231.

62 A. Y. Al-Hassan, ed., *Science and Technology in Islam: Technology and Applied Sciences* (Paris: United Nations Educational, Scientific, and Cultural Organization, 2001).

Conclusion: Moral over Legal, Pluralistic over Monolithic

Every economic system claims its moral primacy.[1] It is apparent that the jugular vein of liberalism lies in its economic lookout; the current economic system dominates the very understanding of key concepts employed by economists in how we perceive economic activities, ideas, norms, laws, and its methodology and epistemology. Making an economic system more humane (purportedly the domain of business ethics) is a noble endeavor in itself, yet humanizing economics does not include restructuring the foundations of the conventional economic structures, which rests upon the scientific, philosophical, political, and cultural predispositions of early modern Europe.

This book inquired into how Islamic economic thought emerged as a distinct field and what forces contributed to its development. The Muslim revivalists treated economics as part of their agenda in imagining an Islamic state and society. Only when Islamic economics became a constitutional force in the second half of the twentieth century, in that it asserted a particular religious identity, did it maintain a convincing foothold in the politico-economic landscape of Muslim-majority countries. Further, proponents of the Islamization process, such as Isma'il al-Faruqi, Nejatullah Siddiqi, Alam Choudhury, Umer Chapra, and others, considered Islamic economics as a tenacious discipline that was, however, conceived within the existing division of social sciences or as a result of Islamization efforts. I contend that such a development can be attributed to the structural changes that occurred in Muslim-majority countries at the turn of the century and to the consequent political variance of Muslim revivalists who contested, reacted to, and struggled with the colonial legacy by trying to create solutions to scientific, social, and constitutional setbacks. Nonetheless, this *making*

[1] Ayn Rand, "The Moral Meaning of Capitalism," in *The Market Economy: A Reader*, ed. James L. Doti and Dwight R. Lee (Los Angeles, CA: Roxbury Publishing, 1991), 12–14.

of a discipline culminated in a particular, that is monolithic, explication of Islamic economic thought.

Given the nature of the discipline of (Islamic) economics, modern Muslim intellectuals are faced with a twofold predicament: how to reconcile the ontological fact of the nation-state and its power structure,[2] and how to negotiate *Sharīʿa* as a moral-legal mechanism into contemporary discourse. This issue precludes an economic theory that would examine real-life socioeconomic circumstances in Muslim-majority countries, and their social and educational institutions,[3] as well as the study of moral-economic concepts in Islamic intellectual history, beyond the popular terms of *zakāt* and *ribā*. Reviewing the relations between these elements and *Sharīʿa* moral values – and not simply applying Western-style economic mechanisms – is what the theory of moral cosmology explicates. Because of a disconnect between economic doctrine and the rule of civil law, as well as the role of governments in managing economic development, in the context of contemporary Islamic economics, the legal aspect of economic and financial theories and mechanisms also has to be revisited. Economic doctrine is a collection of the basic theories treating the problems of economic life, whereas civil law is legislative enactment that also regulates monetary policy. It would be a mistake to propose Islamic ordinances (rules of law) related to Islamic economic doctrine as separate from moral restructuring, for the metaphysical substrate of economic activities has laid rules for the structure of the law and not the opposite.

Economic laws in Islamic intellectual tradition are virtuous laws. The *longue durée* of Islamic economic history that comprises mystical influences, legal precepts, and twentieth-century-based methodological developments consists of a structural crisis that stems from the development of natural and social sciences rooted in the modernist discourse, which have impacted the emergence of contemporary Islamic economics. One of the first steps in recovering the Islamic intellectual history of economic teachings is to reshape the modern understanding of metaphysics and its relation to knowledge, science, and technology.[4] The combination of ethics and economics has to break out from the

2 For more see, Hallaq, *Impossible State*, x.
3 Khan, "Islamic Economics: The State of the Art," 289.
4 Burckhardt, *Alchemy*; Schumacher, *Small Is Beautiful*, 120.

cycle of the utilitarian philosophy and its vision of nature, in order to recuperate the virtuous objectives of economics that have been either lost or discredited.[5] Moral restructuring – to borrow Hallaq's reappropriation of Foucault's phrase, as the spiritual and socioeconomic technology of the self – will be effectively applied only insofar as premodern tradition is scrutinized in view of affirming its polyvalent theories on poverty, wealth, production, and earning as ethical-economic conceptualizations.

The distinct and ubiquitous existence of Islamic economics has to reexamine its relation to its own subject matter, its methodological constraints, and its epistemological inconsistences, not only in how it addresses the socioeconomic problems of today's (Muslim) societies but also, first and foremost, in how it negotiates fact and value, *is* and *ought*, and *ʿilm* and *ʿamal*. What one calls "Islamic economics," "Islamic economic thought," "Islamic economic system," "Islam's moral economy," or "Islamic economic philosophy" can be justifiably established as its own discipline and on its own terms only insofar that it is grounded in cosmologically comprehensive theories of the universe as an *akhlāqi* premise according to various trends within Islamic intellectual tradition. Such postulates set forth a pluralistic epistemology, combining and merging knowledge of theological, philosophical, mystical, legal, and scientific reasoning. The call for past knowledge is not a nostalgic one echoing a long-past wisdom; rather, it incites an Islamic intellectual history that promotes a multitude of knowledge – likewise including the translation of concepts and their meanings whose value was mitigated. A pluralistic epistemology is in itself never solely attached to one epistemic domain in particular, but fluctuates between various realms of knowledge, while being fashioned around moral categories. Precisely such an application of a hermeneutical reasoning is requisite for, first, understanding economic behavior in order to reestablish economic reasoning from the bottom up and, second, critically motivating the contemporary project of (Islamic) economics toward its intellectual *and* moral apotheosis.

[5] "Positivism is marked by the final recognition that science provides the only valid form of knowledge and that facts are the only possible objects of knowledge." Kieran Egan, *The Educated Mind* (Chicago, IL: University of Chicago Press, 1997), 115–116.

Appendix

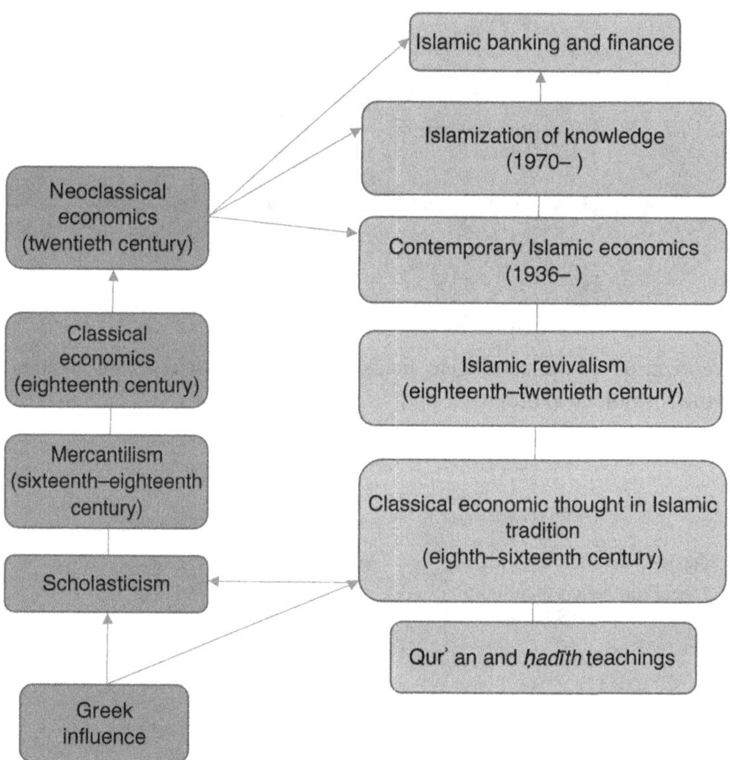

1 History and development of economic thought in Islamic tradition

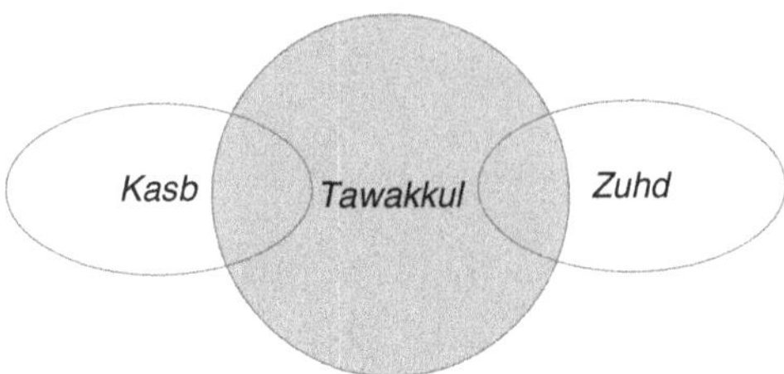

2 *Kasb–zuhd* amalgam under the banner of *Tawakkul*

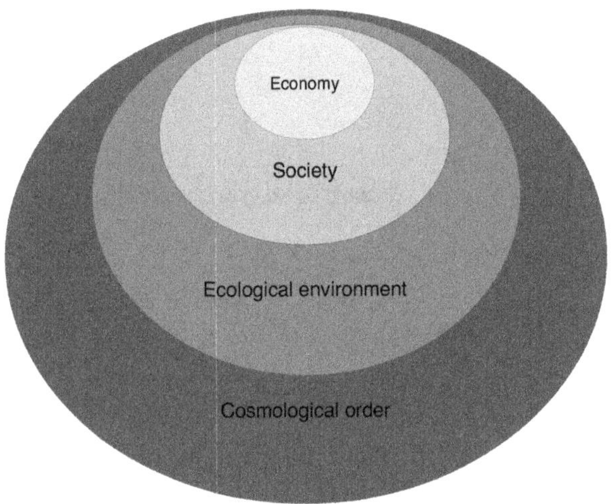

3 Categorization of the contingent fields of economy, society, and ecology within the cosmological order

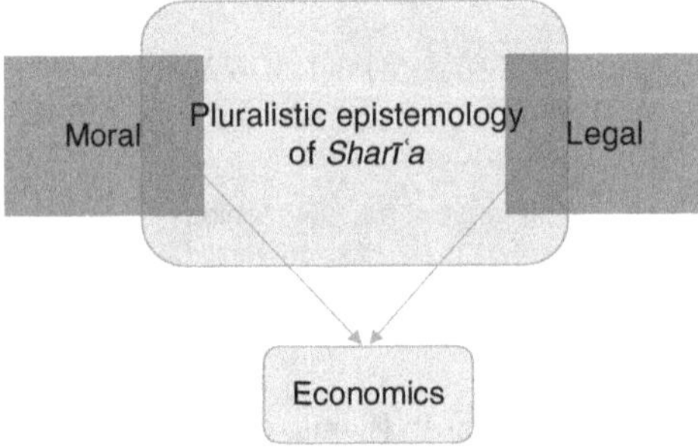

4 Economic behavior and pluralistic epistemology of *Sharīʿa*

Bibliography

Sources in Arabic

Abū Jayb, Sa'dī. *Al-Qāmūs al-Fiqhī*. Damascus: Dār al-Fikr, 1982.

Abū Sulaymān, 'Abdul Ḥamīd. *Mafahīm fī I'ādat Binā' Manhajīyāt al-Fikr al-Islāmī al-Mu'āṣir*. Herndon, VA: IIIT, 1989.

Abū Yūsuf. *Kitāb al-Kharaj*. Cairo: Dār al-Matba'ah al-Salafiyyah, 1972.

Kitāb al-Kharaj. Beirut: Dār al-Ma'rifa, 1979.

Abū Zahra, Muḥammad. *Uṣūl al-Fiqh*. Cairo: Dār al-Fikr al-'Arabī, 1958.

Al-Takaful al-Ijtimā'i fī al-Islām. Cairo: Dār al-Fikr al-'Arabī, 1964.

al-Afghānī, Jamāl al-Dīn. *Al-'Amal al-Kāmilah*. Edited by Muḥammad 'Imārah. Cairo: Dār al-Kitāb al-'Arabī li al-Tab'ah wa al-Nahar, 1968.

al-Barrawi, Rashīd. *Al-Iqtiṣād al-Islāmi*. Cairo: Kitāb al-Ḥurriyyah, 1986.

al-Dimashqī, Abū al-Faḍl Ja'far. *Al-Ishārah ilā Maḥāsin al-Tijāra*. Cairo: Maktaba al-Kulliyyat al-Azhariyyah, 1977.

al-Dunyā, Ibn Abī. *Iṣlāḥ al-Māl*. Beirut: Mu'assasa al-Kutub al-Thaqāfiyya, 1993.

al-Fanjarī, Muḥammad Shawqī. *Al-Madhab al-Iqtiṣādī fī al-Islām*. Cairo: al-Hai'at al-Miṣriyāt al-'Ammah li al-Kitāb,1986.

al-Ghazālī, Abū Ḥamid. *Iḥyā' 'Ulūm al-Dīn*. 4 vols. Beirut: Dār al-Nadwah, n.d.

Mīzān al-'Amal. Cairo: Dār al-Ma'ārif, 1964.

Al-Mustaṣfā'. 4 vols. Medina: Sharika al-Madīna al-Munawwara li al-Ṭabā'at, 2008.

al-Ghazzālī, Muḥammad. *Al-Islām wa al-Manāhij al-Ishtirākiyya*. Cairo: Dār al-Kitāb al-'Arabī, 1954.

Ibn al-Muqaffa'. *Athār Ibn al-Muqaffa'*. Beirut: Dār al-Kutub al-'Ilmīyya, 1989.

Ibn al-Ukhūwwah. *Ma'ālim al-Qūrbah fī Aḥkām al-Ḥisba*. Edited by Reuben Levy. London: Luzac, 1938.

Ibn 'Āshūr. *Maqāsid al-Sharī'a al-Islāmiyya*. Edited by El-Tahir el-Mesawi. Kuala Lumpur: al-Fajr, 1999.

Ibn Bayyah, 'Abd Allāh ibn al-Shaykh al-Mahfūz. *Tawḍīḥ Awjuh Ikhtilāf al-Aqwāl fī Masā'il min Mu'āmalāt al-Amwāl* Beirut: Dār Ibn Hazm, 1998.

Ibn Hazm. *Al-Muhalla*. 3 vols. Egypt: Matba'a al-Nahdah, 1928.
Al-Iḥkām fi Uṣūl al-Aḥkām. Damascus: al-Maktaba al-Islāmiyya, 1981.
Ibn Khaldūn. *Muqaddima*. 3 vols. Beirut: Dār al-Fikr, 1967.
Ibn Manẓūr. *Lisān al-'Arab*. Qom: Adab al-Hawza, 1984.
Ibn Nujayam. *Al-Ashbāh wa al-Naẓā'ir*. Beirut: Dār al-Kutub al-'Ilmīyyah, 1980.
Ibn Qayyim al-Jawziyya. *Zād al-Ma'ād*. Cairo: Matba'a al-Miṣrriyya, n.d.
I'lām al-Muwaqqi'īn. Cairo: Maktaba al-Sa'āda, 1955.
I'lām al-Muwaqqi'īn. Cairo: Maktaba al-Tijāriyah al-Kubrā, 1955.
I'lām al-Muwaqqi'īn. Beirut: Dār al-Jīl, 1973.
Zād al-Ma'ād. Beirut: Dār al-Kitāb al-'Arabī, 1982.
Al-Ṭuruq al-Ḥukmiyyah fī al-Siyāsa al-Shar'iyya. Edited by Muḥammad Ḥāmid al-Fāqi. Cairo: Maṭba'āt al-Sunnah al-Muḥammadiyyah, 1993.
Madārij al-Salikīn. 3 vols. Cairo: al-Mu'asasa al-Mukhtār li al-Nashar wa al-Awzīa', 2001.
Ibn Rushd. *Bidāyat al-Mujtahid*. Beirut: Dār al-Ma'rifa, 1988.
Ibn Sallām, Abū 'Ubayd al-Qāsim. *Kitāb al-Amwāl*. al-Manṣūrah: Dār al-Hadī al-Nabawī, 2007.
Ibn Taymiyya. *Al-Qawā'id al-Nurīniyah*. Cairo: Matba'ah al-Sunnah al-Muḥammadiyah, 1951.
Majmū' Fatāwā Shaykh al-Islām Aḥmad Ibn Taymiyya. Al-Riyāḍ: Matābi' al-Riyāḍ, 1963.
Al-Siyāsa Shar'iyya fī Iṣlāḥ al-Rā'ī wa al-Ra'īya. Cairo: al-Sha'b, 1971.
Al-Ḥisba fī al-Islām. Cairo: Dār al-Sha'b, 1976.
Jum'a, 'Ali. *Al-Naskh 'inda al-Uṣūliyyīn*. Cairo: Nahḍat Miṣr li al-Ṭibā' wa al-Nashr wa al-Tawzī', 2004.
al-Juwaynī, Abū al-Ma'ālī. *Kitāb al-Irshād ilā Qawāṭi' al-Adilla fī Uṣūl al-I'tiqād*. Cairo: Maktaba al-Thaqāfiyya al-Dīnīyya, 2009.
Khallāf, 'Abd al-Wahhāb. *'Ilm Uṣūl al-Fiqh*. Kuwait: Dār al-Qalam, 1978.
Maḥmaṣānī, Ṣubḥī Rajab. *Falsafat al-Tashrī' fī al-Islām*. Beirut: Dār al-'Ilm li al-Malāyīn, 1961.
al-Makkī. *Qūt al-Qulūb*. Beirut: Dār al-Kutub al-'Ilmiyyah, 1997.
al-Maqdīsī, Ibn Qudāmah. *Al-Sharḥ al-Kabīr*. Beirut: Dār al-Kitāb al-'Arabī, 1972.
al-Maqrīzī, Muḥammad 'Alī. *Ighāthah al-Ummah bi Kashf al-Ghummah*. Cairo: 'Ayn al-Dirāsāt al-Ba'ūth al-Insāniyya wa al-Ijtimā'iyya, 2007.
Kitāb al-Sulūk. Cairo: Lajna al-Ta'lif wa al-Tarjama, 1956.
al-Maṣry, Rafīq Yūsuf. *Uṣūl al-Iqtiṣād al-Islāmi*. Damascus: Dār al-Qalam, 1987.
al-Māwardī. *Adab al-Wazir*. Cairo: Maktaba al-Khanji, 1929.
Al-Aḥkām al-Sulṭāniyyah. Cairo: al-Bābī al-Ḥalabī, 1973.

Mawdūdī, Abū al-A'lā. *Mabādi'ī al-Islām*. Damascus: Dhakhā'ir al-Fikr al-Islāmī, 1961.
al-Mubārak, Allāh ibn. *Kitāb al-Zuhd wa al-Rāqa'iq*. Riyāḍ: Dār al-Mu'rāj al-Dawlīyya li Nashr, 1990.
al-Muḥāsibī. *Kitāb al-Waṣāyā*. Edited by 'Abd al-Qādir Aḥmad Aṭā. Beirut: Dār al-Kutub al-'Ilmiyyah, 1986.
Al-Makāsib wa al-Wara'. Beirut: Mu'ssasa al-Kutub al-Thaqāfiyya, 1987.
Nūr, Maḥmūd Muḥammad. *Al-Iqtiṣād al-Islāmi*. Cairo: Maktabāt al-Tijārah wa Ta'āwun, 1978.
Ouda, Jasser. *Maqāṣid al-Sharī'a*. Herndon, VA: al-Ma'had al-'Ālami li al-Fikr al-Islāmī, 2012.
al-Quradāghī, 'Alī. *Al-Bahth fī al-Iqtisād al-Islāmī*. Beirut: Dār al-Bashā'ir al-Islāmiyya, 2002.
Quṭb, Sayyid. *Ma'ālīm fī al-Tarīq*. Beirut: Dār al-Shurūq, 1979.
Al-'Adālat al-Ijtimā'īyya fī al-Islām. Beirut: Dār al-Shurūq, 1990.
al-Rāghib al-Iṣfahānī, Abū al-Ḳāsim al-Ḥusayn b. Muḥammad b. al-Mufaḍḍal. *Kitāb al-Dharī'a ilā Makārim al-Sharī'a*. Cairo: Dār al-Salām, 2007.
Riḍā, Rashīd. *Al-Ribā wa al-Mu'āmalāt fī al-Islām*. Edited by Muḥammad Bahjat al-Bitar. Beirut: Dār Ibn Zaydūn, 1986.
al-Ṣadr, Muḥammad Bāqir. *Al-Bank al-Ribāwi fī al-Islām*. Kuwait: Jami' al-Naqi, 1970.
Durūs fī 'Ilm Uṣūl al-Fiqh. Beirut: Dār al-Kitāb al-Lubnānī, 1978.
Iqtiṣādunā. 3 vols. Beirut: Dār al-Ta'ārif, 1987.
al-Shāfi'ī. *Kitāb al-Umm*. Cairo: al-Dār al-Miṣrriyya, n.d.
al-Shāṭibī. *Al-Muwāfaqāt fī Uṣūl al-Sharī'a*. Edited by 'Abdullāh al Darrāz. Cairo, n.d.
al-Shaybānī, Muḥammad bin al-Ḥasan. *Al-Iktisāb fī al-Rizq al-Mustaṭāb*. Beirut: Dār al-Kutub al-'Ilmiyyah, 1986.
Kitāb al-Kasb. Ḥalab: Maktaba al-Maṭbu'āt al-Islāmiyya, 1997.
al-Shayzarī, 'Abdur Raḥman bin Naṣr. *Aḥkām al-Ḥisba*. Beirut: Dār al-Thaqāfa, n.d.
al-Sibā'ī, Muṣṭafā. *Ishtirākiyya al-Islām*. Damascus: Mu'assasat al-Matba'at al-'Arabiyyah, 1960.
Ṭanṭāwī, Muḥammad Sayyid. "'Asi'lah 'an al-Ribā." *Al-Ahram*, November 21, 1993.
al-Tirīqī, 'Abdullāh bin 'Abd al-Muḥsin. *Al-Iqtiṣād al-Islāmī: Usus wa Mabādī wa Ahdāf*. Riyad: Mu'asasat al-Jarīsī, 2009.
al-Tirmidhī, Abū 'Isā Muḥammad bin 'Isā bin Surah. *Al-Jāmi' al-Ṣaḥīḥ*. Edited by Ibrāhīm 'Awaḍ. Beirut: Dār Iḥyā' al-Turāth al-'Arabī, 1963.
al-Ṭūfī, Najm ad-Dīn Abū al-Rabī' Sulaymān ibn 'Abd al-Qawī. *Kitāb al-Ta'yīn fī Sharḥ al-Arba'īn*. Beirut: al-Rayyān, 1998.

al-Ṭūsī, Abū Naṣr al-Sarrāj. *Kitāb al-Luma' fī al-Taṣawwuf*. Edited by Reynold Alleyne Nicholson. Leyden: Brill, 1914.

Zarqa, Muḥammad. "Taḥqīq Islāmiyyāt 'Ilm al-Iqtiṣād: al-Mahfum wa al-Manhaj." *Journal of King Abdul Aziz University: Islamic Economics*, vol. 2 (1990).

Sources in European Languages

Abū Hanīfah. *Al-Fiqh al-Akbar*. Translated by Ali Ghandour. Istanbul: Kalbi Kitaplar, 2009.

Abaza, Mona. "Some Reflections on the Question of Islam and Social Sciences in the Contemporary Muslim World." *Social Compass*, vol. 40, no. 2 (1993): 301–321.

Abaza, Mona and Stauth, Georg. "Occidental Reason, Orientalism, Islamic Fundamentalism: A Critique." In *Globalization, Knowledge and Society: Readings from International Sociology*, edited by Martin Albrow and Elizabeth King, 209–230. London: Sage Publications, 1990.

'Abduh, Muhammad. *Risālat al-tawḥīd (The Theology of Unity)*. Translated by I. Musa'ad and K. Cragg. London: George Allen & Unwin, 1966.

Abū Yūsuf. *Kitāb al-Kharaj*. Translated by Abid Ahmad Ali. Lahore: Islamic Book Center, 1979.

Adams, Charles J. "The Ideology of Mawlana Mawdudi." In *South Asian Politics and Religion*, edited by Donald E. Smith, 371–391. Princeton, NJ: Princeton University Press, 1966.

Addas, Waleed. *Methodology of Economics: Secular vs. Islamic*. Kuala Lumpur: International Islamic University Malaysia, 2008.

Agamben, Giorgio. *The Signature of All Things*. New York: Zone Books, 2009.

The Kingdom and the Glory. Stanford, CA: Stanford University Press, 2011.

Ahmad, Irfan. "Genealogy of the Islamic State: Reflections on Maududi's Political Thought and Islamism." *Journal of the Royal Anthropological Institute*, vol. 15 (2009): 145–162.

Ahmad, Khurshid. *The Religion of Islam*. Lahore: Islamic Publication, 1960.

Economic Development in an Islamic Framework. Leicester, UK: Islamic Foundation, 1979.

"Economic Development in an Islamic Framework." In *Studies in Islamic Development*, edited by Khurshid Ahmad. Jeddah: International Centre for Research in Islamic Economics, 1980.

Studies in Islamic Economics. Leicester, UK: Islamic Foundation, 1981.

"The Nature of Islamic Resurgence," In *Voices of Resurgent Islam*, edited by John L. Esposito, 218–229. New York: Oxford University Press, 1983.

"Nature and Significance of Islamic Economics." In *Lectures on Islamic Economics*, edited by Ahmad Ausaf and Kazim R. Awan, 19–31. Jeddah: IDB, 1992.

Islamic Approach to Development: Some Policy Implications. Islamabad: Institute of Policy Studies, 1994.

"The Challenge of Global Capitalism: An Islamic Perspective." *Policy Perspectives*, vol. 1, no. 1 (2004): 1–29.

"Global Economic Crisis Need for a Paradigm Shift." *Policy Perspectives*, vol. 8, no. 2 (2011): 1–17.

"Western Philosophies of Research and Fundamentals of Islamic Paradigm." *Policy Perspectives*, vol. 10, no. 1 (2013): 45–62.

Ahmad, Mumtaz. "Islamization and the Structural Crises of the State in Pakistan." *Issues in Islamic Thought*, vol. 12 (1993): 304–310.

Ahmed, Abdulrahman Yousri. "The Scientific Approach to Islamic Economics: Philosophy, Theoretical Construction and Applicability." In *Theoretical Foundations of Islamic Economics*, edited by Habib Ahmed, 19–58. Jeddah: Islamic Development Bank, Islamic Research and Training Institute, 2002.

Ahmed, Shahab. *What Is Islam? The Importance of Being Islamic*. Princeton, NJ: Princeton University Press, 2015.

Alatas, Syed Farid. "Reflections on the Idea of Islamic Social Science." *Comparative Civilizations Review*, vol. 17, no. 17 (1987): 60–86.

"The Sacralization of the Social Sciences: A Critique of an Emerging Theme in Academic Discourse." *Archives de sciences sociales des religions*, vol. 91 (1995): 89–111.

"Islam and Modernization." In *Islam in Southeast Asia: Political, Social and Strategic Challenges for the 21st Century*, edited by K. S. Nathan and Mohammad Hashim Kamali, 209–230. Singapore: ISEAS, 2005.

Alternative Discourses in Asian Social Science: Responses to Eurocentrism. London: Sage, 2006.

Ibn Khaldun. Oxford: Oxford University Press, 2013.

Applying Ibn Khaldun: The Recovery of a Lost Tradition in Sociology. Abingdon, UK: Routledge, 2014.

Ali, Ameer and Thompson, Herb. "The Schumpeterian Gap and Muslim Economic Thought." *Journal of Interdisciplinary Economics*, vol. 10 (1999): 31–49.

Allouche, Adel. *Mamluk Economics: A Translation and Study of al-Maqrīzī's Ighāthah*. Salt Lake City: University of Utah Press, 1994.

Al-Daghistani, Sami. "Al-Ghazali and the Intellectual History of Islamic Economics." *ZIT Jahrbuch für Islamische Theologie und Religionspädagogik: Islamische Gelehrten neu gelesen*, vol. 3 (2014): 97–134.

"Semiotics of Islamic Law, Maṣlaḥa, and Islamic Economic Thought." *International Journal of the Semiotics of Law*, vol. 29, no. 2 (2016): 389–404. doi:10.1007/s11196-016-9457-x

Ethical Teachings of Abū Ḥāmid al-Ghazālī: Economics of Happiness. London: Anthem Press, 2021.

al-Alwani, Taha Jabir. *Issues in Contemporary Islamic Thought.* Herndon, VA: IIIT, 2005.

Islamic Thought: An Approach to Reform. Herndon, VA: IIIT, 2006.

al-Alwani, Taha J. and El-Ansary, Waleed. "Linking Ethics and Economics." In *Islamic Finance: Islamic Finance into the 21st Century: Proceedings of the Second Harvard University Forum on Islamic Finance*, 99–126. Cambridge, MA: Harvard University, 1999.

Amanat, Abbas and Griffel, Frank, eds. *Shari'a: Islamic Law in the Contemporary Context.* Stanford, CA: Stanford University Press, 2007.

Amin, Muhammad. *An Analytical Appraisal of Islamization of Knowledge.* Lahore: Safa Educational Reforms Trust Pakistan, 2009.

Anderson, Lisa. "The State in the Middle East and North Africa." *Comparative Politics*, vol. 20, no. 1 (1987): 1–18.

An-Na'im, Abdullahi Ahmed. *Islam and the Secular State: Negotiating the Future of Shari'a.* Cambridge, MA: Harvard University Press, 2008.

Ann, K. S. *State and Government in Medieval Islam.* Oxford: Oxford University Press, 1981.

Ansari, Abdul Haq. "Islamic Ethics: Concepts and Prospects." *American Journal of Islamic Social Sciences*, vol. 6, no. 1 (1989): 81–91.

Ansari, Muhammad Abul Haq. *Sufism and Sharī'a.* Leicester, UK: Islamic Foundation, 1986.

El-Ansary, Waleed. "Recovering the Islamic Economic Intellectual Heritage." In *Proceedings of the Third Harvard University Forum on Islamic Finance: Local Challenges, Global Opportunities*, 7–14. Cambridge: Cambridge University Press, 1999.

"The Quantum Enigma and Islamic Sciences of Nature: Implications for Islamic Economic Theory." In *Proceedings of the 6th International Conference on Islamic Economics and Finance*, 143–175. Jeddah: Islamic Development Bank, 2005.

"The Spiritual Significance of *Jihād* in the Islamic Approach to Markets and the Environment." PhD dissertation, George Washington University, 2006.

"Islamic Science and the Critique of Neoclassical Economic Theory." In *Contemporary Islamic Finance: Innovations, Applications, and Best Practices*, edited by Karen Hunt-Ahmed, 75–101. Hoboken, NJ: John Wiley & Sons, 2013. doi:10.1002/9781118653814.

"Linking Ethics and Economics for Integral Development: The Need for a New Economic Paradigm and the Three Dimensions of Islam." Al-Alwani Lectures, Washington Theological Consortium.

Anwar, Zainah. *Islamic Revivalism in Malaysia: Dakwah among the Students*. Petaling Jaya, Selangor: Peladunk, 1987.

Aquinas, Thomas. *Summa Theologica*. Translated by Fathers of the English Dominican Province. Perrysburg, OH: Benziger Bros., 1947.

Arif, Khalid Mahmud. *Working with Zia: Pakistan's Power Politics, 1977–88*. Karachi: Oxford University Press, 1995.

Ariff, Mohammad. "Toward a Definition of Islamic Economics: Some Scientific Considerations." *Journal of Research in Islamic Economics*, vol. 2 (1985): 87–103.

Arnsperger, Christian and Varoufakis, Yanis. "What Is Neoclassical Economics? The Three Axioms Responsible for Its Theoretical Oeuvre, Practical Irrelevance and, thus, Discursive Power." *Panoeconomicus*, vol. 53, no. 1 (2006): 5–18.

Asad, Talal. "The Idea of an Anthropology of Islam." Paper presented at the Annual Distinguished Lecture in Arab Studies, Center for Contemporary Arab Studies, Georgetown University, Washington DC, March 1986.

Formations of the Secular. Stanford, CA: Stanford University Press, 2003.

El-Ashker, Ahmed and Wilson, Rodney. *Islamic Economics: A Short History*. Leiden: Brill, 2006.

Asutay, Mehmet. "A Political Economy Approach to Islamic Economics." *Kyoto Bulletin of Islamic Area Studies*, vol. 1–2 (2007): 3–18.

Atasoy, Yildiz. *Islam's Marriage with Neoliberalism: State Transformation in Turkey*. London: Palgrave Macmillan, 2009.

al-Attas, Muhammad Naquib. *Islam, Secularism and the Philosophy of Future*. London: Mansell, 1985.

Islam and the Philosophy of Science. Kuala Lumpur: ISTAC, 1989.

Islam and Secularism. Kuala Lumpur: ISTAC, 1993.

Prolegomena to the Metaphysics of Islam. Kuala Lumpur: ISTAC, 2001.

Auda, Jasser. *Maqāsid al-Sharī'a: An Introductory Guide*. Herndon, VA: IIIT, 2008.

Aydin, Necati. "Redefining Islamic Economics As a New Economic Paradigm." *Islamic Economic Studies*, vol. 21, no. 1 (2013): 1–34.

Azhar, Rauf. *Economics of an Islamic Economy*. Leiden: Brill, 2009.

al-ʿAzm, Sadiq Jalal. "Orientalism and Orientalism in Reverse." In *Forbidden Agendas: Intolerance and Defiance in the Middle East*, edited by John Rothschild, 349–376. London: Al-Saqi Books, 1984.

Bakar, Osman. *Classification of Knowledge in Islam*. Cambridge: Islamic Texts Society, 1998.

Badeen, Dennis and Murray, Patrick. "A Marxian Critique of Neoclassical Economics' Reliance on Shadows of Capital's Constitutive Social Forms." *Crisis & Critique*, vol. 3, no. 3 (2016): 9–28.

Bauer, Thomas. *Die Kultur der Ambiguität: Eine andere Geschichte des Islams*. Berlin: Verlag der Weltreligionen, 2011.

Behdad, Sohrab. "Property Rights in Contemporary Islamic Economic Thought." *Review of Social Economy*, vol. 47, no. 2 (1989): 185–211.

Bentham, Jeremy. *An Introduction to the Principles of Moral Legislation*. Kitchener, Ontario: Batoche Books, 2001.

Berlin, Isaiah. *Liberty*. Oxford: Oxford University Press, 2002.

Blaut, J. M. "Colonialism and the Rise of Capitalism." *Science & Society*, vol. 53, no. 3 (1989): 260–296.

Bonner, Michael. "The Kitab al-Kasb Attributed to al-Shaybānī: Poverty, Surplus, and the Circulation of Wealth." *Journal of the American Oriental Society*, vol. 121, no. 3 (2011): 410–427.

Boukhatem, Jamel and Ben Moussa, Fatma. "The Effect of Islamic Banks on GDP Growth: Some Evidence from Selected MENA Countries." *Borsa Istanbul Review*, vol. 18, no. 3 (2018): 231–247.

Braudel, Fernand. *Civilization and Capitalism 15th–18th Century*. London: Commerce, 1983.

Bucknill, John A. Strachey, trans. *The Imperial Ottoman Penal Code*. Oxford: Oxford University Press, 1913.

Burckhardt, Titus. *Alchemy: Science of the Cosmos, Science of the Soul*. Louisville, KY: Fons Vitae, 1997.

Calder, Norman. "The Limits of Islamic Orthodoxy." In *Intellectual Traditions in Islam*, edited by Farhad Daftary, 66–86. London: I. B. Tauris, 2000.

Caldwell, Bruce. *Beyond Positivism: Economic Methodology in the Twentieth Century*. London: Routledge, 1994.

Celarent, Barbara. Review of *On the Sociology of Islam; Marxism and Other Western Fallacies*, by Ali Shariʾati, *American Journal of Sociology*, vol. 117, no. 4 (January 2012).

Chapra, Muhammad Umer. "The Need for a New Economic System?" *Review of Islamic Economics*, vol. 1, no. 1 (1991): 9–47. (Reproduced in Tim Niblock and Rodney Wilson, eds. *The Political*

Economy of the Middle East, vol. 3, 76–114. Cheltenham, UK: Edward Elgar, 1999.)

Islam and the Economic Challenge. Herndon, VA: IIIT, 1992.

What Is Islamic Economics? Jeddah: Islamic Development Bank, Islamic Research and Training Institute, 1996.

The Future of Economics: An Islamic Perspective. Leicester, UK: Islamic Foundation, 2000.

"Islamic Economic Thought and the New Global Economy." *Islamic Economic Studies*, vol. 9, no. 1 (2001): 1–16.

The Islamic Vision of Development in the Light of Maqasid al-Shari'a. Herndon, VA: IIIT, 2008.

"Ethics and Economics: An Islamic Perspective." *Islamic Economic Studies*, vol. 16, no. 1 & 2 (2008/9): 1–24.

"Islamic Economics: What It Is and How It Developed." *EH.net Online Encyclopedia of Economics and Business History*. Available at http://eh.net/encyclopedia/islamic-economics-what-it-is-and-how-it-developed.

Chatterjee, Partha. *Nationalist Thought and the Colonial World: A Derivative Discourse*. London: Zed Books, 1993.

Choudhury, Masudul Alam. *The Principles of Islamic Political Economy: A Methodological Enquiry*. London: Macmillan, 1992.

"A Critique of Modernist Synthesis in Islamic Thought: Special Reference to Political Economy." *American Journal of Islamic Social Sciences*, vol. 11, no. 4 (1994): 475–503.

"Toward Islamic Political Economy at the Turn of the Century." *American Journal of Islamic Social Sciences*, vol. 13, no. 3 (1996): 366–381.

"Critique of Current Thinking in Islamic Political and Economic Issues." *Islamic Quarterly*, vol. 42, no. 2 (1998): 125–143.

Studies in Islamic Social Sciences. Basingstoke: Macmillan, 1998.

The Islamic Worldview. London: Kegan Paul, 2000.

The Islamic World-System: A Study in Polity–Market Interaction. New York: Routledge, 2004.

"Development of Islamic Economic and Social Thought." In *Handbook of Islamic Banking*, edited by M. Kabir Hassan and Mervyn K. Lewis, 21–37. Cheltenham, UK: Edward Elgar, 2007.

"A Critique of Economic Theory and Modeling: A Meta-epistemological General-System Model of Islamic Economics." *Social Epistemology: A Journal of Knowledge, Culture and Policy*, vol. 25, no. 4, (2011): 423–446. http://dx.doi.org/10.1080/02691728.2011.604447

Islamic Economics and Finance: An Epistemological Inquiry, Bingley, UK: Emerald Group Publishing, 2011.

"Islamic Political Economy: An Epistemological Approach." *Social Epistemology Review and Reply Collective*, vol. 3, no. 11 (2014): 53–103.

Çizakça, Murat. "Awqaf in History and Its Implications for Modern Islamic Economics." *Islamic Economic Studies*, vol. 6, no. 1 (1998).

Colander, David, et al. *The Changing Face of Economics*. Ann Arbor: University of Michigan Press, 2004.

Comte, Auguste. *A General View of Positivism*. Cambridge: Cambridge University Press, 2009.

Coulson, N. J. *A History of Islamic Law*. Chicago, IL: Aldine Transaction, 1994.

Introduction to Islamic Law. Edinburgh: Edinburgh University Press, 1964.

Crone, Patricia. "Did al-Ghazālī Write a Mirror for Princes? On the Authorship of Nasīḥat al-Mulūk." *Jerusalem Studies of Arabic and Islam*, vol. 10 (1987): 167–197.

"Weber, Islamic Law, and the Rise of Capitalism." In *Max Weber and Islam*, edited by Toby E. Huff and Wolfgang Schluchter, 247–272. New Brunswick, NJ: Transaction Publishers, 1999.

Crone, Patricia and Hinds, Martin. *God's Caliph: Religious Authority in the First Centuries of Islam*. Cambridge: Cambridge University Press, 1986.

Crouch, Harold. *Government and Society in Malaysia*. Ithaca, NY: Cornell University Press, 1996.

Dabashi, Hamid. *Theology of Discontent*. New York: New York University Press, 1993.

Al-Darir, Siddiq. *Al-Gharar in Contracts and Its Effects on Contemporary Transaction*. Eminent Scholars Lecture Series, no. 16. Jeddah: IRTI, IDB, 1997.

Davison, Roderic H. *Reform in the Ottoman Empire, 1856–1876*. Princeton, NJ: Princeton University Press, 1963.

Dawson, Christopher. *The Making of Europe*. New York: Meridian Books, 1956.

Descartes, René. *Meditationes III*. Translated by Gerhart Schmidt. Stuttgart, 1986.

Discours de la méthode et essais. 3 vols. Edited by Marie Beyssade and Denis Kambouchner. Paris: Gallimard, 2009.

Dilley, Roy, ed. *Contesting Markets*. Edinburgh: Edinburgh University Press, 1992.

Donohue, John and Esposito, John, eds. *Islam in Transition*. New York: Oxford University Press, 1982.

Doti, James L and Lee, Dwight R., eds. *The Market Economy: A Reader*. Los Angeles, CA: Roxbury Publishing, 1991.

Egan, Kieran. *The Educated Mind*. Chicago, IL: University of Chicago Press. 1997.

Egri, Taha and Kizilkaya, Necmettin, eds. *Islamic Economics: Basic Concepts, New Thinking and Future Directions*. Cambridge: Cambridge Scholars Publishing, 2015.

Emon, Anver M. *Islamic Natural Law Theories*. Oxford: Oxford University Press, 2010.

Essid, Yassine. *A Critique of the Origins of Islamic Economic Thought*. Leiden: Brill, 1995.

Fadel, Mohammad. "The Social Logic of Taqlīd and the Rise of the Mukhataṣar." *Islamic Law and Society*, vol. 3, no. 2 (1996): 193–233.

"Is Islamic Purposivism (*maqāṣid al-sharīʿa*) a Thinly-Disguised Form of Utilitarianism?," Accessed December 28, 2019, https://islamiclaw.blog/2019/09/05/is-islamic-purposivism-maqaṣid-al-shariʿa-a-thinly-disguised-form-of-utilitarianism.

El Fadl, Khaled Abu. *Speaking in God's Name: Islamic Law, Authority and Women*. Oxford: Oneworld, 2001.

Fakhry, Majid. *A History of Islamic Philosophy*. New York: Columbia University Press, 2004.

al-Faruqi, Ismaʿil Raji. *Tawhid: Its Implications for Thought and Life*. Herndon, VA: IIIT, 1982.

Islamization of Knowledge. Herndon, VA: IIIT, 1989.

The Essence of Islamic Civilization. Herndon, VA: IIIT, 2013.

Florens, Aleksander. *Zivilisation oder Barbarei? Der Islam im historischen Kontext*. Berlin: Suhrkamp Verlag, 2015.

Foucault, Michel. *Discipline and Punishment*. New York: Vintage Books, 1979.

"What Is Enlightenment?" In *The Foucault Reader*, edited by P. Rabinow, 32–50. New York: Pantheon Books, 1984.

The Order of Things. New York: Vintage Books, 1994.

"Technologies of the Self." In *Ethics, Subjectivity, and Truth*, edited by P. Rabinow, 223–251. New York: The New Press, 1994.

Friedman, Milton. *Essays in Positive Economics*. Chicago, IL: University of Chicago Press, 1953.

Capitalism and Freedom. Chicago, IL: Chicago University Press, 1962.

Friedrich, Carl J. *The Philosophy of Law in Historical Perspective*. Chicago, IL: University of Chicago Press, 1963.

Fullbrook, Edward. "Introduction: Lawson's Reorientation." In *Ontology and Economics: Tony Lawson and His Critics*, edited by Edward Fullbrook, 1–12. London: Routledge, 2009.

Furqani, Hafas and Haneef, Muhammad Aslam. "Methodology of Islamic Economics: Typology of Current Practices, Evaluation and

Way Forward." Paper presented at the Eighth International Conference on Islamic Economics and Finance, Doha Qatar, December 19–21, 2011.

al-Ghazzali, Abu Hamid. *The Alchemy of Happiness*. Translated by Claud Field. London: J. Murray, 1910.

Nasihat al-Muluk. Translated by F. R. Bagley as *The Book of Counsel for Kings*. Oxford: Oxford University Press, 1964.

Kīmiyā-yi Sa'ādat (Alchemy of Eternal Bliss). Translated by Muhammad Asim Bilal. Lahore: Kazi, 2001.

Mīzān al-'Amal, translated by Muhammad Hozien. Available at http://ghazali.org/works/mizan-en.htm.

Ghazanfar, S. Mohammad. *Medieval Islamic Thought: Filling the "Great Gap" in European Economics*. London: Routledge, 2003.

Ghazanfar, S. Mohammad and Islahi, Abdul Azim. "Economic Thought of an Arab Scholastic: Abu Hamid Al-Ghazali." *History of Political Economy*, vol. 22, no. 2, (1990): 381–403.

Economic Thought of al-Ghazali. Jeddah: Scientific Publishing Centre King Abdulaziz University, 1997.

Giddens, Anthony. *Positivism and Sociology*, 2nd ed. Aldershot, UK: Ashgate Publishing, 1974.

Goitein, Shelomo Dov. *Studies in Islamic History and Institutions*. Leiden: E. J. Brill, 1966.

Griffel, Frank. *Al-Ghazali's Philosophical Theology*. Oxford: Oxford University Press, 2009.

Guenon, Rene. "Al-Faqr or 'Spiritual Poverty'." *Studies in Comparative Religion*, vol. 7, no. 1 (1973): 16–20.

Hadden, Jeffrey K. "Toward Desacralizing Secularization Theory." *Social Forces*, vol. 65, no. 3 (1987): 587–611.

Hallaq, Wael. "Usul Al-Fiqh: Beyond the Tradition." *Journal of Islamic Studies*, vol. 3. no. 2 (1992): 172–202.

"Was al-Shafi the Master Architect of Islamic Jurisprudence?" *International Journal of Middle East Studies*, vol. 25, no. 4 (1993): 587–605.

"From Fatwas to Furu: Growth and Change in Islamic Substantive Law." *Islamic Law and Society*, vol. 1, no. 1 (1994): 29–65.

A History of Islamic Legal Theories. Cambridge: Cambridge University Press, 1997.

The Origins and Evolution of Islamic Law. Cambridge: Cambridge University Press, 2005.

Sharī'a: Theory, Practice, Transformations. Cambridge: Cambridge University Press, 2009.

"Groundwork of the Moral Law: A New Look at the Qur'an and the Genesis of Shari'a." *Islamic Law and Society*, vol. 16 (2009): 239–279.

An Introduction to Islamic Law. Cambridge: Cambridge University Press, 2009.

"Maqāṣid and the Challenges of Modernity." *Al-Jāmi'ah*, vol. 49, no. 1 (2011): 1–31.

"Qur'anic Constitutionalism and Moral Governmentality: Further Notes on the Founding Principles of Islamic Society and Polity." *Comparative Islamic Studies*, vol. 8, no. 1–2 (2012): 1–51.

The Impossible State. New York: Columbia University Press, 2013.

"God's Word: Between the Intentional and the Political." Lecture at IRCPL, Columbia University, February 13, 2015.

Hamidullah, Muhammad. "Islam's Solution to the Basic Economic Problems: The Position of Labour." *Islamic Culture*, vol. 10, no. 2 (1936): 213–233.

"Haidarabad's Contribution to Islamic Economic Thought and Practice." *Die Welt des Islams*, vol. 4, no. 2/3 (1955): 73–78.

Introduction to Islam. Paris: Centre Culturel Islamique, 1957; second edition 1969.

Ḥammād, Aḥmad Zakī Mansūr. "Abu Hamid al-Ghazali's Juristic Doctrine in al-Mustasfa min 'ilm al'usul." PhD dissertation. 2 vols. University of Chicago, 1987.

Haneef, Muhammad Aslam. *Contemporary Islamic Economic Thought: A Selected Comparative Analysis*. Kuala Lumpur: S. Abdul Majeed & Co, 1995.

"Islam, the Islamic Worldview and Islamic Economics." *IIUM Journal of Economics and Management*, vol. 5, no. 1 (1997): 39–65.

A Critical Survey of Islamization of Knowledge. Kuala Lumpur: International Islamic University Malaysia, 2005.

Haneef, Muhammad Aslam and Furqani, Hafas. "Contemporary Islamic Economics: The Missing Dimension of Genuine Islamization." *Thoughts on Economics*, vol. 19, no. 4 (2004): 29–48.

"Usul al-Iqtisad: The Missing Dimension in Contemporary Islamic Economics and Finance." In *Readings in Islamic Economics and Finance*, edited by Nur Azura Sanusi et al., 1–15. Sintok: University Utara Malaysia Press 2007.

"Developing the Ethical Foundations of Islamic Economics: Benefitting from Toshihiko Izutsu." *Intellectual Discourse*, vol. 17, no. 2 (2009): 173–199.

Hanna, Sami A. and Gardner, George H., eds. *Arab Socialism: A Documentary Survey*. Leiden: Brill, 1969.

Hanssen, Jens and Weiss Max. *Arabic Thought beyond the Liberal Age*. Cambridge: Cambridge University Press 2016.

Hasan, Zubair. Review of *An Introduction to Islamic Economics*, by Muhammad Akram Khan. *American Journal of Islamic Social Sciences*, vol. 13, no. 4 (1996): 580–585.

"Islamization of Knowledge in Economics: Issues and Agenda." *IIUM Journal*, Special Issue, vol. 6, no. 2 (1998): 1–40.

Review of *Teaching Economics in Islamic Perspective*, by Siddiqi. *Islamic Economic Studies*, vol. 6, no. 1 (1998): 111–132.

al-Hasani Baqir and Mirakhor, Abbas, eds. *Essays on Iqtisād: The Islamic Approach to Economic Problems*. Silver Spring, MD: Nur Corporation, 1989.

Hasanuzzaman, S. M. "Definition of Islamic Economics." *Journal of Research in Islamic Economics*, vol. 1, no. 2 (1984): 49–50.

Hashim, Rosnani and Rossidy, Imron. "Islamization of Knowledge: A Comparative Analysis of the Conceptions of Al-Attas and Al-Fārūqī." *Intellectual Discourse*, vol. 8, no. 1 (2000): 19–44.

Hassan, Abdullah Alwi bin Haji. "Al-Mudarabah and Its Identical Islamic Partnership in Early Islam." *Hamdard Islamicus*, vol. 12, no. 2 (1989): 11–38.

al-Hassan, A. Y., ed. *Science and Technology in Islam: Technology and Applied Sciences*. Paris: United Nations Educational, Scientific, and Cultural Organization, 2001.

Hathaway, Robert M. and Lee, Wilson, eds. *Islamization and the Pakistani Economy*. Washington, DC: Woodrow Wilson International Center for Scholars, 2004.

Hayek, Friedrich. *Individualism and Economic Order*. Chicago, IL: University of Chicago Press, 1948.

The Counter Revolution of Science. London: Free Press of Glencoe Collier-Macmillan, 1955.

The Road to Serfdom. Chicago, IL: University of Chicago Press, 2007.

Hermann, Rainer. "Islamisches Recht und Seine wirtschaftspolitischen Implikationen." In *Wirtschaft und Fundamentalismus*, edited by Gerhard Schich, 75–84. Berlin: Stiftung Marktwirtschaft, 2003.

Hicks, J. R. "Léon Walras." *Econometrica*, vol. 2, no. 4 (1934): 338–348.

Hillenbrand, Carole. "A Little-Known Mirror for Princes by al-Ghazālī," in Gerhard Endress, Arnzen Rüdiger, and J. Thielmann, eds., *Words, Texts, and Concepts Cruising the Mediterranean Sea: Studies on the Sources, Contents and Influences of Islamic Civilization and Arabic Philosophy and Science: Dedicated to Gerhard Endress on his Sixty-Fifth Birthday*. Leuven: Peeters, 2004.

Hodges, Donald Clark. "Historical Materialism." *Ethics, Philosophy and Phenomenological Research*, vol. 23 (1962): 1–22.

Hoffman, Murad. Review of *The Future of Economics: An Islamic Perspective*, by Umer Chapra. *Intellectual Discourse*, vol. 10, no. 1 (2002): 91–97.

Hossein, Hamid. "Understanding the Market Mechanism before Adam Smith: Economic Thought in Medieval Islam." In *Medieval Islamic Economic Thought*, edited by S. M. Ghazanfar, 88–107. London: Routledge, 2003.

"Inaccuracy of the Schumpeterian ʿGreat Gapʾ Thesis: Economic Thought in Medieval Iran (Persia)." In *Medieval Islamic Economic Thought*, edited by S. M. Ghazanfar, 108–126. London: Routledge, 2003.

Huff E. Toby and Schluchter, Wolfgang, eds. *Max Weber and Islam*. New Brunswick, NJ: Transactions, 1999.

Hume, David. *A Treatise of Human Nature*. Auckland, New Zealand: The Floating Press, 2009.

Hussein, Fahim and Helmer, Katherine. "Indigenous Anthropology in Non-Western Countries: A Further Elaboration." *Current Anthropology*, vol. 21, no. 5 (1980): 644–650.

Hussein, Ishrat. *Pakistan: The Economy of an Elitist State*. Karachi: Oxford University Press, 1999.

Hussin, Iza. *The Politics of Islamic Law*. Chicago, IL: Chicago University Press, 2016.

Ibn ʿĀshūr. *Treatise on Maqāsid al-Sharīʿa*. Translated by Muhammad al-Tahir el Mesawi. Washington, DC: IIIT, 2006.

Ibn Khaldūn. *Muqaddima*. Translated by Hasan Šušić. Sarajevo: IRO Veselin Masleša, 1982.

Ibn Rushd. *The Distinguished Jurist Primer*. 2 vols. Doha: Garnet Publishing, 2000.

Ibn Sallam, Abū ʿUbayd al-Qasim. *The Book of Revenue: Kitāb al-Amwāl*. Translated by Imran Ahsan Khan Nyazee. Doha: Garnet Publishing, Center for Muslim Contribution to Civilization, 2005.

Ibn Taymiyya. *Public Duties in Islam: The Institution of the Hisbah*. Translated by Muhtar Holland. Leicester, UK: Islamic Foundation, 1982.

Iqbal, Afzal. *Islamisation of Pakistan*, Lahore: Vanguard, 1986.

Iqbal, Muhammad. *The Reconstruction of Religious Thought in Islam*. Electronic version, available at https://ia902701.us.archive.org/31/items/cover_201501/the_reconstruction_of_religious_thought_in_islam.pdf.

Ilmul Iqtisad (The Science of Economics). Lahore: Khadimul-Taleem Steam Press of Paisa Akhba, 1904; 2nd edition, Karachi: Iqbal Academy, 1961.

Asrar-i Khudī. Translated by R. A. Nicholson as *The Secrets of the Self*. London, 1920.

Islahi, Abdul Azim. "Ibn Taymiyyah's Concept of Market Mechanism." *Journal of Research in Islamic Economics*, vol. 2, no. 2, (1985): 51–60.

Economic Concepts of Ibn Taymiyyah. Leicester, UK: Islamic Foundation, 1988.

History of Economic Thought in Islam. Aligharh, India: Department of Economics, Aligharh Muslim University, 1996.

Contribution of Muslim Scholars to Economic Thought and Analysis, 11–905 AH/632–1500 AD. Jeddah: Islamic Economics Research Centre, King Abdulaziz University, 2004.

"Linkages and Similarities between Economics Ideas of Muslim Scholars and Scholastics." *Wednesday Dialogue* (2010–11): 1–26.

"The Genesis of Islamic Economics." *Islamic Economic Studies*, vol. 23, no. 2 (2015): 1–28.

ed. *Muhammad Hamidullah and His Pioneering Works on Islamic Economics*. Jeddah: Islamic Economics Institute, King Abdulaziz University, 2014.

Izutsu, Toshihiko. *Ethico-Religious Concepts in the Qur'an*. Montreal: McGill-Queen's University Press, 2002.

Jackson, Roy. *Mawlana Mawdudi and Political Islam*. London: Routledge, 2010.

Jackson, Sherman. *Islamic Law and the State: The Constitutional Jurisprudence of Shihāb al-Dīn al-Qarāfi*. Leiden: Brill, 1996.

Jameelah, Maryam. "An Appraisal of Some Aspects of Maulana Sayyid Ala Maudoodi's Life and Thought." *Islamic Quarterly*, vol. 31, no. 2 (1987): 116–130.

James, Lawrence. *Raj: The Making and Remaking of British India*. New York: St. Martin's Griffin, 1997.

al-Jāzirī, ʿAbd al-Raḥmān. *Islamic Jurisprudence According to the Four Sunni Schools*. Translated by Nancy Roberts. Louisville, KY: Fons Vitae, 2009.

Jevons, W. Stanley. *The Theory of Political Economy*. New York: Augustus M. Kelley, 1960.

Johansen, Baber. "Das islamische Recht." *Die islamische Welt*, vol. 1 (1984): 129–145.

"The Changing Limits of Contingency in the History of Muslim Law." Third Annual Levtzion Lecture, Nehemia Levtzion Center for Islamic

Studies, Institute for Asian and African Studies, Hebrew University of Jerusalem, 2013.

al-Juwayni. *A Guide to the Conclusive Proofs for the Principles of Belief.* Translated by Paul E. Walker. Reading: Garnet, 2001.

Kader, Radia Abdul and Ariff, Mohamed. "The Political Economy of Islamic Finance: The Malaysian Experience." In *Islamic Political Economy in Capitalist Globalization: An Agenda for Change*, edited by Masudul Alam Choudhry, Abdad M. Z., and Muhammad Syukri Salleh, 262–263. Kuala Lumpur: IPIPE, 1997.

Kahf, Monzer. "Islamic Economics: Notes on Definition and Methodology." *Review of Islamic Economics*, vol. 13 (2003): 23–47.

al-Kalābādhī, Abū Bakr. *The Doctrine of the Sufis.* Translated by Arthur John Arberry. Cambridge: Cambridge University Press, 1977.

Kalam, Abul. "The Basic Principles of Islamic Economics." *Journal of Islamic Banking and Finance*, vol. 8 (1991): 16–24.

Kamali, Mohammad Hashim. "Siyasa Shari'a or the Policies of Islamic Government." *American Journal of Islamic Social Sciences*, vol. 6, no. 1 (1989): 59–80.

Islamic Commercial Law: An Analysis of Futures and Options. Cambridge: I. B. Tauris in association with the Islamic Texts Society, 1990.

"Islamic Commercial Law: An Analysis of Options." *American Journal of Islamic Social Sciences*, vol. 14, no. 3 (2000): 17–37.

Principles of Islamic Jurisprudence. Cambridge: Islamic Texts Society, 2005.

Islamic Finance Law, Economics, and Practice. Cambridge: Cambridge University Press, 2006.

Shariah Law: An Introduction. Oxford: Oneworld, 2008.

Kamenka, Eugene. *The Ethical Foundations of Marxism.* London: Routledge & Kegan Paul, 1962. Electronic edition.

Kant, Immanuel. "Was ist Afklärung?" *UTOPIE kreativ*, vol. 159 (2004): 5–10.

Kato, Hiroshi. "Reconsidering al-Maqrīzī's View on Money in Medieval Egypt." *Mediterranean World*, vol. 21 (2012): 33–44.

Keddie, Nikki R. *Sayyid Jamal ad-Din "al-Afghāni": A Political Biography.* Berkeley, CA: UCLA, 1972.

An Islamic Response to Imperialism: Political and Religious Writings of Sayyid Jamal ad-Din "al-Afghani." Berkeley: University of California Press, 1983.

Kennedy, Charles H. *Bureaucracy in Pakistan.* Karachi: Oxford University Press, 1987.

Keynes, John Maynard. *The Collected Writings of John Maynard Keynes*, vol. 7: *The General Theory of Employment, Interest and Money.* Cambridge: Cambridge University Press, 2013.

Khalili, Imas al-Din. *Islamization of Knowledge: A Methodology*. Herndon, VA: IIIT, 1991.
Khan, Mohsin S. and Mirakhor, Abbas. "The Framework and Practice of Islamic Banking." *Finance and Development*, vol. 23, no. 3 (1986): 32–36.
Khan, Muhammad Akram. "Methodology of Islamic Economics." *Journal of Islamic Economics*, vol. 1, no. 1 (1987): 17–33.
"Islamic Economics: The State of the Art." *Toward Islamization of Disciplines*, 273–292. Herndon, VA: IIIT, 1989.
"The Future of Islamic Economics." *Futures*, vol. 23, no. 3 (1991): 248–261.
An Introduction to Islamic Economics. Islamabad: International Institute of Islamic Thought, 1994.
What Is Wrong with Islamic Economics? Analysing the Present State and Future Agenda. Cheltenham, UK: Edward Elgar, 2013.
Khan, Muhammad Fahim. *Essays in Islamic Economics*. Leicester, UK: Islamic Foundation, 1995.
"*Fiqh* Foundations of the Theory of Islamic Economics: A Survey of Selected Contemporary Writings on Economics Relevant Subjects of *Fiqh*." In *Theoretical Foundation of Islamic Economics*, edited by Habib Ahmed, 59–86. Jeddah: Islamic Development Bank, Islamic Research and Training Institute, 2002
Khomeini, Ruhollah. *Islamic Government*. Translated by Joint Publications Research Service. Dublin: Manor Books, 1979.
Khorchide, Mouhanad. *Islam ist Bahrherzichkeit*. Freiburg im Breisgau: Herder, 2012.
Scharia – der missverstandene Gott. Der Weg zu einer moderne islamischen Ethik. Freiburg: Herder, 2013.
Khun, Thumas. *The Structure of Scientific Revolutions*. Chicago, IL: University of Chicago Press, 1970.
Knysh, Alexander. *Sufism*. Princeton, NJ: Princeton University Press, 2017.
Koehler, Benedikt. *Early Islam and The Birth of Capitalism*. Lanham, MD: Lexington Books, 2014.
Kojiro, Nakamura. "Was Al-Ghazali an Ash'arite." *The Memories of the Toyo Bunko*, vol. 51 (1993): 1–24. Originally published as "Gazali and Ash'arite Theology" in *Isuramu Sekai* (The World of Islam).
Kuran, Timur. "The Economic System in Contemporary Islamic Thought: Interpretations and Assessment." *International Journal for Middle East Studies*, vol. 18 (1986): 135–164.
"Further Reflections on the Behavioral Norms of Islamic Economics." *Journal of Economic Behavior and Organization*, vol. 27 (1995): 159–163.

"Islamic Economics and the Islamic Subeconomy." *Journal of Economic Perspectives*, vol. 9, no. 4 (1995): 155–173.

"The Discontents of Islamic Economic Morality." *American Economic Review*, vol. 86, no. 2 (1996): 438–443.

"The Genesis of Islamic Economics: A Chapter in the Politics of Muslim Identity." *Islam and Mammon*. Princeton, NJ: Princeton University Press, 2004.

Islam and Mammon. Princeton, NJ: Princeton University Press, 2004.

The Long Divergence: How Islamic Law Held Back the Middle East. Princeton, NJ: Princeton University Press, 2010.

Laliwala, Jafarhusein. "Islamic Economics: Some Issues in Definition and Methodology." *Journal of King Abdulaziz University: Islamic Economics*, vol. 1 (1989): 129–131.

Lama, Abu-Odeh. Review of *The Impossible State* by Wael Hallaq. *Georgetown Law Faculty Publications and Other Works*, paper 1269. 2013.

Lambton, Ann K. S. "The Theory of Kingship in the Nasīḥat al-Mulūk." *The Islamic Quarterly*, vol. 1 (1954): 47–55.

Lapidus, I. M. "The Separation of State and Religion in the Development of Early Islamic Society." *Journal of Middle East Studies*, vol. 6, no. 4 (1975): 363–385.

"State and Religion in Islamic Societies." *Past & Present*, no. 151 (1996): 3–27.

Lawson, Tony. *Economics and Reality*. London: Routledge, 1997.

Reorienting Economics. London: Routledge, 2003.

Leshem, Dotan. *The Origins of Neoliberalism*. New York: Columbia University Press, 2016.

Lewis, Bernard. "Siyasa." In *Quest of an Islamic Humanism: Arabic and Islamic Studies in Memory of Muhammad al-Nowaihi*, edited by A. H. Green, 3–13. Cairo: American University in Cairo Press, 1984.

Lieberman, David. "Adam Smith on Justice, Rights, and Law." UC Berkeley Public Law and Legal Theory Working Paper No. 13, December 1999. Available at http://dx.doi.org/10.2139/ssrn.215213.

Lohlker, Rüdiger. *Islamisches Recht*. Vienna: Facultas wuv, 2011.

Lutz, Mark and Lux, Kenneth. *Humanistic Economics: The New Challenge*. New York: The Bootstrap Press, 1988.

Maas, Harro. *William Stanley Jevons and the Making of Modern Economics*. Cambridge: Cambridge University Press, 2005.

MacIntyre, Alasdair. *A Short History of Ethics*. London: Routledge, 1998.

After Virtue. Notre Dame, IN: Notre Dame Press, 2007.

Mahmood, Saba. *Religious Difference in a Secular Age: A Minority Report*. Princeton, NJ: Princeton University Press, 2015.

"Secularism, Hermeneutics, and Empire: The Politics of Islamic Reformation." *Public Culture*, vol. 18, no. 2 (2006): 323–347.

Makdisi, George. "The Shari'a Court Records of Ottoman Cairo and Other Resources for the Study of Islamic Law." American Research Center in Egypt Newsletter, no. 114 (1982): 3–10.

Mannan, Muhammad Abdul. *The Frontiers of Islamic Economics*. Delhi: Idarah-i Adabiyat-i Delli, 1984.

The Making of Islamic Economic Society: Islamic Dimensions in Economic Analysis. Cairo: International Association of Islamic Banks; Turkish Federated State of Kibris, Turkish Cyprus: International Institute for Islamic Banking and Economics, 1984.

Islamic Economics: Theory and Practice. Sevenoaks, Kent: Hodder & Stoughton, 1986.

Manzo, Kate. "Modernist Discourse and the Crisis of Development Theory." *Studies in Comparative International Development*, vol. 26, no. 2 (1991): 3–36.

Marshall, Alfred. *Principles of Economics*, 8th ed. London: Macmillan and Co., 1920.

Martineau, Harriet, trans. *The Positive Philosophy of Auguste Comte*. Kitchener, Ontario: Batoche Books, 2000.

Marx, Karl. *Das Kapital*. Hamburg: Verlag von Otto Meissner, 1883.

Marx, Karl and Engels, Friedrich. *Die deutsche Ideologie*. Berlin: Akademie Verlag, 2003.

Masud, Muhammad Khalid. "'Classical' Islamic Legal Theory As Ideology: Nasr Abu Zayd's Study of al-Shafi'i's Risala," draft.

Shatibi's Philosophy of Islamic Law. Islamabad: Islamic Research Institute, International Islamic University, 1995.

"The Doctrine of *Siyāsa* in Islamic Law." *Recht van de Islam*, vol. 18 (2001): 1–29.

"Muslim Jurists' Quest for the Normative Basis of Shari'a." Inaugural lecture. International Institute for the Study of Islam, Leiden, 2001.

"Ikhtilaf al-Fuqaha: Diversity in Fiqh As a Social Construction." In *Wanted: Equality and Justice in the Muslim Family*, edited by Zainah Anwar, 66–92. Selangor, Malaysia, Musawah, 2009.

Masud, Muhammad Khalid, Messick, Brinkly and Powers, David, eds. *Islamic Legal Interpretation: The Muftis and Their Fatwas*. Cambridge, MA: Harvard, 1996.

Masuzawa, Tomoko. *The Invention of World Religions*. Chicago, IL: University of Chicago Press, 2005.

Mawdūdī, Sayyid Abū al-A'lā. *Nationalism and India*. Lahore: Maktaba-e-Jama'at-e-Islami, 1947.

The Economic Problem of Man and Its Islamic Solution. Lahore: Markazi Maktaba Jama'at-e-islami Pakistan, 1955.

First Principles of the Islamic State. Lahore: Islamic Publications, 1960.

Islamic Law and Constitution. Translated by Khurshid Ahmad. Lahore: Islamic Publications, 1960.

Towards Understanding Islam (Risalah Diniyat). Lahore: UKIM Dawah Center, 1960.

A Short History of the Revivalist Movement in Islam. Translated by al-Ash'ari. Lahore: Islamic Publication, 1963.

Islami Riyasat. Lahore: Islamic Publications, 1969.

Islam: Its Meaning and Message. Edited by Khurshid Ahmad. London: Council of Europe, 1976.

Capitalism, Socialism, and Islam. Kuwait: Islamic Book Publishers, 1977.

Fundamentals of Islam. Delhi: Markazi Maktabah-i Islami, 1978.

Islamic Economic System: Principles and Objectives. Delhi: Markazi Maktabah Islami, 1980.

Als Muslim leben. Karlsruhe: Cordoba Verlag, 2001.

First Principles of Islamic Economics. Leicester, UK: Islamic Foundation, 2011.

Meloy, John L. "The Merits of Economic History: Re-reading al-Maqrīzī Ighāthah and Shudhūr." *Mamlūk Studies Review*, vol. 7, no. 2 (2003): 1–19.

Menger, Carl. *Principles of Economics*. Auburn, AL: Ludwig von Mises Institute, 2007.

Midgeley, James. Review of *The Principles of Islamic Political Economy*, and *Comparative Development Studies: In Search of the World View*, by Masudul Alam Choudhury, *Journal of Sociology and Social Welfare*, vol. 21, no. 3 (2015).

Mill, John Stuart. *Utilitarianism*. London: Parker, Son and Bourn, 1863.

A System of Logic. Harper & Brothers, 1882. Electronic edition by eBooks@Adelaide.

The Collected Works of John Stuart Mill, vol. 4: *Essays on Economics and Society*, part I. Edited by John M. Robson. Toronto: University of Toronto Press, 1967.

"On the Definition and Method of Political Economy." In *The Philosophy of Economics: An Anthology*, edited by Daniel Hausman, 41–58. Cambridge: Cambridge University Press, 2007.

Miklós Maróth, "Qiyās", in *Encyclopedia of Arabic Language and Linguistics*, Managing Editors Online Edition: Lutz Edzard, Rudolf de Jong. Accessed 20 August 2021 <http://dx.doi.org/10.1163/1570-6699_eall_EALL_SIM_0114>

Mirakhor, Abbas. "Muslim Scholars and the History of Economics: A Need for Consideration." *American Journal of Islamic Social Sciences*, vol. 4, no. 2 (1987): 245–276.

A Note on Islamic Economics. Jeddah: Islamic Development Bank, Islamic Research and Training Institute, 2007.

Mirowski, Philip. *Never Let a Serious Crisis Go to Waste: How Neoliberalism Survived the Financial Meltdown*. London: Verso, 2014.

Mises, Ludwig. *Nation, Staat, Wirtschaft: Beiträge zur Politik und Geschichte der Zeit*. Vienna: Manzsche Verlags und Universitäts-Buchhandlung, 1919.

Mishan, Ezra J. *Economic Myths and the Mythology of Economics*. Atlantic Highlands, NJ: Humanities Press International, 1986.

Mitchell, Timothy. "The Limits of the State: Beyond Statist Approaches and Their Critics." *American Political Science Review*, vol. 85, no. 1 (1991): 77–96.

Mohamed, Yasien. *The Path to Virtue: The Ethical Philosophy of al-Rāghib al-Iṣfahānī*. Kuala Lumpur: International Institute of Islamic Thought and Civilization, 2006.

Mohammed, Mustafa Omar. "Economic Consumption Model Revisited: *Infaq* Based on *Al-Shaybani's* Levels of *Al-Kasb*." *International Journal of Economics, Management and Accounting*, no. 19 (2011): 115–132.

Mottahedeh, Roy P. *Loyalty and Leadership in an Early Islamic Society*. Princeton, NJ: Princeton University Press, 1980.

Motzki, Harald. *Die Anfänge der islamischen Jurisprudenz: Ihre Entwicklung in Mekka bis zur Mitte des 2./8. Jahrhunderts*. Stuttgart: Steiner, 1991.

Moussalli, Ahmad S. "Islamism: Modernization of Islam, or Islamization of Knowledge." In *Cosmopolitanism, Identity and Authenticity in the Middle East*, edited by Roel Meijer, 87–102. London: Routledge, 1999.

Muhammad, Mahathir. "Islamization of Knowledge and the Future of the Ummah." In *Toward Islamization of Disciplines*, 13–25. Herndon, VA: IIIT, 1995.

Mujani, Wan Kamal and Yaakub, Noor Inayah. "Al-Maqrizi (d. 1442) and Abd Al-Basit (d. 1514) and Their Accounts on the Economy in Egypt." International Conference on the Modern Development of Humanities and Social Sciences, Hong Kong, December 1–2, 2013.

Nabi, Nasir. "Islamic Economic Thought in the Medieval Times: Some Reflections." *Journal of Islamic Thought and Civilization*, vol. 3, no. 2 (2013): 21–32.

Najjar, Fawzi M. "Siyāsa in Islamic Political Philosophy." In *Islamic Theology and Philosophy: Studies in Honor of George F. Hourani*, edited by M. E. Marmura, 92–110. Albany: State University of New York Press, 1984.

Nakissa, Aria. "An Epistemic Shift in Islamic Law: Educational Reform at al-Azhar and Dār al-ʿUlūm." *Islamic Law and Society*, vol. 21 (2014): 209–251.

Naqvi, Syed Nawab Haider. *Ethics and Economics: An Islamic Synthesis*. Leicester, UK: Islamic Foundation, 1981.

Islam, Economics, and Society. London: Kegan Paul International, 1994.

"The Dimensions of an Islamic Economic Model." *Islamic Economic Studies*, vol. 4, no. 2 (1997): 1–23.

Nasr, Seyyed Hossein. *Islamic Science: An Illustrated Study*. London: World of Islam Festival Trust, 1976.

"Reflections on Methodology in the Islamic Sciences." *Hamdard Islamicus*, vol. 3, no. 3 (1980): 3–13.

The Need for a Sacred Science: The Gifford Lectures. Edinburgh: Edinburgh University Press, 1981.

Knowledge and the Sacred. New York: State University of New York, 1989.

"Perennial Ontology and Quantum Mechanics: A Review Essay of Wolfgang Smith's *The Quantum Enigma: Finding the Hidden Key*." *Sophia: A Journal of Traditional Studies*, vol. 3, no. 1 (1997): 135–159.

"Islam and the Problem of Modern Sciences." *Islam and Science*, vol. 8, no. 1 (2010): 63–74.

Nasr, Seyyed Vali Reza. "Toward a Philosophy of Islamic Economics." *Muslim World*, vol. 77, no. 3–4 (1987): 175–196.

"Islamic Economics: Novel Perspectives." *Middle Eastern Studies*, vol. 25, no. 4 (1989): 516–530.

"Islamization of Knowledge: A Critical Overview." *Islamic Studies*, vol. 30, no. 3 (1991): 387–400.

The Vanguard of the Islamic Revolution: The Jama'at-I Islami of Pakistan. Berkeley: University of California Press, 1994.

Mawdudi and the Making of Islamic Revivalism. New York: Oxford University Press, 1996.

Islamic Leviathan. Oxford: Oxford University Press, 2001.

"Islamization, the State and Development." In *Islamization and the Pakistani Economy*, edited by Robert M. Hathaway and Wilson Lee, 91–100. Washington, DC: Woodrow Wilson International Center for Scholars, 2004.

Nayed, Aref Ali. "The Unitary Qur'ānic Hermeneutics of Muhammad Baqir al-Sadr." *Islamic Studies*, vol. 31, no. 4 (1992): 443–449.

Nienhaus, Volker. "Der Beitrag des Islam zur ethnischen Fundierung einer Wirtschaftsordnung." In *Wirtschaft und Fundamentalismus*, edited by Gerhard Schich, 85–100. Berlin: Stiftung Marktwirtschaft, 2003.

"Islamic Economic System: A Threat to Development?" 2006. Available at www.iefpedia.com/english/wp-content/uploads/2009/09/Islamic-Economic-System-%E2%80%93-A-Threat-to-Development.pdf.

"Grundzüge einer islamischen Wirtschaftsordnung im Vergleich zur sozialen Marktwirtschaft." *Kas Auslandsinformationen*, vol. 11 (2010): 80–102.

Nietzsche, Friedrich. *Sämtliche Werke*, edited by Giorgio Colli and Mazzino Montinari. Berlin: de Gruyter, 1967.

Nomani, Farhad and Rahnema, Ali. *Islamic Economic Systems*. London: Zed Books, 1994.

Nyazee, Imran Ahsan Khan. *Theories of Islamic Law: The Methodology of Ijtihad*. Kuala Lumpur: The Other Press, 1994.

Theories of Islamic Jurisprudence. Cambridge: Islamic Texts Society, 2003.

Oberauer, Nobert. *Religiöse Verpflichtung im Islam. Ein ethischer Grundbegriff und seine theologische, rechtliche und sozialgeschichtliche Dimension*. Würzburg: Ergon, 2004.

Oleck, Howard L. "Historical Nature of Equity Jurisprudence." *Fordham Law Review*, vol. 20, no. 1 (1951): 23–44.

Opwis, Felicitas. "Maslaha in Contemporary Islamic Legal Theory." *Islamic Law and Society*, vol. 12, no. 2, (2005): 182–223.

Pal, Din. *Pakistan, Islam and Economics*. Karachi: Oxford University Press, 1999.

Peffer, Rodney G. *Marxism, Morality, and Social Justice*. Princeton, NJ: Princeton University Press, 1990.

Peters, E. Francis. *Allah's Commonwealth*. New York: Simon and Schuster, 1973.

Philipp, Thomas. "The Idea of Islamic Economics." *Die Welt des Islams*, new series, vol. 30, no. 1/4 (1990): 117–139.

Piketty, Thomas. *Capital in the Twenty-First Century*. Cambridge, MA: Belknap Press of Harvard University Press, 2014.

Polanyi, Karl. *The Great Transformation*. Boston: Beacon Press, 2001.

Prichard, H. A. "Does Moral Philosophy Rest on a Mistake." *Mind*, vol. 21, issue 81 (January 1, 1912): 21–37. https://doi.org/10.1093/mind/XXI.81.21.

al-Qaraḍāwī, Yūsuf. *Economic Security in Islam*. Translated by Muhammed Iqbal Siddiqi. New Delhi: Islamic Book Services, 1997.

Quasem, Muhammad Abdul. *The Ethics of Al-Ghazali*. Petaling Jaya, Selangor: Quasem, 1975.

Quṭb, Sayyid. "Humanity Needs Us." Translated by M. Hafez. *Al-Muslimūn*, vol. 3, no. 2 (1953).

Social Justice in Islam. Translated by John B. Hardie. New York: Islamic Publication International, 1953.

"The America I Have Seen: In the Scale of Human Values." In *America in an Arab Mirror: Images of America in Arabic Travel Literature: An Anthology*, edited by Kamal Abdel-Malek. New York: St. Martin's Press, 2000.

Milestones. Birmingham: Maktabah, 2006.

Raghavan, Srinath. *India's War: World War II and the Making of Modern South Asia*. New York: Basic Books, 2016.

Rahim, Dayangku Aslinah Abd. "An Analysis of Selected Fundamental Concepts in Islamic Economics." Proceedings of the Second Islamic Conference, organized by Faculty of Economics and Muamalat, Islamic Science University of Malaysia, 2007.

Rahman, Fazlur. *Islam and Modernity*. Chicago, IL: Chicago University Press, 1982.

Islam. Chicago, IL: Chicago University Press, 2002.

"Islamization of Knowledge: A Response." *Islamic Studies*, vol. 50, no. 3/4 (2011): 449–457.

al-Raysuni, Ahmad. *Imam al-Shatibi's Theory of the Higher Objectives and Intents of Islamic Law*. Herndon, VA: IIIT, 2005.

Reinhart A. K. "Islamic Law As Islamic Ethics." *Journal of Religious Ethics*, vol. 11, no. 2 (1983): 186–203.

Ricardo, David. *On the Principles of Political Economy and Taxation*. Kitchener, Ontario: Batoche Books, 2001.

Riddick, John F. *The History of British India: A Chronology*. Westport, CT: Praeger, 2006.

Robbins, Lionel. *An Essay on the Nature and Significance of Economic Science*. New York: St. Martin's Press, 1962.

Roberts, A. and Donaldson J., eds. *The Ante-Nicene Fathers*. Grand Rapids, MI: Wm. B. Eerdmans Publishing, 1962.

Rodinson, Maxime. *Islam and Capitalism*. New York: Pantheon Books, 1974.

Roff, William R. "Patterns of Islamization in Malaysia, 1890s–1990s: Exemplars, Institutions, and Vectors." *Journal of Islamic Studies*, vol. 9, no. 2 (1998): 210–228.

Rohe, Mathias. *Das Islamische Recht*. München: C. H. Beck, 2011.

Rosenthal, Franz. *Muqaddimah of Ibn Khaldūn*. Princeton, NJ: Princeton University Press, 1967.

Rowthorn, Bob. "Neoclassical Economics and Its Critics: A Marxist View." *Social Scientist*, vol. 2, no. 3 (1973): 3–29.

Sadeq Abdul-Hasan Muhammad and Ghazali, Aidit, eds. *Pregled islamske ekonomske misli*. Sarajevo: El-Kalem, 1996.

al-Ṣadr, Muḥammad Bāqir. *Iqtiṣādunā*. Tehran: World Organization for Islamic Services, 1982.

Towards an Islamic Economy. Tehran: Bonyad Be'that, 1984.

Saleem, Muhammad Yusuf. "Methods and Methodologies in Fiqh and Islamic Economics." *Review of Islamic Economics*, vol. 14, no. 1 (2010): 103–123.

Saliba, George. *Islamic Science and the Making of the European Renaissance*. Cambridge, MA: MIT Press, 2007.

Salvatore, Armando. *Islam and the Political Discourse of Modernity*. Reading, UK: Ithaca Press, 1997.

The Sociology of Islam. Chichester, UK: Wiley Blackwell, 2016.

Sardar, Ziauddin. *Islamic Futures*. Kuala Lumpur: Pelanduk Publications, 1988.

al-Sāti, Abdul-Rahim. "The Permissible Gharar (Risk) in Classical Islamic Jurisprudence." *JKAU: Islamic Economics*, vol. 16, no. 2 (2003): 3–19.

Saud, Mahmud Abu. "The Methodology of the Islamic Behavioural Sciences." *American Journal of Islamic Social Sciences*, vol. 10, no. 3, (1993): 382–395.

"Toward Islamic Economics." In *Toward Islamization of Disciplines*, 265–723. Herndon, VA: IIIT, 1995.

Schacht, Joseph. *An Introduction to Islamic Law*. Oxford: Clarendon Press, 1982.

Schmidt, Godfrey P. "An Approach to the Natural Law." *Fordham Law Review*, vol. 18, no. 1 (1950): 1–42. Available at http://ir.lawnet.fordham.edu/flr/vol19/iss1/1.

Schmitt, Carl. *Der Begriff des Politischen*. Berlin: Dunckner & Humbolt, 1979.

The Concept of the Political. Translated by George Schwab. Chicago, IL: Chicago University Press, 1996.

Schultz, Warren C. "Mamluk Monetary History: A Review Essay." *Mamlūk Studies Review*, vol. 3 (1999): 183–205.

Schumacher, Ernst F. *Small Is Beautiful*. London: Perennial Library, 1973.

Good Work. New York: Harper & Row, 1979.

Schumpeter, Joseph. *History of Economic Analysis*. Abingdon, UK: Taylor & Francis, 2006.

Schuon, Frithjof. *Understanding Islam*. Translated by D. D. Matheson. London: Allen & Unwin, 1963.

Scott, James C. *Political Ideology in Malaysia: Reality and the Beliefs of an Elite*. Kuala Lumpur: University of Malaya Press, 1968.

Searle, John. *Social Construction of Reality*. New York: The Free Press, 1995.

Making the Social World. Oxford: Oxford University Press, 2010.

Sen, Amartya. *Development Is Freedom*. New York: Anchor, 2000.

Setia, Adi. *The Book of Earning a Livelihood.* Kuala Lumpur: IBFIM, 2011.

"Imam Muḥammad Ibn al-Ḥasan al-Shaybāni on Earning a Livelihood: Seven Excerpts from his Kitāb al-Kasb." *Islam and Science*, vol. 10, no. 2 (2012): 99–116.

"The Restoration of Wealth: Introducing Ibn Abī al-Dunyā's *Iṣlāḥ al-māl.* " *Islamic Sciences*, vol. 13, no. 2 (2015): 77–94.

"Al-Muḥāsibī: On Scrupulousness and the Pursuit of Livelihoods: Two Excerpts from His *al-Makāsib wa al-Wara'.*" *Islamic Sciences*, vol. 14, no. 1 (2016): 67–90.

Kitāb al-Makāsib (The Book of Earnings) by al-Hārith al-Muḥāsibī (751–857 CE). Kuala Lumpur: IBFIM, 2016.

"The Meaning of 'Economy': *Qaṣd, Iqtiṣād, Tadbīr al-Manzil.*" *Islamic Sciences*, vol. 14, no. 1 (2016): 117–124.

al-Shāfi'ī. *Al-Imām Muḥammad Idris al-Shāfi'ī's al-Risāla fī uṣūl al-fiqh: Treatise on the Foundations of Islamic Jurisprudence.* Translated by Majid Khadduri. Cambridge, UK: Islamic Text society, 1997.

Shalakany, Amr A. "Islamic Legal Histories." *Berkeley Journal of Middle Eastern and Islamic Law*, vol. 1 (2008): 1–82.

Sharī'atī, 'Alī. *Marxism and Other Western Fallacies.* Translated by R. Campbell. Berkeley, CA: Mizan Press, 1980.

On the Sociology of Islam. Translated by Hamid Algar, Berkeley, CA: Mizan Press, 1979.

al-Shayzarī. *The Book of the Islamic Market Inspector. Nihāyat al-Rutba fī Ṭalab al-Ḥisba.* Translated by R. P. Buckley. Oxford: Oxford University Press, 1999.

Shinsuke, Nagaoka. "Critical Overview of the History of Islamic Economics: Formation, Transformation, and New Horizons." *Asian and African Area Studies*, vol. 11, no. 2 (2012): 114–136.

Siddiqi, Mohammad Nejatullah. *Economic Enterprise in Islam.* Delhi: Markazi Maktaba Islami; Lahore: Islamic Publications, 1972.

Contemporary Literature on Islamic Economics. Jeddah: International Centre for Research on Islamic Economics, King Abdul Aziz University; Leicester, UK: Islamic Foundation, 1978.

Some Aspects of the Islamic Economy. Lahore: Islamic Publications, 1978.

"Tawhid, the Concept and the Process." In *Islamic Perspectives: Studies in Honour of Mawlana Sayyid Abul A'la Mawdudi*, edited by Khurshid Ahmad and Zafar Ishaq Ansari, 17–33. Leicester, UK: Islamic Foundation, 1979.

"Muslim Economic Thinking: A Survey of Contemporary Literature." In *Studies in Islamic Economics*, edited by Khurshid Ahmad. Leicester, UK: Islamic Foundation, 1980.

Muslim Economic Thinking: A Survey of Contemporary Literature. Leicester, UK: Islamic Foundation, 1981.

Recent Writings on History of Economic Thought in Islam. Jeddah: International Centre for Research in Islamic Economics King Abdulaziz University, 1982.

"An Islamic Approach to Economics." In *Islam: Source and Purpose of Knowledge*, 153–175. Herndon, VA: IIIT, 1988.

"Islamizing Economics." In *Toward Islamization of Disciplines*, 253–264. Herndon, VA: IIIT, 1995.

Teaching Economics in Islamic Perspective. Jeddah: Centre for Research in Islamic Economics, KAAU, 1996.

An Islamic Approach to Economics. Islamabad and London: Institute of Policy Studies and Islamic Foundation, 2001.

Riba, Bank Interest and the Rationale of Its Prohibition. Jeddah: Islamic Development Bank, Islamic Research & Training Institute, 2004.

Teaching Economics in Islamic Perspective. Jeddah: Scientific Publishing Centre, King Abdulaziz University, 2005.

"Islamization of Knowledge: Reflections and Priorities." *American Journal of Islamic Sciences*, vol. 28, no. 3 (2011): 15–34.

Smith, Adam. *The Theory of Moral Sentiments*. MetaLibri, 2005. Electronic edition.

The Wealth of Nations. MetaLibri, 2007. Electronic edition.

Smith, Wolfgang. *The Quantum Enigma: Finding the Hidden Key*. Hillsdale, NY: Sophia Perennis, 2005.

Cosmos and Transcendence: Breaking through the Barrier of Scientistic Belief. San Rafael, CA: Sophia Perennis, 2008.

The Wisdom of Ancient Cosmology: Contemporary Science in Light of Tradition. Oakton, VA: Foundation for Traditional Studies, 2009.

Soroush, Abdolkarim. *Reason, Freedom, and Democracy in Islam*. Edited by Mahmoud Sadri and Ahmad Sadri. Oxford: Oxford University Press, 2000.

Strassmann, Diana. "Feminist Thought and Economics; or, What do the Visigoths Know?" *American Economic Review*, vol. 84, no. 2 (1994): 153–158.

Tāliqānī, Seyyed Maḥmūd. *Society and Economics in Islam*. Translated by R. Campbell, Berkeley, CA: Mizan Press, 1982.

Islām va Mālkīyāt. Translated by Ahmad Jabbari and Farhang Rajaee as *Islam and Ownership*. Lexington, KY: Mazda, 1983.

Taylor, Charles. "Modes of Secularism." In *Secularism and Its Critics*, edited by Rajeev Bhargava, 31–53. New Delhi: Oxford University Press, 1998.

A Secular Age. Cambridge, MA: Belknap Press of Harvard University Press, 2007.

Tibi, Bassam. "The Renewed Role of Islam in the Political and Social Development of the Middle East." *Middle East Journal*, vol. 37 (1983): 3–13.

Der Islam und das Problem der kulturellen Bewältigung des sozialen Wandels. Frankfurt: Suhrkamp, 1985.

Die Krise des modernen Islams: Eine vorindustrielle Kultur im wissenschaftlich-technichen Zeitalter. Frankfurt: Suhrkamp, 1991.

Arab Nationalism: Between Islam and Nation-State. London: Palgrave Macmillan, 1997.

Islam between Culture and Politics. New York: Palgrave, Macmillan, 2005.

Tripp, Charles. *Islam and Moral Economy*. Cambridge: Cambridge University Press, 2006.

Turner, Brian. *Weber and Islam: A Critical Study*. London: Routledge & Kegan Paul, 1974.

Ṭūsī, Naṣīr al-Dīn. *The Nasirean Ethics*. Translated by G. M. Wickens. London: G. Allen & Unwin, 1964.

Tyon, E. "Judicial Organization." In *Law in the Middle East*, edited by Majid Khadduri and H. J. Liebesny, 236–278. Washington, DC: Middle East Institute, 1955.

Utvik, Bjørn Olav. *Islamist Economics in Egypt*. Boulder, CO: Lynne Rienner, 2006.

Vahdat, Farzin. *Islamic Ethos and the Specter of Modernity*. London: Anthem Press, 2015.

van Ess, Josef. *Theologie und Gesellschaft im 2. und 3. Jahrhundert Hidschra. Eine Geschichte des religiösen Denkens im frühen Islam*. Berlin: Walter de Gruyter, 1991–7.

Veatch, Henry. *For an Ontology of Morals*. Evanston, IL: Northwestern University Press, 1971.

Veblen, Thorstein. "The Preconceptions of Economic Science – III." *Quarterly Journal of Economics*, vol. 14, no. 2 (1900): 240–269.

The Theory of the Leisure Class. New York: Macmillan Company, 1912.

Vikør, Knut S. *Between God and the Sultan: A History of Islamic Law*. Oxford: Oxford University Press, 2005.

Vogel, Frank E. and Hayes, Samuel L. *Islamic Law and Finance*. The Hague: Kluwer Law International, 1998.

Walbridge, John. *God and Logic in Islam: The Caliphate of Reason*. Cambridge: Cambridge University Press, 2011.

Wallerstein, Immanuel, et al. *Open the Social Sciences*. Stanford, CA: Stanford University Press, 1996.

Walras, Léon. *Éléments d'économie politique pure, ou théorie de la richesse sociale*. Paris, 1926.

Weiss, Bernard G., ed. *Studies in Islamic Legal Theory*. Leiden: Brill, 2002.

Westfall, Richard S. *The Construction of Modern Science: Mechanisms and Mechanics*. Cambridge: Cambridge University Press, 1978.

Wilson, Rodney. "The Contribution of Muhammad Baqir al-Sadr to Contemporary Islamic Economic Thought." *Journal of Islamic Studies*, vol. 9, no. 1 (1998): 46–56.

"Islam and Malaysia's Economic Development." *Journal of Islamic Studies*, vol. 9, no. 2 (1998): 259–276.

"The Development of Islamic Economics: Theory and Practice." In *Islamic Thought in the Twentieth Century*, edited by Suha Taji-Farouki and Basheer M. Nafi, 195–222. London: I. B. Tauris, 2004.

"Islamic Economics and Finances." *World Economics*, vol. 9, no. 1 (2008): 177–195.

Witham, Larry. *Marketplace of the Gods: How Economics Explains Religion*. Oxford: Oxford University Press, 2010.

Wolff, Richard D and Resnick, Stephen. *Contending Economic Theories: Neoclassical, Keynesian, and Marxian*. Cambridge, MA: MIT Press, 2012.

Yazaki, Saeko. *Islamic Mysticism and Abū Ṭālib al-Makkī*. New York: Routledge, 2013.

Yusuf, Muhammad. *Maududi: A Formative Phase*. Karachi: Islamic Research Academy, 1979.

Zaman, Arshad. "Mawlana Mawdudi and the Genesis of Islamic Economics." Paper presented at The Ninth International Conference on Islamic Economics and Finance, Istanbul, Turkey, November 9–11, 2013.

Zaman, Asad. *Islamic Economics: A Survey of the Literature*. Islamabad: International Islamic University of Islamabad, 2008.

Zaratiegui, Jesus M. "The Imperialism of Economics over Ethics." *Journal of Markets and Morality*, vol. 2, no. 2 (1999): 208–219.

Zarqa, Muḥammad. "Islamization of Economics: The Concept and Methodology." *Journal of King Abdul Aziz University: Islamic Economics*, vol. 16, no. 1 (2003): 3–42.

Zubaida, Sami. "Islam, the State and Democracy: Contrasting Conceptions of Society in Egypt." *Middle East Report*, no. 179 (1992): 2–10.

Internet Links

Center for Islamic Economics. Accessed March 18, 2017. www.iium.edu.my/cie.

Constitution of Malaysia of 1957. Accessed September 16, 2017. www.commonlii.org/my/legis/const/1957.

Constitution of the Islamic Republic of Iran 1979. Accessed January 7, 2020. www.constituteproject.org/constitution/Iran_1989.pdf?lang=en.

Constitution of the Islamic Republic of Pakistan 1973. Senate of Pakistan. Accessed September 17, 2017. www.senate.gov.pk/uploads/documents/3.%20Special%20Publication%20to%20mark%20Constitution%20Day.pdf.

International Monetary Fund. "Regional Economic Outlook: Middle East and Central Asia." 2019. Accessed April 4, 2021. www.imf.org/en/Publications/REO/MECA/Issues/2019/10/19/reo-menap-cca-1019.

Islamic Development Bank. "Facts and Figures on IDB Member Countries 2017." Accessed March 21, 2021. www.isdb.org/pub/fact-figures/2017/facts-and-figures-1438h-2017.

Islamic Economics Institute. Last modified November 13, 2014. http://iei.kau.edu.sa/Pages-E-DirectorMessage.aspx.

Islamic Finance.com. "A History of Islamic Finance." Last modified February 8, 2015. www.islamicfinance.com/2015/02/an-overview-of-the-history-of-islamic-finance.

Islamic Foundation. "Islamic Economics Unit." Last modified October 18, 2017. www.islamic-foundation.org.uk.

Jamaat-e-islami Pakistan. Accessed May 17, 2017. https://web.archive.org/web/20140418092730/http://jamaat.org/beta/site/page/3.

Index

Abbasid Caliphate, 182
ʿAbduh, Muḥammad, 36, 49, 51–53
adab, 27, 86, 159, 181
ʿadāla, 101
ʿadl (justice), 33, 39, 86, 116, 117, 151, 172, 177, 200, 207, 209, 261
ʿadl wa al-iḥsān (equilibrium), 118, 119, 261
al-Afghānī, Jamāl al-Dīn, 36, 49–52
agriculture, 203, 208, 216, 265
aḥādīth, 116, 138, 181, 183
aḥkām (legal rulings), 111, 129, 152, 153, 169
aḥkām al-sulṭāniyya, 179
al-Aḥkām al-Sulṭāniyya (al-Māwardī), 171
ahl al-taṣawwuf, 174, 189, *See* Sufism
Ahmad, Khurshid, 36, 48, 49, 64, 75, 103
Ahmad, Shaikh Mahmud, 48, 74
Ahmed, Shahab, 258
akhlāq (ethics), 31, 149, 178, 179, 270
Alatas, Syed Farid, 40, 222, 264
Al-Alwani, Taha Jabir, 81, 83
ʿamal (action), 5, 41, 151, 166, 193, 261, 276
ʿāmma (common people), 218
amwāl, 186
al-ʿaqār (property), 199
ʿaql (reason), 82, 161
ʿaqlīyya, 215
Aristotelian logic, 162
ʿaṣabiyyah (social cohesion), 210
Asad, Muhammad, 36
al-Ashʿarī, Abū Mūsā, 213
āthārī, 181
athmān (prices), 200
al-Attas, Muhammad Naquib, 28, 48, 83, 85–87, 249
  and Islamization of knowledge, 81, 94, 248
Auda, Jasser, 134
Azhar, Rauf, 102, 104, 138, 222

baʿḍ al-nufūs, 186
Bakr, Abū, 192
al-Bannā, Ḥasan, 36, 49, 52, 228
Barqūq, 216
barter exchange, 148, 176, 194, 206
bāṭin, 272
Bauer, Thomas, 247
bayt al-māl (fiscus or treasury), 150
Behdad, Sohrab, 123, 222
Bhutto, Zulfikar Ali, 88
bi ghayr haqq, 192
bi haqq, 192
British Raj, 68

Caliphs, 72, 170, 171, 173, 180, 182, 183, 210, 213, 229, 230
capitalism, 22, 30, 36, 51, 53, 54, 59, 60, 63, 73, 76, 78, 79, 95, 98, 105, 115, 121, 122, 123, 124, 143, 176, 235, 236, 238, 239, 244, 254, 268
  and colonialism, 62
  and Islamic economics, 80, 99, 101, 124, 142, 223, 246
  and market economy, 240
  free-market, 22
  neoliberal, 1, 234
Cartesian bifurcation, 7, 9, 85, 248, 266, *See* Descartes, René
Chapra, Umer, 36, 37, 102, 103, 116, 118, 132, 139, 142, 274
  and Islamic economic thought, 139–140
  and Islamic economics, 141
  on the state, 115

Choudhury, Alam, 37, 102, 103, 141, 241, 274
 epistemology of Islamic economics, 110–112
colonialism, 2, 3, 28, 35, 47, 50, 62, 95, 226, 237, 238, 244, 248, 251, 252, 267
 and mercantilism, 11
 and Muslim reformists, 36, 44–45, 50
 and Muslim revivalists, 50, 61, 97, 274
 and *Sharīʿa*, 229
 and the state, 27, 45, 62
 British, 46, 64
 in Egypt, 52
 in India, 69
 in Pakistan, 89–90
 Mawdūdī on, 67–69
commodities, 18, 130, 138, 150, 156, 202, 203, 206, 207, 241
 and price, 17, 183, 185–187, 212
 licit, 32
 money as commodity, 63
 unlawful, 210–211
commodity exchange, 7, 198, 201
communism, 59, 77, 79, *See* socialism
Companion era, 158
Comte, Auguste, 10, 14
consumerism, 111, 125, 237
counterfeiting, 194, 196, 199, 207

danāʾa, 188
ḍarūriyyāt (necessities), 161
 ḍarūrah, 187
 ḍarūri, 164, 166
al-ḍarūriyyāt, 197
dawla (state or governmental authority), 213
al-Dawwānī, 140
democracy, 70, 91
 economic, 13
 liberal, 56
 secular, 80
Descartes, René, 8
dhikr, 120, 191
al-Dimashqī, 39, 140, 147, 208
 on wealth, 199
dīn, 64, 65, 73, 78, 93, 161
dīn wa dawla (religion and state), 60
dīnārs, 196, 198, 201, 202, *See* money
dirhams, 196, 198, 201, 202, 217, 218 *See* money
Divine Recognition, 193
Divine Unity, 57, 66, 82, 111, 151, *See tawḥīd*
dunyā, 179, 196
al-Dunyā, Ibn Abī, 32, 39, 147, 175, 185, 192, 203, 206
 and Islamic economic thought, 181–182

earnings, 147, 178, 180, 181–182, 194, 195, 276
 and moral conduct, 186–189
 types of, 203
economic inequalities, 124, 133
Economic Problem of Man and Its Islamic Solution, The (Mawdūdī), 36, 48, 78–79
Economic System of Islam, The (Seoharwi), 73
economics, 1, 5, 11, 13, 20, 22, 36, 40, 42, 64, 77, 80, 88, 104, 110, 113, 118, 139, 141, 143, 178, 219, 230, 233, 244, 250, 251, 252, 261, 262, 263, 269, 270, 272, 274, 275
 and deductivism, 9
 as a discipline, 13–14, 47, 140, 177, 240
 as science, 6–7, 18, 20, 21, 257, 266
 as social science, 23, 26, 245
 Austrian School, 22
 Chicago school, 259
 classical, 15–16, 266
 conventional, 93, 101, 123, 142, 237, 246, 252, 263, 269, 272
 ethical, 179
 evolutionary, 16
 free-market, 5, 21, 22, 62, 113, 118, 122, 138, 220, 240, 242, 245, 270, 272, *See laissez faire*
 al-Ghazālī on, 194
 in Islam, 33, 34, 36, 38, 39, 44, 113, 114, 263, 273
 Keynesian, 22
 mainstream, 31, 227, 238, 259, 260
 medieval, 175
 modern, 25, 31, 80
 moral, 20, 42, 60, 63, 135, 139, 143

economics (cont.)
  neoclassical, 15, 16, 24, 26, 28, 37, 98, 107, 121, 122, 126, 127, 128, 236, 240, 257, 260, 262, 266
  neoliberal, 12, 40
  profit-based, 144
  resource-based, 273
  secular, 122, 238, 239, 240, 273
  spiritual, 194, 268
  traditional, 121
  Western, 176, 259, 263
Economics of Islam: A Comparative Study (Ahmad), 74
Egypt, 52, 53, 62, 148, 216, 217, 218
Enlightenment, the, 5, 9, 122, 177, 229, 259, 262
  and Adam Smith, 12
  and economic thought, 9–11
epistemology of Unity, 105, 241
equality, 109, 113
equity, 119, 133, 167, 185, 193, 194, 205, 206
  of price, 185–186

al-fa'idah, 137
al-falāḥ, 107, 108, 119
faqr (poverty), 33, 193, 219, 261
al-Farābi, 175
farḍ, 118, 131
farḍ 'ayn, 85
farḍ kifāya, 39, 85, 272
al-Farra, 174
al-Faruqi, Isma'il, 28, 48, 49, 81, 83, 93, 94, 95, 248, 274
  and Islamization of knowledge, 83–85, 94, 249, 250
fasid, 205
fatāwa, 169
Fatimid Caliphate, 148, 216
fatwas, 163
fiqh, 1, 30, 35, 38, 39, 77, 99, 147, 154, 156, 162, 166, 169, 172, 180, 185, 189, 234, 235, 237, 264
  and Islamic economic thought, 224–226
  and Islamic economics, 95, 102, 107, 126, 128, 252
  and Islamic law, 65
  and justice, 161
  and *mu'āmalāt*, 130
  and *ribā*, 137–138
  and *Sharī'a*, 146, 150, 152, 153, 233, 268
  and *siyāsa*, 169–170, 171
  and wealth, 190
  science of, 155, 162–163, 181
fitna, 192, 197
food, 156, 181, 183, 188, 196, 198, 199, 206, 208, 209, 217
  hoarding of, 138, 207, 213
  production of, 204
  waste of, 190
Foucault, Michel, 228, 276
freedom, 25, 155
  and *maqāṣid*, 134
  economic, 124
  free will, 160
  in Islam, 118
  individual, 79, 108, 116, 122
  moral, 113
  of enterprise, 113, 133
  al-Ṣadr on, 123
Friedman, Milton, 21, 22, 259
fulūs, 196, 200, *See* money
  and Egyptian economic crisis, 216
fuqahā' (legal specialists), 109, 137, 152, 174, 188

ghalā' (inflation), 218
ghanī, 190
gharār (risk), 132
ghayb (the unseen), 57
al-Ghazālī, Abū Ḥāmid, 32, 39, 134, 140, 147, 153, 159, 161, 163, 165, 175, 191, 193, 195, 201, 204, 208, 209, 210, 212
  and Islamic economic thought, 193–196
  on *fiqh*, 162–163
  on governmental authority, 214, 215
  on *maṣlaḥa*, 163–165
  on *muḥtasib*, 212
  on price control, 185
  on *ribā*, 201–202
  on *siyāsa*, 171
  on trade, 207–208
  on wealth, 196–198
Gilani, Manazir Ahsan, 48, 73–74
Griffel, Frank, 151, 227

ḥadīth, 71, 185, 187, 246, 265
and price control, 185
and wealth, 60, 192, 197
science of, 162, 181
al-ḥājah al-ʿamah, 161
haji, 164, 166
hajj, 198
ḥalāl, 254
goods, 106, 109
Hallaq, Wael, 19, 32, 153, 276
on law, 228
on the state, 210
Hamidullah, Muhammad, 28, 36, 48, 74, 75–76
Haneef, Muhammad Aslam, 94, 98
Ḥanīfa, Abū, 180, 184
haqīqa (truth), 86
haqq, 119, 261
al-haqq, 190
ḥarām, 131, 161, 196
ḥasab al-māl, 192
Hayek, Friedrich, 22–24
al-ḥaywān, 199
Hereafter, the, 33, 139, 179, 197, 202, 204, 220
and Islamic economic thought, 194–196, 204
and *maṣlaḥa*, 164
and *siyāsa*, 171
and *tazkiyya*, 270
and wealth, 192
sciences of, 163
al-ḥifẓ, 164
ḥifẓ al-māl, 160
hikma, 132
ḥisba, 39, 148, 150, 211, 212, 216, 219, 220
and governmental authority, 211–212
hoarding, 109, 113, 138, 184, 189, 194, 198, 205, 207, 212, 213
Hofmann, Murad W., 142
homo islamicus, 82, 114, 240, 252
hudūd, 155
ḥukm, 132, 152
Hume, David, 9
Hyderabad, 67, 74, 75

ʿibādāt, 132, 181, 204, 262
Ibn al-Haytham, 174
Ibn al-Muqaffaʿ, 184
Ibn Ḥanbal, 183
Ibn Hazm, 140, 148, 209
Ibn Khaldūn, 39, 148, 177, 265
and Islamic economic thought, 140–141, 175, 209–210
categories of knowledge, 265
on agriculture, 208
on governmental authority, 215
on *siyāsa*, 173
Ibn Qayyim, 180, 200, 203
Ibn Rushd, 140, 148, 175, 202
Ibn Sīnā, 174, 175
Ibn Taymiyya, 32, 39, 140, 148, 172, 175, 177, 185, 208, 209, 210
and economic activity, 205
on governmental authority, 215
on *ḥisba*, 211–213
on price, 186, 200
on *ribā*, 202–203
Ibn Ṭufayl, 174, 175
iḍāʿat al-māl, 192
iḥsān, 33, 185
Iḥyāʾ ʿUlūm al-Dīn (al-Ghazālī), 162, 194, 201, 213
al-ijāra, 203
ijmāʿ, 138, 152
ijtihād, 49, 66, 161, 173, 232
and *istiḥsān*, 166
ikhlāṣ (sincerity), 191
ikhtiyār (free will), 118
ikrāh bi ghayr ḥaqq, 186
ʿilla, 132, 160
ʿilm (knowledge), 5, 28, 31, 41, 82, 151, 166, 249, 261, 276
ʿilm al-iktisāb wa al-infāq, 178
al-ʿilm al-kullu, 162
ʿilm al-madani (political science), 179
ʿilm Sharʿī (legal knowledge), 166
ʿilm tadbīr al-manzil (household management), 33, 173, 178, 179
ʿilm ṭarīq al-ākhira, 163
imām, 147, 171, 181, 182, 183
imperialism, 50–51, 69
of economics, 14
India, 55, 64, 126
and Mawdūdī, 67–69
Indian philosophy, 265
Muslims in, 74, 78

indigenization, 264, 268
of knowledge, 265, 267
of social sciences, 220, 253, 264
individualism, 59
methodological, 22, 24
Indonesia, 94, 95, 234
infāq, 120
al-infāq fī ghayr haqq, 193
interest, 202–203, 205, 207, 239, 254
and *ribā*, 136–138
interest-free banks, 75, 90, 239, 251, *See* Islamic banking
International Center for Research in Islamic Economics, 104, 125
International Institute of Islamic Thought (IIIT), 81, 83, 92
International Monetary Fund, 242
Iqbal, Muhammad, 36, 49, 54–56, 228
iqtiṣād (economics), 178, 270–271
al-iʿrāḍ, 199
Iran, 46, 56, 63, 73, 234, 239, 255
Iranian philosophy, 265
Islamic State of, 62, 234
Iraq, 73, 115
al-Rāghib al-Iṣfahānī, 32, 39, 148
al-ishtirāqiyya (socialism), 51
Al-Ishtirāqiyya fī al-Islām (al-Afghānī), 51
Iṣlāḥ al-Māl (al-Dunyā), 147, 181
Islam, 26, 42, 46, 47, 49, 51, 53, 56, 59, 60–61, 70, 80, 83, 94, 105, 109, 118, 126, 138, 142, 147, 151, 157, 176, 177, 215, 234, 235, 239, 241, 246, 248, 250, 251, 253, 258, 263, 265, 267
ʿAlī Sharīʿatī and, 56–57
and anticolonialism, 51
and critique of mainstream economics, 76–77
and economic philosophy, 146
and economic theory, 116, 117
and economic thought, 225
and economics, 80, 100, 104, 177, 241, 256, 268
and Muslim revivalism, 52
and ownership, 114
and Pakistan, 78
and social justice, 53
and the state, 27
and theocracy, 71
classical, 168, 173, 249
Mawdūdī and, 55, 64–66, 68
modernization of, 73, 230
moral cosmology of, 257
moral economy of, 146
moral philosophy of, 141
Muḥammad ʿAbduh and, 52
Muhammad Iqbal and, 54
Muḥammad Zarqa on, 93
pluralistic epistemology of, 255
political, 28, 230
premodern, 222
Shahab Ahmed on, 258
Sunni, 160, 193
Islam and the Theory of Interest (Qureshi), 74
Islamic banking, 3, 4, 29, 48, 87, 91, 92, 93, 94–95, 96, 101, 104–105, 143–144, 225, 238, 254
and Islamic law, 254–255
and *ribā*, 136, 138
al-Ṣadr on, 239
Islamic economic thought, 1, 3, 4, 5, 29, 32, 33, 37, 38, 41, 42, 106, 132, 140, 146, 164, 244, 252, 257, 258–259, 269, 272, 273, 274, 275, 276
Abū Ḥāmid al-Ghazālī and, 193, 213
and Islamic law, 173–175
and Islamic states, 128
and positivism, 10
and *Sharīʿa*, 145–146, 157, 226
and social sciences, 5
and the Qurʾan, 152
classical, 31, 32, 34, 102, 110, 140, 146–147, 155, 179–180, 221
contemporary, 159
epistemology of, 177, 219, 255, 263
Ibn Khaldūn and, 209
Ibn Taymiyya and, 185
intellectual history of, 35
modern, 225, 226, 250
moral cosmology of, 219, 262
Muhammad Akram Khan and, 245
Muḥammad Zarqa and, 93
Islamic economics, 5, 9, 29, 32, 35, 36, 39, 44–45, 47, 60–61, 62, 64, 66, 82, 98, 101, 102, 105, 109, 110, 114, 120, 123–126, 128, 141, 143,

160, 222, 235–236, 242, 247, 250, 251, 252, 254, 268, 270, 274, 276
Abū al-A'lā Mawdūdi on, 67, 78–79
Alam Choudhury on, 111–112
and ethics, 115–117, 119
and Islamic banking, 91–92, 94, 254
and Islamic law, 105–106, 128–129, 132, 155–156, 224–226, 237
and Islamic states, 230, 232–234
and law, 29, 38
and mainstream economics, 142, 223–224, 236, 238–240, 245, 246
and Muslim reformists, 36, 50
and Muslim revivalists, 63, 102–104
and nation-states, 27, 80
and neoclassical economic thought, 30
and Pakistan, 88–89, 90
and rationality, 139
and *ribā*, 134, 136, 138, 243
and *Sharī'a*, 80, 128
and *zakāt*, 135
as social science, 142, 270
contemporary, 2–4, 5, 28, 29, 31, 34, 37, 44, 48, 77, 81, 93, 94, 97, 101, 103, 109, 113, 141, 143, 146, 157, 220, 221, 222, 234, 244, 246, 252–253, 262, 263, 264, 271, 275, 276
definitions of, 106–109
discipline of, 100, 242, 244, 246, 275
epistemology of, 34, 42, 93, 98–100
intellectual history of, 219, 275
Islamization of, 37, 46, 84, 93, 95–96, 247, 248, 249
methodology of, 120, 240, 242
modern, 10, 40, 41
Mohammad Nejatullah Siddiqi on, 112–113, 126
moral cosmology of, 7
Muhammad Akram Khan on, 113–114
Muhammad Hamidullah on, 75
philosophy of, 114, 118, 121, 205
pluralistic epistemology of, 41
scholars of, 73–75
science of, 104, 109, 127, 245, 251, 264
Islamic Economics: Theory and Practice (Mannan), 124
Islamic Economics (Gilani), 73–74
Islamic Economics Institute, The, 92, 100
Islamic finance, 2, 80, 91, 92, 93, 94–95, 96, 101, 102, 104–105, 134, 225, 238, 239, 243, 252, 254, *See* Islamic banking
and Islamic states, 87
and mainstream economics, 30, 121, 254
and *mu'āmalāt*, 130
contemporary, 44, 93
Islamic Foundation, The, 92, 100
Islamic law, 35, 40, 112, 128, 129, 130, 132, 150, 155, 158, 160, 162, 165, 168, 169, 224, 225, 227, 236, 248, 252, 258
Abū al-A'lā Mawdūdi on, 55
and capitalism, 115
and *ḥisba*, 211
and Islamic banking, 254
and Islamic economics, 38, 146, 156, 224, 237, 275
and *istiḥsān*, 166–167
and *maṣlaḥa*, 134, 157, 160, 164
and price, 183
and private property, 115
and *Sharī'a*, 151, 152, 229
and *siyāsa*, 171
and state, 230–231
and the Qur'an, 130
commercial, 130
Islamic sciences, 44, 84, 98, 181, 194, 247, 248, 250
and Islamic economics, 222, 267
and *siyāsa*, 170
and *tawḥīd*, 111
and Western knowledge, 52, 82
Islamism, 3, 5, 27, 37, 42, 44, 45, 55, 61, 66, 90, 248, 251, 252, 253, 268, *See* Muslim revivalism
Islamization, 44, 47, 64, 66, 83, 85, 86–87, 90, 102, 246, 248, 249, 251, 253, 255, 265, 270, 274
in Pakistan, 88, 89–90
Islamization of knowledge (IOK) process, 3, 28, 29, 34, 35, 36, 39–40, 44, 45, 47–48, 58, 63, 81, 85, 92, 94, 95, 100, 104, 110, 116, 119, 142, 247, 248, 249, 250, 269

Islamization (cont.)
of economics, 50, 97, 127, 139, 141
of Islam, 247, 248
of science, 3, 83, 95
Islamization of Knowledge (al-Faruqi), 83
is–ought dichotomy, 9, 20, 35, 227, 276, *See* Hume, David
isrāf (wasteful behavior), 111
istiḥsān (equity), 39, 101, 112, 157, 160, 164, 166–168
istiṣlāḥ, 39, 157, 166–168
ʿiwaḍ al-mithl, 186

Jamaʿat-i Islami, 64, 69
al-Jawziyya, Ibn Qayyim, 32, 39, 148, 158, 159, 200
on *Sharīʿa*, 160
on *siyāsa*, 171
Jevons, William Stanley, 12, 15, 16
jihād, 191, 206
jins, 186
jurisprudence, 34, 35, 94, 95, 99, 105, 128, 138, 150, 160, 161, 181, 186, 189, 191, 197, 224, 235, 265
Abū Ḥāmid al-Ghazālī on, 162, 194, 214
categories of, 131
economic, 130
Ḥanafī school, 147, 151, 166
Ḥanbalī school, 148, 151, 200, 248
Mālikī school, 148, 151, 166
Shāfiʿī school, 147, 151, 160, 162, 163, 191, 199
jurists, 33, 38–39, 130, 147, 160, 179, 180, 191, 199, 200, 202, 209, 216, 226, 267
Abū Ḥāmid al-Ghazālī, 162–163
and Islamic economic thought, 177, 179
and Islamic economics, 221, 224
and *istiḥsān*, 167
and price control, 183, 184
and *qādis*, 171
and *ribā*, 137
and *uṣūl al-fiqh*, 153–153
classical, 131
juristic-economics, 116
justice, 5, 34, 77, 119, 120, 139, 142, 169, 172, 180, 194, 209, 214, 267, *See ʿadl* (justice)
Adam Smith on, 11–12
and *fiqh*, 161
and governmental authority, 214–215
and Islamic economics, 79, 107, 109
and *maqāṣid*, 134, 141, 158, 160
and *maṣlaḥa*, 121
and *muḥtasib*, 212
and *ribā*, 202
and *siyāsa*, 171–172
economic, 37, 38, 41, 101, 118, 125, 129, 157, 177, 179
in price control, 184–187
in trade, 205
in Western economics, 11
al-Ṣadr on, 116
socioeconomic, 29
al-Juwaynī, 159, 161, 162, 163, 165

Kahf, Monzer, 36, 94, 102
kalām, 4, 35, 158, 170, 258, 265
kasb, 39, 159, 180, 187–190, 219, 261, 271
-zuhd amalgam, 219
kashf (unveiling), 86, 179
Keynes, John Maynard, 22, 25
Keynesian economics, 107, 111, 127, 236
Khan, Muhammad Akram, 36, 37, 40, 102, 104, 113, 119, 143, 222
on Islamic economics, 48–49, 99, 121, 245
on *ribā*, 136
Khan, Muhammad Fahim, 37, 102
al-kharāj (land tax), 179
khilāfa (viceregency), 70, 116, 117
Khilafat movement, 64
Khomeini, Ruhollah, 62
khudi (selfhood), 54, 55
khushūʿ, 120
Kīmīya-i al-saʿādat (al-Ghazālī), 198, 207
Kinānī, 174
Kitāb Adāb al-Kasb wa al-Maʿāsh (al-Ghazālī), 147
Kitāb al-Isharāh ilā Maḥāsin al-Tijārah (al-Dimashqī), 147

Kitāb al-Kasb (al-Shaybānī), 147, 181, 182
Kitāb al-Kharaj (Yūsuf), 182
Kitāb al-Luma' (al-Ṭūsī), 193
Kitāb al-Sijar (al-Shaybānī), 147
Kitāb Naṣīḥat al-Mulūk (al-Ghazālī), 213–214
knowledge, 82, 85, 87, 108, 158, 248, 249, 250, 252, 253, 260, 262, 263, 265, 267, 272
  contemporary, 248
  decolonization of, 264
  division of, 244
  economic, 139
  human, 166, 263, 269, 270
  Islamic, 85
  Islamic theory of, 91
  of God, 204
  of *Sharī'a*, 153
  scientific, 66, 223
  sociology of, 226
  unity of, 111
  Western, 82, 95, 244, 247, 268
kuliyyāt, 165
Kuran, Timur, 40, 99, 222, 239

labor, 11, 16, 17, 21, 197, 203, 206–207, 268
  and justice, 206
  and private property, 115
  and utilitarianism, 13
  division of, 139, 204, 272
  value of, 79, 180, 198, 201
labor theory of value, 16
laissez-faire, 12, 21, 76, 245
law, 5, 12–13, 19, 21, 23, 25, 38, 46–47, 57, 62, 72, 107, 108, 116, 126, 147, 148, 152, 154, 155, 161, 170, 177, 188, 212, 228, 231, 261, 263, 274
  civil, 275
  commercial, 38, 130, 146, 151, 254
  criminal, 129, 231
  Divine, 28, 111, 115, 118, 150, 177, 215, 219, 241
  economic, 7, 18, 78, 80
  inheritance, 76, 246
  labor, 242
  methodology of, 180
  moral, 4, 27, 111, 173, 182, 233
  natural, 149
  objective, 131
  positive, 167
  religious, 225
  state, 20, 27, 125, 233
  Western, 226, 228
Lawson, Tony, 10, 26
liberalism, 19, 61, 62, 98, 223, 233, 244, 245, 274

ma'rifa, 28, 86, 193, 204
madhāhib (legal schools), 52
madhhab, 166, 171
mafāsid, 165
mafsada (corruption), 165
makāsib, 188
al-Makāsib wa al-Wara' (al-Muḥāsibī), 191
al-Makkī, 148
makrūh, 131
al-makrumāt, 161
māl (wealth), 31, 39, 133, 179, 187, 196–197
  and *maqāṣid*, 162
  categories of, 199
Malaysia, 45, 46, 62, 63, 81, 88, 90, 92, 100
  and Islamization, 84, 89, 94, 95, 255
Mālik, Imām, 184
Mamluk Sultanate, 200, 216
manāfi' (profit), 186
al-mandūbāt, 161
manhaj (method), 248
Mannan, Muhammad Abdul, 50, 102–103, 115, 116, 124
maqādir al-amwāl, 200
maqāmāt, 193, 270
maqāṣid, 108, 116, 130, 132–134, 141, 145, 158–159, 160, 164, 165, 166, 231
  levels of, 161
maqāṣid al-Sharī'a, 35, 39, 157, 158, 159, 164
al-Maqrīzī, 39, 140, 148, 175, 177, 210, 216, 217, 218
  on Egyptian economic crisis, 217–219
maqsūd, 197
marginal revolution, the, 16

Marshall, Alfred, 16, 17
Marx, Karl, 18, 22
Marxism, 1, 18, 111, 123, *See* socialism
  and Islam, 56–57
maṣlaḥa (common good), 17, 33, 39, 121, 132, 134, 149, 150, 161, 166, 168, 172, 195, 219, 224, 231, 255, 261, 263
  Abū Ḥāmid al-Ghazālī on, 163–165
  and economic justice, 101
  and Islamic law, 112, 169
  and *Sharīʿa*, 34, 157, 159–160
  and *siyāsa*, 231
  categories of, 165–166
maṣāliḥ, 165, 168
maṣlaḥa mursala, 134, 160, 164
Masud, Muhammad Khan, 171
materialism, 51, 57, 60, 115, 122, 223, 235, 269
al-Māwardī, 140, 148, 171, 175, 209, 211
Mawdūdī, Abū al-Aʿlā, 28, 36, 44, 46, 49–50, 52, 63, 69–70, 78–80, 93, 102, 228
  and Fazlur Rahman, 58–59
  and Islamic economics, 74–75
  and Islamic states, 66–67, 71–72, 95
  and Muhammad Iqbal, 55–56
  and political Islam, 68
  and theo-democracy, 64, 70
maẓālim, 233
Medina, 70
mercantilism, 10–11, 215
methodological pluralism, 123, 141
miʿyār al-amwāl, 200
Middle East, 3, 36, 44–47, 48, 50, 52, 142, 143, 213, 221, 226
  and Islamic economics, 101, 238, 242, 243
  and Islamic finance, 88, 91
  and Islamic states, 61–63
  and Islamization, 81
Mill, John Stuart, 13–14, 266
miqdār, 186
Mirakhor, Abbas, 138, 222
mīzān, 261
Mīzān al-ʿAmal (al-Ghazālī), 196
modernism, 98, 223, 235, 241, 251, 264
  and Islamic economics, 85, 95, 254, 270, 275
modernity, 41, 47, 67, 70, 72–73, 223, 234, 252, 253, 267, 269
  and economics, 25
  and Islamic economics, 77, 220, 236, 246, 247, 263
  and Islamic states, 72
  and Islamization, 83, 90
  and law, 228
modernization, 7, 28, 52–53, 66, 89, 223, 235
  and Islamic states, 78
  and Islamization, 37
  and nation-states, 46
  of Islam, 58
monetarism, 22
money, 21, 39, 63, 75, 79, 109, 139, 148, 156, 160, 181, 187, 188, 191, 192–193, 199–200, 206, 224, 251, 273
  Abū Ḥāmid al-Ghazālī on, 193–199
  and Egyptian economic crisis, 216–218
  and *ribā*, 201–202
  quantity theory of, 22
muʿāmalāt (commercial law), 40, 132, 151, 181, 191, 219, 262
  and *fiqh*, 130
mubāḥ, 131–132
muḍāraba (profit-sharing), 111
mufti, 52, 231
Mughal Empire, 64
muḥāsaba (introspection), 191, 193
al-Muḥāsibī, 32, 39, 148, 175, 191–192
muḥtāj, 186
muḥtasib, 211–213
munāsaba (suitability), 163
Muqaddima (Ibn Khaldūn), 209
al-Muqaffaʿ, ʿAbd Allah Ibn, 173
murāqaba, 193
mushāraka (equity participation), 111
Muslim Brotherhood, 52
Muslim economists, 4, 37, 44, 64, 75, 76, 81, 92–94, 95, 98–99, 101, 103, 109, 122, 142, 222, 223–224, 235, 244–245, 250, 251–252, 254, 264, 267, 269, 273
  and Islamic economics, 114, 120–121, 237–239

and Islamic states, 233–234
contemporary, 6, 38, 42, 101–102, 105, 110–111, 113, 128, 135, 138–139, 140, 143, 146, 156, 220, 221, 241, 262
modern, 29–31, 45, 60, 73, 77
Western-trained, 83
Muslim reformists, 2, 27, 35–36, 42, 44–45, 50, 59, 63, 83, 106, *See* Muslim revivalists
modernists, 36, 60, 136
neo-revivalists, 36
Muslim revivalism, 34, 35, 44, 70, 72, 141
Muslim revivalists, 48, 61, 63, 66, 92, 97, 102, 221, 229, 232, 235, 244, 249, 251, 274
modernists, 49, 99
Muslim scholars, 1–3, 5, 27, 28, 35, 40, 44, 47, 95, 98, 115, 175–176, 203, 224, 228, 234, 240, 247, 250
classical, 28, 32–33, 38–39, 42, 109, 139–140, 144, 146–147, 150–151, 158, 178–180, 205, 215, 219–220, 222, 226, 235, 237, 254, 262, 263, 265, 271
contemporary, 34, 101, 110, 134, 160, 251
medieval, 138
modern, 78, 82, 85
premodern, 30, 60, 161, 254
religious, 62
mustaḥab, 131
Mustaṣfā (al-Ghazālī), 162
muta'affifan (temperance), 188
mutakallimūn, 174
al-mutaqashshifa, 188

nadar (proletariat), 54
nafs, 161
Nagaoke, Shinsuke, 222
al-nahḍa, 27, 48, *See* Muslim reformists
al-Na'im, 230
Naqvi, Haider, 37, 102, 109, 114, 136, 141
on Islamic economics, 118–119, 128, 129
Naṣīḥat al-Mulūk (al-Ghazālī), 214
nasl, 162
Nasr, Seyyed Vali Reza, 40, 99, 222, 262
nationalism, 28, 45, 68, 72
Arab, 52
Egyptian, 52
Hindu, 64, 65, 69
Islamic, 72
Nienhaus, Volker, 222, 242
nineteenth century, 35, 60, 103
economics, 6, 13, 110
Europe, 26, 30, 40
Middle East, 2, 47, 226
Muslim revivalists, 48
Muslim societies, 50
philosophy, 223
social sciences, 9
niyya, 187, 197, 227
niẓām (system), 248
North Africa, 45, 50
and Islamic finance, 88, 91
nufūs, 186

orientalism, 229, 247, 268
Ottoman Empire, 45–47, 154, 227, 242

Pakistan, 46, 58, 62–63, 67, 69, 74–76, 78, 80, 81, 88, 92, 94–95, 124, 234, 235, 239, 255
and Islamization, 45, 87–91
Phillipp, Thomas, 222
physiocrats, 11
Piketty, Thomas, 26
pluralistic epistemology, 41, 255, 263, 267–268, 270, 272, 276
Polanyi, Karl, 20
political economy, 11, 17, 20, 26, 32, 65, 209–210, 219, 234, 252, 259, 268, 269, *See* economics
Abū al-A'lā Mawdūdī and, 66–67, 95
Islamic, 64, 111, 241, 251
liberal, 111
positivism, 6, 10, 14, 23, 34, 118, 139, 235, 249, 255, 269
and mathematical deductivism, 10
and sociology, 244
economic, 30, 47, 220, 222, 245
in social sciences, 5, 40, 264
legal, 225, 253
scientific, 3, 125

poverty, 12, 53, 119, 133, 135, 177, 180, 181, 189, 190–191, 193, 197, 200, 202, 209, 215, 219, 271, 276
spiritual, 261, 271
price, 17, 181, 186, 199, 200, 206
Abū Ḥāmid al-Ghazālī on, 207–208
and Egyptian economic crisis, 216–217
and *ḥisba*, 211–213
and money, 22
control, 148, 182–186, 222
of the equivalent, 182, 186, 187
theory, 147
private ownership, 57, 79, 124
private property, 113, 115, 122, 124
production processes, 32, 180, 194, 197, 203, 204, 219, 251, 261, 268, 270, 272
secularization of, 11
profit, 124, 136, 184, 185, 186, 198, 199–200, 206, 218, 219, 243, 255, 270
Abū Ḥāmid al-Ghazālī on, 207–208
profit-sharing, 203, 207
Prophet Muḥammad, 52, 66, 71, 162, 177, 206, 213
on price control, 183–184
psychological hedonism, 13, 24
Punjab, 69

qaḍā (fate), 193
qādis, 171, 180
qalb (heart), 193, 219
qanūn (state law), 46, 227
qaṣd, 178
qaṣd al-māl, 181, 193
qast, 261
qiyās, 152, 163, 166, 168
quality to quantity reduction, 17, 34, 35, 266, *See* Descartes, René

Qur'an, 39, 52, 57, 59, 66, 116, 118, 127, 128, 130–131, 164, 166, 187, 197, 203, 226, 257, 260, 262, 265, 267
and *fiqh*, 65
and *ḥisba*, 211, 212
and Islamic economic thought, 177, 181
and Islamic economics, 99, 105, 111–112, 117, 143, 146, 246
and Islamic law, 149–151, 152, 156, 163, 228
and Islamic states, 64
and *ribā*, 136
and *Sharīʿa*, 127, 225, 229
and *siyāsa*, 171–172
and *tawḥīd*, 111, 241
and *zakāt*, 135
Mawdūdī on, 66–67, 71
Qureshi, Anwar Iqbal, 74
Quṭb, Sayyid, 36, 49, 53, 228

ra'smāliyya (capitalism), 51
ra'y, 168, 173
Rahman, Fazlur, 36, 49, 58–59, 249
al-Rashīd, Hārūn, 180, 182
Rashidun Caliphate, 52, 177, 183
al-Rāzī, Fakhr ad-Dīn, 174
ribā (usury), 89, 104, 111, 120, 132, 134, 136–138, 139, 144, 180, 201–202, 211, 219, 222, 224, 243, 246, 275
types of, 201, 203
al-ribḥ al-ma'rūf, 186
al-ribḥ al-mu'atād, 186
Riḍā, Rashīd, 36, 49, 52
riḍā', 193
rizq, 191, 206

saʿāda (eternal happiness), 163, 194, 204
Saadī, 271
ṣabr (patience), 193
ṣadaqa, 150, 202
al-Ṣadr, Muḥammad Bāqir, 36, 49, 50, 102, 115, 123, 129, 138, 143, 239
and Islamic economics, 115–116, 125, 129
critique of mainstream economics, 124
Salafism, 148
ṣalāt, 135
Saljuq dynasty, 213
Sallam, Abū 'Ubayd al-Qāsim Ibn, 174
al-ṣāmit, 199
al-Sarakhsī, 140, 174, 181
Sardar, Ziauddin, 249
sarf, 193

sarmayahdar (capitalism), 54
Saudi Arabia, 81, 92, 100, 234
Schacht, Joseph, 168
Schmitt, Carl, 19
scholasticism, 175, 182
Schumacher, Ernst, 25
Scientific Revolution, the, 8, 9
secularism, 64, 82, 85, 94, 103, 238, 247, 249, 258
  and economics, 28, 80, 110, 114, 118, 122–123
  and Islamic states, 61–62, 87–88
  and nation states, 19–20, 98, 233
secularization, 7, 11, 40, 47, 83, 87, 90
  of economics, 17
  of knowledge, 83
Seoharwi, Hifzur Rahman, 47–48
al-Shāfiʿī, 160, 171, 183
al-shakhṣiyāt al-islamiyyah (Islamic personality), 114
sharʿī, 165
Sharīʿa, 28, 34, 64, 65, 86, 100, 109, 110, 114, 134, 151–154, 160, 165, 167, 171, 179, 191, 195, 200, 205, 210, 215, 217, 219, 221–222, 234, 245, 257
  and economic law, 105–107, 131–132
  and *ḥisba*, 211
  and Islamic banking, 254–255
  and Islamic economic thought, 2–5, 30–31, 32, 93–94, 112, 145–146, 157–158, 177, 180–181, 224–227
  and Islamic economics, 126–127, 128, 138, 237, 272, 275
  and Islamic states, 51, 52, 62
  and Islamization, 248, 250, 253
  and *maṣlaḥa*, 159, 160, 163–164
  and price, 184
  and *ribā*, 202
  and *siyāsa*, 168–169, 171–173, 231–234
  and state law, 27, 46, 125, 227–229, 252
  al-Ghazālī on, 196–197, 207, 213
  Mawdūdī on, 64–65, 70, 78, 80
  moral cosmology of, 4, 31, 32, 38–39, 40, 144, 145, 146, 149–150, 156, 194, 219, 254, 260–261, 268
Sharīʿatī, ʿAlī, 49, 56–57
al-Shāṭibī, 134, 165
  and Islamic law, 165–166
al-Shaybānī, Muḥammad Ibn al-Ḥasan, 32, 39, 147, 160, 175, 180, 181, 189
  on earnings, 180–181, 187, 189, 203
al-Shayzarī, 148, 212
Shiʿism, 56–57
Shūrā, 112
shūrā (Islamic consultation), 71
Siddiqi, Mohammad Nejatullah, 36, 37, 94, 102, 103, 109, 110, 115, 118, 129, 139, 141, 274
  on Islamic economics, 112, 126–127
ṣifa al-faqr, 190
ṣināʿa, 203
siyāsa, 145, 169–172, 173, 178, 231–232
  and *fiqh*, 233–234
  types of, 171, 173
siyāsa ʿādila, 171
siyāsa Sharʿiyya, 151, 168–169, 172–173, 231
siyāsaẓ ālima, 171
Smith, Adam, 9, 11–12, 21
Smith, Wolfgang, 266
  on measurements, 8
social justice, 53, 57, 92, 119, 125–126, 128, 139, 182, 250
  and Islamic economics, 116
  and private ownership, 79, 115
  and *zakāt*, 201
  Muslim reformists and, 44, 46, 50
social sciences, 5, 9–10, 13, 15, 16, 20, 26, 34, 40, 105, 113, 127, 148, 220, 221–223, 242, 245, 247, 263–266, 267, 275
  and Islamic economics, 101, 107, 109, 125, 141, 142, 221, 237, 253, 270, 274
  and Islamization of knowledge, 83–84, 249–250
  Hayek on, 22–24
  modern, 2
  Muhammad Akram Khan and, 246
  Western, 243, 247

social welfare, 270
and *fiqh*, 161
and *maqāṣid*, 158, 160
and *maṣlaḥa*, 163
and *zakāt*, 135, 242
socialism, 30, 36, 50, 51, 53, 54, 76, 78, 95, 98, 105, 122, 124, 142, 224, 235
critique of, 60, 73
Islamic, 59, 238
South Asia, 2, 35–36, 47, 54, 73, 75, 92, 95, 142, 143, 221
and Islamic economics, 101, 238
colonialism in, 44–45
Islamic states in, 60–62
nationalism in, 28
state, 11–12, 18, 22, 25, 42, 53, 59–61, 68, 75–77, 83, 91, 113, 117, 121, 122–123, 125, 132, 182, 209, 228, 234–235, 245
and ownership, 114–115, 124, 129
authority, 210–211, 215
colonial, 63, 232
industrialized, 63
Islamic, 3, 35, 42, 44, 46, 50, 52, 56–57, 61–62, 63, 64–66, 70–72, 74, 78, 80, 83, 88, 95, 98, 128, 230, 234, 235, 251, 252, 274
modern, 9, 35, 41, 45, 63, 225, 230–231, 253
Muslim, 28, 142
nation-state, 10, 19–21, 27, 28, 34, 45, 46, 62, 68, 71, 80, 98, 101, 172, 229–230, 232–233, 239, 240, 244, 251, 271, 273, 275
Pakistani, 87–90
postcolonial, 2, 45, 67, 88, 90
secular, 46, 90, 230
Western, 80
Sufism, 99, 160, 162, 174, 193, 218, 226, 258, 267
and Islamic economic thought, 32–33, 38–39, 146–147, 179
al-Attas and, 248–249
al-Muḥāsibī and, 191–192
and wealth, 182, 188–189, 200, 271
Sunna, 129, 146, 152

al-taḍāmun al-ijtimāʿī (social solidarity), 51
tadbīr al-nafs, 178
tafsīr (exegesis), 99, 185, 264
ṭahāra, 188
ṭahārat al-qulūb, 191
taḥsīni, 164, 166
tajdīd (renewal process), 67
al-takāful al-ijtimāʿī (social responsibility), 51
Tāliqānī, Maḥmūd, 50, 102
Tanzimat reform period, the, 46
al-taqarrub, 191
taqwā, 120, 181, 191
tasʿīr (price control), 149
taṣawwuf, 4, 85, 179, 191, 193, 249, 264
and Islamic economic thought, 34–35
and Islamic sciences, 248, 265
tawakkul, 189, 191, 193, 207
tawba (repentance), 120, 191, 193
tawḥīd, 45, 54, 57, 82, 83, 103, 110–111, 118, 152, 241, 248
and Islamic economics, 113, 116
Mawdūdī on, 64–66
Muhammad Iqbal on, 56
Taylor, Charles, 19, 228
al-taʿzīrāt, 161
tazkiyya, 33, 120, 261, 270
thaman al-mithl (price of the equivalent), 182
Theory of Moral Sentiments, The (Smith), 11, 12
al-tijāra (trade), 203
trade, 10, 109, 131, 139, 168, 176, 181, 186, 205–206, 215, 217, 243
and *ḥisba*, 211
and Islamic banking, 255
and *ribā*, 201, 243
al-Ghazālī on, 194–195, 198, 207–208
Tripp, Charles, 60
al-Ṭūfi, 159
al-Tūsi, Abū Naṣr al-Sarrāj, 140, 175, 193
twentieth century, 3, 28, 40, 44, 46, 61, 67, 72, 83, 154, 250
capitalism, 60
economics, 16, 22
Islamic economics, 36, 47, 92, 253
Islamists, 251

Middle East, 62
Muslim reformists, 27, 44
Muslim revivalists, 35, 249
South Asia, 36

'ulamā', 76, 99–100, 122, 131, 153, 209, 214, 232, 264
ul-Haq, Muhammad Zia, 62, 88
al-'ulūm al-'aqliyya, 265
al-'ulūm al-naqliyya, 265
umma, 27, 45, 55, 66, 129, 170, 192
and Islamic states, 65, 70, 71–72, 83
and Islamization, 84
al-'uqūd al-ṣaḥīḥa, 186
ushr, 183
uṣūl al-fiqh (methodology of Islamic law), 35, 93, 152–153, 179
usury, 99, 130, 166, 177, 202, *See ribā*
utilitarianism, 13–14, 112, 122, 139, 245, 259, 272, 276
utility, 11, 16–17, 18, 21, 25, 164, 204, 255, 263, 272
mono-, 266, 267
social, 121
Utvik, Bjørn Olav, 27

Veblen, Thorstein, 15–16
vicegerency, 70

al-waḥy (revealed knowledge), 82
wājib, 189, 198
wājibāt, 161
Waliyullah, Shah, 140
Walras, Léon, 16
waqf, 150, 163
wara', 181, 191, 193
wasā'il, 160
wealth, 1, 16, 60, 79, 113, 126, 133, 138, 157–159, 160, 180, 181, 185, 187–193, 195, 196, 199–201, 213, 276, *See māl* (wealth)
acquisition of, 124, 147, 177–179, 206, 242, 261, 273
and poverty, 271
and private property, 115
and *ribā*, 138
and *zakāt*, 135–136
distribution of, 129, 236
al-Dunyā on, 181–182
al-Ghazālī on, 196–198
Wealth of Nations, The (Smith), 11, 12
West, the, 6–7, 143, 227, 244, 247, 253
and Islamization of knowledge, 83
economic thought in, 12
Mawdūdī on, 58
social sciences in, 105, 222, 264
westernization, 66, 83, 244
de-, 269
wilāya, 215

ya'khudh, 192
Yūsuf, Abū, 39, 140, 147, 174, 180, 182–183, 210, 212, 213

zakāt (wealth tax), 79, 88, 111, 120, 134–136, 139, 144, 150, 177, 189, 194, 201, 202–203, 209, 219, 224, 239, 242–243, 246, 275
Zarqa, Muḥammad Anas, 36, 93, 103
Zayd, Abu, 263
al-zirā'a (agriculture), 203
zuhd (abstinence), 33, 39, 149, 159, 179, 180, 181, 191, 193, 200, 219, 261
ẓulm, 184, 187

Printed in the United States
by Baker & Taylor Publisher Services